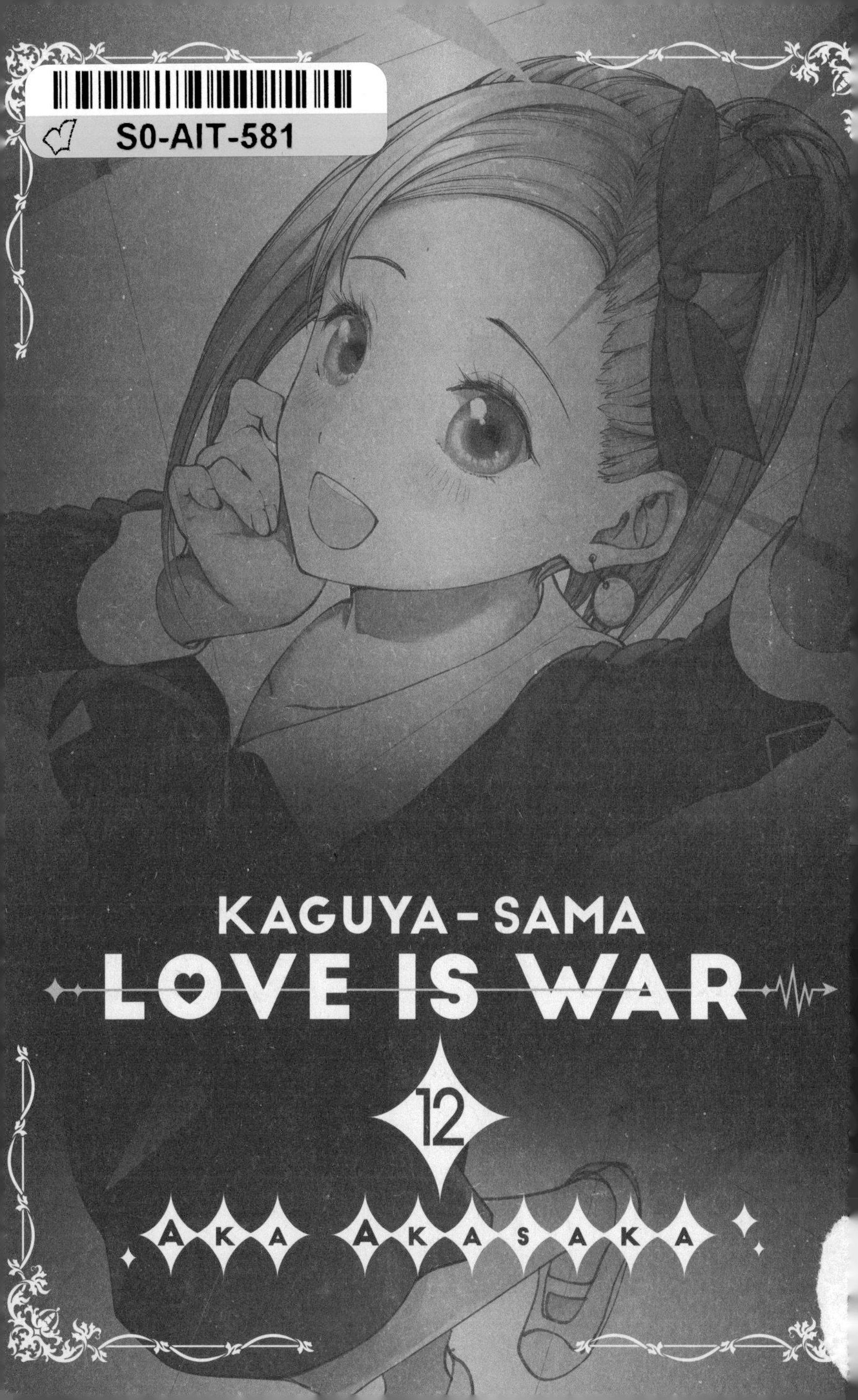
KAGUYA-SAMA
LOVE IS WAR
12
AKA AKASAKA

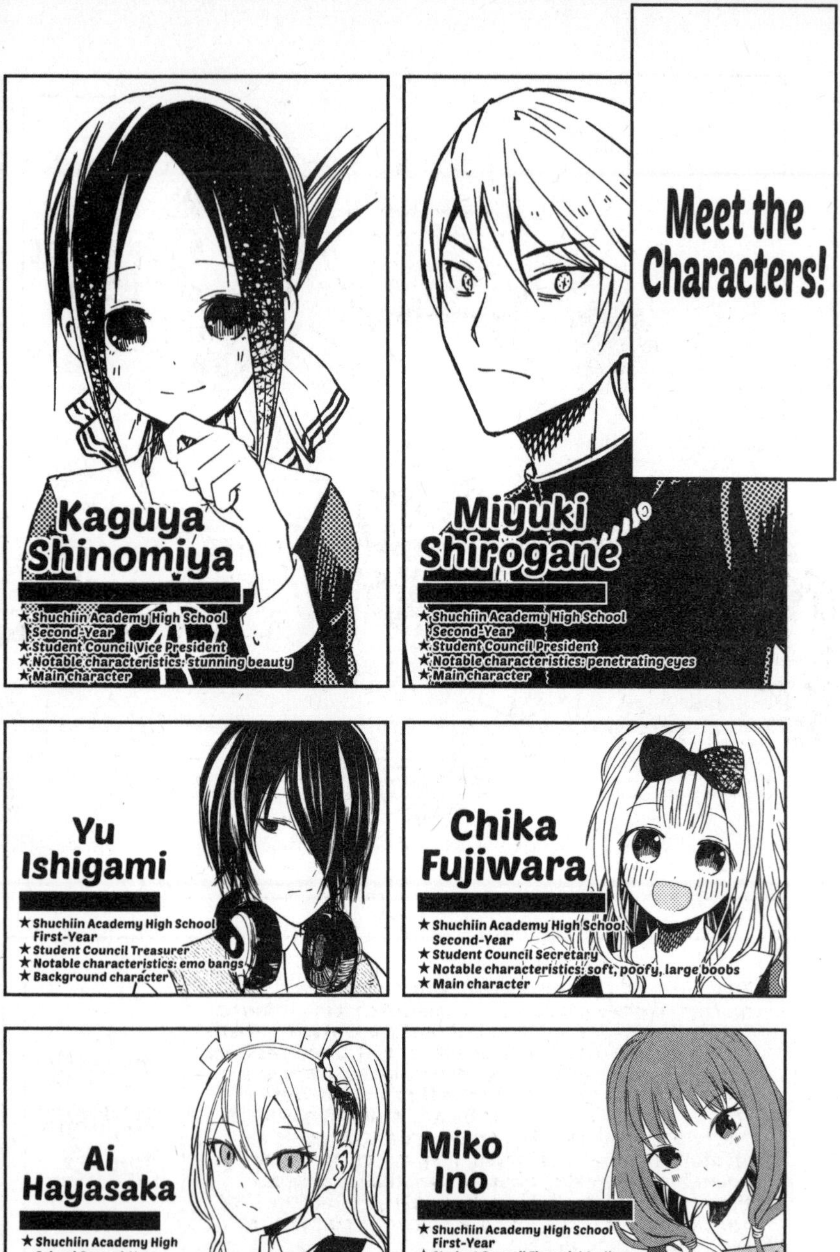
Meet the Characters!
Miyuki Shirogane
★Shuchiin Academy High School Second-Year
★Student Council President
★Notable characteristics: penetrating eyes
★Main character
Kaguya Shinomiya
★Shuchiin Academy High School Second-Year
★Student Council Vice President
★Notable characteristics: stunning beauty
★Main character
Chika Fujiwara
★Shuchiin Academy High School Second-Year
★Student Council Secretary
★Notable characteristics: soft, poofy, large boobs
★Main character
Yu Ishigami
★Shuchiin Academy High School First-Year
★Student Council Treasurer
★Notable characteristics: emo bangs
★Background character
Miko Ino
★Shuchiin Academy High School First-Year
★Student Council Financial Auditor
★Notable characteristics: short
★Background character
Ai Hayasaka
★Shuchiin Academy High School Second-Year
★Notable characteristics: one-quarter Irish
★Profession: Kaguya Shinomiya's personal assistant

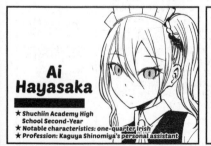

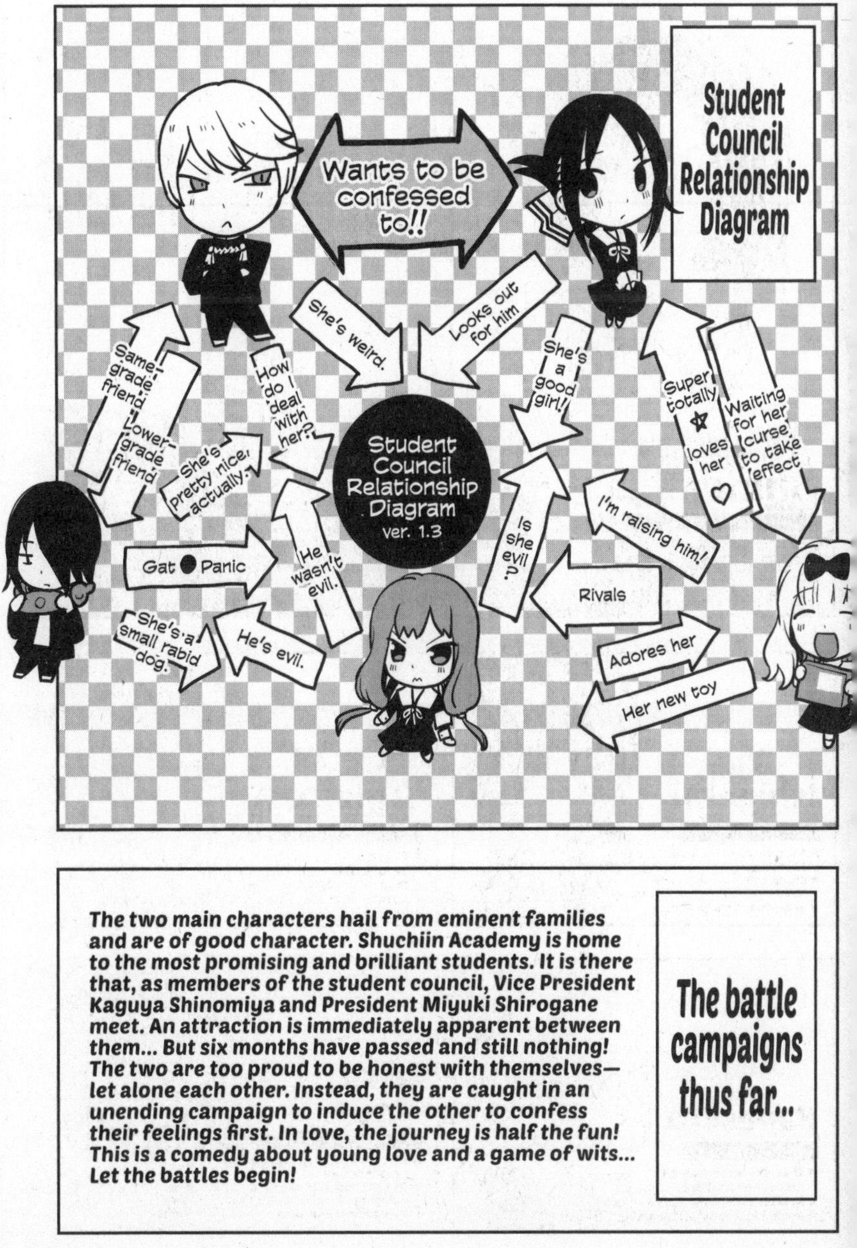
Student Council Relationship Diagram
Wants to be confessed to!!
Looks out for him
She's weird.
She's a good girl!
Super totally ☆ loves her ♡
Waiting for her curse to take effect
Same-grade friend
Lower-grade friend
How do I deal with her?
She's pretty nice, actually.
Student Council Relationship Diagram ver. 1.3
I'm raising him!
Is she evil?
Gat ● Panic
He wasn't evil.
Rivals
She's a small rabid dog.
He's evil.
Adores her
Her new toy

The two main characters hail from eminent families and are of good character. Shuchiin Academy is home to the most promising and brilliant students. It is there that, as members of the student council, Vice President Kaguya Shinomiya and President Miyuki Shirogane meet. An attraction is immediately apparent between them... But six months have passed and still nothing! The two are too proud to be honest with themselves—let alone each other. Instead, they are caught in an unending campaign to induce the other to confess their feelings first. In love, the journey is half the fun! This is a comedy about young love and a game of wits... Let the battles begin!

The battle campaigns thus far...

BATTLE CAMPAIGNS

12

◆ Battle 112 ◆
Miyuki Shirogane Wants to Make Her Confess, Part 1 ········ 5

◆ Battle 113 ◆
Miyuki Shirogane Wants to Make Her Confess, Part 2 ······ 25

◆ Battle 114 ◆
Miyuki Shirogane Wants to Make Her Confess, Part 3 ······ 45

◆ Battle 115 ◆
Miko Ino Can't Love, Part 1 ······························· 65

◆ Battle 116 ◆
Students Wish to Discuss the Culture Festival ·················· 85

◆ Battle 117 ◆
Chika Fujiwara Wants to Battle ··························· 105

◆ Battle 118 ◆
Miyuki Shirogane Wants to Blow It Up ··················· 125

◆ Battle 119 ◆
Kei Shirogane Wants to Show Off ······················· 145

◆ Battle 120 ◆
About Kaguya Shinomiya, Part 2 ······················· 165

◆ Battle 121 ◆
Spring of First Year ····································· 184

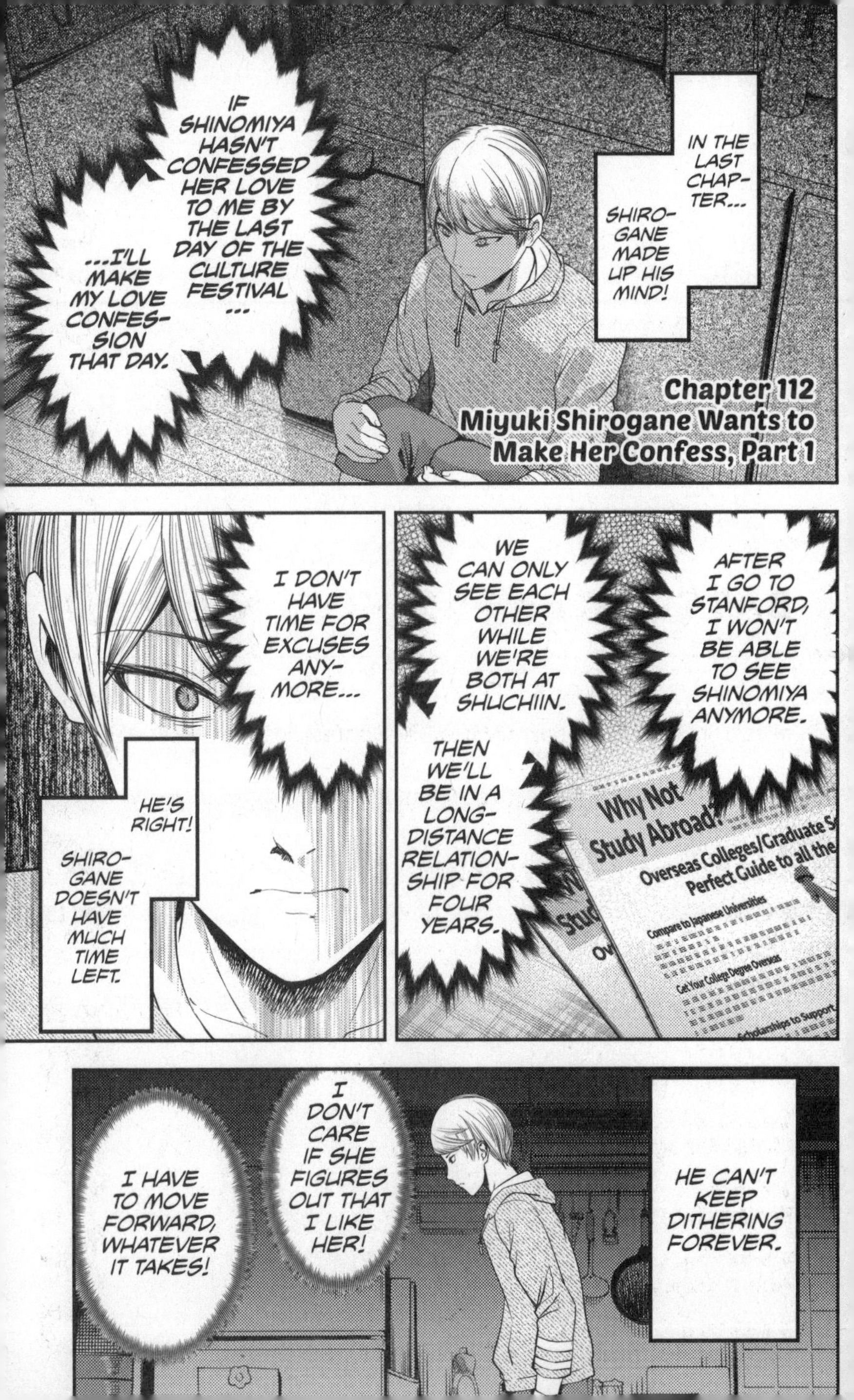
IN THE LAST CHAP-TER... SHIRO-GANE MADE UP HIS MIND!
IF SHINOMIYA HASN'T CONFESSED HER LOVE TO ME BY THE LAST DAY OF THE CULTURE FESTIVAL...
...I'LL MAKE MY LOVE CONFES-SION THAT DAY.
Chapter 112
Miyuki Shirogane Wants to Make Her Confess, Part 1
AFTER I GO TO STANFORD, I WON'T BE ABLE TO SEE SHINOMIYA ANYMORE.
WE CAN ONLY SEE EACH OTHER WHILE WE'RE BOTH AT SHUCHIIN.
THEN WE'LL BE IN A LONG-DISTANCE RELATION-SHIP FOR FOUR YEARS.
Why Not Study Abroad?
Compare to Japanese Universities
Get Your College Degree Overseas
I DON'T HAVE TIME FOR EXCUSES ANY-MORE...
HE'S RIGHT! SHIRO-GANE DOESN'T HAVE MUCH TIME LEFT.
HE CAN'T KEEP DITHERING FOREVER.
I DON'T CARE IF SHE FIGURES OUT THAT I LIKE HER!
I HAVE TO MOVE FORWARD, WHATEVER IT TAKES!

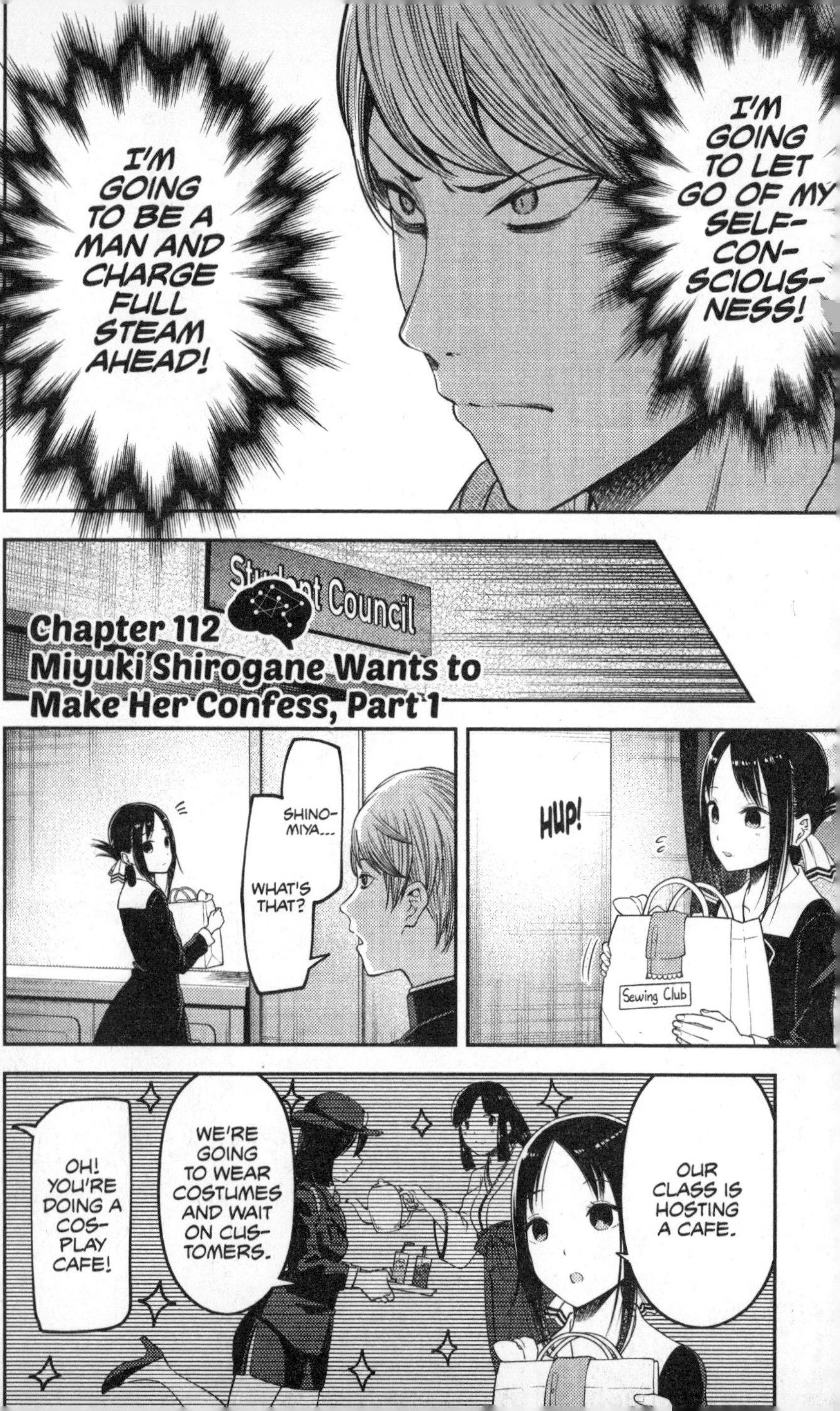
I'M GOING TO LET GO OF MY SELF-CONSCIOUSNESS!
I'M GOING TO BE A MAN AND CHARGE FULL STEAM AHEAD!
Student Council
Chapter 112
Miyuki Shirogane Wants to Make Her Confess, Part 1
HUP!
Sewing Club
SHINOMIYA...
WHAT'S THAT?
OUR CLASS IS HOSTING A CAFE.
WE'RE GOING TO WEAR COSTUMES AND WAIT ON CUSTOMERS.
OH! YOU'RE DOING A COSPLAY CAFE!

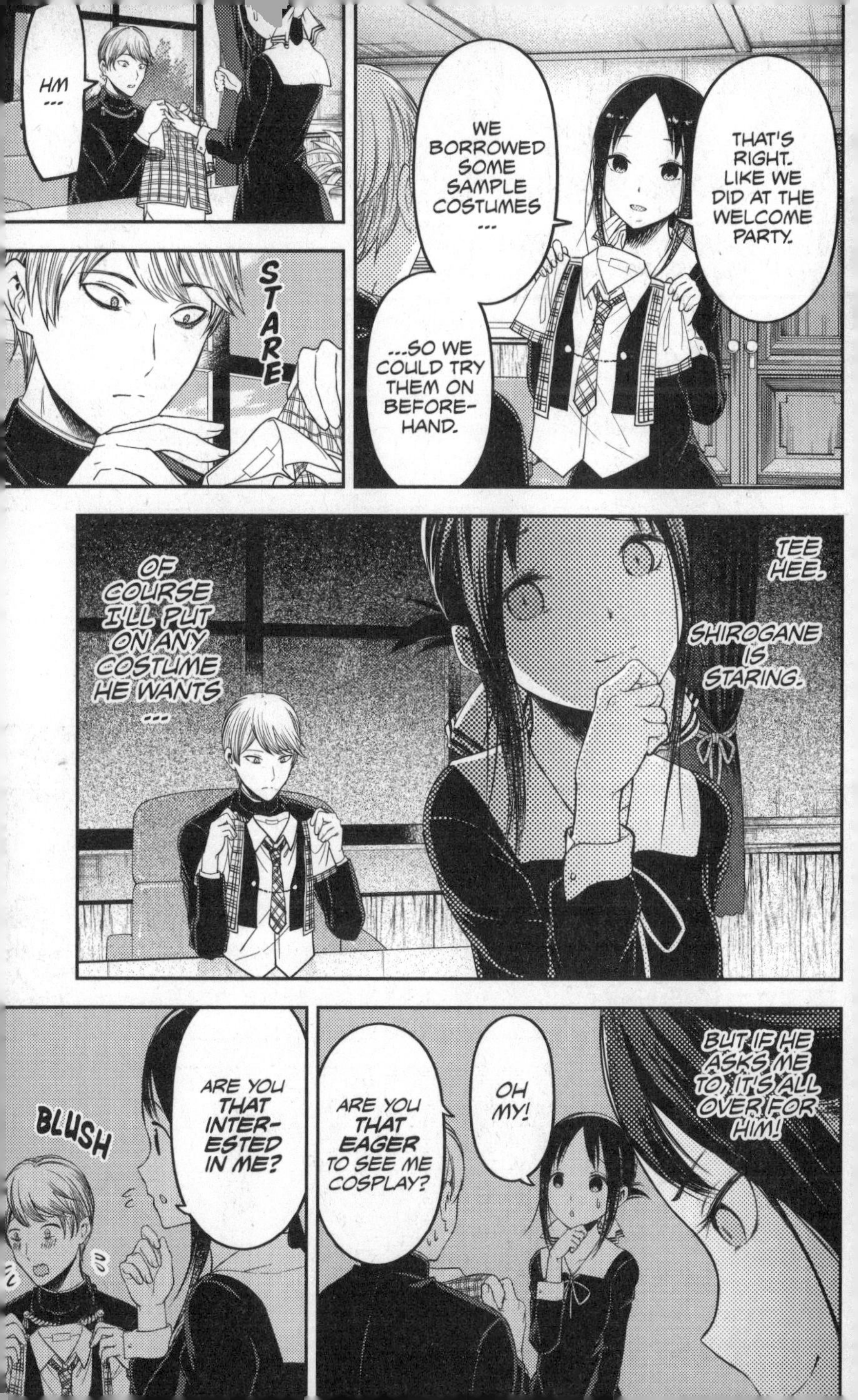
THAT'S RIGHT. LIKE WE DID AT THE WELCOME PARTY.
WE BORROWED SOME SAMPLE COSTUMES...
...SO WE COULD TRY THEM ON BEFORE-HAND.
HM...
STARE
TEE HEE.
SHIROGANE IS STARING.
OF COURSE I'LL PUT ON ANY COSTUME HE WANTS...
BUT IF HE ASKS ME TO, IT'S ALL OVER FOR HIM!
OH MY!
ARE YOU THAT EAGER TO SEE ME COSPLAY?
ARE YOU THAT INTER-ESTED IN ME?
BLUSH

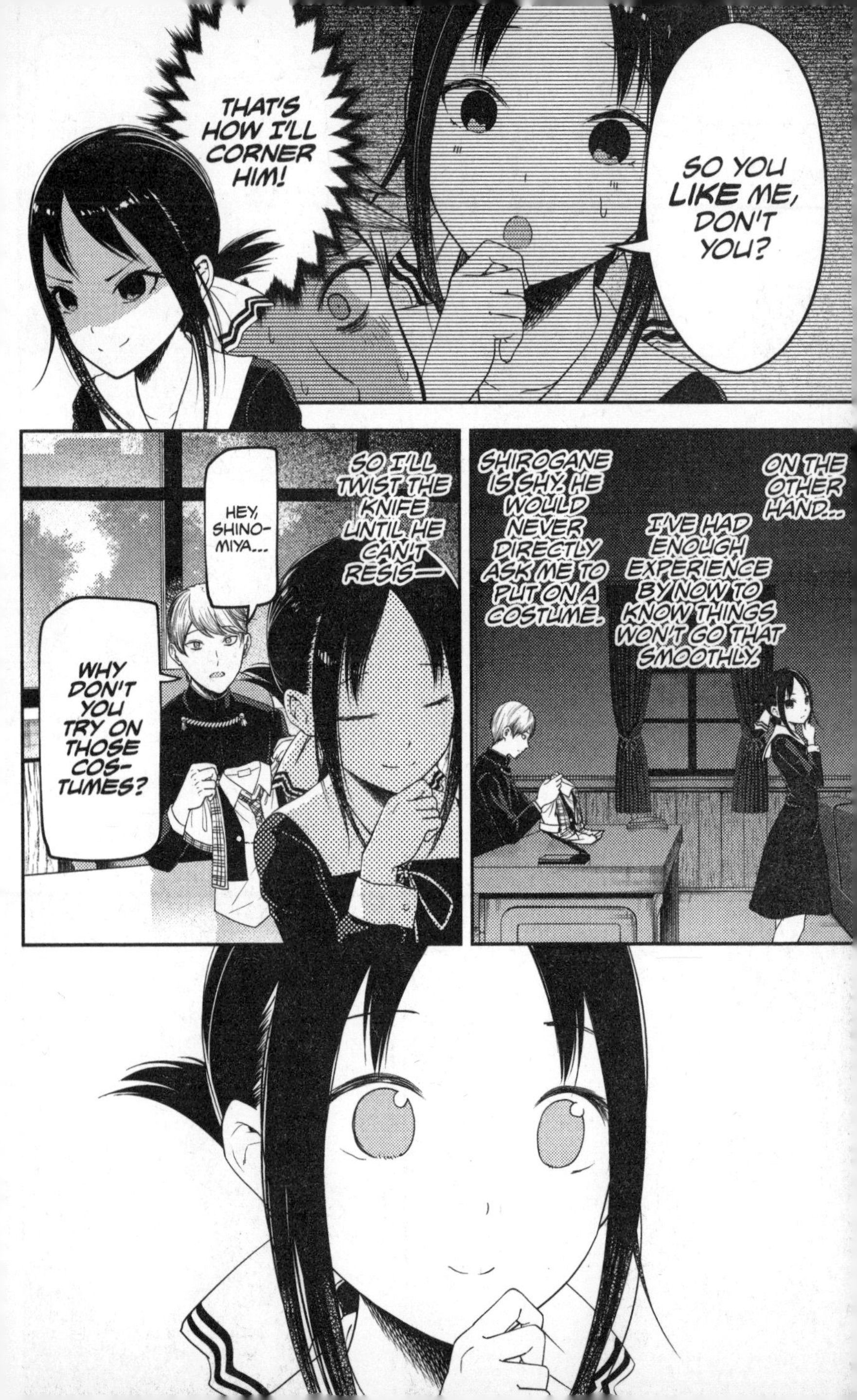
SO YOU LIKE ME, DON'T YOU?
THAT'S HOW I'LL CORNER HIM!
ON THE OTHER HAND...
I'VE HAD ENOUGH EXPERIENCE BY NOW TO KNOW THINGS WON'T GO THAT SMOOTHLY.
SHIROGANE IS SHY. HE WOULD NEVER DIRECTLY ASK ME TO PUT ON A COSTUME.
SO I'LL TWIST THE KNIFE UNTIL HE CAN'T RESIS—
HEY, SHINO-MIYA...
WHY DON'T YOU TRY ON THOSE COS-TUMES?

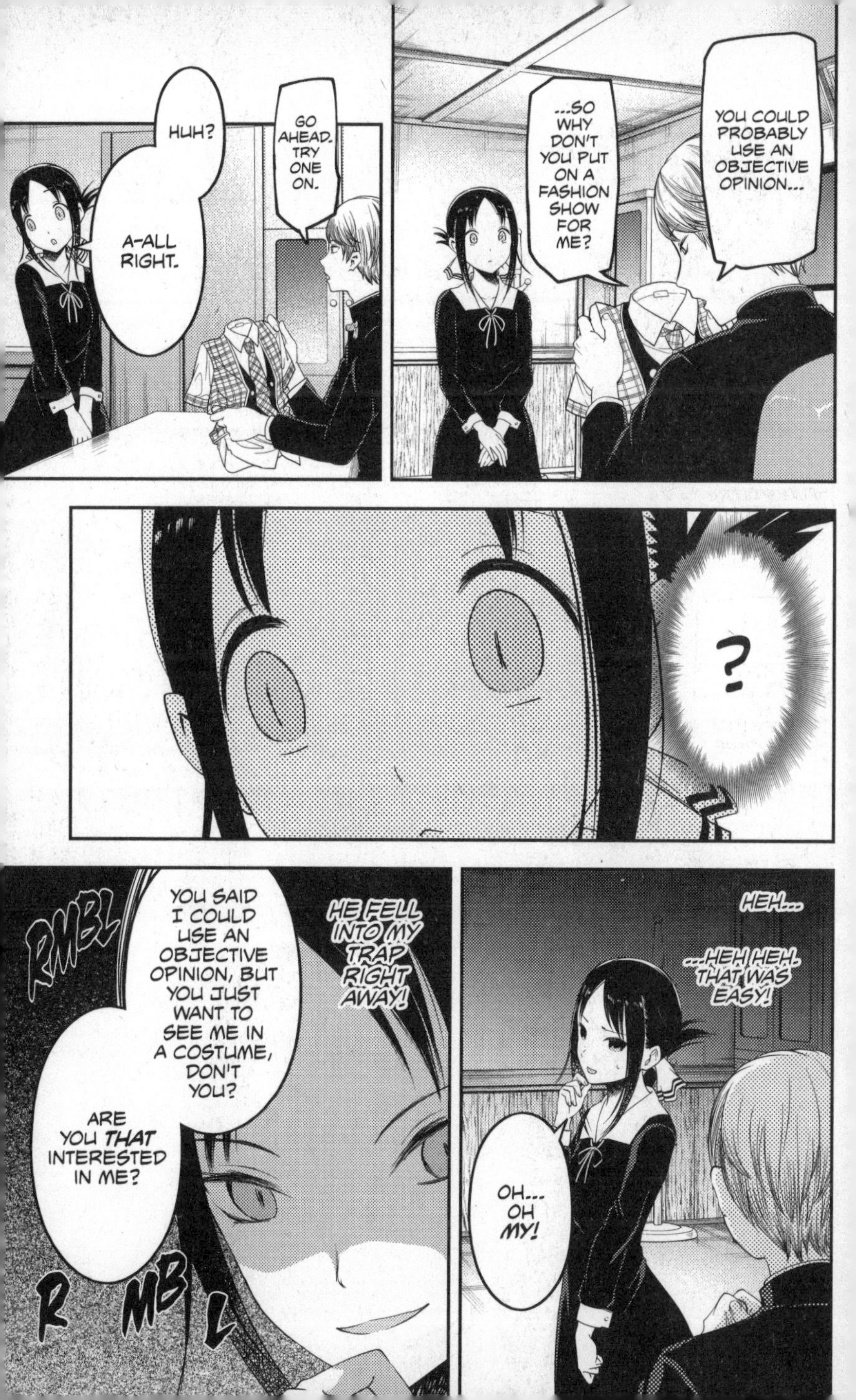
YOU COULD PROBABLY USE AN OBJECTIVE OPINION...
...SO WHY DON'T YOU PUT ON A FASHION SHOW FOR ME?
GO AHEAD. TRY ONE ON.
HUH?
A-ALL RIGHT.
?
HEH...
...HEH HEH. THAT WAS EASY!
OH... OH MY!
HE FELL INTO MY TRAP RIGHT AWAY!
RMBL
YOU SAID I COULD USE AN OBJECTIVE OPINION, BUT YOU JUST WANT TO SEE ME IN A COSTUME, DON'T YOU?
ARE YOU THAT INTERESTED IN ME?
RMBL

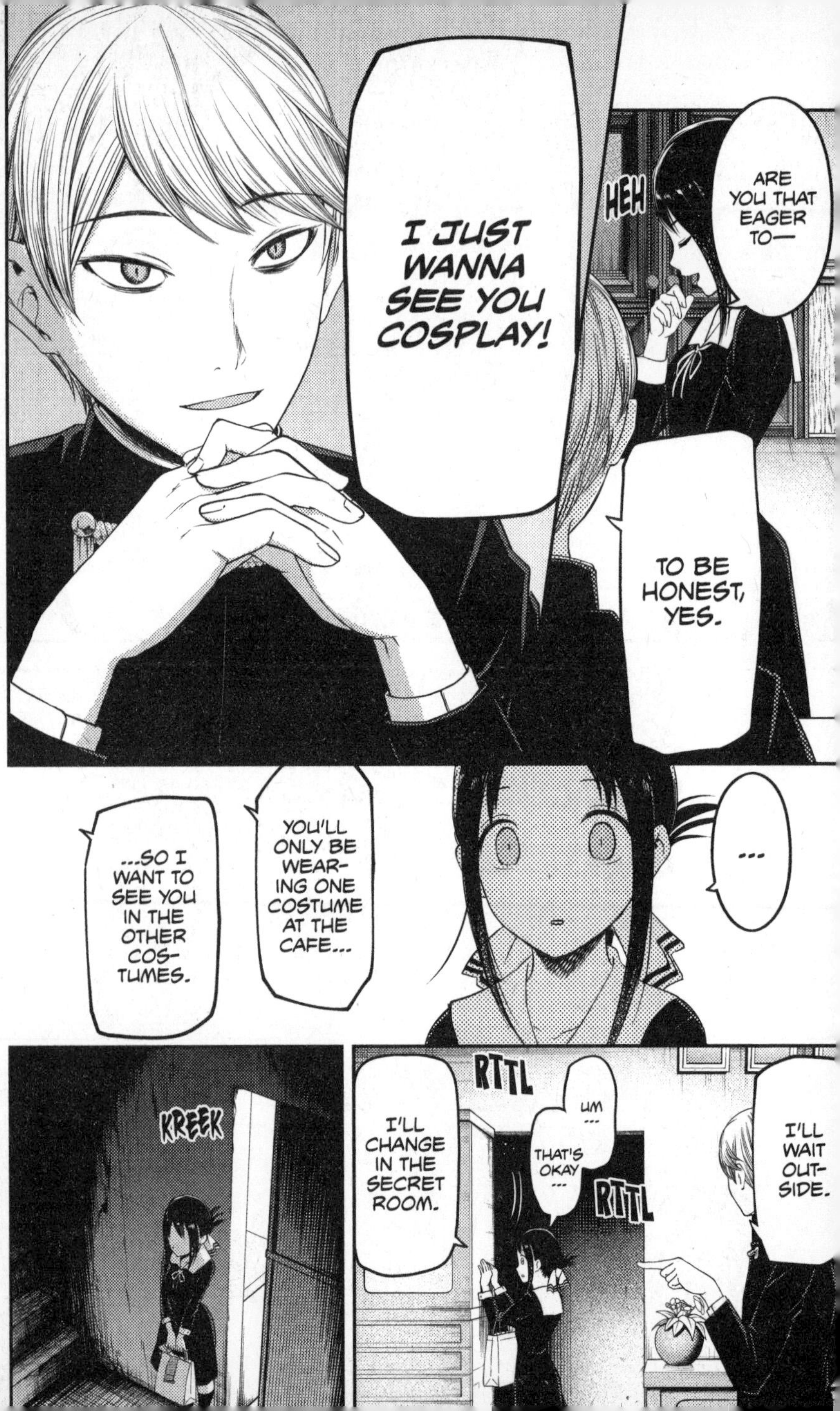
HEH
ARE YOU THAT EAGER TO—
TO BE HONEST, YES.
I JUST WANNA SEE YOU COSPLAY!
...
YOU'LL ONLY BE WEAR-ING ONE COSTUME AT THE CAFE...
...SO I WANT TO SEE YOU IN THE OTHER COS-TUMES.
I'LL WAIT OUT-SIDE.
RTTL
UM... THAT'S OKAY...
RTTL
I'LL CHANGE IN THE SECRET ROOM.
KREEK

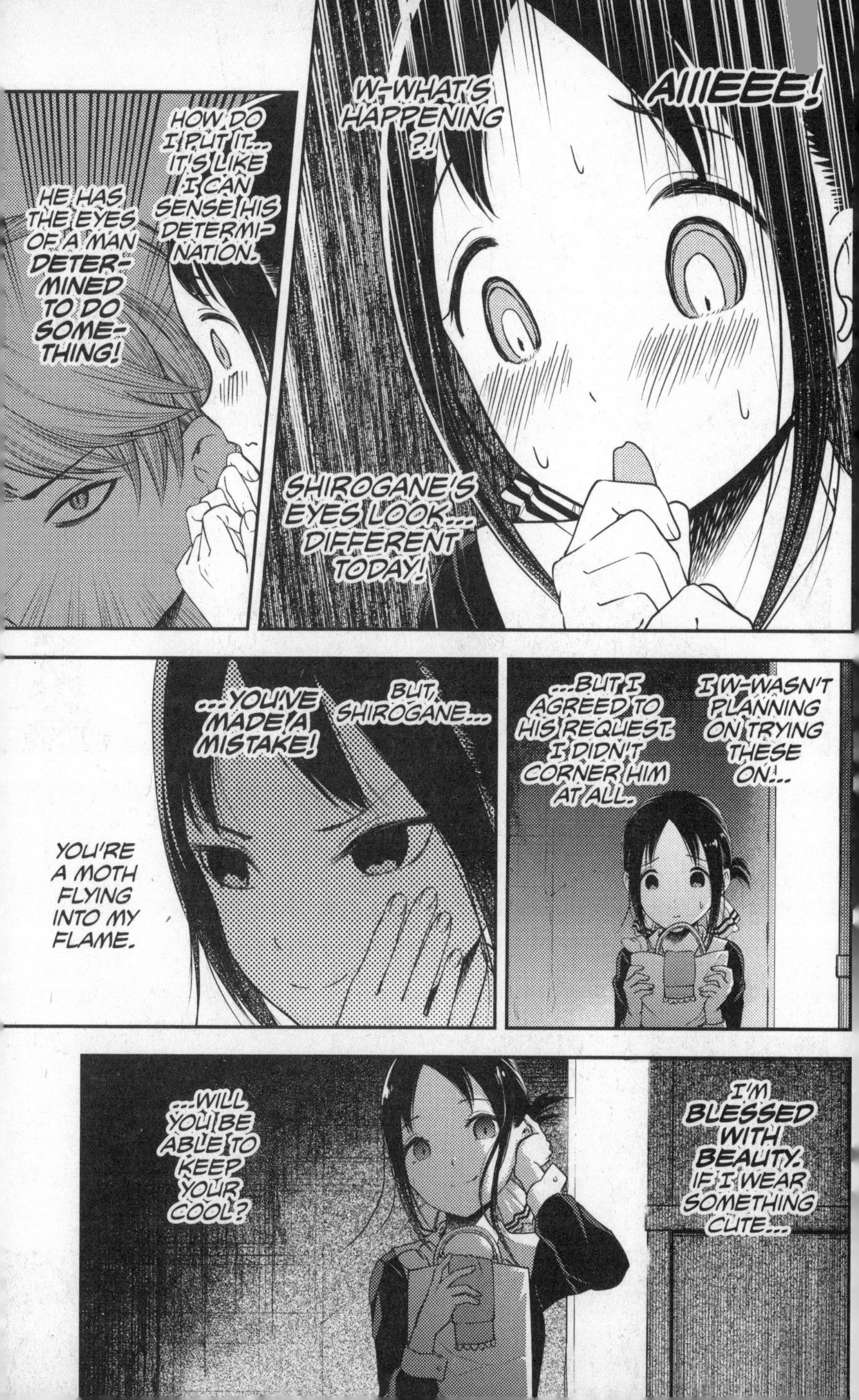
AIIIEEEE!
W-WHAT'S HAPPENING?!
SHIROGANE'S EYES LOOK... DIFFERENT TODAY!
HOW DO I PUT IT... IT'S LIKE I CAN SENSE HIS DETERMINATION.
HE HAS THE EYES OF A MAN DETERMINED TO DO SOMETHING!
I W-WASN'T PLANNING ON TRYING THESE ON...
...BUT I AGREED TO HIS REQUEST. I DIDN'T CORNER HIM AT ALL.
BUT, SHIROGANE...
...YOU'VE MADE A MISTAKE!
YOU'RE A MOTH FLYING INTO MY FLAME.
I'M BLESSED WITH BEAUTY. IF I WEAR SOMETHING CUTE...
...WILL YOU BE ABLE TO KEEP YOUR COOL?

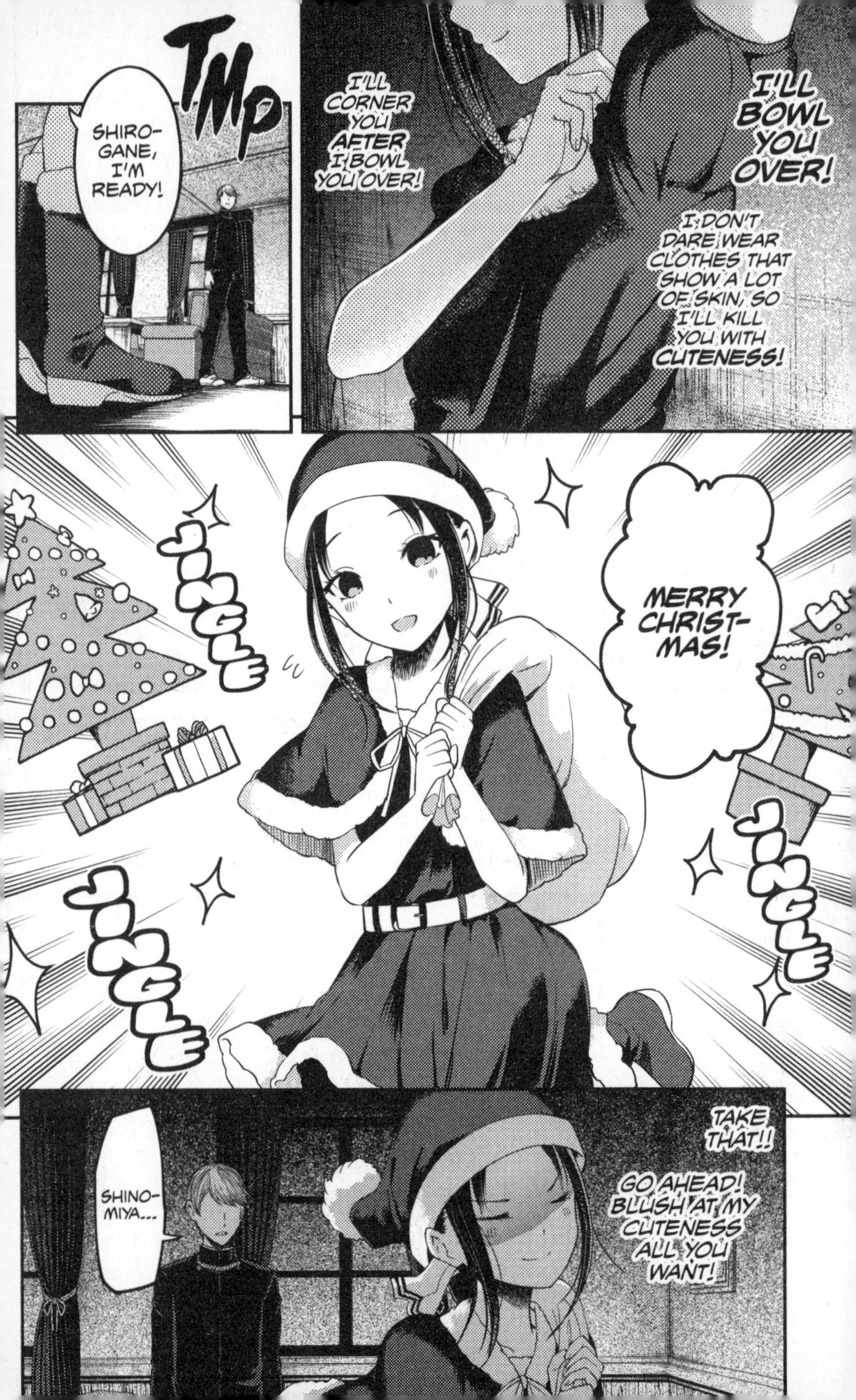
I'LL BOWL YOU OVER!
I'LL CORNER YOU AFTER I BOWL YOU OVER!
I DON'T DARE WEAR CLOTHES THAT SHOW A LOT OF SKIN, SO I'LL KILL YOU WITH CUTENESS!
TMP
SHIRO-GANE, I'M READY!
MERRY CHRIST-MAS!
JINGLE
JINGLE
JINGLE
TAKE THAT!!
GO AHEAD! BLUSH AT MY CUTENESS ALL YOU WANT!
SHINO-MIYA...

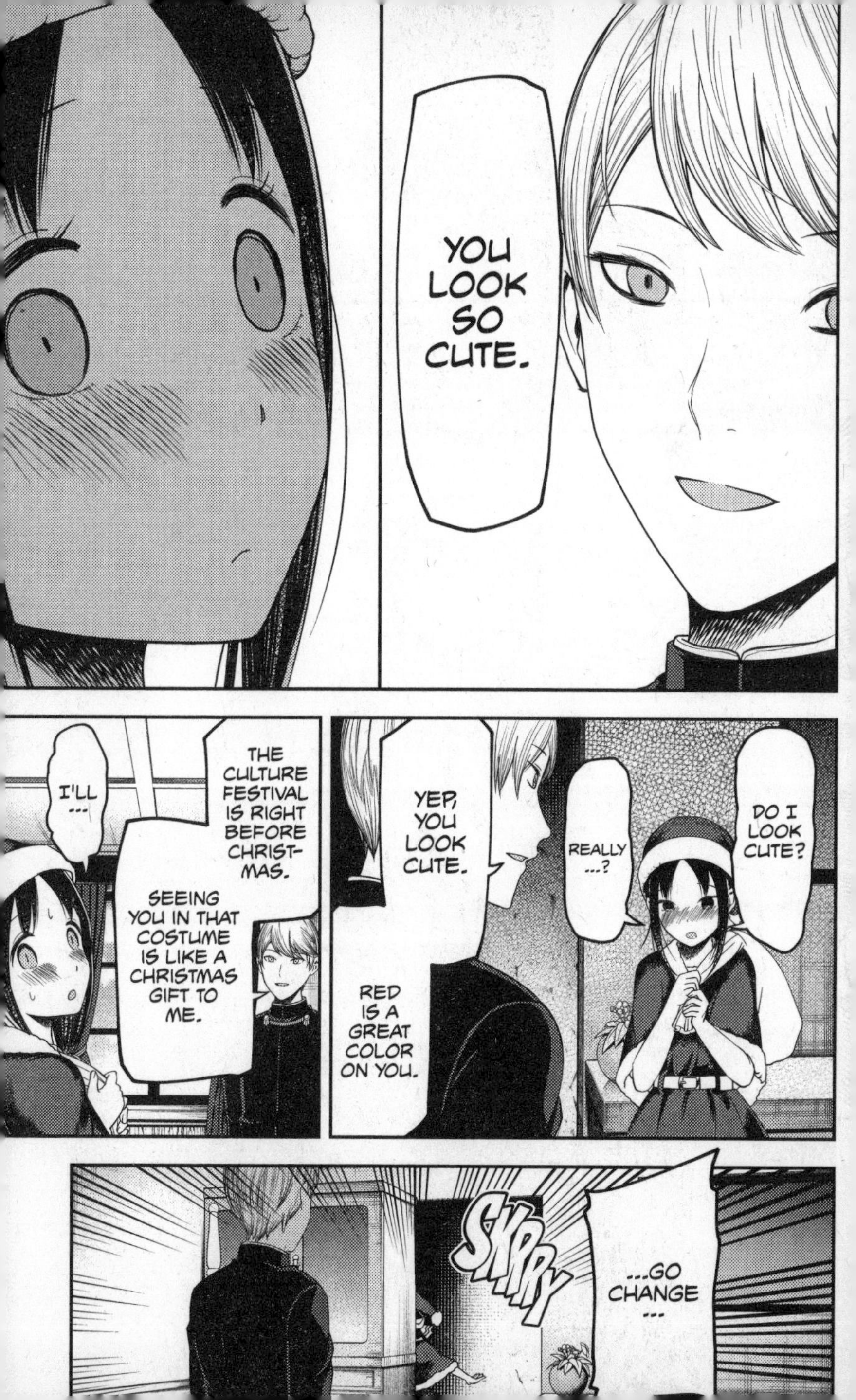
YOU LOOK SO CUTE.
DO I LOOK CUTE?
REALLY ...?
YEP, YOU LOOK CUTE.
RED IS A GREAT COLOR ON YOU.
THE CULTURE FESTIVAL IS RIGHT BEFORE CHRIST-MAS.
SEEING YOU IN THAT COSTUME IS LIKE A CHRISTMAS GIFT TO ME.
I'LL ...
...GO CHANGE ...
SKRRY

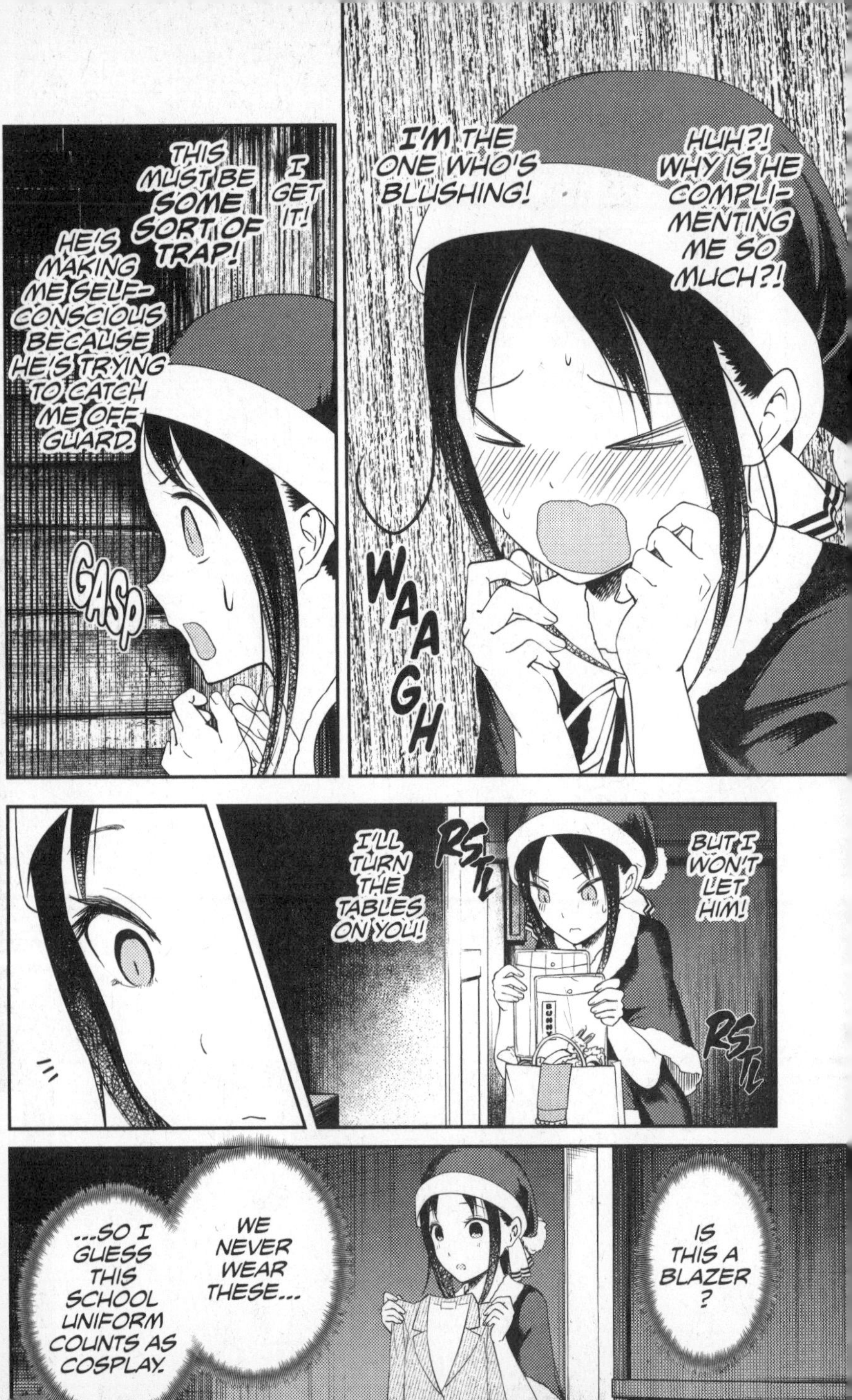
HUH?! WHY IS HE COMPLIMENTING ME SO MUCH?!
I'M THE ONE WHO'S BLUSHING!
WAAAGH
I GET IT!
THIS MUST BE SOME SORT OF TRAP!
HE'S MAKING ME SELF-CONSCIOUS BECAUSE HE'S TRYING TO CATCH ME OFF GUARD.
GASP
BUT I WON'T LET HIM!
RSTL
I'LL TURN THE TABLES ON YOU!
RSTL
IS THIS A BLAZER?
WE NEVER WEAR THESE...
...SO I GUESS THIS SCHOOL UNIFORM COUNTS AS COSPLAY.

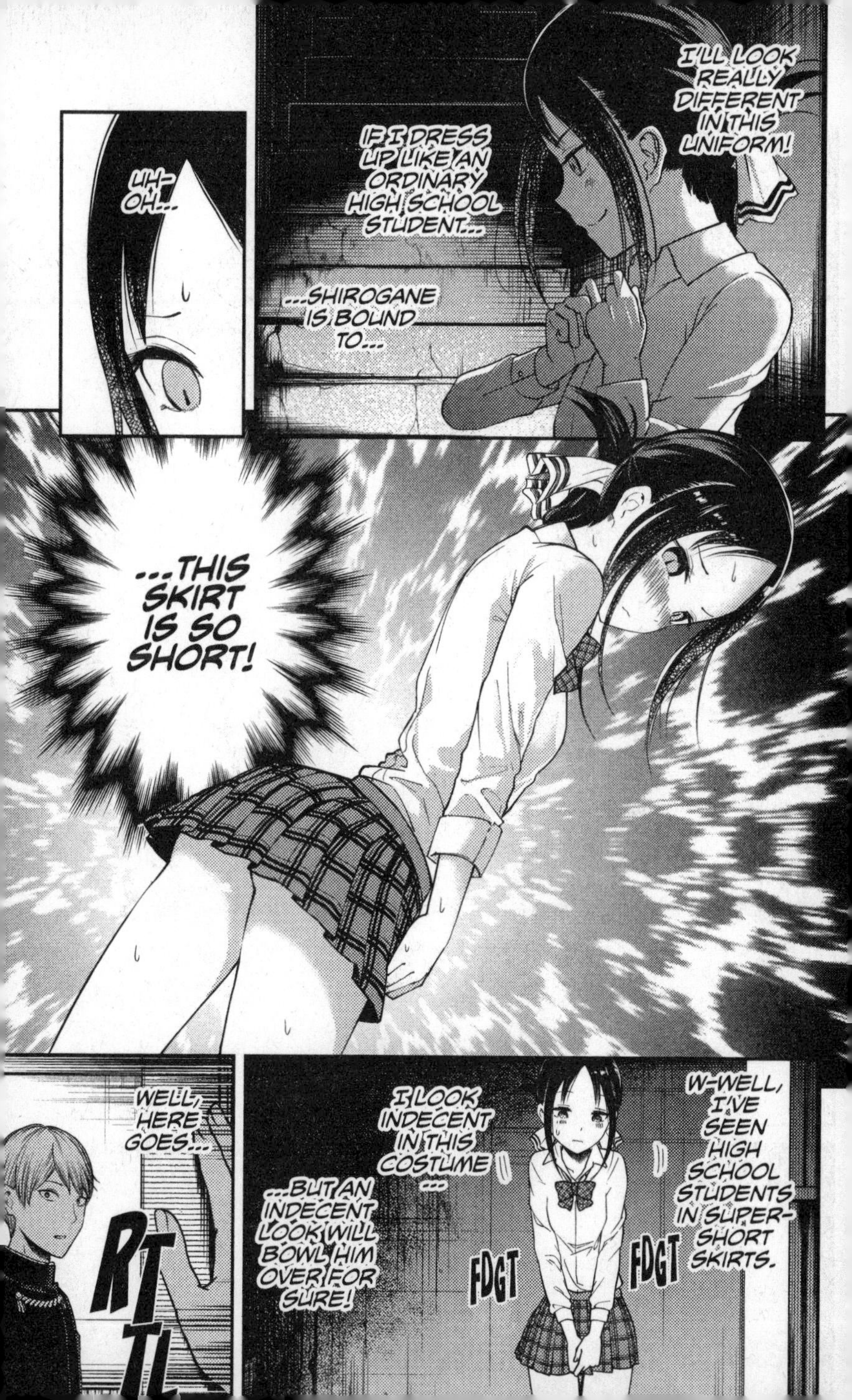
I'LL LOOK REALLY DIFFERENT IN THIS UNIFORM!
IF I DRESS UP LIKE AN ORDINARY HIGH SCHOOL STUDENT...
...SHIROGANE IS BOUND TO...
UH-OH...
...THIS SKIRT IS SO SHORT!
W-WELL, I'VE SEEN HIGH SCHOOL STUDENTS IN SUPER-SHORT SKIRTS.
FDGT
FDGT
I LOOK INDECENT IN THIS COSTUME...
...BUT AN INDECENT LOOK WILL BOWL HIM OVER FOR SURE!
WELL, HERE GOES...
RTTL

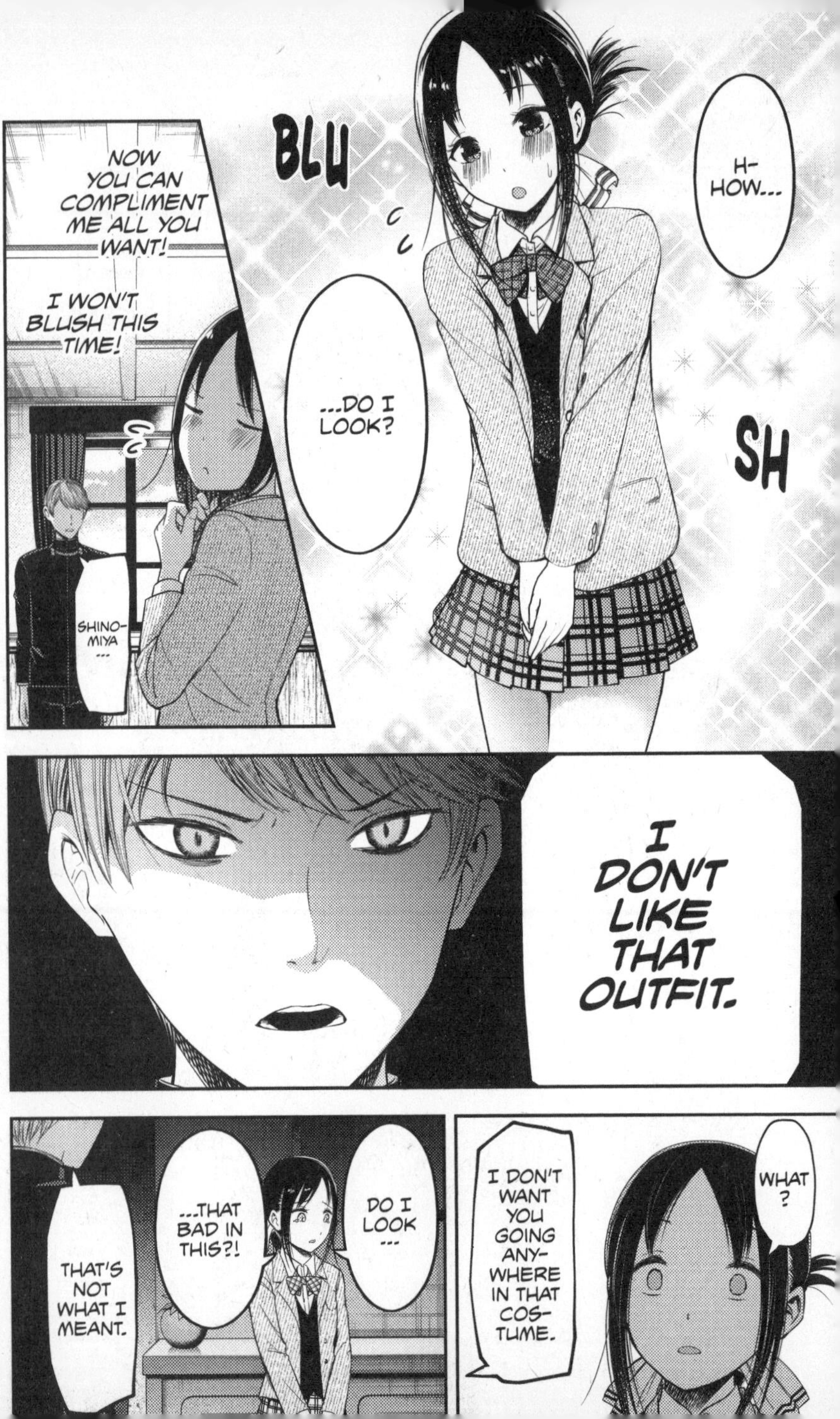
H-HOW...
...DO I LOOK?
SH
BLU
NOW YOU CAN COMPLIMENT ME ALL YOU WANT!
I WON'T BLUSH THIS TIME!
SHINOMIYA...
I DON'T LIKE THAT OUTFIT.
WHAT?
I DON'T WANT YOU GOING ANYWHERE IN THAT COSTUME.
DO I LOOK...
...THAT BAD IN THIS?!
THAT'S NOT WHAT I MEANT.

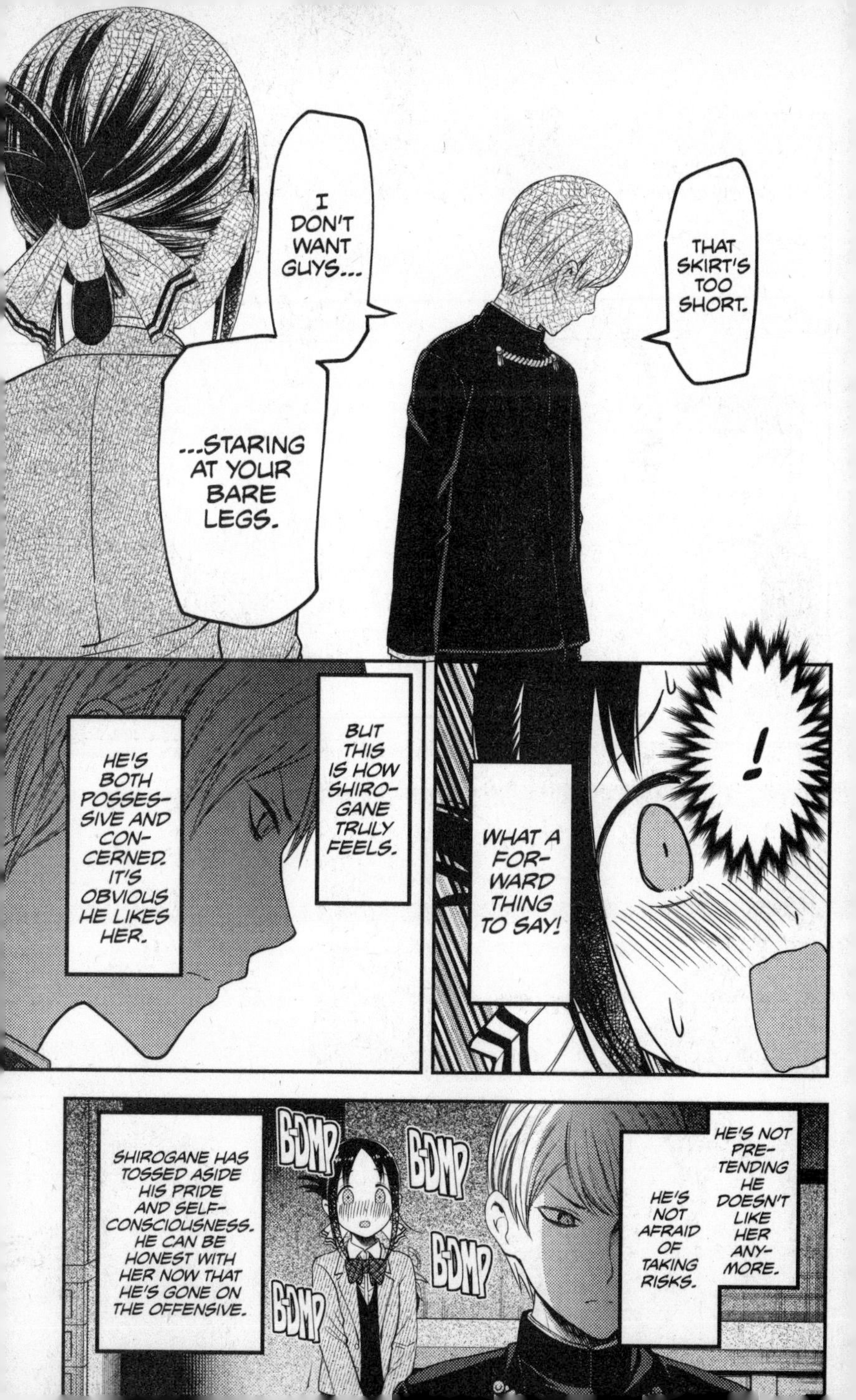
THAT SKIRT'S TOO SHORT.
I DON'T WANT GUYS...
...STARING AT YOUR BARE LEGS.
!
WHAT A FOR-WARD THING TO SAY!
BUT THIS IS HOW SHIRO-GANE TRULY FEELS.
HE'S BOTH POSSES-SIVE AND CON-CERNED. IT'S OBVIOUS HE LIKES HER.
HE'S NOT PRE-TENDING HE DOESN'T LIKE HER ANY-MORE.
HE'S NOT AFRAID OF TAKING RISKS.
B-DMP
B-DMP
B-DMP
B-DMP
SHIROGANE HAS TOSSED ASIDE HIS PRIDE AND SELF-CONSCIOUSNESS. HE CAN BE HONEST WITH HER NOW THAT HE'S GONE ON THE OFFENSIVE.

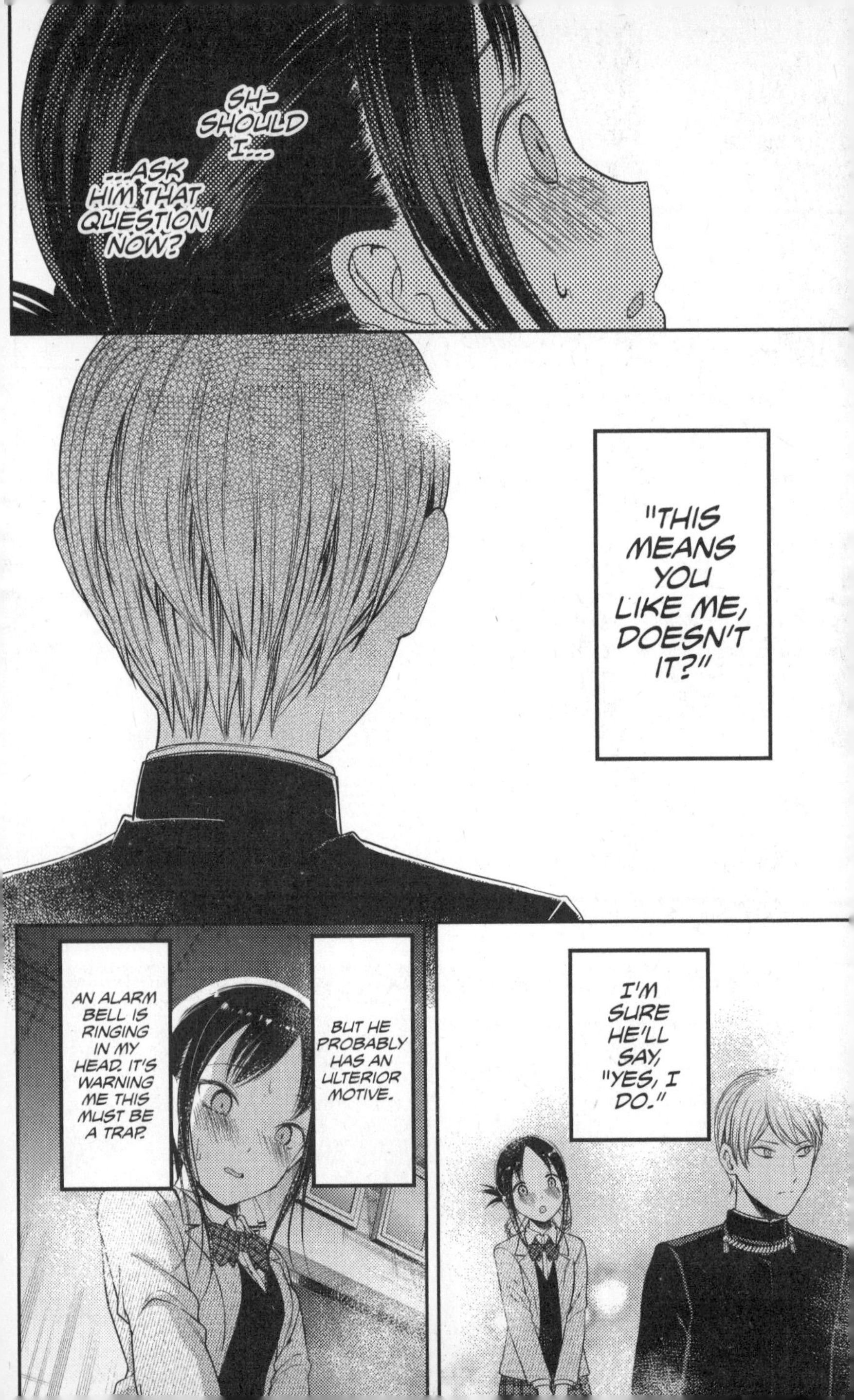
SH- SHOULD I...
...ASK HIM THAT QUESTION NOW?
"THIS MEANS YOU LIKE ME, DOESN'T IT?"
I'M SURE HE'LL SAY, "YES, I DO."
BUT HE PROBABLY HAS AN ULTERIOR MOTIVE.
AN ALARM BELL IS RINGING IN MY HEAD. IT'S WARNING ME THIS MUST BE A TRAP.

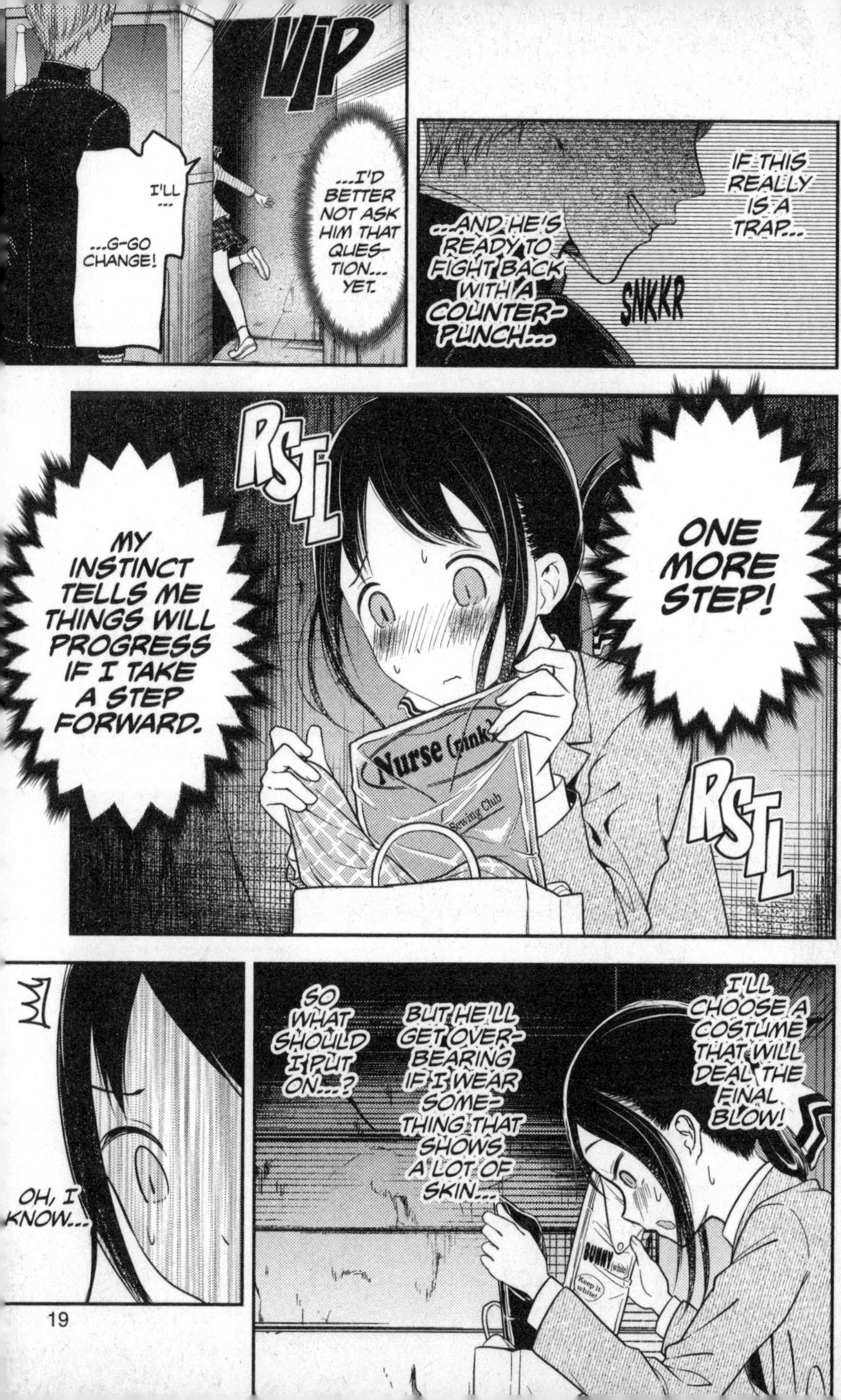
IF THIS REALLY IS A TRAP...
...AND HE'S READY TO FIGHT BACK WITH A COUNTER-PUNCH...
SNKKR
VIP
...I'D BETTER NOT ASK HIM THAT QUESTION... YET.
I'LL ...
...G-GO CHANGE!
ONE MORE STEP!
RSTL
RSTL
MY INSTINCT TELLS ME THINGS WILL PROGRESS IF I TAKE A STEP FORWARD.
Nurse (pink)
Sewing Club
I'LL CHOOSE A COSTUME THAT WILL DEAL THE FINAL BLOW!
BUT HE'LL GET OVER-BEARING IF I WEAR SOME-THING THAT SHOWS A LOT OF SKIN...
SO WHAT SHOULD I PUT ON...?
BUNNY (white)
Keep it white!
OH, I KNOW...

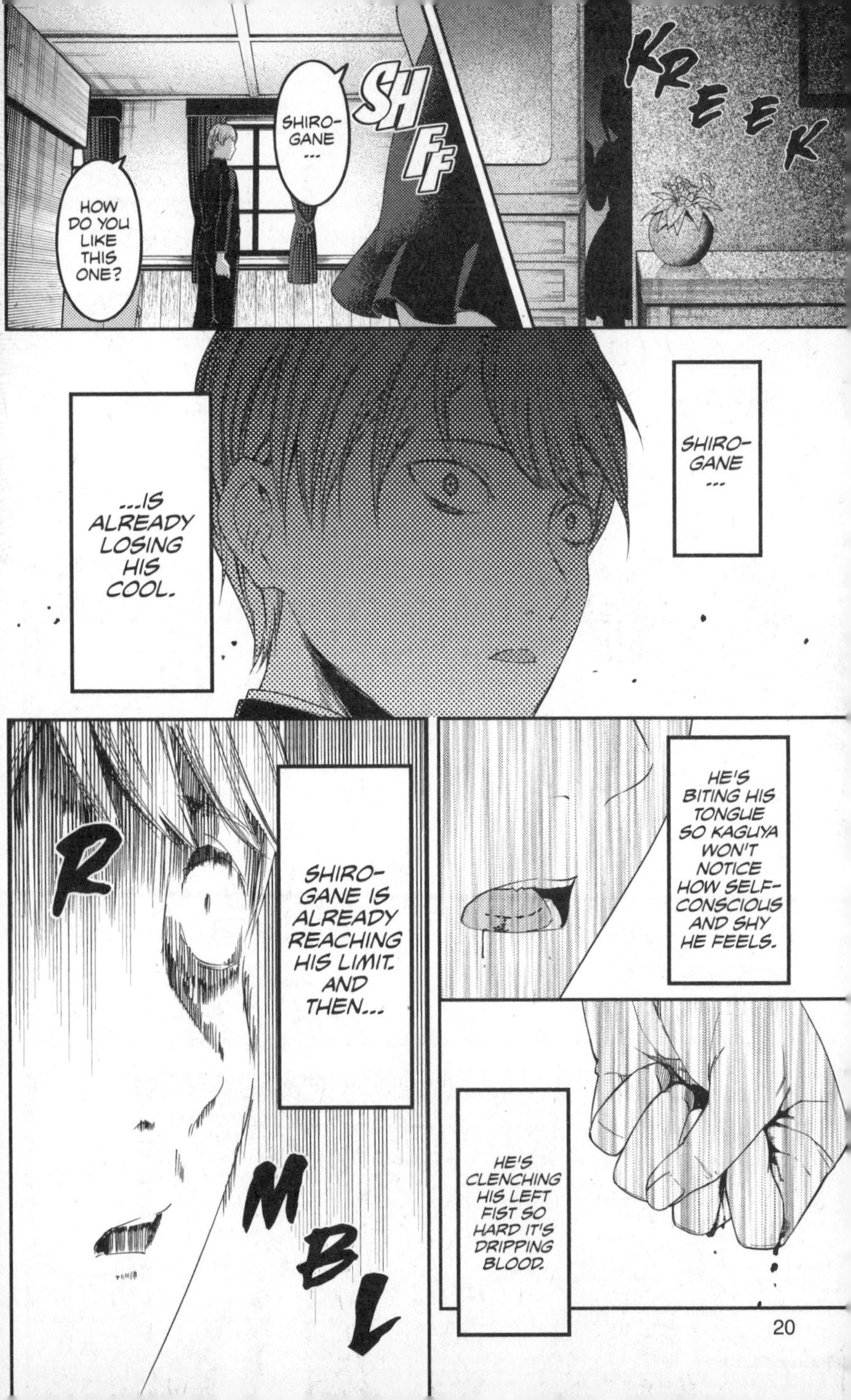
KREEK
SHFF
SHIRO-GANE...
HOW DO YOU LIKE THIS ONE?
SHIRO-GANE...
...IS ALREADY LOSING HIS COOL.
HE'S BITING HIS TONGUE SO KAGUYA WON'T NOTICE HOW SELF-CONSCIOUS AND SHY HE FEELS.
HE'S CLENCHING HIS LEFT FIST SO HARD IT'S DRIPPING BLOOD.
SHIRO-GANE IS ALREADY REACHING HIS LIMIT. AND THEN...
RMBL

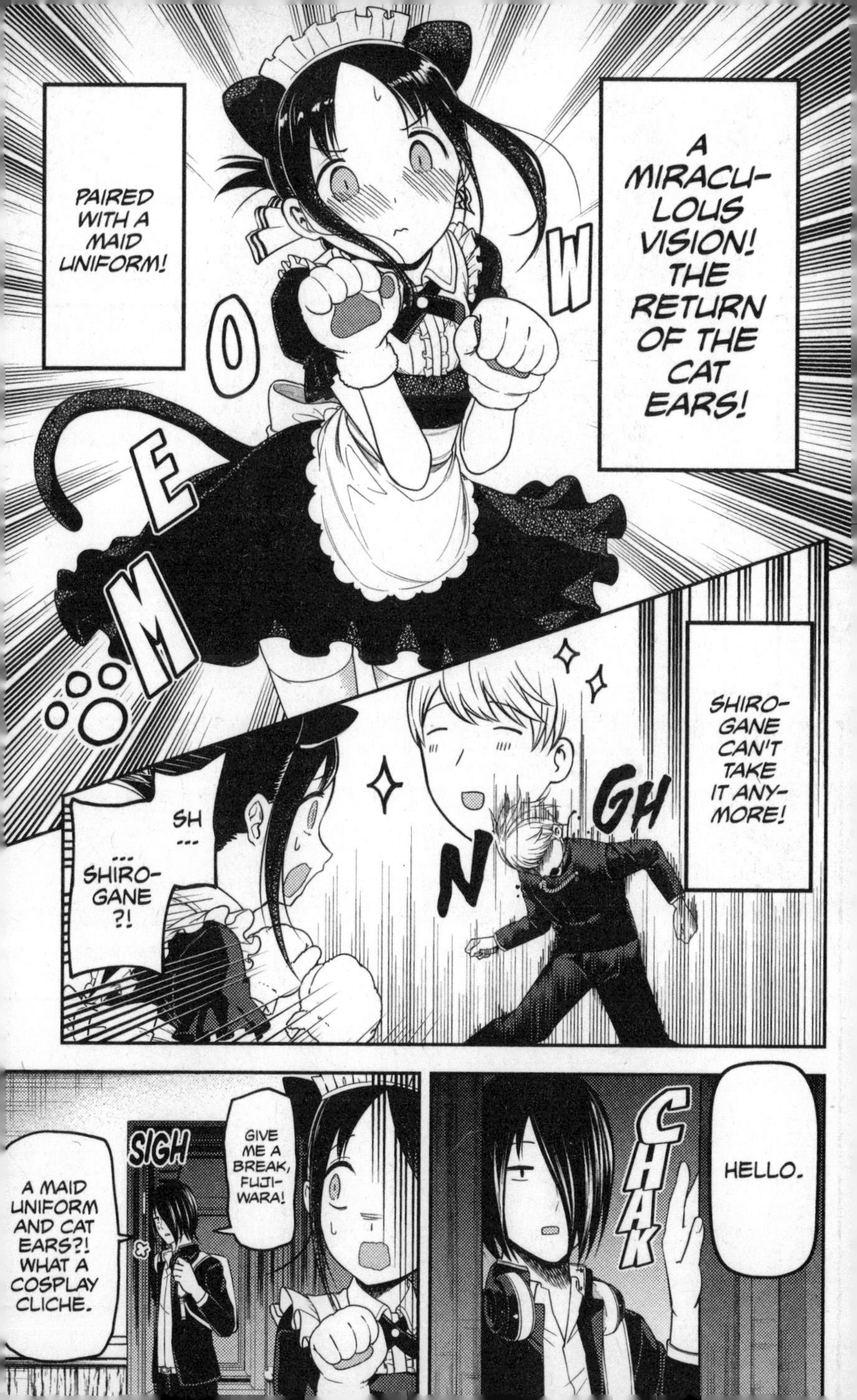

A MIRACULOUS VISION! THE RETURN OF THE CAT EARS!
PAIRED WITH A MAID UNIFORM!
MEOW
SHIROGANE CAN'T TAKE IT ANYMORE!
NGH
SH--- ...SHIROGANE?!
CHAK
HELLO.
GIVE ME A BREAK, FUJIWARA!
SIGH
A MAID UNIFORM AND CAT EARS?! WHAT A COSPLAY CLICHE.

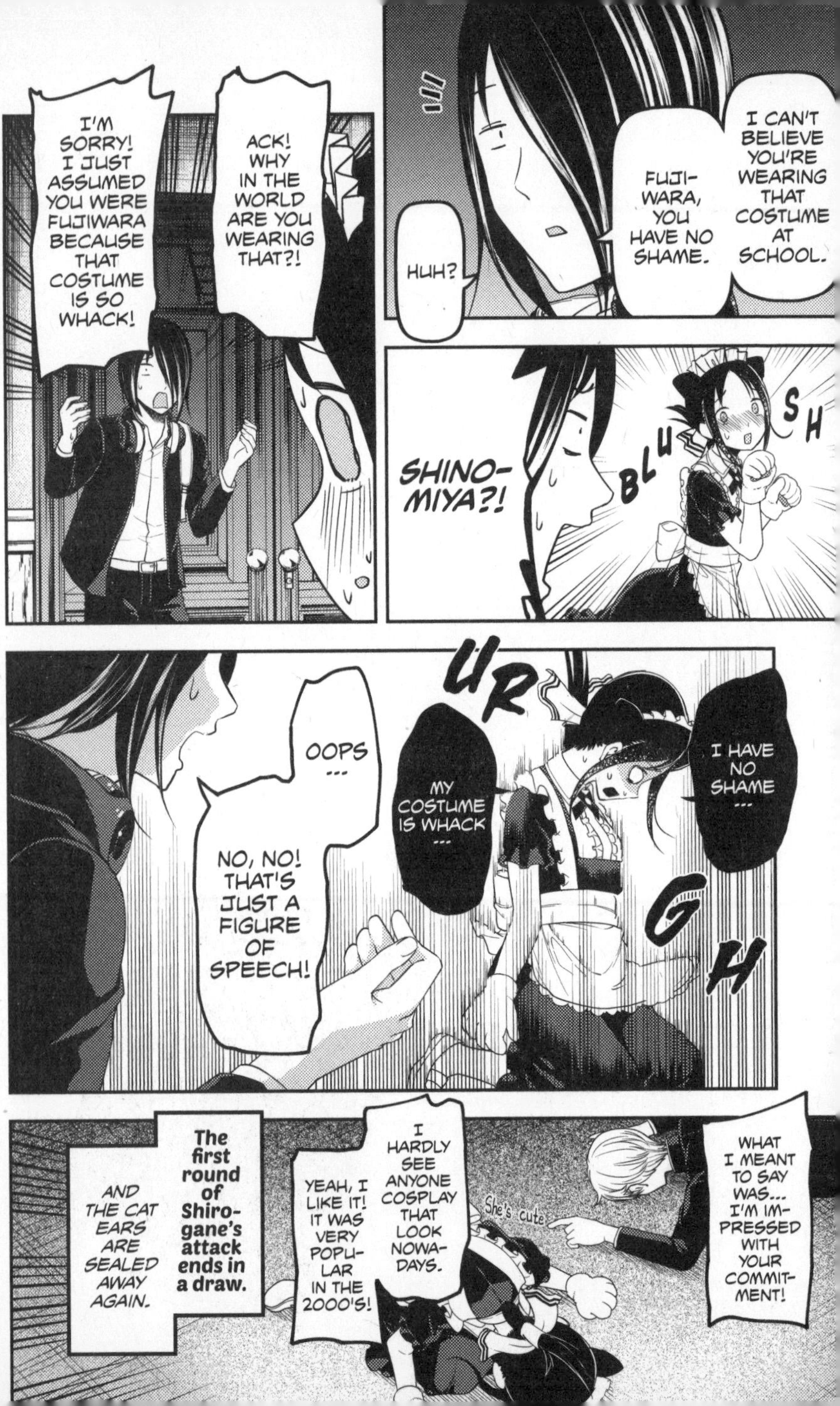
I CAN'T BELIEVE YOU'RE WEARING THAT COSTUME AT SCHOOL.
FUJIWARA, YOU HAVE NO SHAME.
HUH?
BLUSH
SHINOMIYA?!
ACK! WHY IN THE WORLD ARE YOU WEARING THAT?!
I'M SORRY! I JUST ASSUMED YOU WERE FUJIWARA BECAUSE THAT COSTUME IS SO WHACK!
URGH
I HAVE NO SHAME...
MY COSTUME IS WHACK...
OOPS...
NO, NO! THAT'S JUST A FIGURE OF SPEECH!
WHAT I MEANT TO SAY WAS... I'M IMPRESSED WITH YOUR COMMITMENT!
She's cute
I HARDLY SEE ANYONE COSPLAY THAT LOOK NOWADAYS.
YEAH, I LIKE IT! IT WAS VERY POPULAR IN THE 2000'S!
The first round of Shirogane's attack ends in a draw.
AND THE CAT EARS ARE SEALED AWAY AGAIN.

SCHOOL EVENTS

Hoshin Culture
Festival (12/20 to 12/21)
Christmas Eve (12/24)
Second Semester
Closing Ceremony (12/26)
Kaguya's Birthday (1/1)
Third Semester
Opening Ceremony (1/7)
School Trip (2/1 to 2/4)
Valentine's Day (2/14)
Fujiwara and Ishigami's
Birthday (3/3)
Commencement (3/10)
Third Semester
Closing Ceremony (3/22)

Diary

KAGUYA-SAMA
LOVE IS WAR

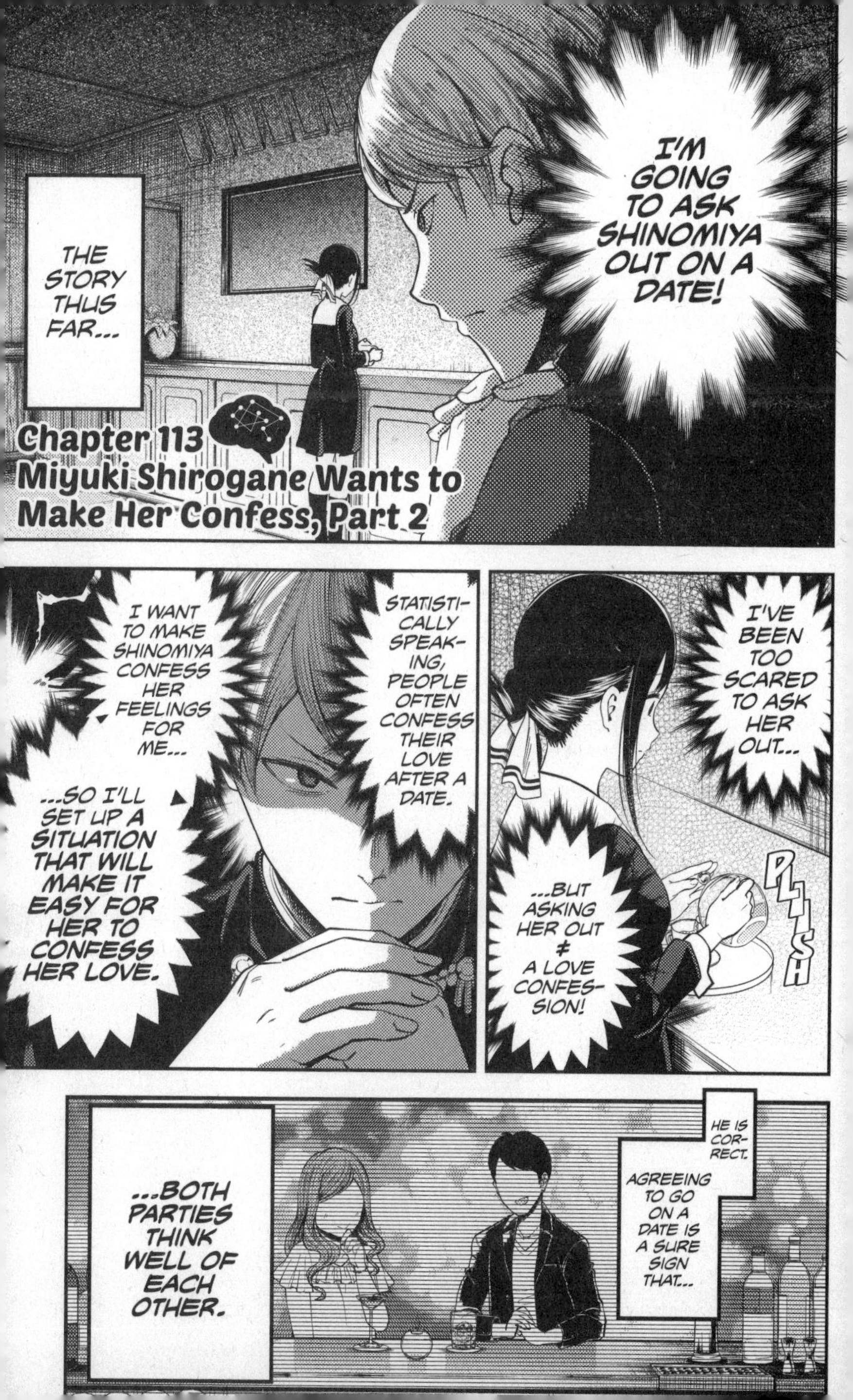
I'M GOING TO ASK SHINOMIYA OUT ON A DATE!
THE STORY THUS FAR...
Chapter 113 Miyuki Shirogane Wants to Make Her Confess, Part 2
I'VE BEEN TOO SCARED TO ASK HER OUT...
...BUT ASKING HER OUT ≠ A LOVE CONFESSION!
PLISH
STATISTICALLY SPEAKING, PEOPLE OFTEN CONFESS THEIR LOVE AFTER A DATE.
I WANT TO MAKE SHINOMIYA CONFESS HER FEELINGS FOR ME...
...SO I'LL SET UP A SITUATION THAT WILL MAKE IT EASY FOR HER TO CONFESS HER LOVE.
HE IS CORRECT.
AGREEING TO GO ON A DATE IS A SURE SIGN THAT...
...BOTH PARTIES THINK WELL OF EACH OTHER.

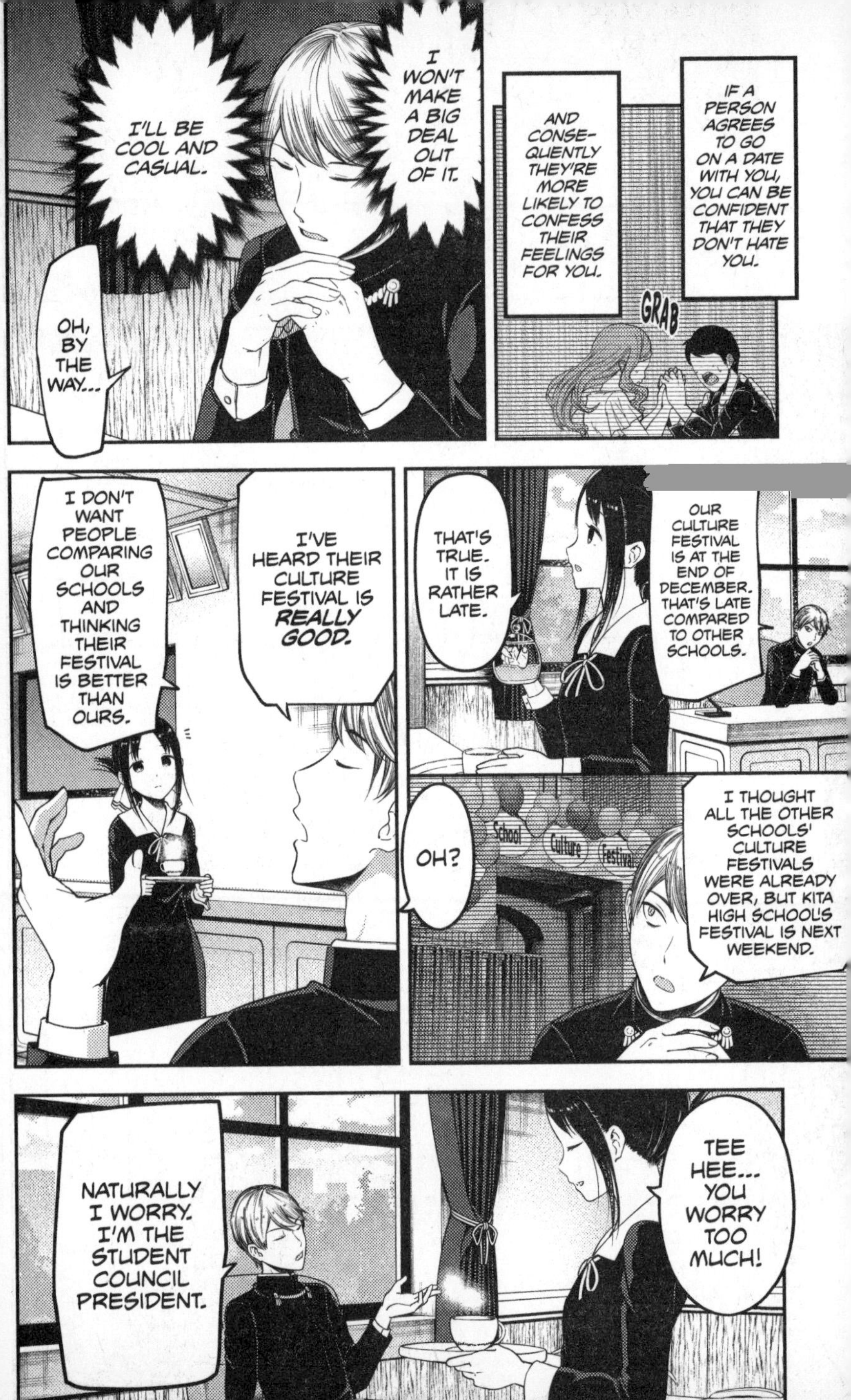
IF A PERSON AGREES TO GO ON A DATE WITH YOU, YOU CAN BE CONFIDENT THAT THEY DON'T HATE YOU.
AND CONSE-QUENTLY THEY'RE MORE LIKELY TO CONFESS THEIR FEELINGS FOR YOU.
GRAB
I WON'T MAKE A BIG DEAL OUT OF IT.
I'LL BE COOL AND CASUAL.
OH, BY THE WAY...
OUR CULTURE FESTIVAL IS AT THE END OF DECEMBER. THAT'S LATE COMPARED TO OTHER SCHOOLS.
THAT'S TRUE. IT IS RATHER LATE.
I THOUGHT ALL THE OTHER SCHOOLS' CULTURE FESTIVALS WERE ALREADY OVER, BUT KITA HIGH SCHOOL'S FESTIVAL IS NEXT WEEKEND.
OH?
School Culture Festival
I'VE HEARD THEIR CULTURE FESTIVAL IS REALLY GOOD.
I DON'T WANT PEOPLE COMPARING OUR SCHOOLS AND THINKING THEIR FESTIVAL IS BETTER THAN OURS.
TEE HEE... YOU WORRY TOO MUCH!
NATURALLY I WORRY. I'M THE STUDENT COUNCIL PRESIDENT.

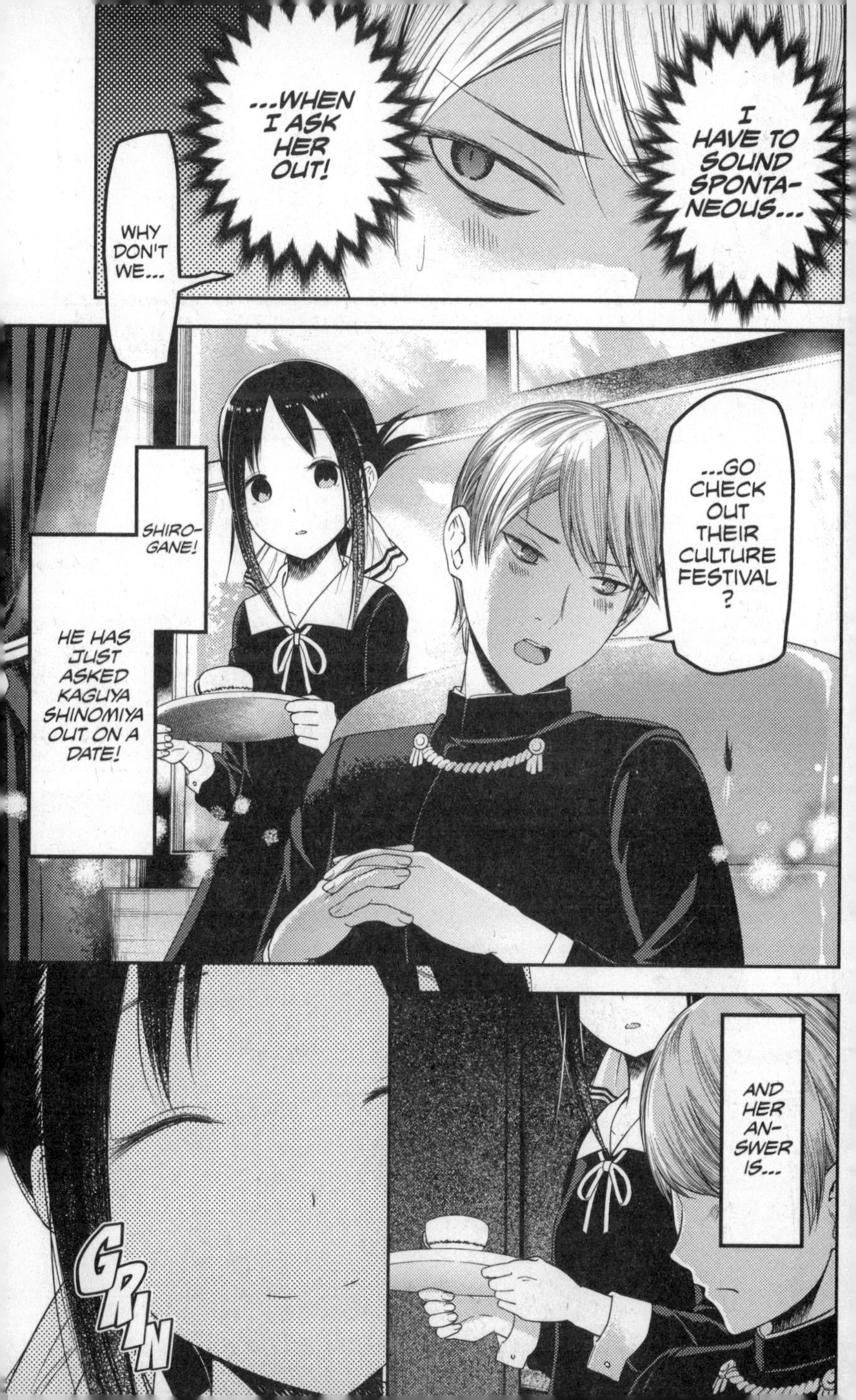
I HAVE TO SOUND SPONTANEOUS...
...WHEN I ASK HER OUT!
WHY DON'T WE...
...GO CHECK OUT THEIR CULTURE FESTIVAL?
SHIROGANE!
HE HAS JUST ASKED KAGUYA SHINOMIYA OUT ON A DATE!
AND HER ANSWER IS...
GRIN

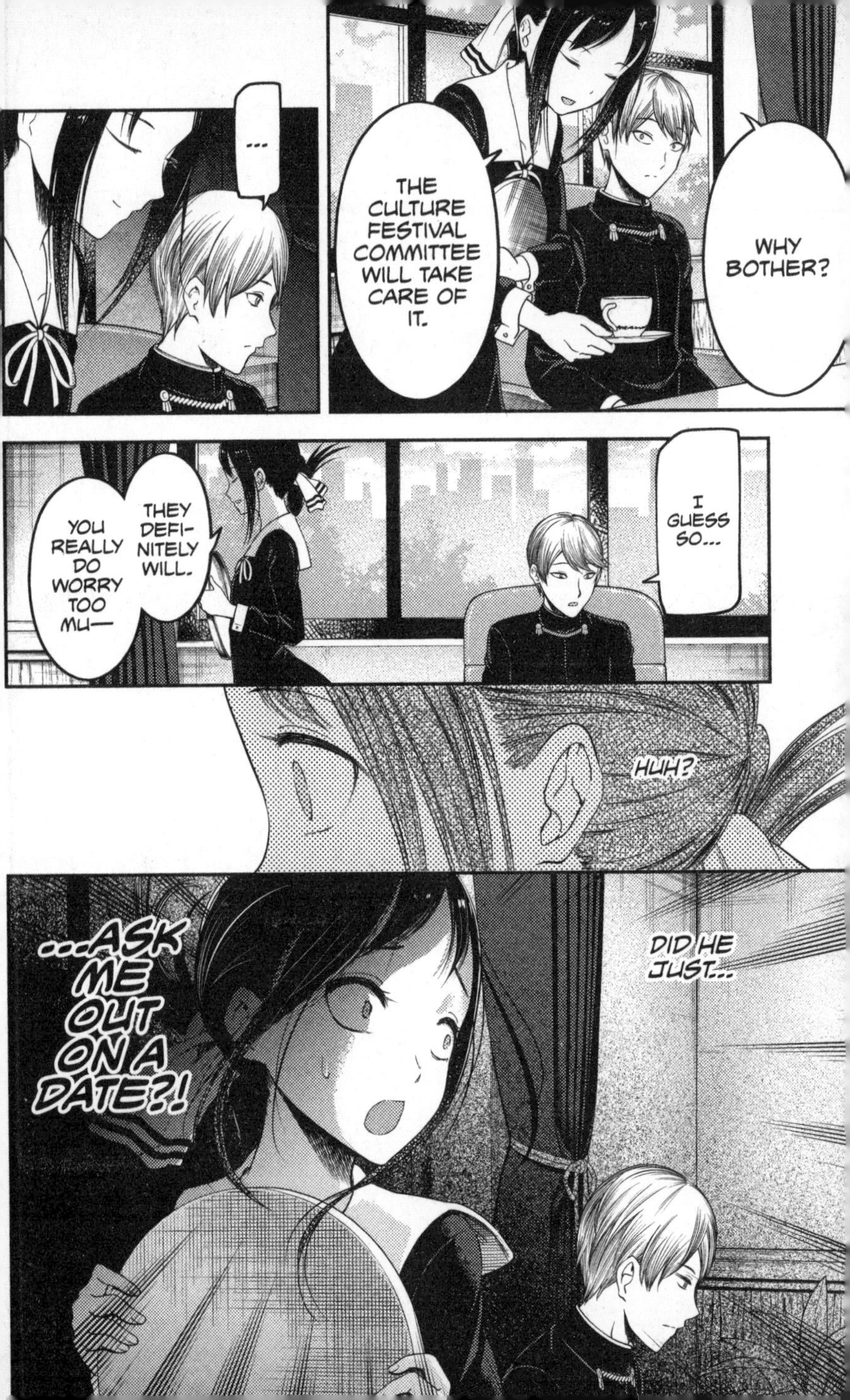
WHY BOTHER?
THE CULTURE FESTIVAL COMMITTEE WILL TAKE CARE OF IT.
...
I GUESS SO...
THEY DEFI-NITELY WILL.
YOU REALLY DO WORRY TOO MU—
HUH?
DID HE JUST...
...ASK ME OUT ON A DATE?!

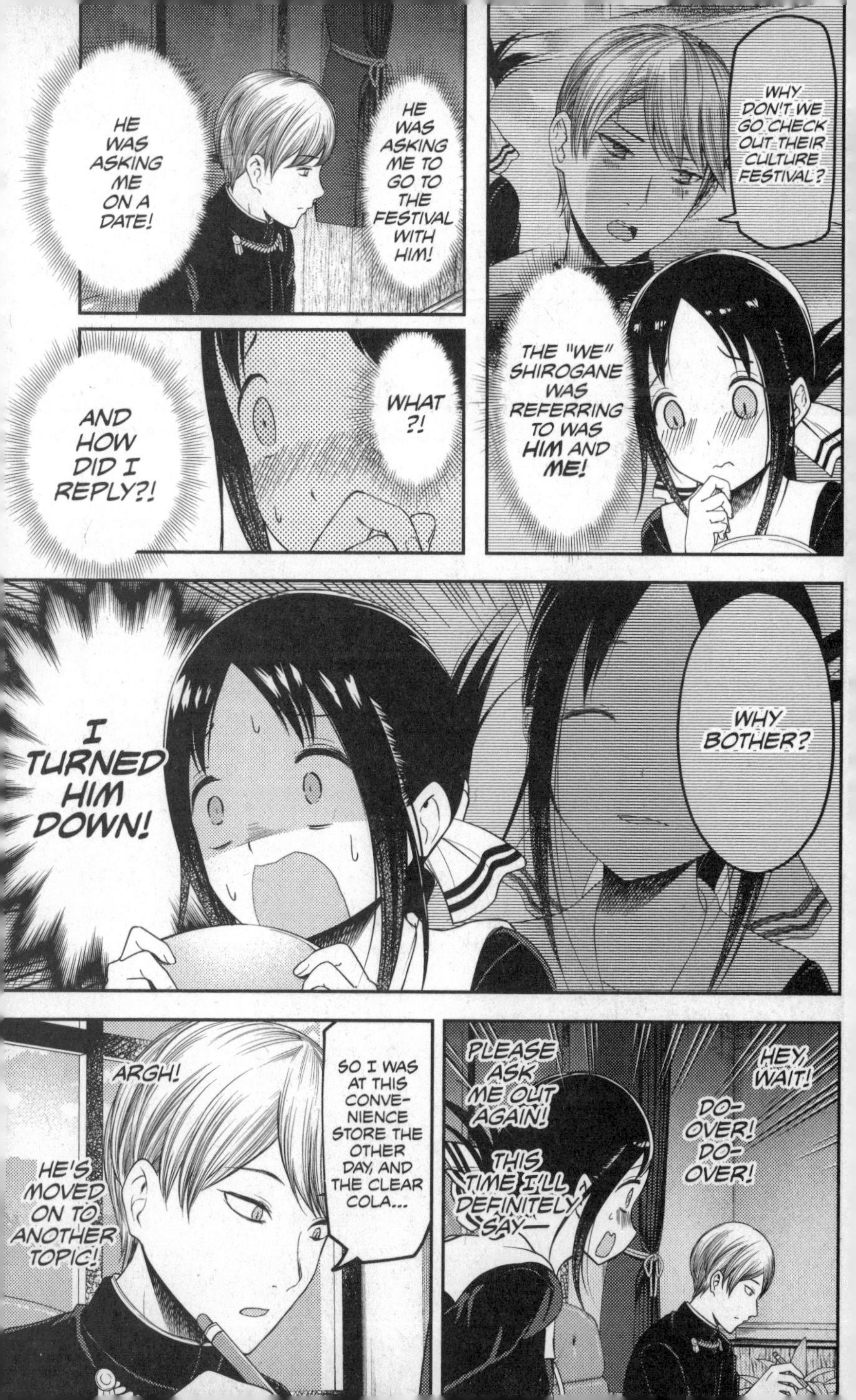
WHY DON'T WE GO CHECK OUT THEIR CULTURE FESTIVAL?
THE "WE" SHIROGANE WAS REFERRING TO WAS HIM AND ME!
HE WAS ASKING ME TO GO TO THE FESTIVAL WITH HIM!
HE WAS ASKING ME ON A DATE!
WHAT?!
AND HOW DID I REPLY?!
WHY BOTHER?
I TURNED HIM DOWN!
HEY, WAIT!
DO-OVER! DO-OVER!
PLEASE ASK ME OUT AGAIN!
THIS TIME I'LL DEFINITELY SAY—
SO I WAS AT THIS CONVENIENCE STORE THE OTHER DAY, AND THE CLEAR COLA...
ARGH!
HE'S MOVED ON TO ANOTHER TOPIC!

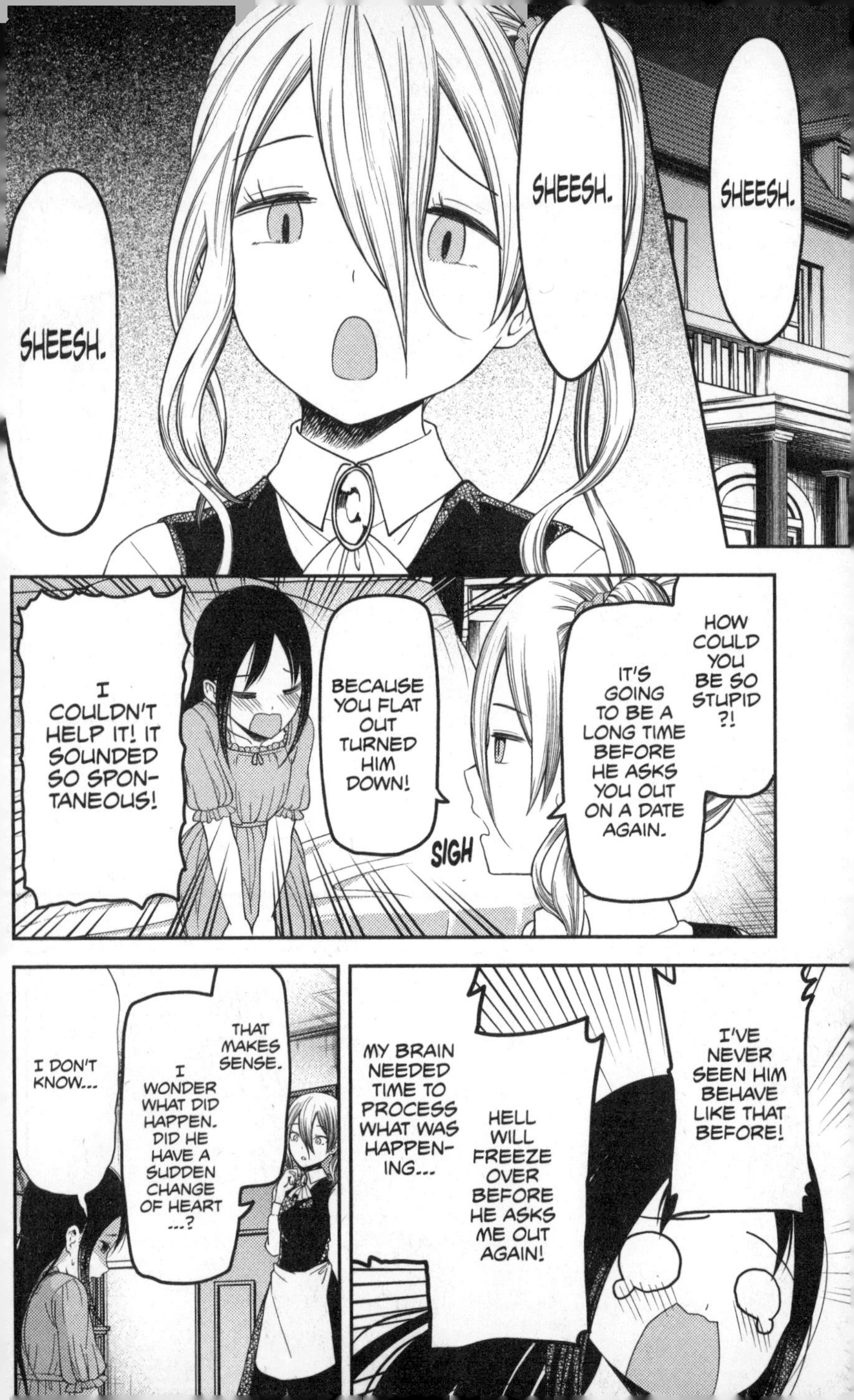
SHEESH.
SHEESH.
SHEESH.
HOW COULD YOU BE SO STUPID?!
IT'S GOING TO BE A LONG TIME BEFORE HE ASKS YOU OUT ON A DATE AGAIN.
SIGH
BECAUSE YOU FLAT OUT TURNED HIM DOWN!
I COULDN'T HELP IT! IT SOUNDED SO SPONTANEOUS!
I'VE NEVER SEEN HIM BEHAVE LIKE THAT BEFORE!
HELL WILL FREEZE OVER BEFORE HE ASKS ME OUT AGAIN!
MY BRAIN NEEDED TIME TO PROCESS WHAT WAS HAPPENING...
THAT MAKES SENSE.
I WONDER WHAT DID HAPPEN. DID HE HAVE A SUDDEN CHANGE OF HEART...?
I DON'T KNOW...

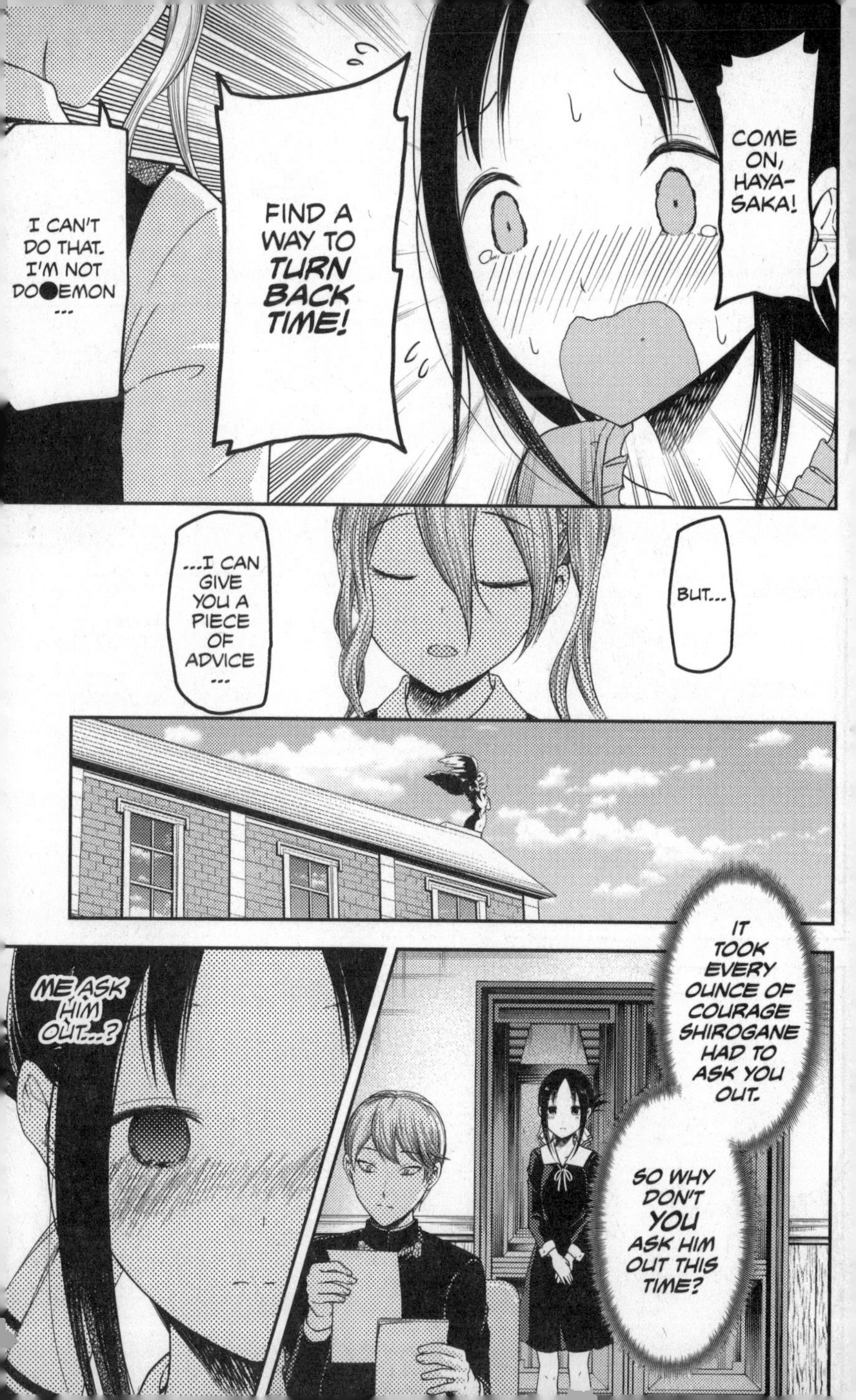
COME ON, HAYA-SAKA!
FIND A WAY TO TURN BACK TIME!
I CAN'T DO THAT. I'M NOT DO●EMON...
BUT...
...I CAN GIVE YOU A PIECE OF ADVICE...
IT TOOK EVERY OUNCE OF COURAGE SHIROGANE HAD TO ASK YOU OUT.
SO WHY DON'T YOU ASK HIM OUT THIS TIME?
ME ASK HIM OUT...?

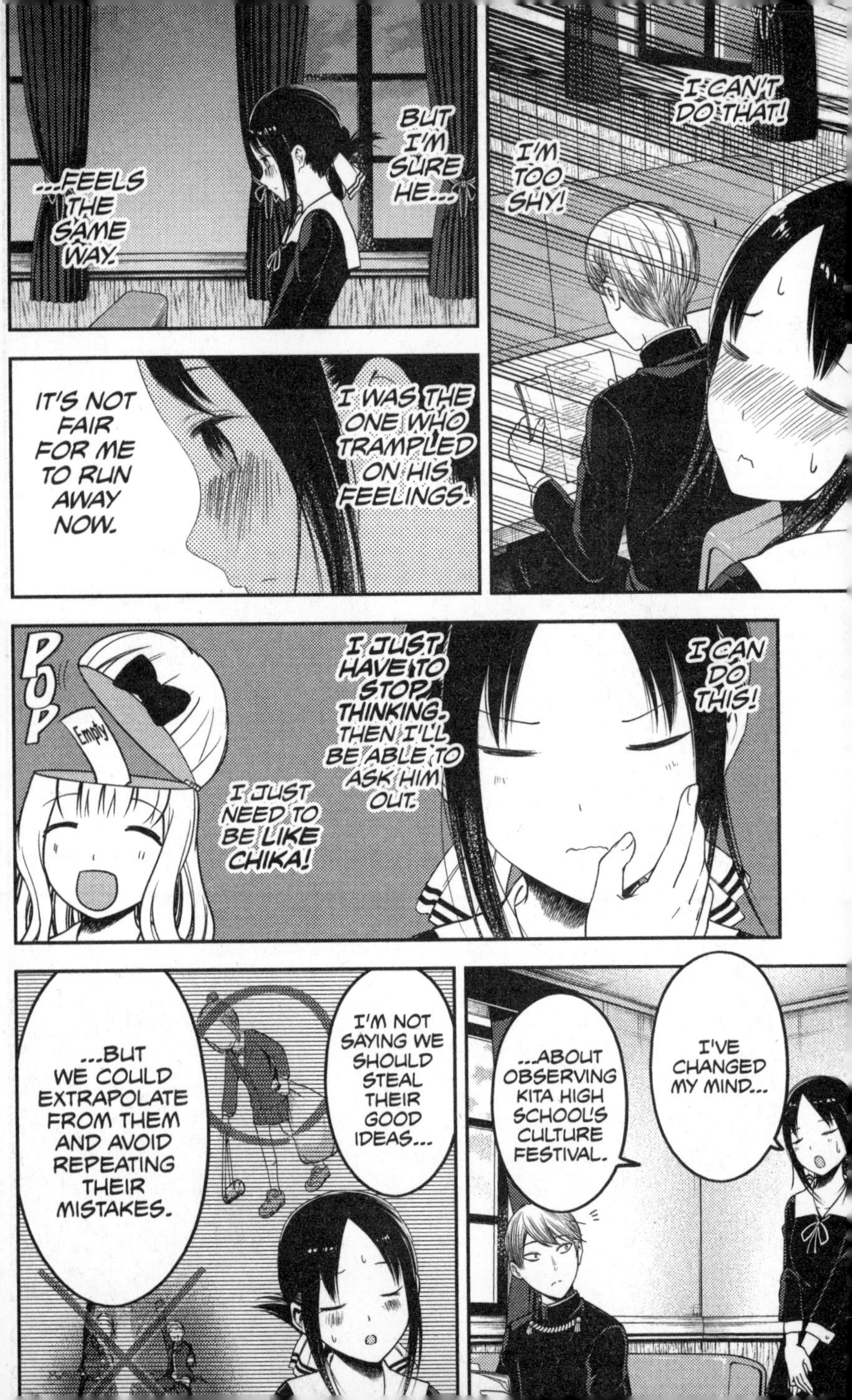
I CAN'T DO THAT!
I'M TOO SHY!
BUT I'M SURE HE...
...FEELS THE SAME WAY.
I WAS THE ONE WHO TRAMPLED ON HIS FEELINGS.
IT'S NOT FAIR FOR ME TO RUN AWAY NOW.
I CAN DO THIS!
I JUST HAVE TO STOP THINKING. THEN I'LL BE ABLE TO ASK HIM OUT.
I JUST NEED TO BE LIKE CHIKA!
Empty
POP
I'VE CHANGED MY MIND...
...ABOUT OBSERVING KITA HIGH SCHOOL'S CULTURE FESTIVAL.
I'M NOT SAYING WE SHOULD STEAL THEIR GOOD IDEAS...
...BUT WE COULD EXTRAPOLATE FROM THEM AND AVOID REPEATING THEIR MISTAKES.

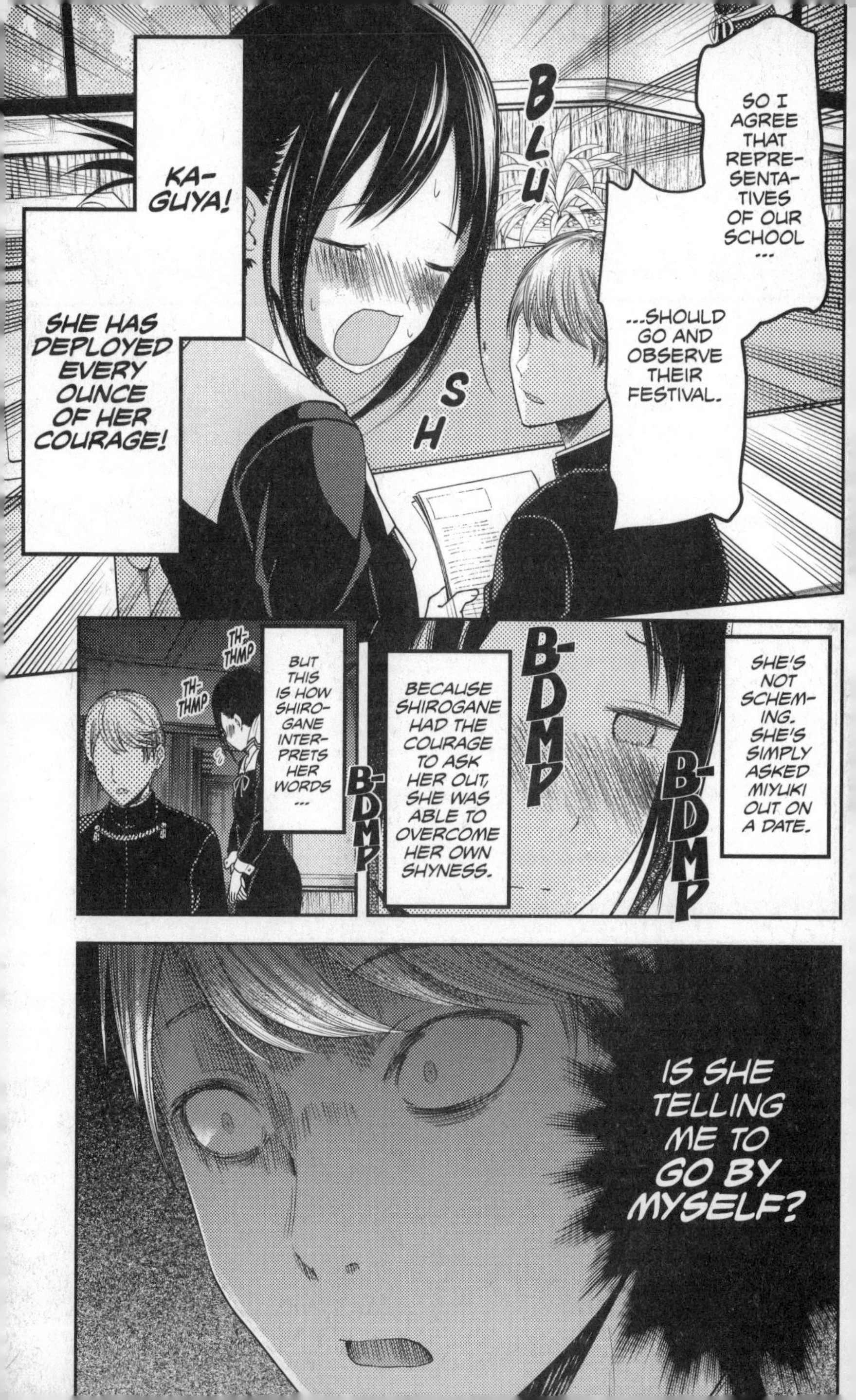
SO I AGREE THAT REPRESENTATIVES OF OUR SCHOOL...
...SHOULD GO AND OBSERVE THEIR FESTIVAL.
BLUSH
KA-GUYA!
SHE HAS DEPLOYED EVERY OUNCE OF HER COURAGE!
SHE'S NOT SCHEMING. SHE'S SIMPLY ASKED MIYUKI OUT ON A DATE.
B-BDMP
B-BDMP
BECAUSE SHIROGANE HAD THE COURAGE TO ASK HER OUT, SHE WAS ABLE TO OVERCOME HER OWN SHYNESS.
B-BDMP
BUT THIS IS HOW SHIROGANE INTERPRETS HER WORDS...
TH-THMP
TH-THMP
IS SHE TELLING ME TO GO BY MYSELF?

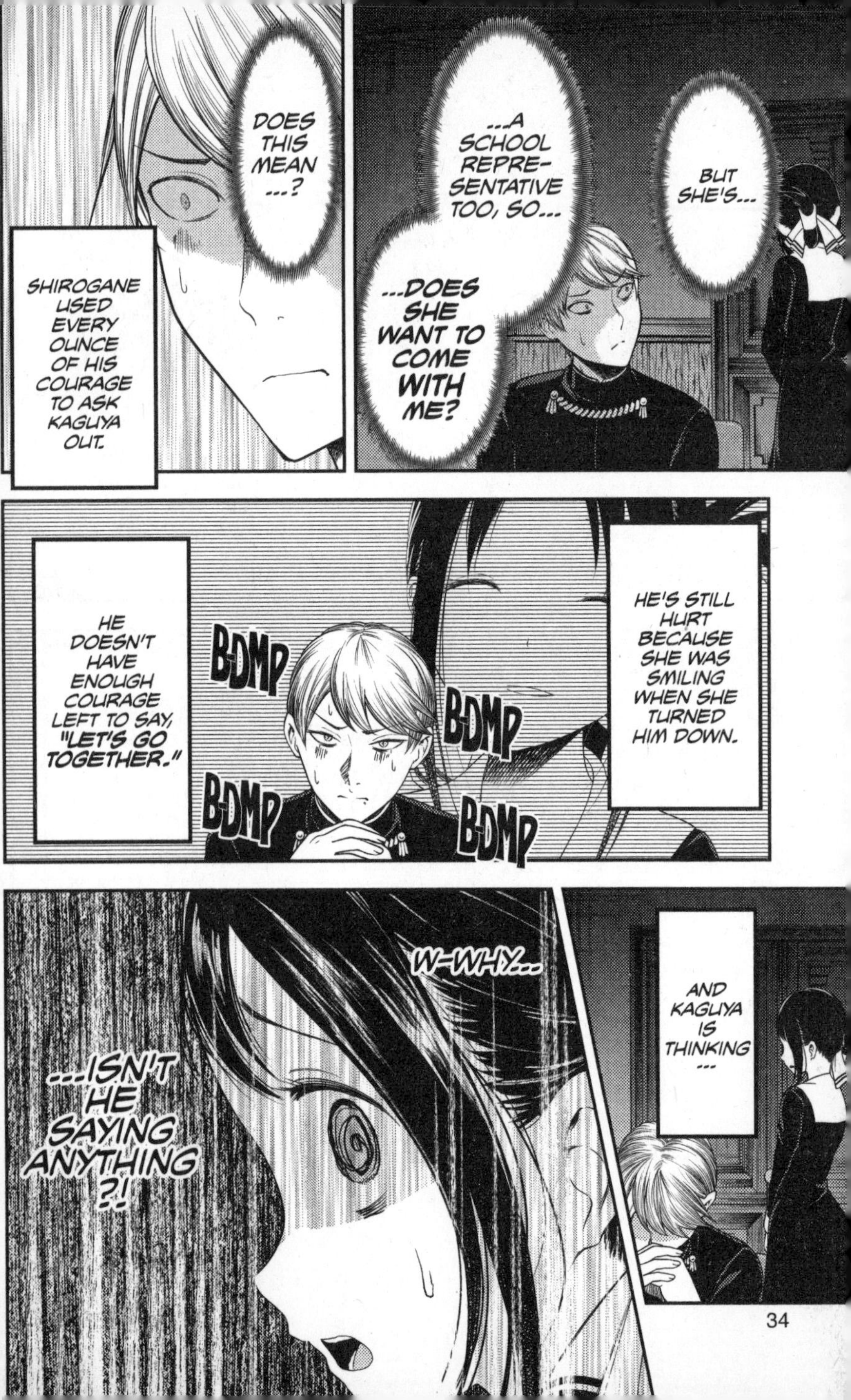
BUT SHE'S...
...A SCHOOL REPRESENTATIVE TOO, SO...
...DOES SHE WANT TO COME WITH ME?
DOES THIS MEAN...?
SHIROGANE USED EVERY OUNCE OF HIS COURAGE TO ASK KAGUYA OUT.
HE'S STILL HURT BECAUSE SHE WAS SMILING WHEN SHE TURNED HIM DOWN.
B-DMP
B-DMP
B-DMP
B-DMP
HE DOESN'T HAVE ENOUGH COURAGE LEFT TO SAY, "LET'S GO TOGETHER."
AND KAGUYA IS THINKING...
W-WHY...
...ISN'T HE SAYING ANYTHING?!

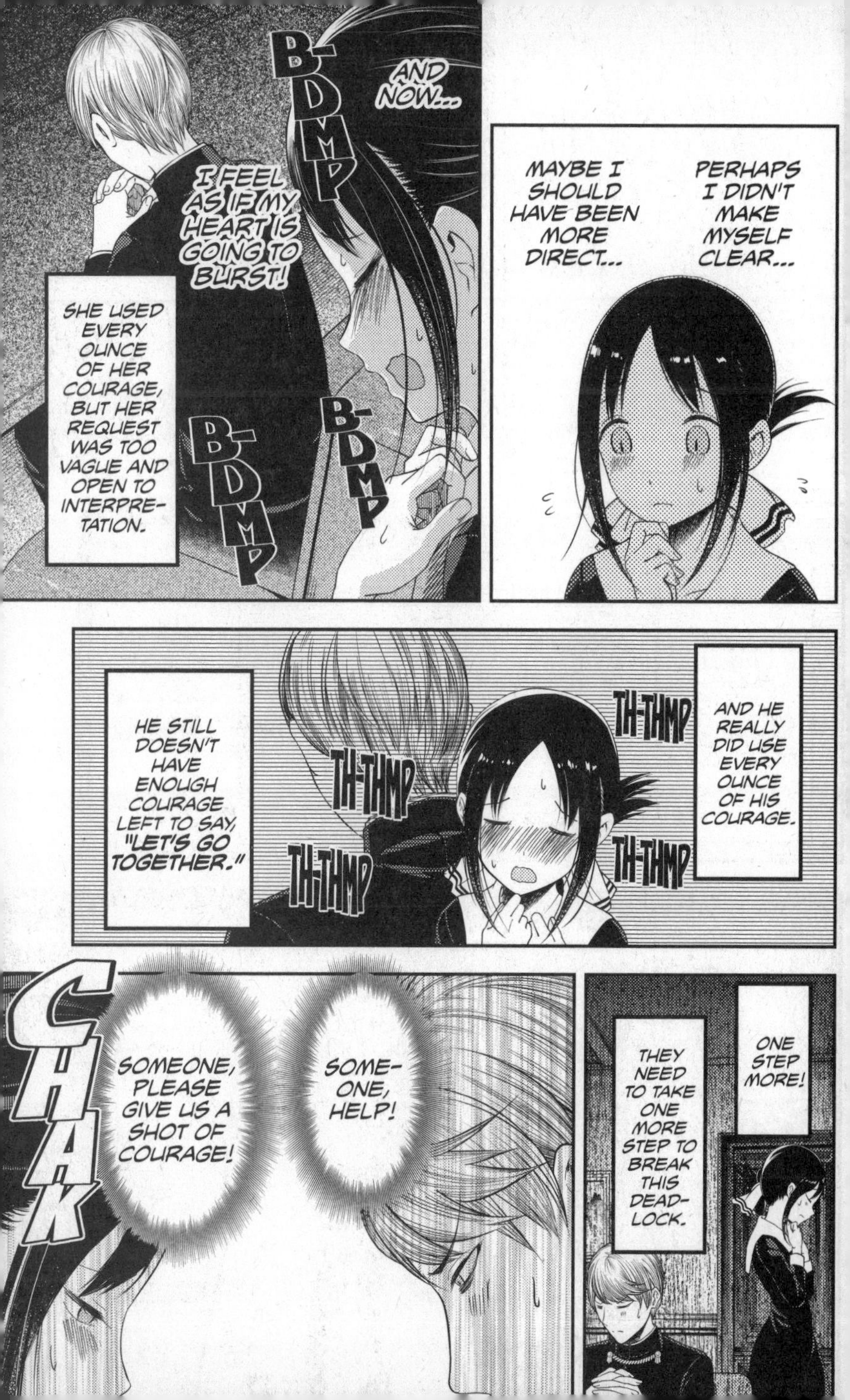
PERHAPS I DIDN'T MAKE MYSELF CLEAR...
MAYBE I SHOULD HAVE BEEN MORE DIRECT...
AND NOW...
B-DMP
I FEEL AS IF MY HEART IS GOING TO BURST!
B-DMP
B-DMP
SHE USED EVERY OUNCE OF HER COURAGE, BUT HER REQUEST WAS TOO VAGUE AND OPEN TO INTERPRE-TATION.
AND HE REALLY DID USE EVERY OUNCE OF HIS COURAGE.
TH-THMP
TH-THMP
TH-THMP
TH-THMP
HE STILL DOESN'T HAVE ENOUGH COURAGE LEFT TO SAY, "LET'S GO TOGETHER."
ONE STEP MORE!
THEY NEED TO TAKE ONE MORE STEP TO BREAK THIS DEAD-LOCK.
SOME-ONE, HELP!
SOMEONE, PLEASE GIVE US A SHOT OF COURAGE!
CHAK

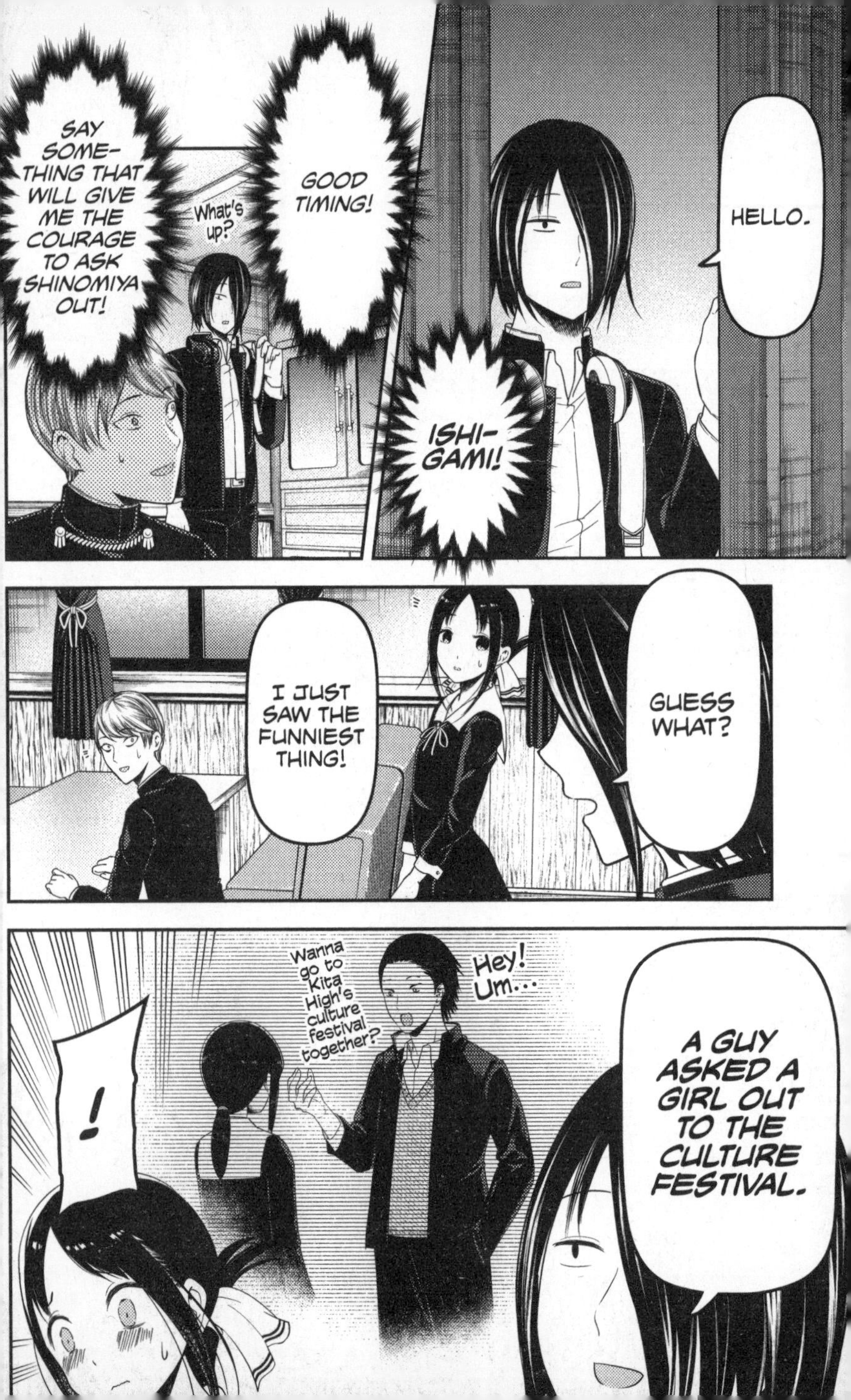
HELLO.
ISHIGAMI!
GOOD TIMING!
What's up?
SAY SOMETHING THAT WILL GIVE ME THE COURAGE TO ASK SHINOMIYA OUT!
GUESS WHAT?
I JUST SAW THE FUNNIEST THING!
A GUY ASKED A GIRL OUT TO THE CULTURE FESTIVAL.
Hey! Um...
Wanna go to Kita High's culture festival together?
!

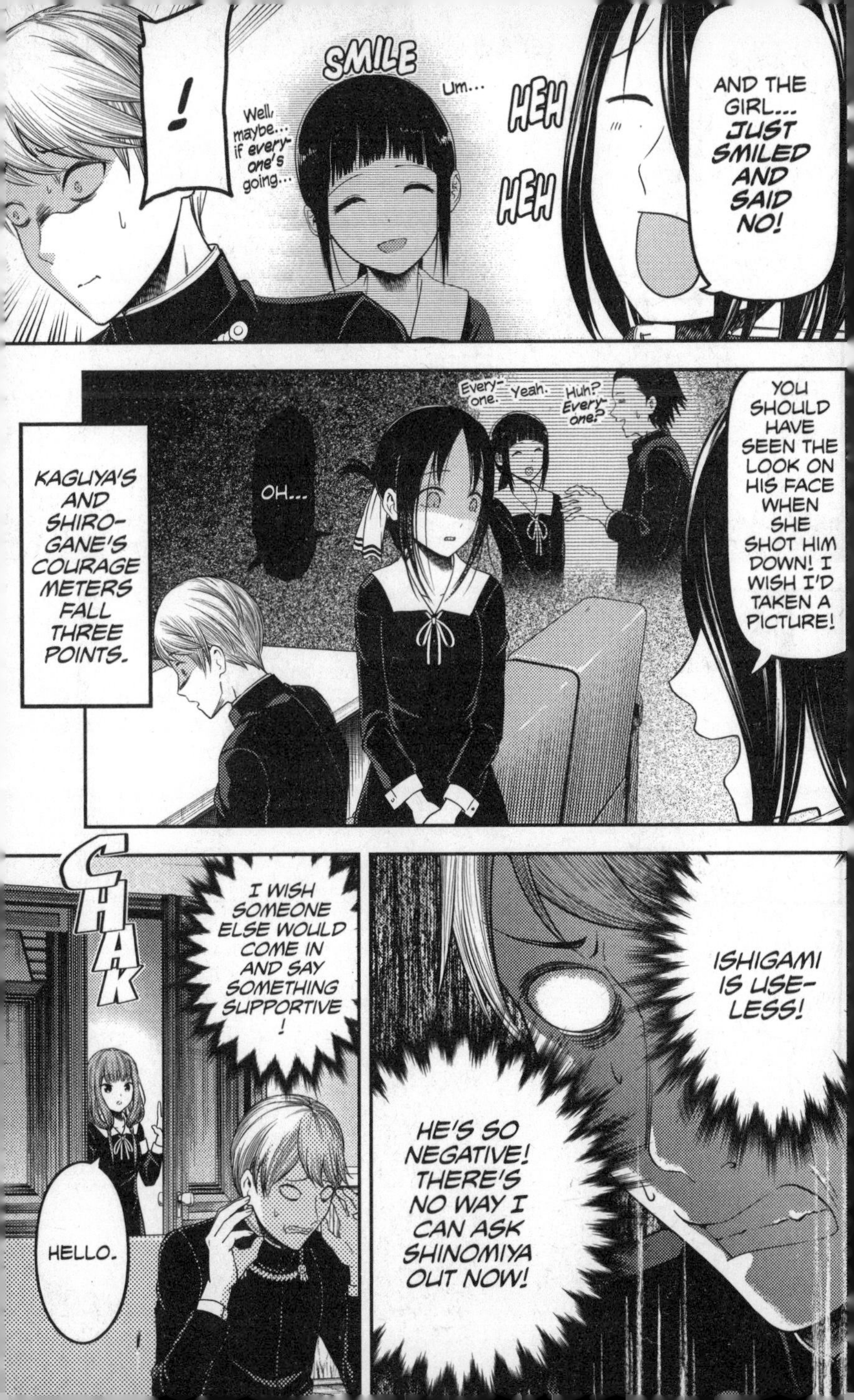
AND THE GIRL... JUST SMILED AND SAID NO!
HEH
HEH
Um...
SMILE
Well, maybe... if every-one's going...
!
YOU SHOULD HAVE SEEN THE LOOK ON HIS FACE WHEN SHE SHOT HIM DOWN! I WISH I'D TAKEN A PICTURE!
Huh? Every-one?
Yeah.
Every-one.
OH...
KAGUYA'S AND SHIRO-GANE'S COURAGE METERS FALL THREE POINTS.
ISHIGAMI IS USE-LESS!
HE'S SO NEGATIVE! THERE'S NO WAY I CAN ASK SHINOMIYA OUT NOW!
I WISH SOMEONE ELSE WOULD COME IN AND SAY SOMETHING SUPPORTIVE!
CHAK
HELLO.

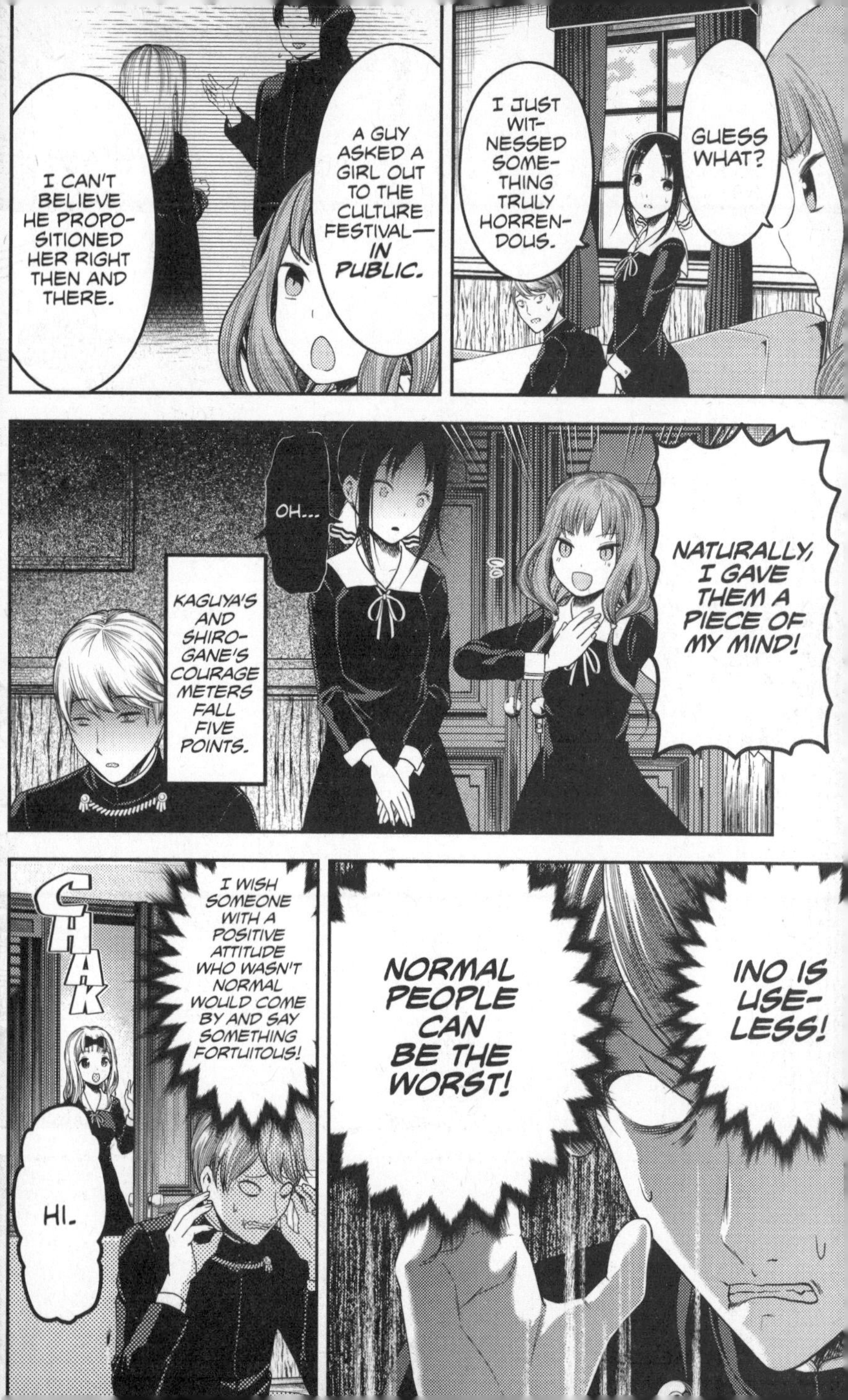
GUESS WHAT?
I JUST WIT-NESSED SOME-THING TRULY HORREN-DOUS.
A GUY ASKED A GIRL OUT TO THE CULTURE FESTIVAL—IN PUBLIC.
I CAN'T BELIEVE HE PROPO-SITIONED HER RIGHT THEN AND THERE.
NATURALLY, I GAVE THEM A PIECE OF MY MIND!
OH...
KAGUYA'S AND SHIRO-GANE'S COURAGE METERS FALL FIVE POINTS.
INO IS USE-LESS!
NORMAL PEOPLE CAN BE THE WORST!
I WISH SOMEONE WITH A POSITIVE ATTITUDE WHO WASN'T NORMAL WOULD COME BY AND SAY SOMETHING FORTUITOUS!
CHAK
HI.

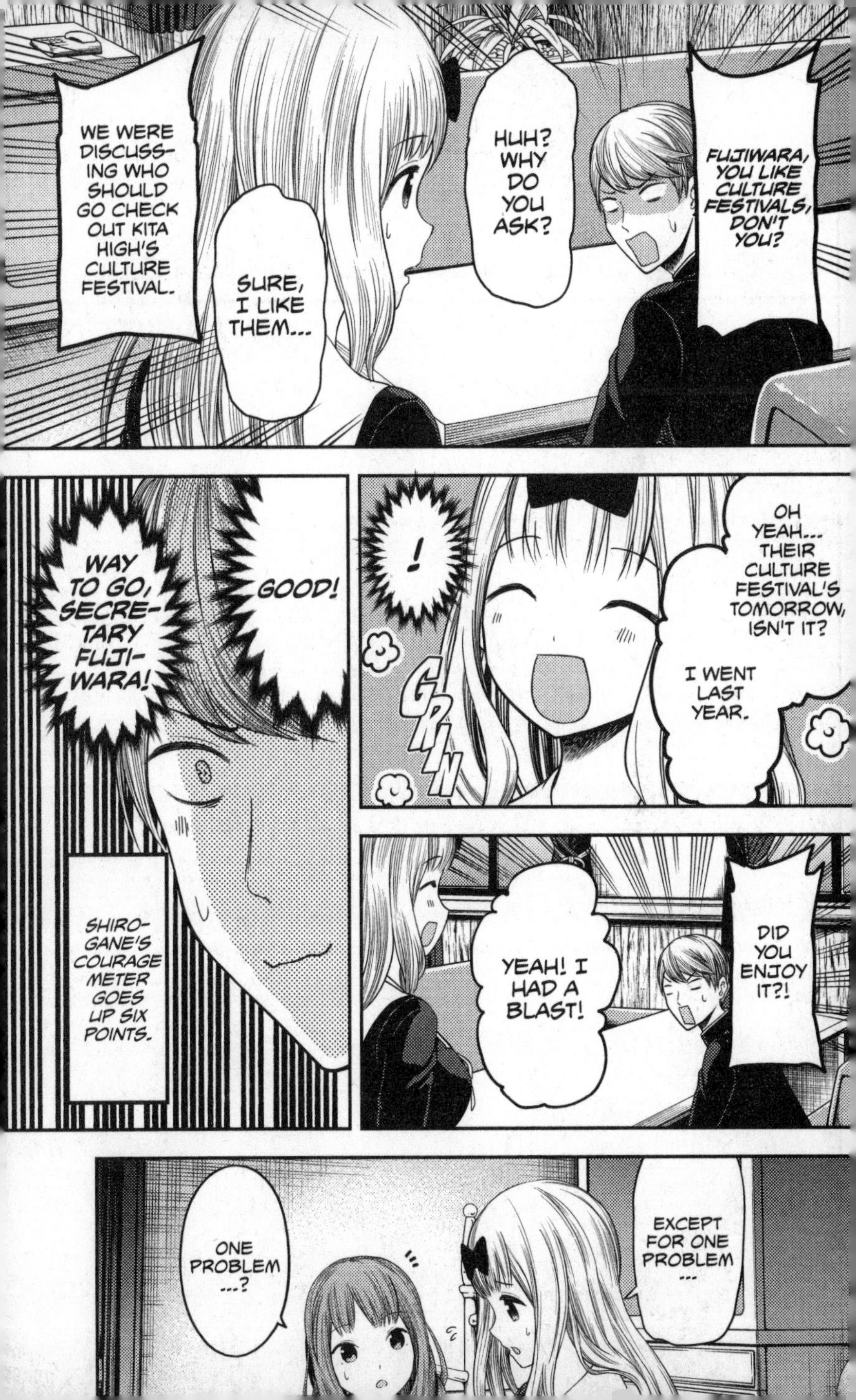
FUJIWARA, YOU LIKE CULTURE FESTIVALS, DON'T YOU?
SURE, I LIKE THEM...
HUH? WHY DO YOU ASK?
WE WERE DISCUSSING WHO SHOULD GO CHECK OUT KITA HIGH'S CULTURE FESTIVAL.
OH YEAH... THEIR CULTURE FESTIVAL'S TOMORROW, ISN'T IT?
I WENT LAST YEAR.
!
GRIN
DID YOU ENJOY IT?!
YEAH! I HAD A BLAST!
GOOD!
WAY TO GO, SECRETARY FUJIWARA!
SHIROGANE'S COURAGE METER GOES UP SIX POINTS.
EXCEPT FOR ONE PROBLEM...
ONE PROBLEM...?

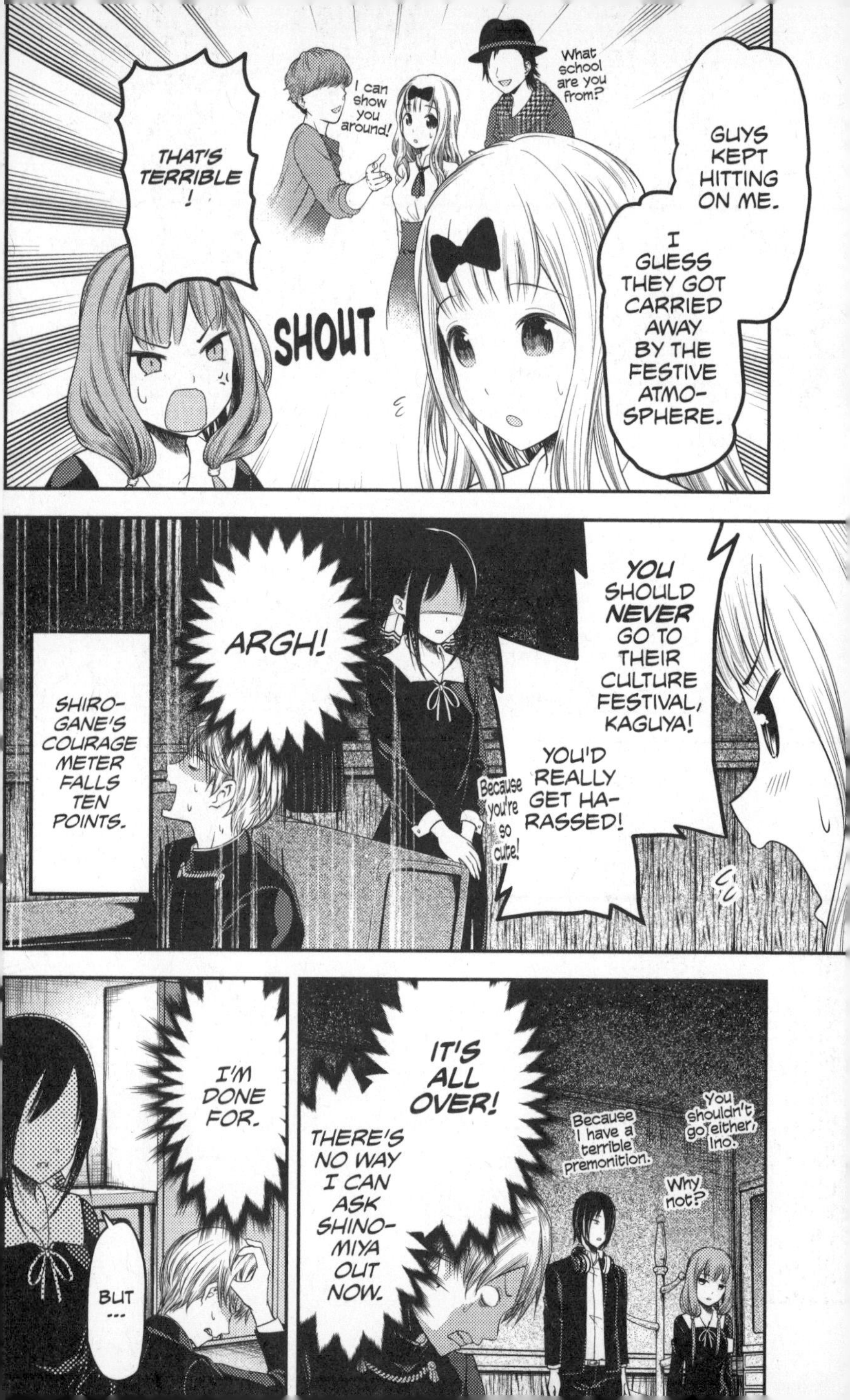
GUYS KEPT HITTING ON ME.
I GUESS THEY GOT CARRIED AWAY BY THE FESTIVE ATMOSPHERE.
What school are you from?
I can show you around!
THAT'S TERRIBLE!
SHOUT
YOU SHOULD NEVER GO TO THEIR CULTURE FESTIVAL, KAGUYA!
YOU'D REALLY GET HARASSED!
Because you're so cute!
ARGH!
SHIROGANE'S COURAGE METER FALLS TEN POINTS.
You shouldn't go either, Ino.
Why not?
Because I have a terrible premonition.
IT'S ALL OVER!
THERE'S NO WAY I CAN ASK SHINOMIYA OUT NOW.
I'M DONE FOR.
BUT ...

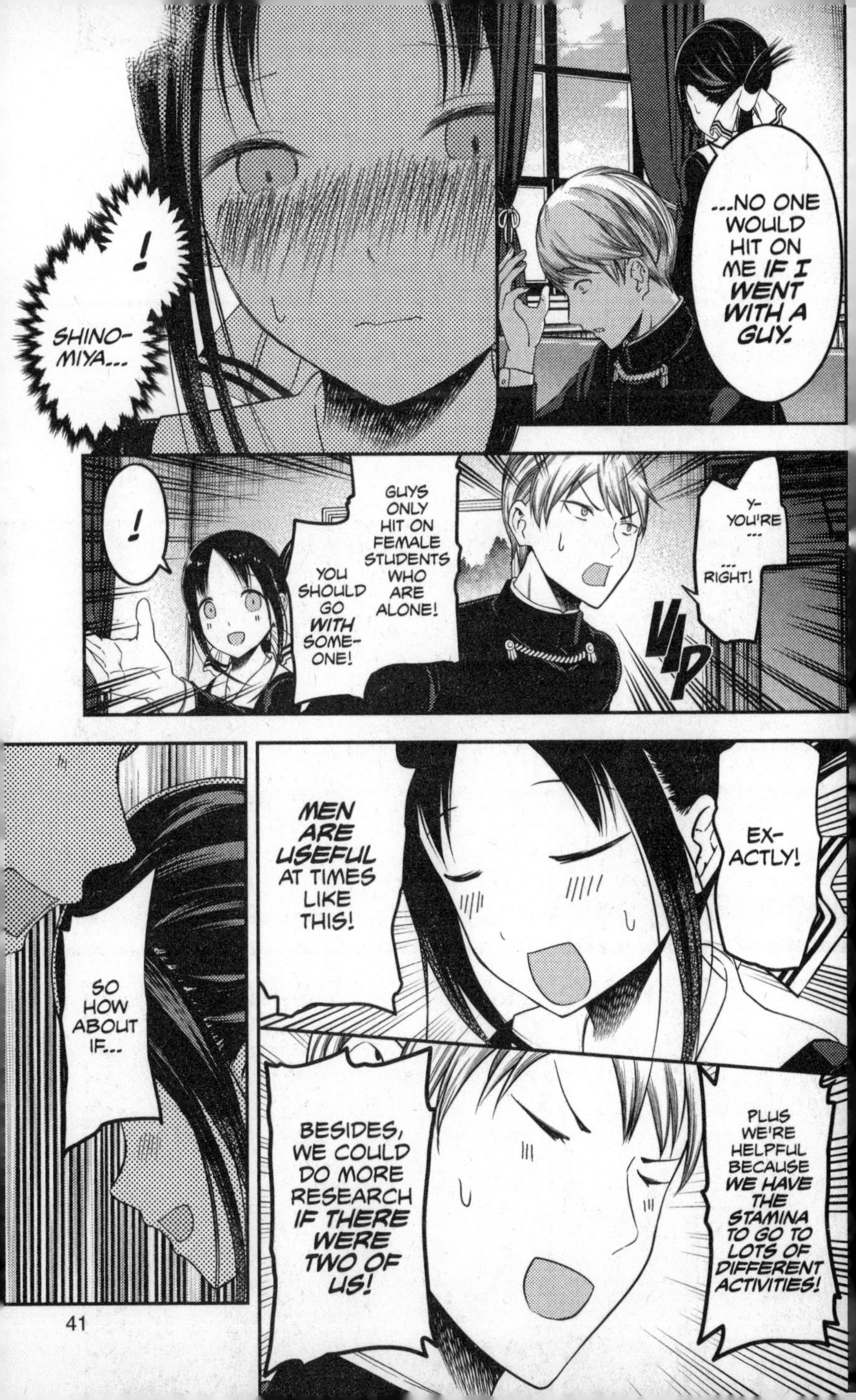
...NO ONE WOULD HIT ON ME *IF I WENT WITH A GUY.*
!
SHINO-MIYA...
Y-YOU'RE... ...RIGHT!
VIP
GUYS ONLY HIT ON FEMALE STUDENTS WHO ARE ALONE!
YOU SHOULD GO *WITH* SOME-ONE!
!
EX-ACTLY!
MEN ARE USEFUL AT TIMES LIKE THIS!
PLUS WE'RE HELPFUL BECAUSE *WE HAVE THE STAMINA TO GO TO LOTS OF DIFFERENT ACTIVITIES!*
BESIDES, WE COULD DO MORE RESEARCH *IF THERE WERE TWO OF US!*
SO HOW ABOUT IF...

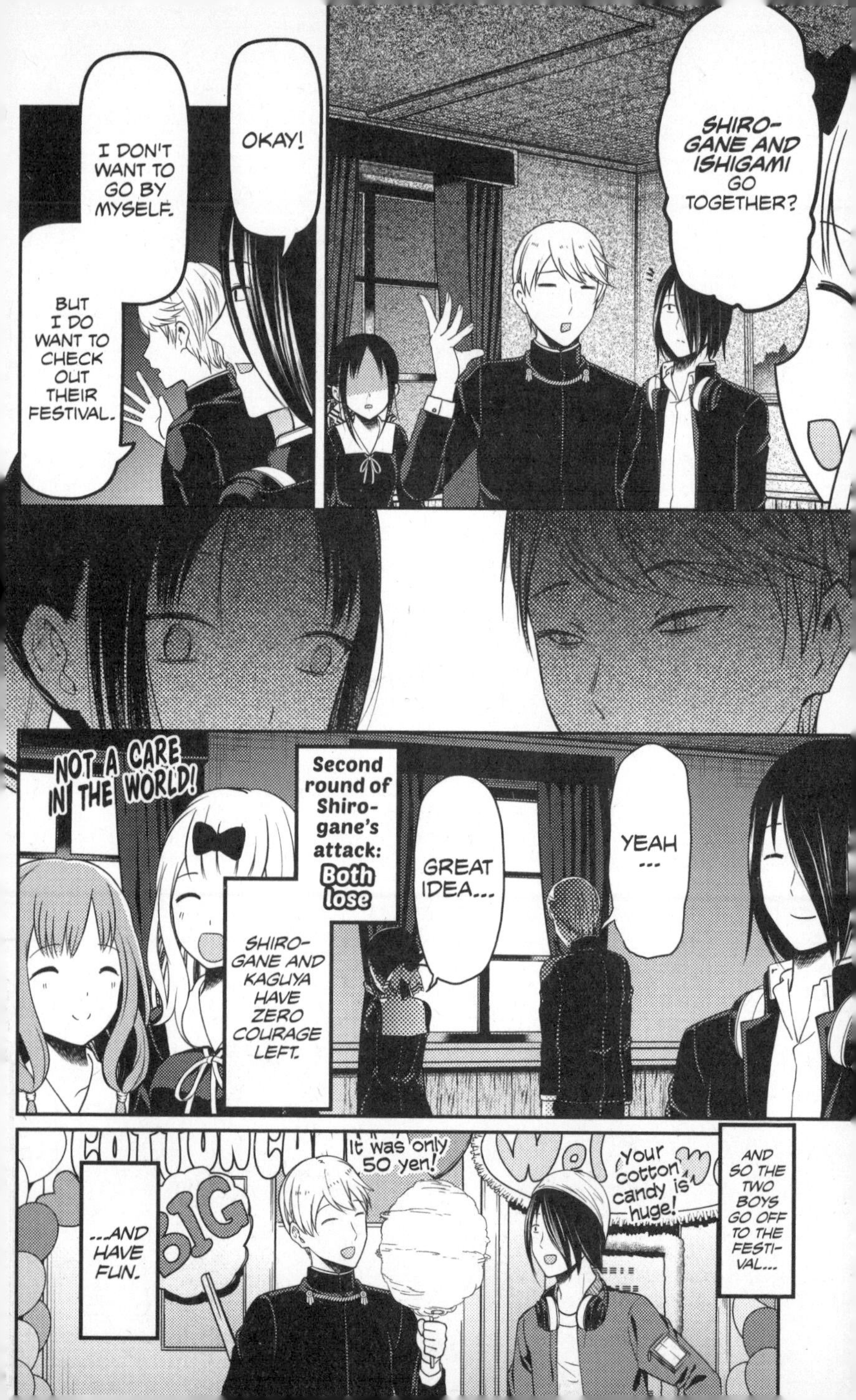
SHIRO-GANE AND ISHIGAMI GO TOGETHER?
OKAY!
I DON'T WANT TO GO BY MYSELF.
BUT I DO WANT TO CHECK OUT THEIR FESTIVAL.
YEAH...
GREAT IDEA...
Second round of Shiro-gane's attack: Both lose
SHIRO-GANE AND KAGUYA HAVE ZERO COURAGE LEFT.
NOT A CARE IN THE WORLD!
AND SO THE TWO BOYS GO OFF TO THE FESTI-VAL...
Your cotton candy is huge!
It was only 50 yen!
BIG
...AND HAVE FUN.

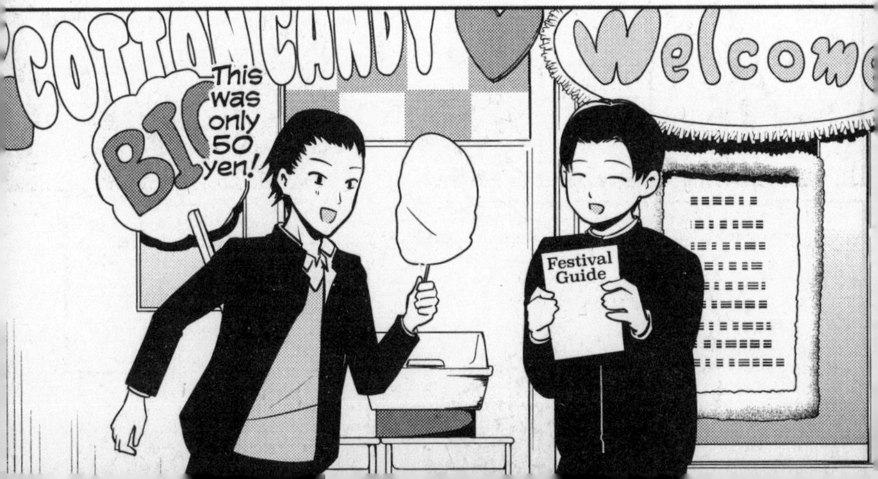
Welcome
Festival Guide
COTTON CANDY
This was only 50 yen!

KAGUYA-SAMA
LOVE IS WAR

Chapter 114
Miyuki Shirogane Wants to Make Her Confess, Part 3

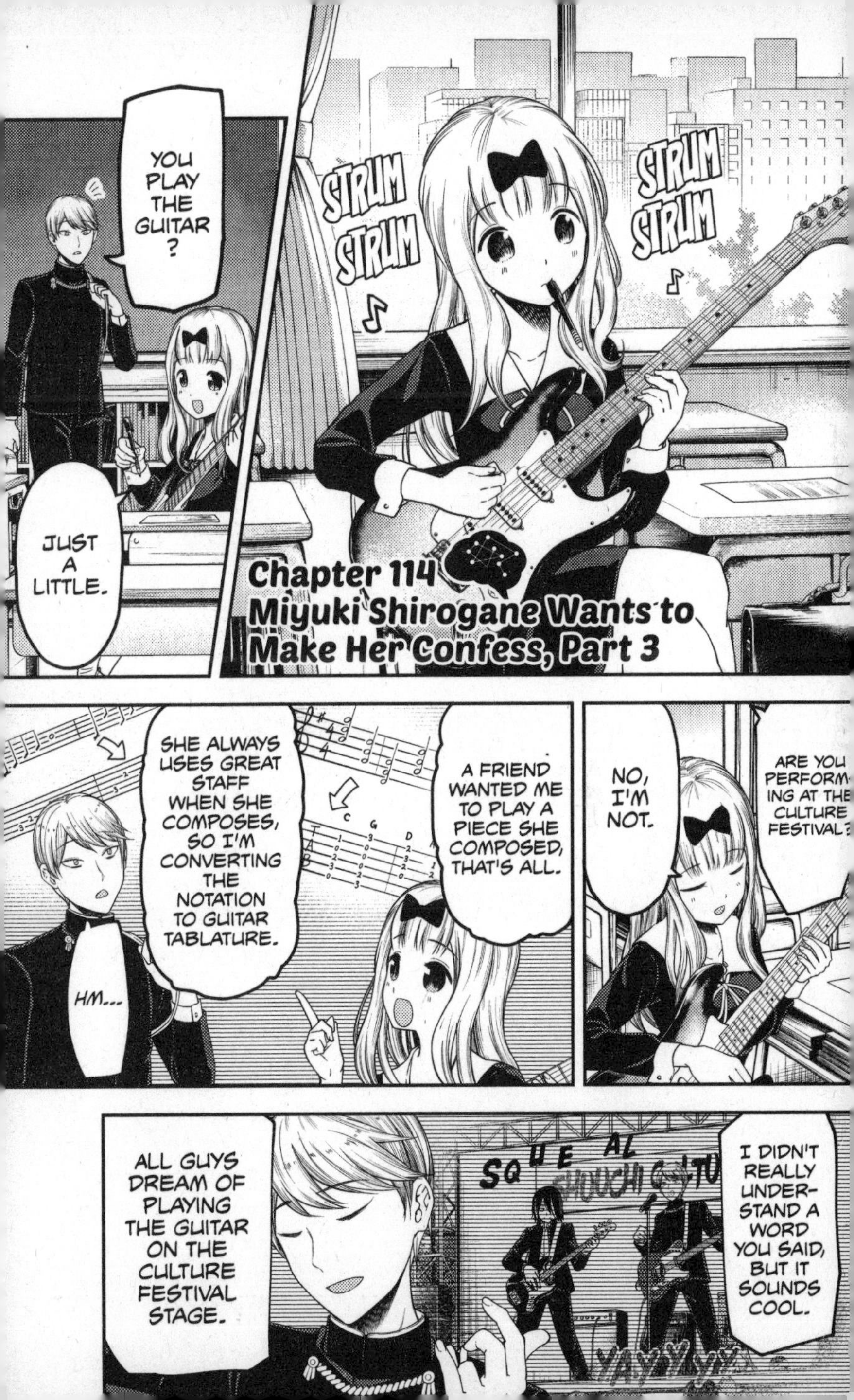

STRUM STRUM
STRUM STRUM
YOU PLAY THE GUITAR?
JUST A LITTLE.
ARE YOU PERFORMING AT THE CULTURE FESTIVAL?
NO, I'M NOT.
A FRIEND WANTED ME TO PLAY A PIECE SHE COMPOSED, THAT'S ALL.
SHE ALWAYS USES GREAT STAFF WHEN SHE COMPOSES, SO I'M CONVERTING THE NOTATION TO GUITAR TABLATURE.
HM...
I DIDN'T REALLY UNDERSTAND A WORD YOU SAID, BUT IT SOUNDS COOL.
ALL GUYS DREAM OF PLAYING THE GUITAR ON THE CULTURE FESTIVAL STAGE.
SQUEAL

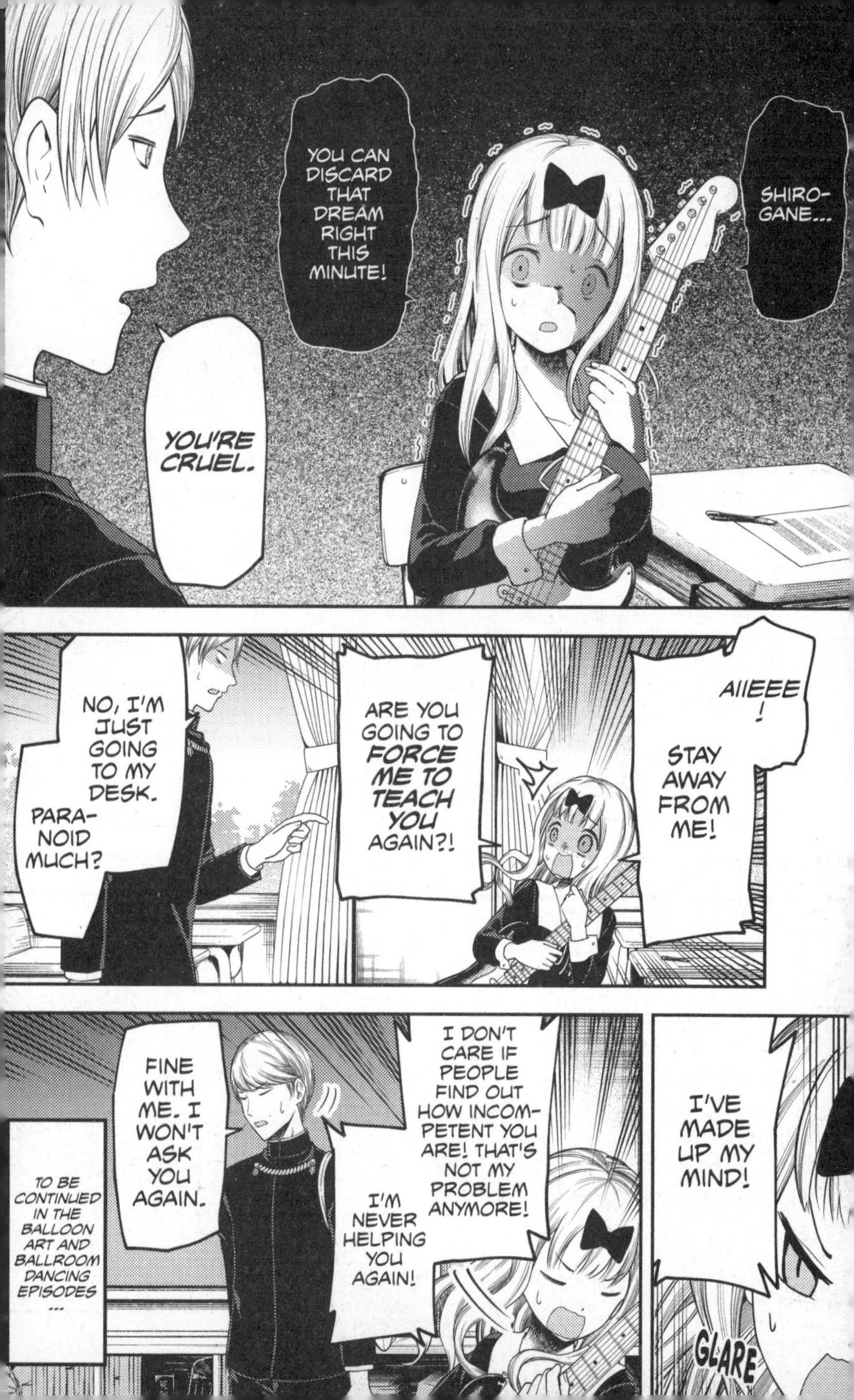
SHIRO-GANE...
YOU CAN DISCARD THAT DREAM RIGHT THIS MINUTE!
YOU'RE CRUEL.
AIIEEE!
STAY AWAY FROM ME!
ARE YOU GOING TO FORCE ME TO TEACH YOU AGAIN?!
NO, I'M JUST GOING TO MY DESK.
PARA-NOID MUCH?
I'VE MADE UP MY MIND!
GLARE
I DON'T CARE IF PEOPLE FIND OUT HOW INCOM-PETENT YOU ARE! THAT'S NOT MY PROBLEM ANYMORE!
I'M NEVER HELPING YOU AGAIN!
FINE WITH ME. I WON'T ASK YOU AGAIN.
TO BE CONTINUED IN THE BALLOON ART AND BALLROOM DANCING EPISODES...

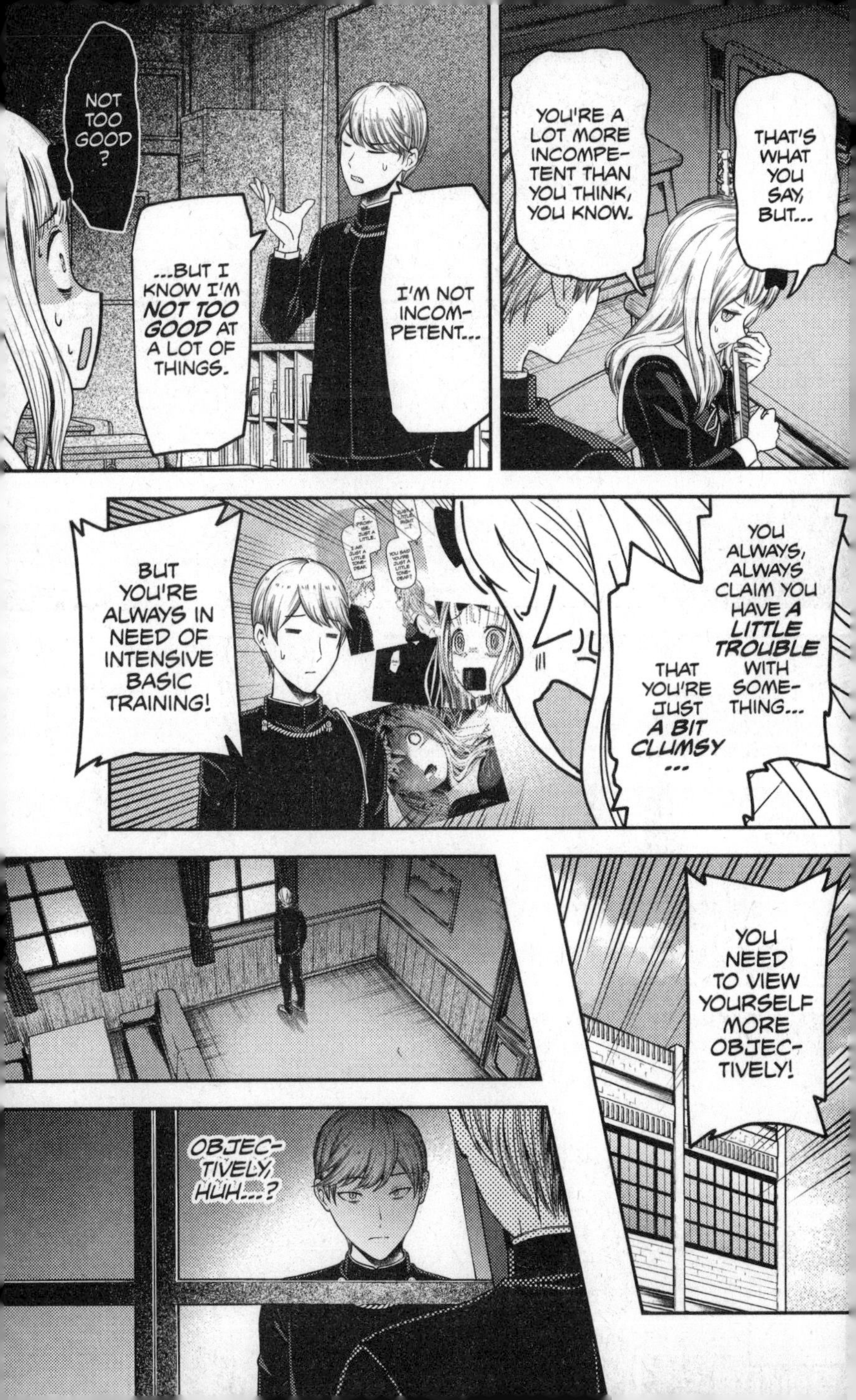
THAT'S WHAT YOU SAY, BUT...
YOU'RE A LOT MORE INCOMPETENT THAN YOU THINK, YOU KNOW.
I'M NOT INCOMPETENT...
...BUT I KNOW I'M NOT TOO GOOD AT A LOT OF THINGS.
NOT TOO GOOD?
YOU ALWAYS, ALWAYS CLAIM YOU HAVE A LITTLE TROUBLE WITH SOMETHING...
THAT YOU'RE JUST A BIT CLUMSY...
JUST A LITTLE, RIGHT...?
YOU SAID YOU'RE JUST A LITTLE TONE-DEAF?
I PROMISE JUST A LITTLE.
I AM JUST A LITTLE TONE-DEAF.
BUT YOU'RE ALWAYS IN NEED OF INTENSIVE BASIC TRAINING!
YOU NEED TO VIEW YOURSELF MORE OBJECTIVELY!
OBJECTIVELY, HUH...?

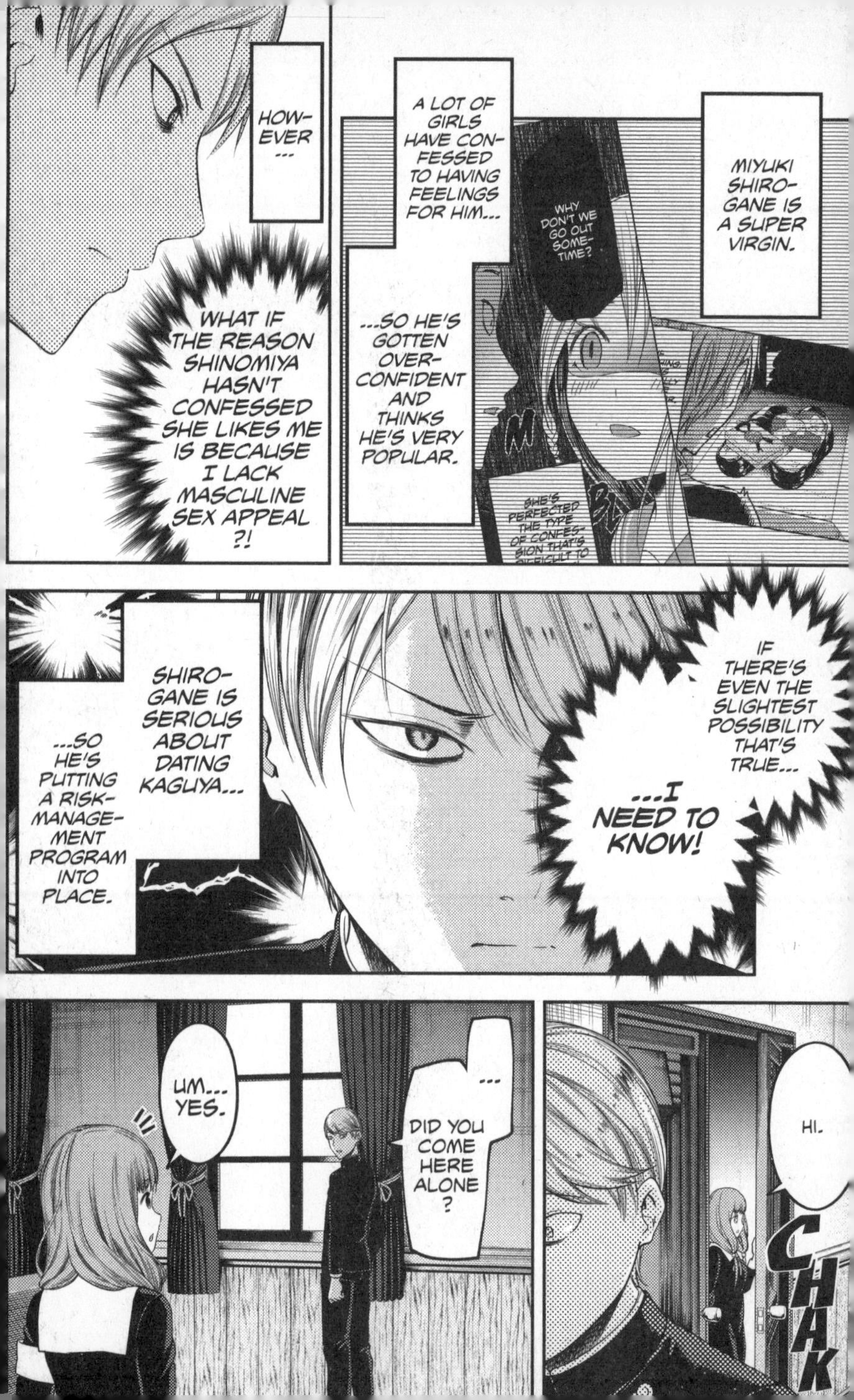
MIYUKI SHIROGANE IS A SUPER VIRGIN.
A LOT OF GIRLS HAVE CONFESSED TO HAVING FEELINGS FOR HIM...
WHY DON'T WE GO OUT SOMETIME?
...SO HE'S GOTTEN OVERCONFIDENT AND THINKS HE'S VERY POPULAR.
SHE'S PERFECTED THE TYPE OF CONFESSION THAT'S
HOWEVER...
WHAT IF THE REASON SHINOMIYA HASN'T CONFESSED SHE LIKES ME IS BECAUSE I LACK MASCULINE SEX APPEAL?!
IF THERE'S EVEN THE SLIGHTEST POSSIBILITY THAT'S TRUE...
...I NEED TO KNOW!
SHIROGANE IS SERIOUS ABOUT DATING KAGUYA...
...SO HE'S PUTTING A RISK-MANAGEMENT PROGRAM INTO PLACE.
CHAK
HI.
...
DID YOU COME HERE ALONE?
UM... YES.

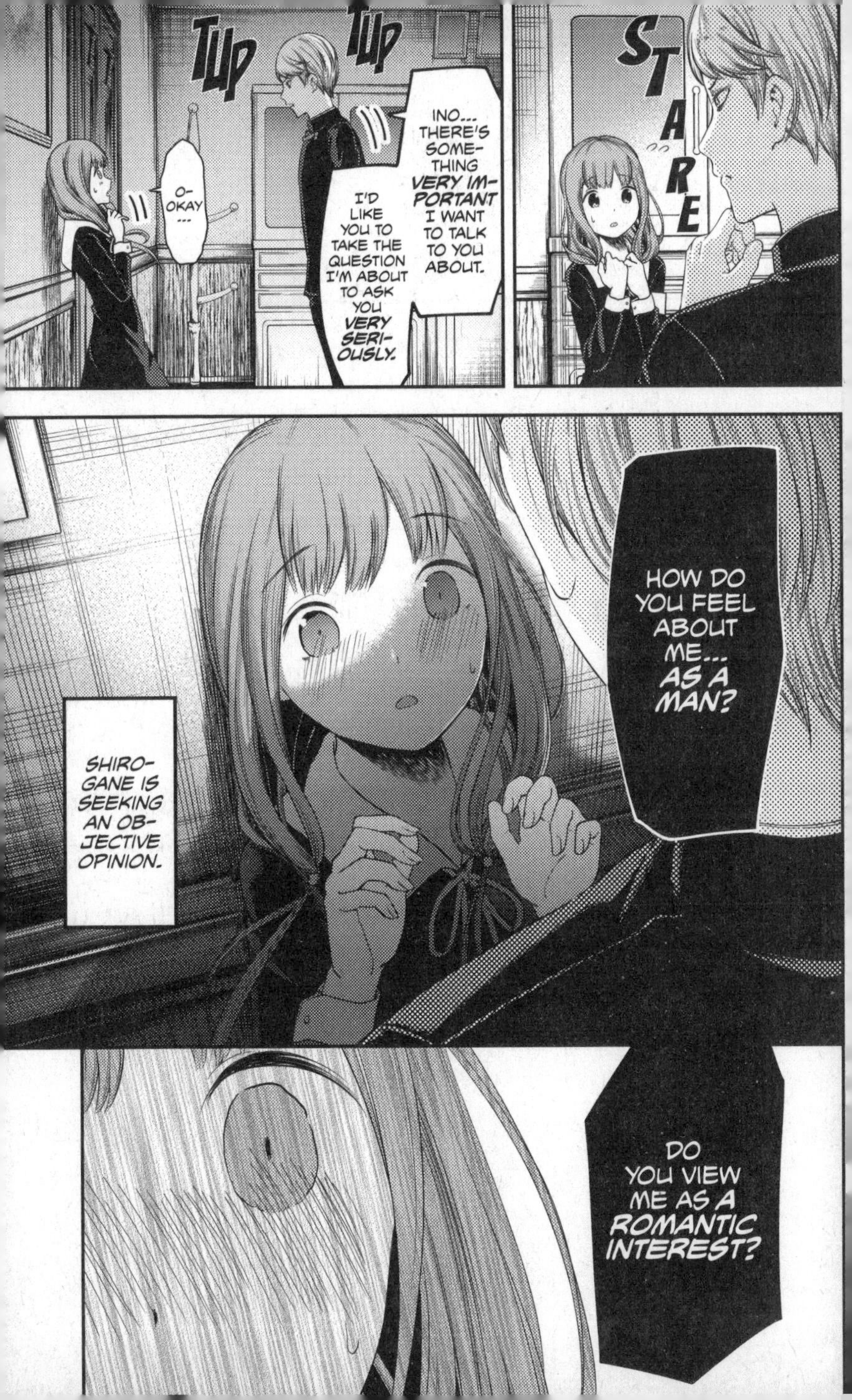
STARE
TUP TUP
INO... THERE'S SOMETHING VERY IMPORTANT I WANT TO TALK TO YOU ABOUT.
I'D LIKE YOU TO TAKE THE QUESTION I'M ABOUT TO ASK YOU VERY SERIOUSLY.
O-OKAY...
HOW DO YOU FEEL ABOUT ME... AS A MAN?
SHIROGANE IS SEEKING AN OBJECTIVE OPINION.
DO YOU VIEW ME AS A ROMANTIC INTEREST?

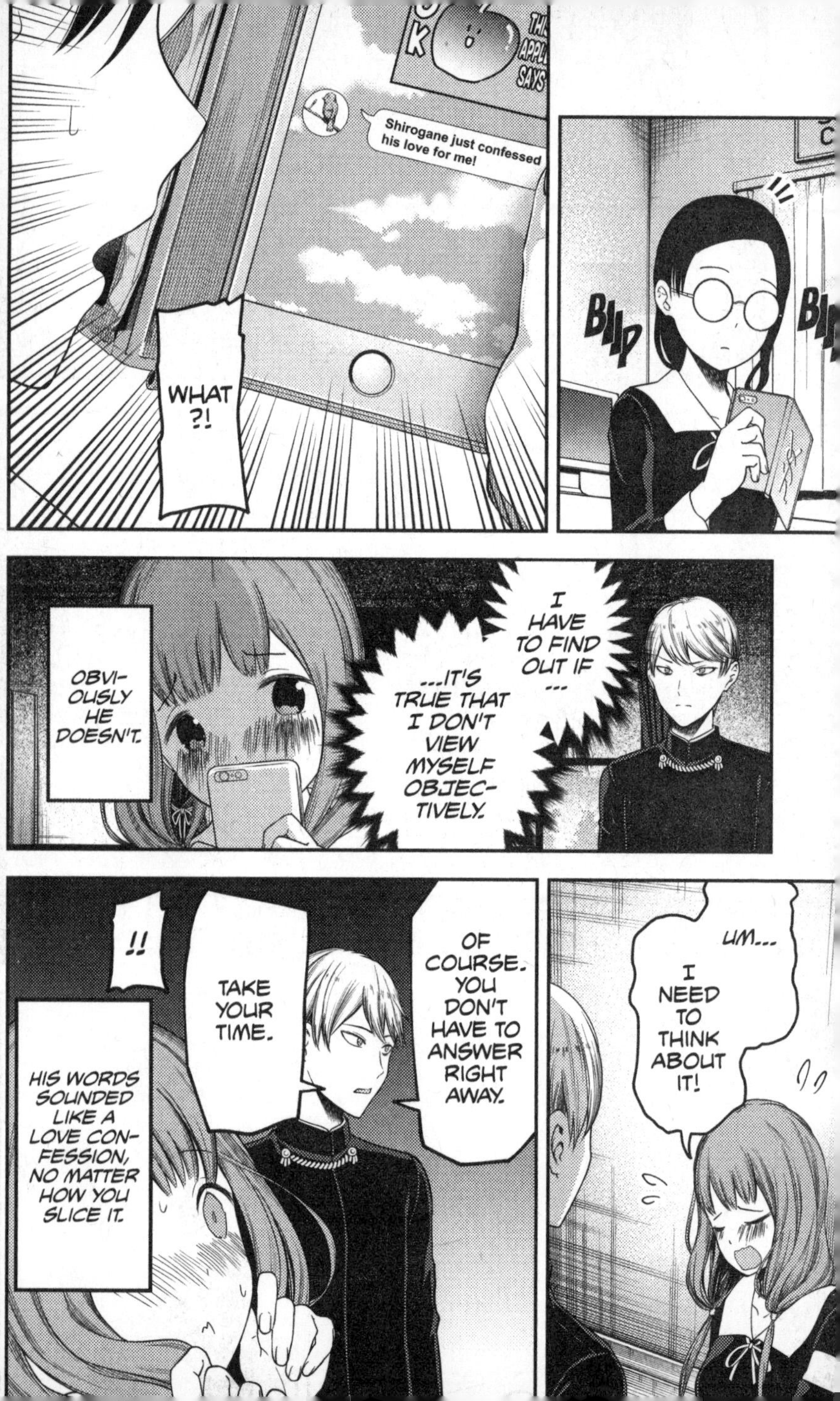
BIIP
Shirogane just confessed his love for me!
WHAT?!
I HAVE TO FIND OUT IF ...
...IT'S TRUE THAT I DON'T VIEW MYSELF OBJECTIVELY.
OBVIOUSLY HE DOESN'T.
UM...
I NEED TO THINK ABOUT IT!
OF COURSE. YOU DON'T HAVE TO ANSWER RIGHT AWAY.
TAKE YOUR TIME.
!!
HIS WORDS SOUNDED LIKE A LOVE CONFESSION, NO MATTER HOW YOU SLICE IT.

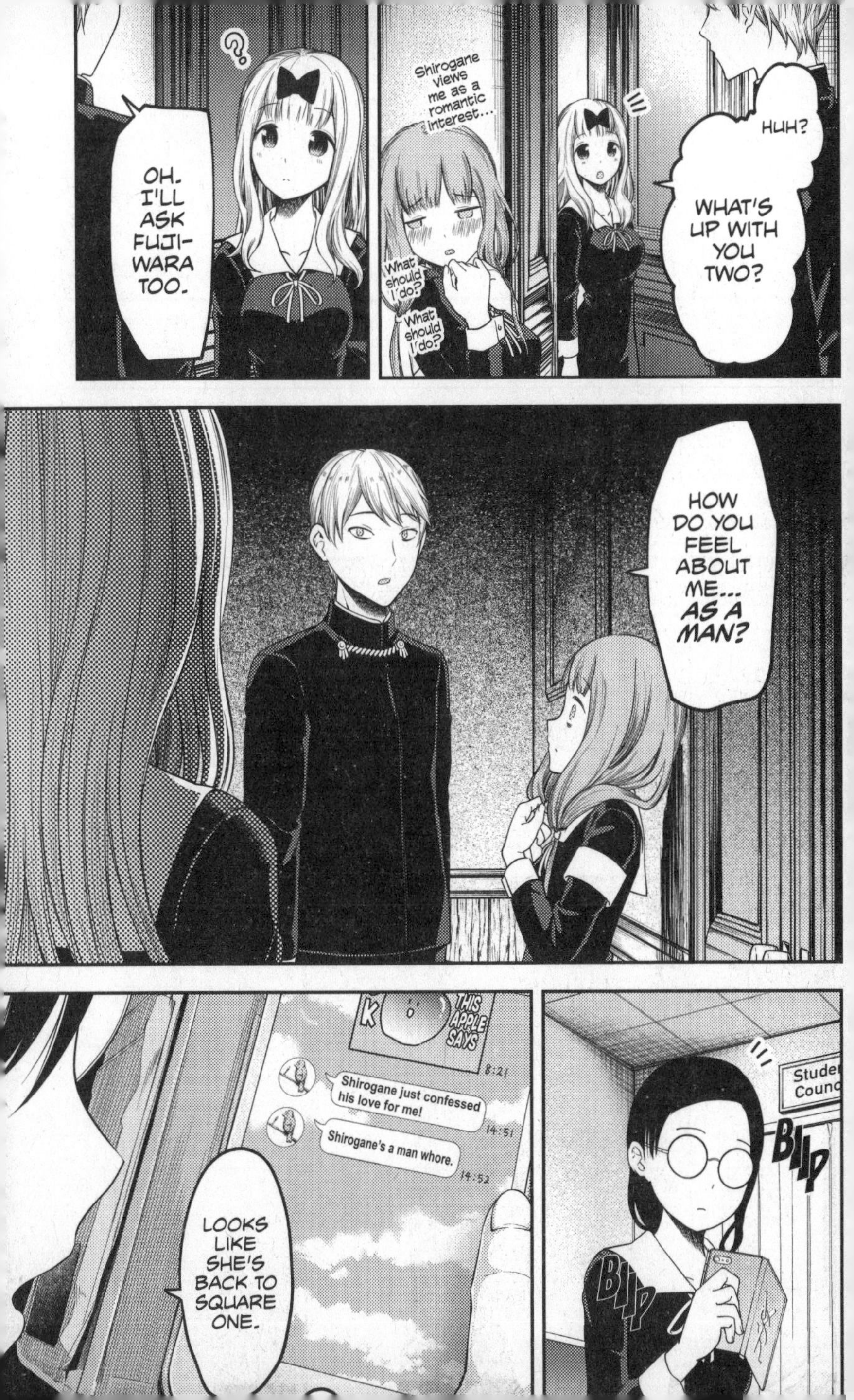
HUH?
WHAT'S UP WITH YOU TWO?
Shirogane views me as a romantic interest...
What should I do?
What should I do?
OH. I'LL ASK FUJIWARA TOO.
HOW DO YOU FEEL ABOUT ME... AS A MAN?
Stude
Counc
BIIP
BIIP
THIS APPLE SAYS
K
8:21
Shirogane just confessed his love for me!
14:51
Shirogane's a man whore.
14:52
LOOKS LIKE SHE'S BACK TO SQUARE ONE.

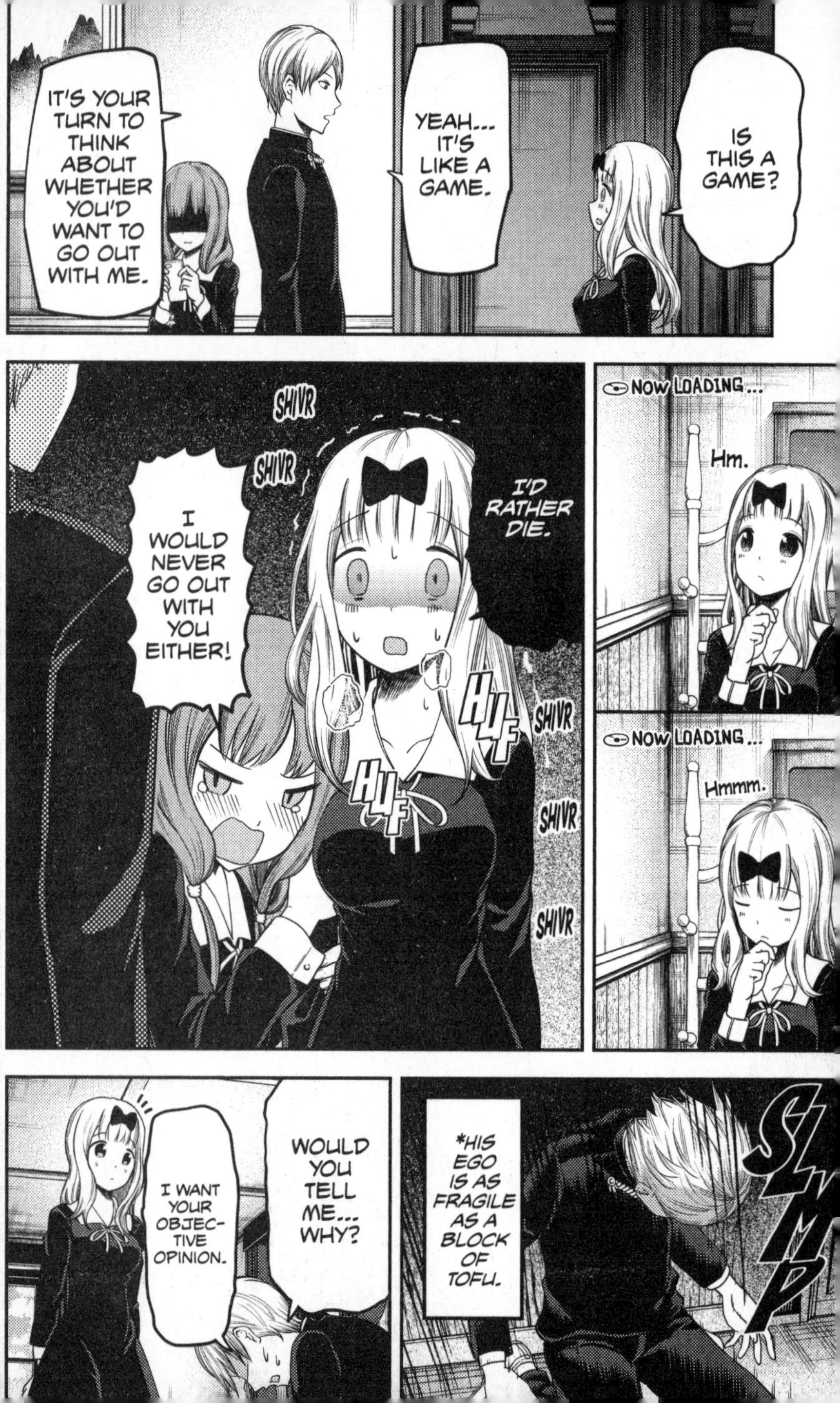
IS THIS A GAME?
YEAH... IT'S LIKE A GAME.
IT'S YOUR TURN TO THINK ABOUT WHETHER YOU'D WANT TO GO OUT WITH ME.
NOW LOADING...
Hm.
NOW LOADING...
Hmmm.
I'D RATHER DIE.
SHIVR
SHIVR
HUF
HUF
SHIVR
SHIVR
SHIVR
I WOULD NEVER GO OUT WITH YOU EITHER!
*HIS EGO IS AS FRAGILE AS A BLOCK OF TOFU.
WOULD YOU TELL ME... WHY?
I WANT YOUR OBJECTIVE OPINION.

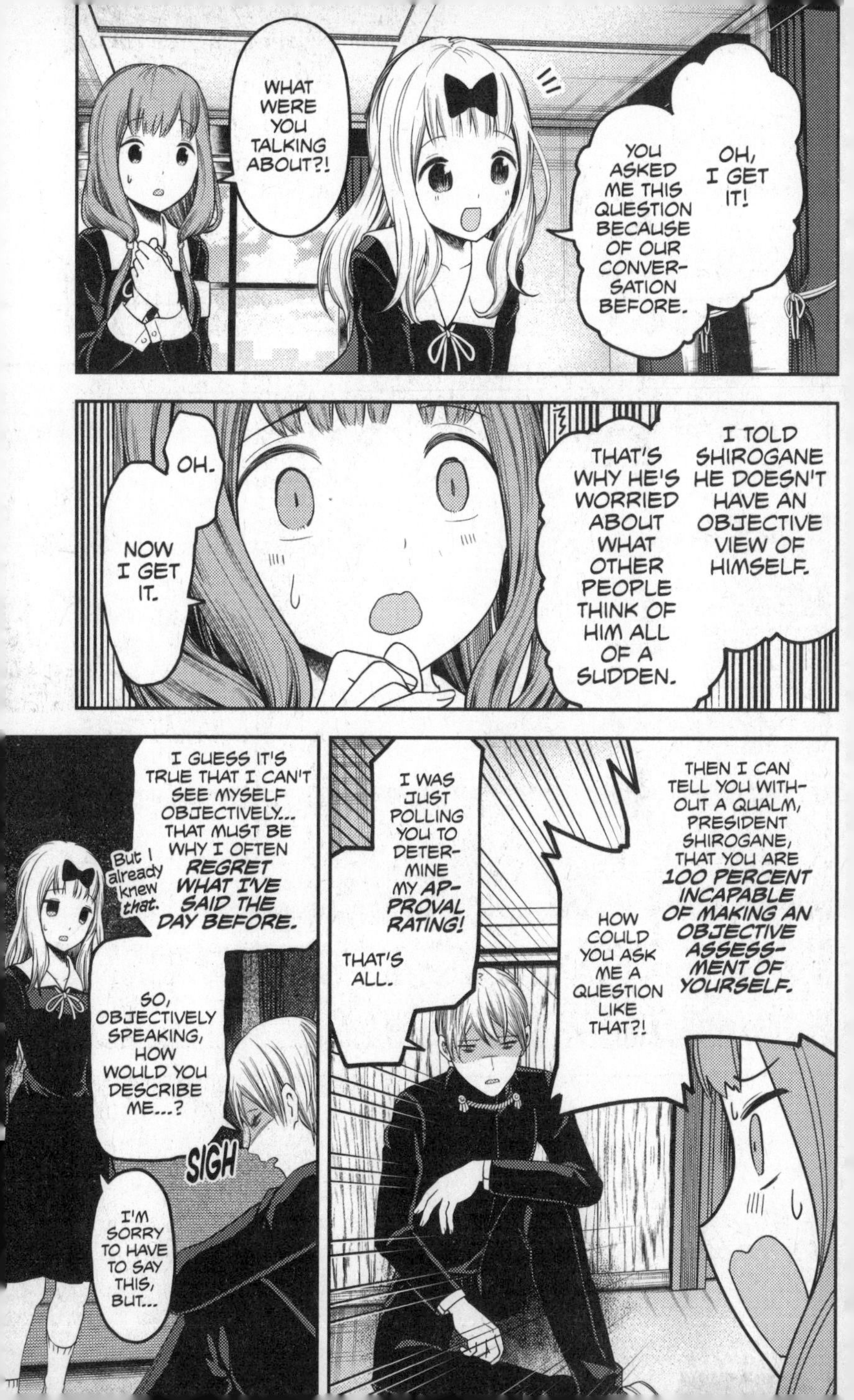
OH, I GET IT!
YOU ASKED ME THIS QUESTION BECAUSE OF OUR CONVERSATION BEFORE.
WHAT WERE YOU TALKING ABOUT?!
I TOLD SHIROGANE HE DOESN'T HAVE AN OBJECTIVE VIEW OF HIMSELF.
THAT'S WHY HE'S WORRIED ABOUT WHAT OTHER PEOPLE THINK OF HIM ALL OF A SUDDEN.
OH.
NOW I GET IT.
THEN I CAN TELL YOU WITHOUT A QUALM, PRESIDENT SHIROGANE, THAT YOU ARE 100 PERCENT INCAPABLE OF MAKING AN OBJECTIVE ASSESSMENT OF YOURSELF.
HOW COULD YOU ASK ME A QUESTION LIKE THAT?!
I WAS JUST POLLING YOU TO DETERMINE MY APPROVAL RATING!
THAT'S ALL.
I GUESS IT'S TRUE THAT I CAN'T SEE MYSELF OBJECTIVELY... THAT MUST BE WHY I OFTEN REGRET WHAT I'VE SAID THE DAY BEFORE.
But I already knew that.
SO, OBJECTIVELY SPEAKING, HOW WOULD YOU DESCRIBE ME...?
SIGH
I'M SORRY TO HAVE TO SAY THIS, BUT...

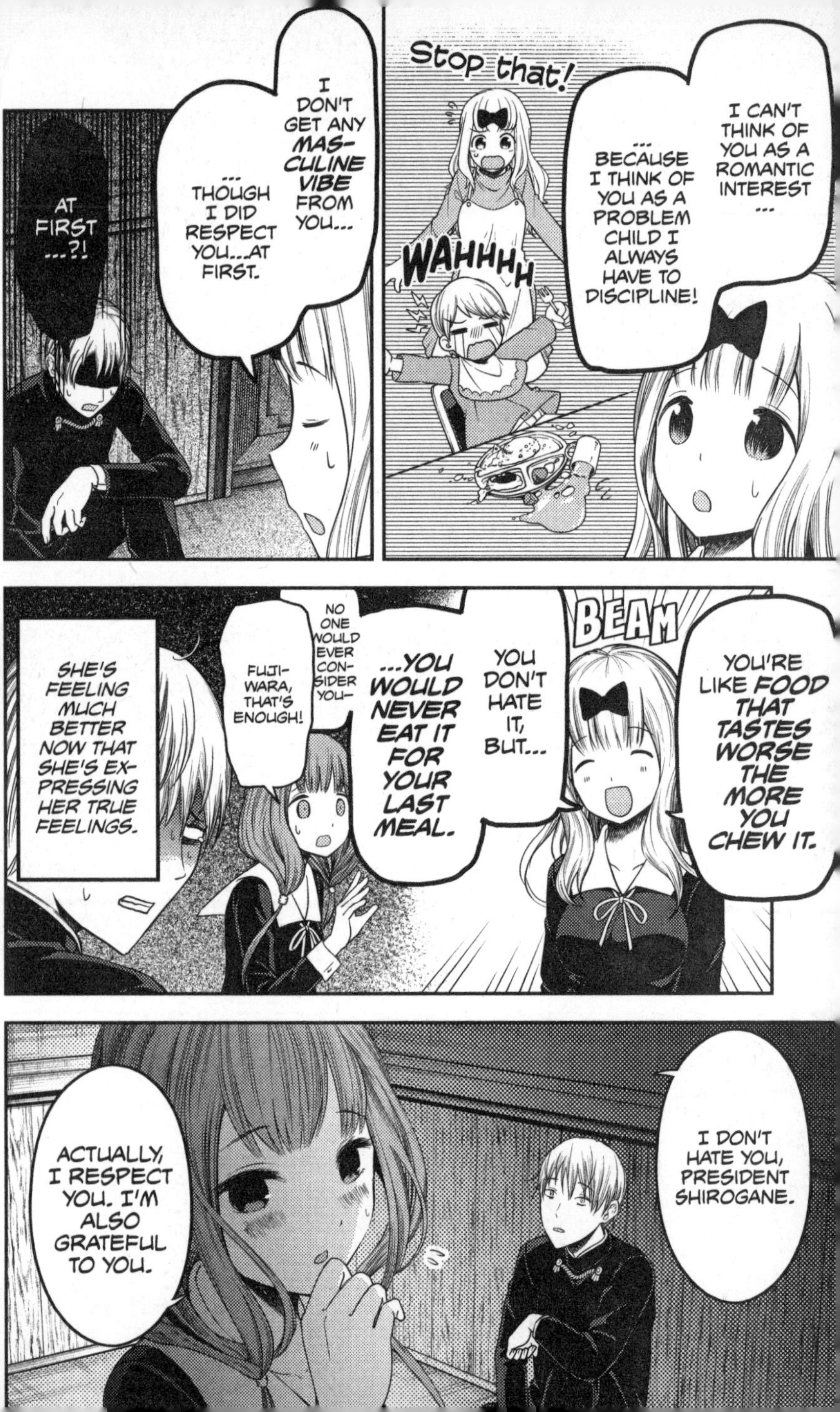
I CAN'T THINK OF YOU AS A ROMANTIC INTEREST...
...BECAUSE I THINK OF YOU AS A PROBLEM CHILD I ALWAYS HAVE TO DISCIPLINE!
Stop that!
WAHHHH
I DON'T GET ANY MASCULINE VIBE FROM YOU...
...THOUGH I DID RESPECT YOU...AT FIRST.
AT FIRST...?!
BEAM
YOU'RE LIKE FOOD THAT TASTES WORSE THE MORE YOU CHEW IT.
YOU DON'T HATE IT, BUT...
...YOU WOULD NEVER EAT IT FOR YOUR LAST MEAL.
NO ONE WOULD EVER CONSIDER YOU—
FUJIWARA, THAT'S ENOUGH!
SHE'S FEELING MUCH BETTER NOW THAT SHE'S EXPRESSING HER TRUE FEELINGS.
I DON'T HATE YOU, PRESIDENT SHIROGANE.
ACTUALLY, I RESPECT YOU. I'M ALSO GRATEFUL TO YOU.

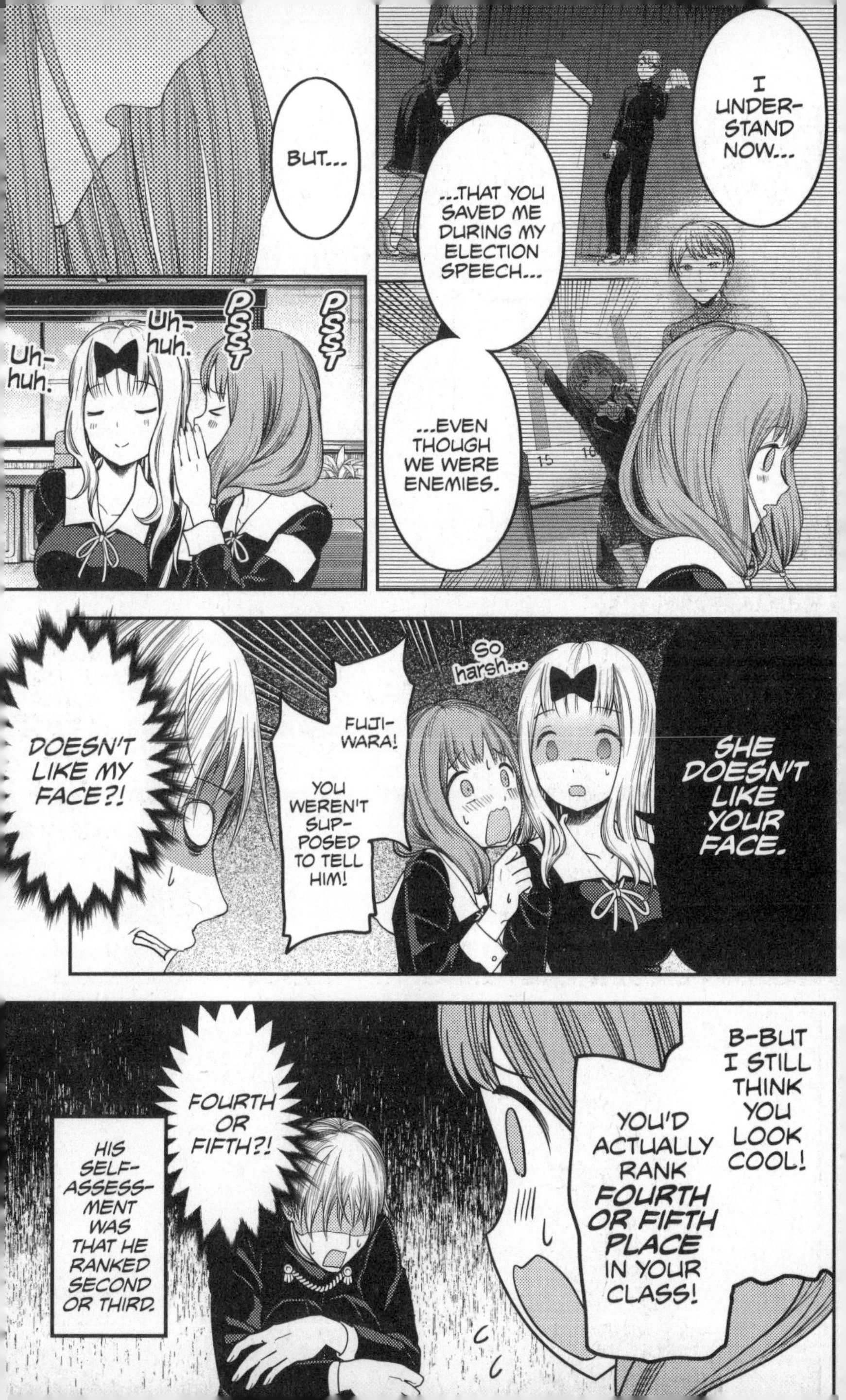
I UNDER-STAND NOW...
...THAT YOU SAVED ME DURING MY ELECTION SPEECH...
...EVEN THOUGH WE WERE ENEMIES.
BUT...
PSST PSST
Uh-huh.
Uh-huh.
SHE DOESN'T LIKE YOUR FACE.
So harsh...
FUJI-WARA!
YOU WEREN'T SUP-POSED TO TELL HIM!
DOESN'T LIKE MY FACE?!
B-BUT I STILL THINK YOU LOOK COOL!
YOU'D ACTUALLY RANK FOURTH OR FIFTH PLACE IN YOUR CLASS!
FOURTH OR FIFTH?!
HIS SELF-ASSESS-MENT WAS THAT HE RANKED SECOND OR THIRD.

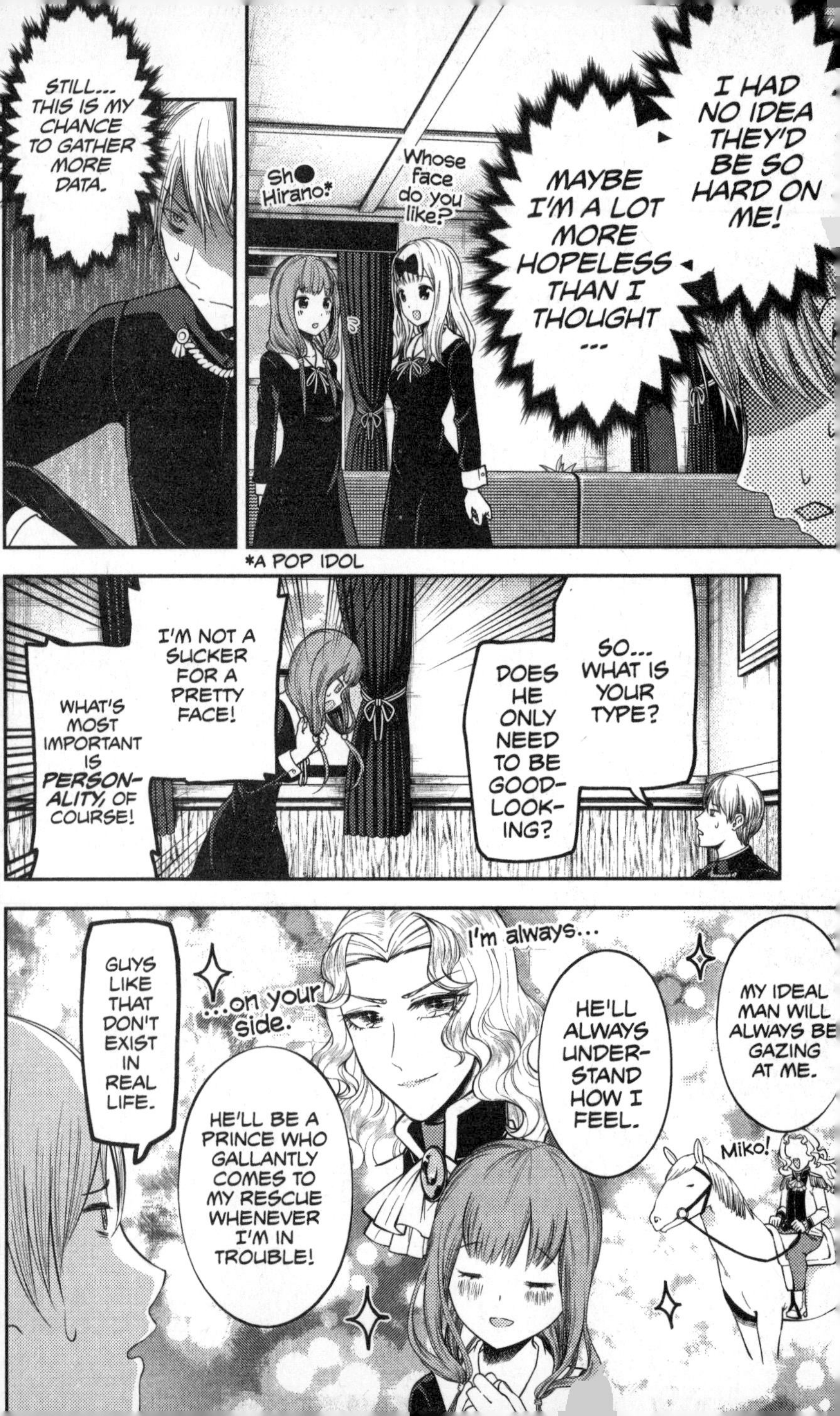
I HAD NO IDEA THEY'D BE SO HARD ON ME!
MAYBE I'M A LOT MORE HOPELESS THAN I THOUGHT...
Whose face do you like?
Sh● Hirano*
STILL... THIS IS MY CHANCE TO GATHER MORE DATA.
*A POP IDOL
SO... WHAT IS YOUR TYPE?
DOES HE ONLY NEED TO BE GOOD-LOOKING?
I'M NOT A SUCKER FOR A PRETTY FACE!
WHAT'S MOST IMPORTANT IS PERSONALITY, OF COURSE!
MY IDEAL MAN WILL ALWAYS BE GAZING AT ME.
Miko!
HE'LL ALWAYS UNDERSTAND HOW I FEEL.
I'm always...
...on your side.
HE'LL BE A PRINCE WHO GALLANTLY COMES TO MY RESCUE WHENEVER I'M IN TROUBLE!
GUYS LIKE THAT DON'T EXIST IN REAL LIFE.

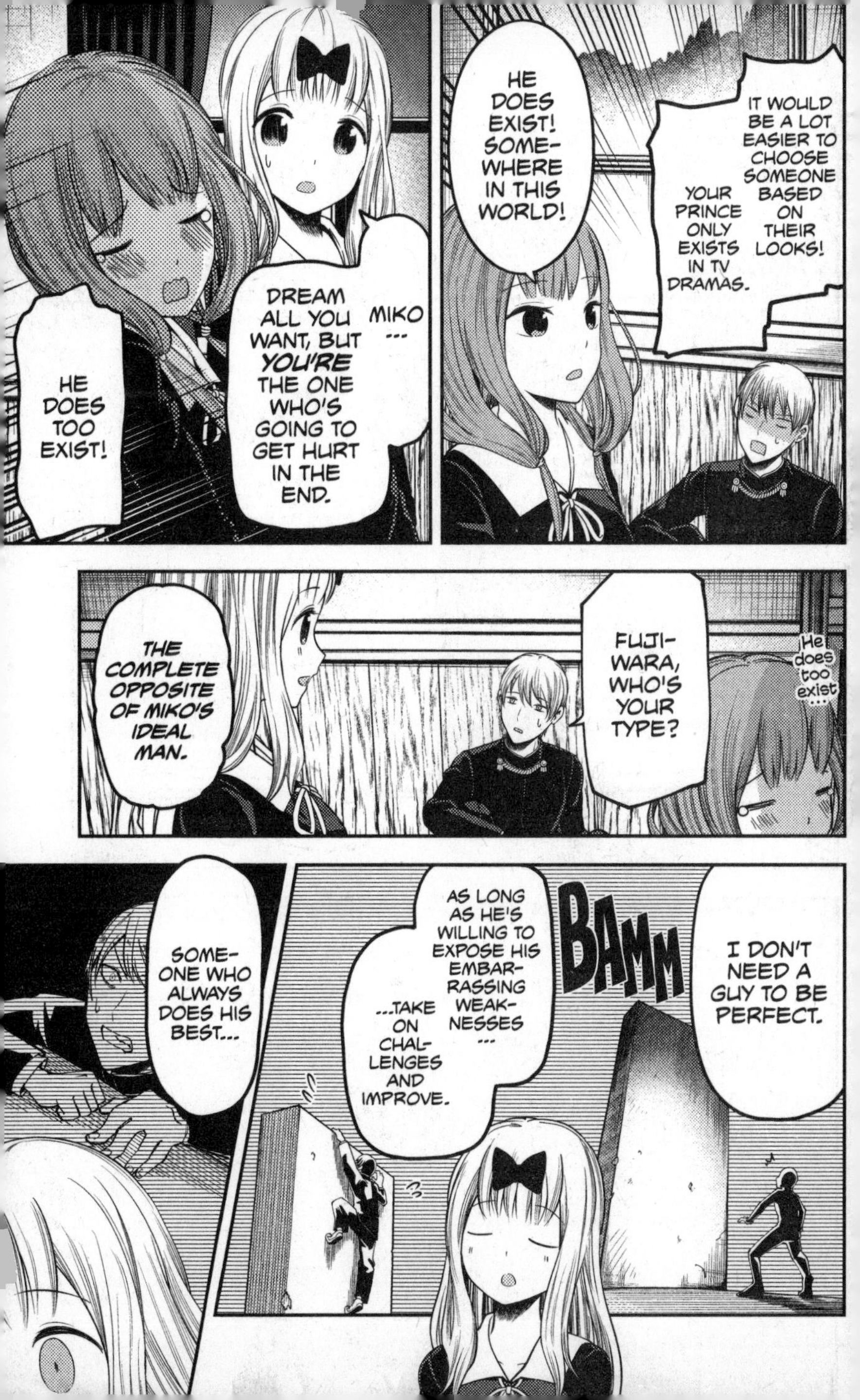
IT WOULD BE A LOT EASIER TO CHOOSE SOMEONE BASED ON THEIR LOOKS!
YOUR PRINCE ONLY EXISTS IN TV DRAMAS.
HE DOES EXIST! SOME-WHERE IN THIS WORLD!
MIKO...
DREAM ALL YOU WANT, BUT *YOU'RE* THE ONE WHO'S GOING TO GET HURT IN THE END.
HE DOES TOO EXIST!
He does too exist...
FUJI-WARA, WHO'S YOUR TYPE?
THE COMPLETE OPPOSITE OF MIKO'S IDEAL MAN.
I DON'T NEED A GUY TO BE PERFECT.
BAMM
AS LONG AS HE'S WILLING TO EXPOSE HIS EMBAR-RASSING WEAK-NESSES...
...TAKE ON CHAL-LENGES AND IMPROVE.
SOME-ONE WHO ALWAYS DOES HIS BEST...

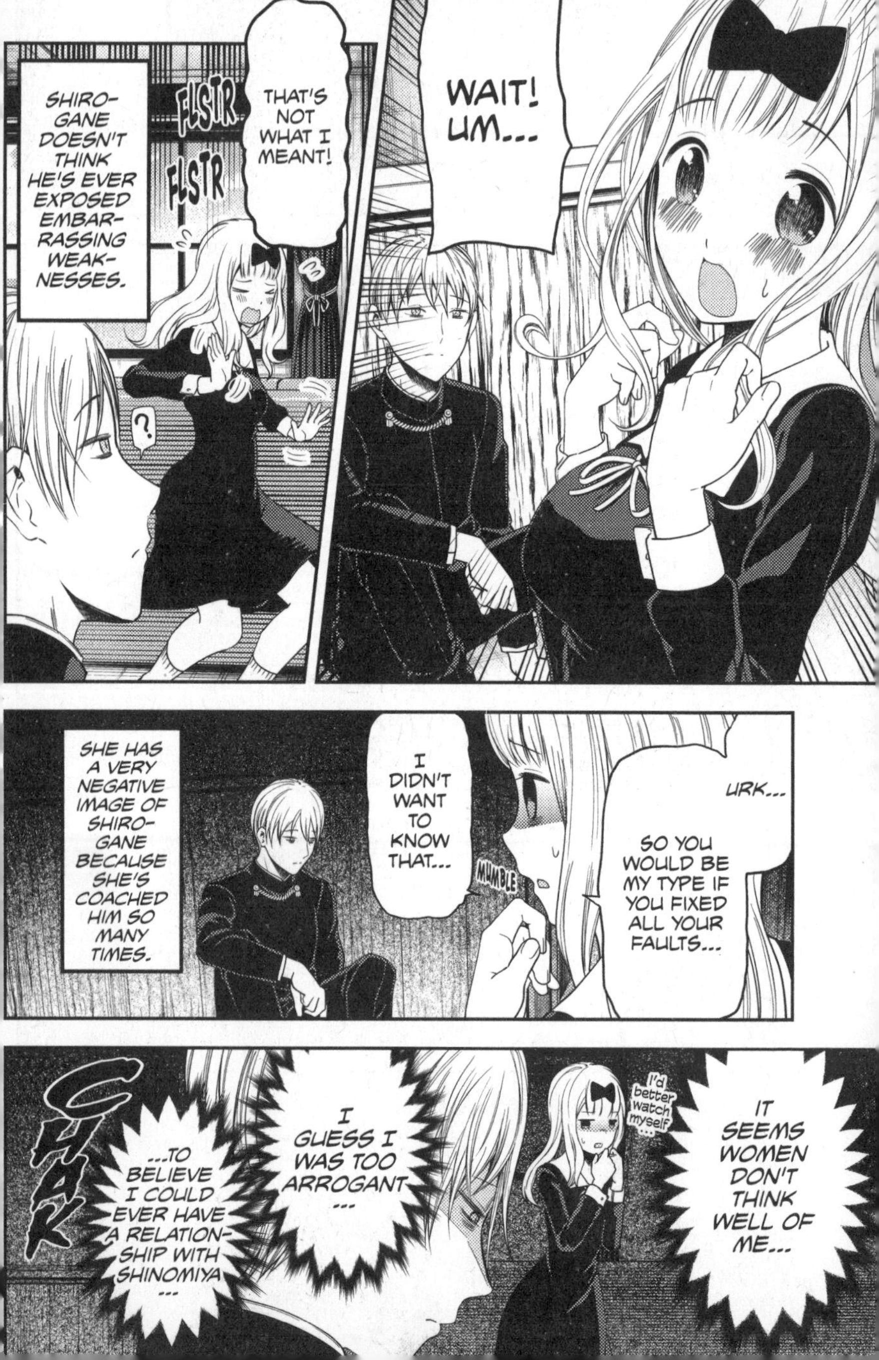
WAIT! UM...
THAT'S NOT WHAT I MEANT!
FLSTR
FLSTR
SHIRO-GANE DOESN'T THINK HE'S EVER EXPOSED EMBARRASSING WEAKNESSES.
URK...
SO YOU WOULD BE MY TYPE IF YOU FIXED ALL YOUR FAULTS...
MUMBLE
I DIDN'T WANT TO KNOW THAT...
SHE HAS A VERY NEGATIVE IMAGE OF SHIROGANE BECAUSE SHE'S COACHED HIM SO MANY TIMES.
IT SEEMS WOMEN DON'T THINK WELL OF ME...
I'd better watch myself...
I GUESS I WAS TOO ARROGANT...
...TO BELIEVE I COULD EVER HAVE A RELATIONSHIP WITH SHINOMIYA...
CHAK

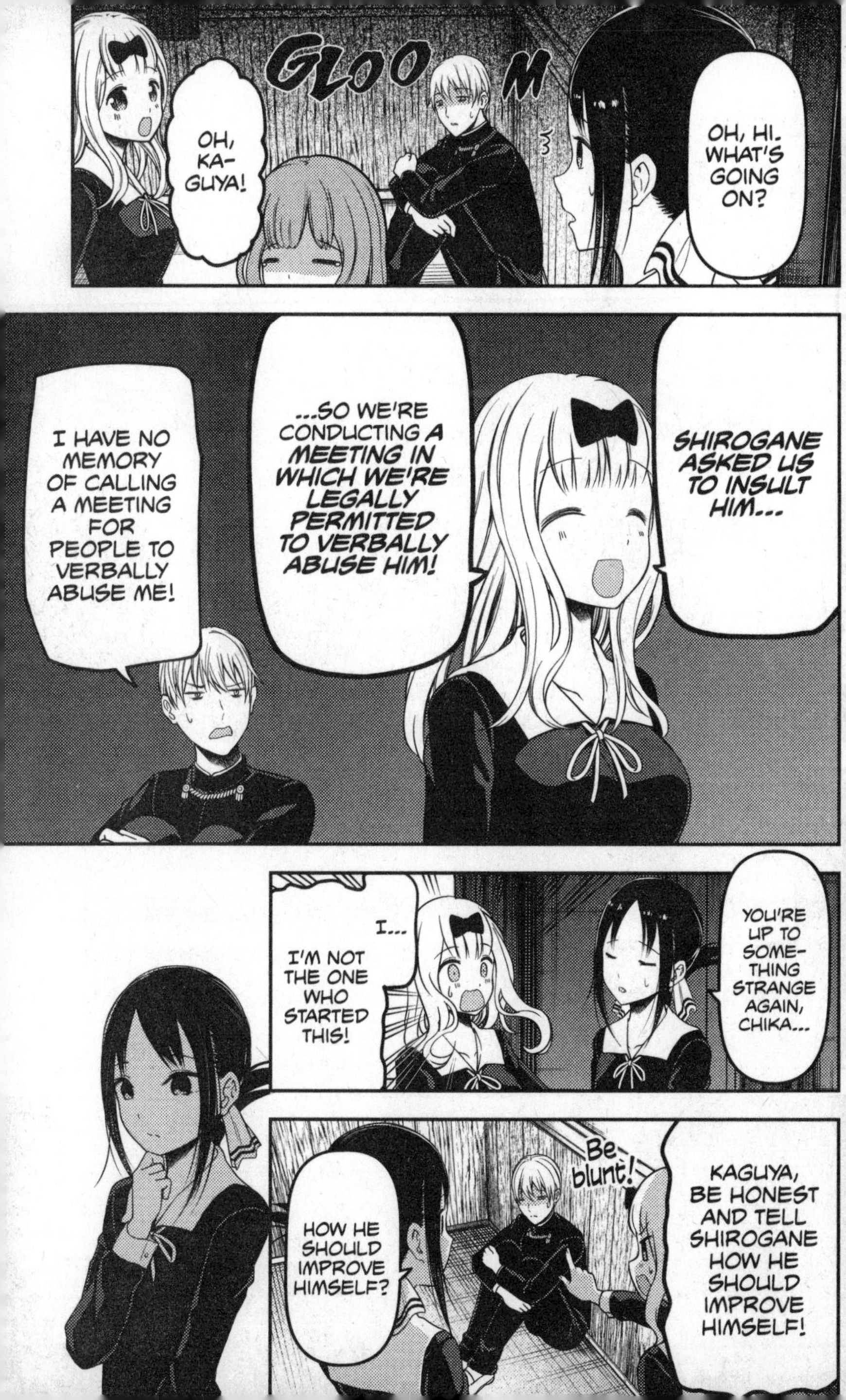
OH, HI. WHAT'S GOING ON?
GLOOM
OH, KAGUYA!
SHIROGANE ASKED US TO INSULT HIM...
...SO WE'RE CONDUCTING A MEETING IN WHICH WE'RE LEGALLY PERMITTED TO VERBALLY ABUSE HIM!
I HAVE NO MEMORY OF CALLING A MEETING FOR PEOPLE TO VERBALLY ABUSE ME!
YOU'RE UP TO SOMETHING STRANGE AGAIN, CHIKA...
I...
I'M NOT THE ONE WHO STARTED THIS!
KAGUYA, BE HONEST AND TELL SHIROGANE HOW HE SHOULD IMPROVE HIMSELF!
Be blunt!
HOW HE SHOULD IMPROVE HIMSELF?

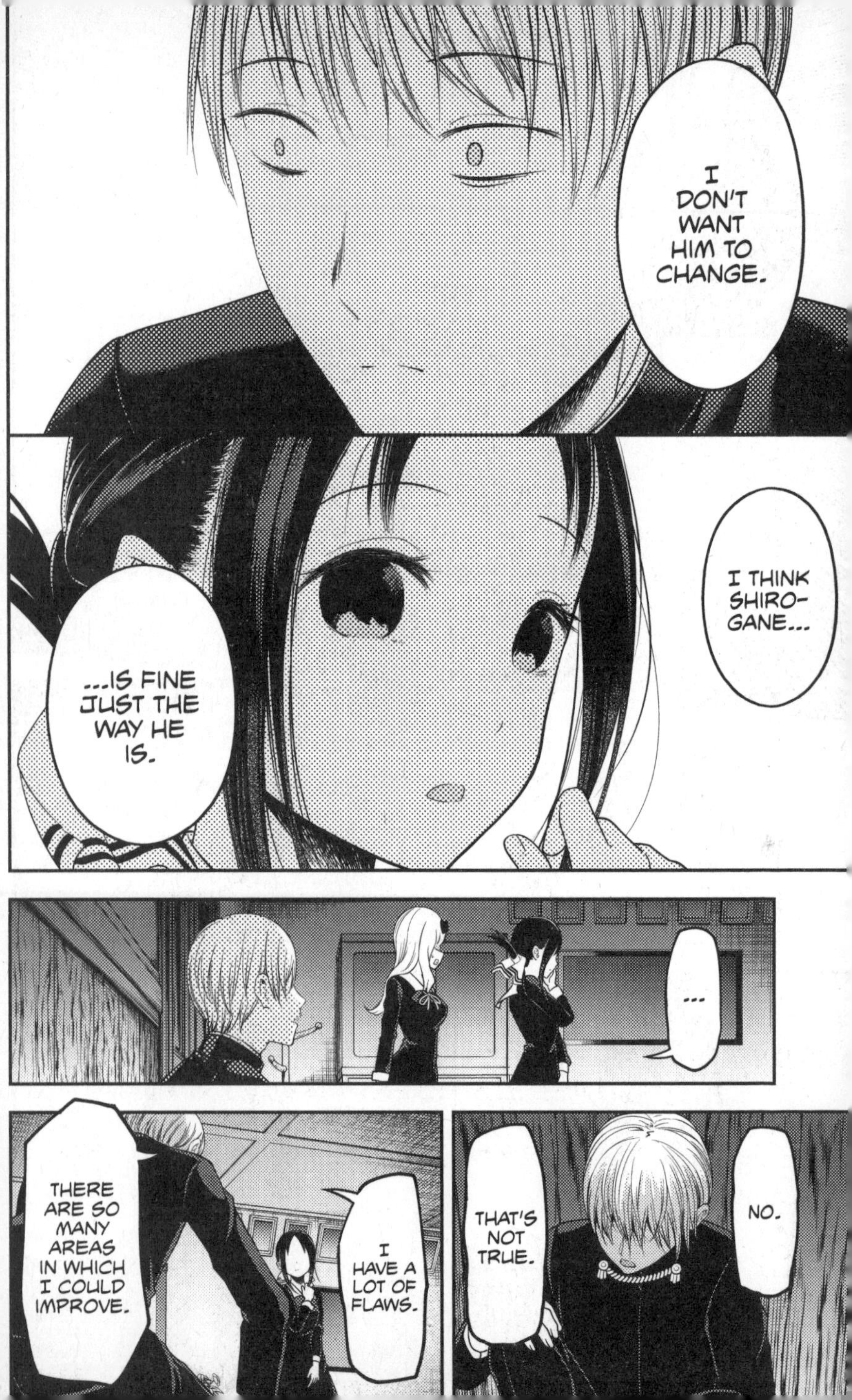
I DON'T WANT HIM TO CHANGE.
I THINK SHIRO-GANE...
...IS FINE JUST THE WAY HE IS.
......
NO.
THAT'S NOT TRUE.
I HAVE A LOT OF FLAWS.
THERE ARE SO MANY AREAS IN WHICH I COULD IMPROVE.

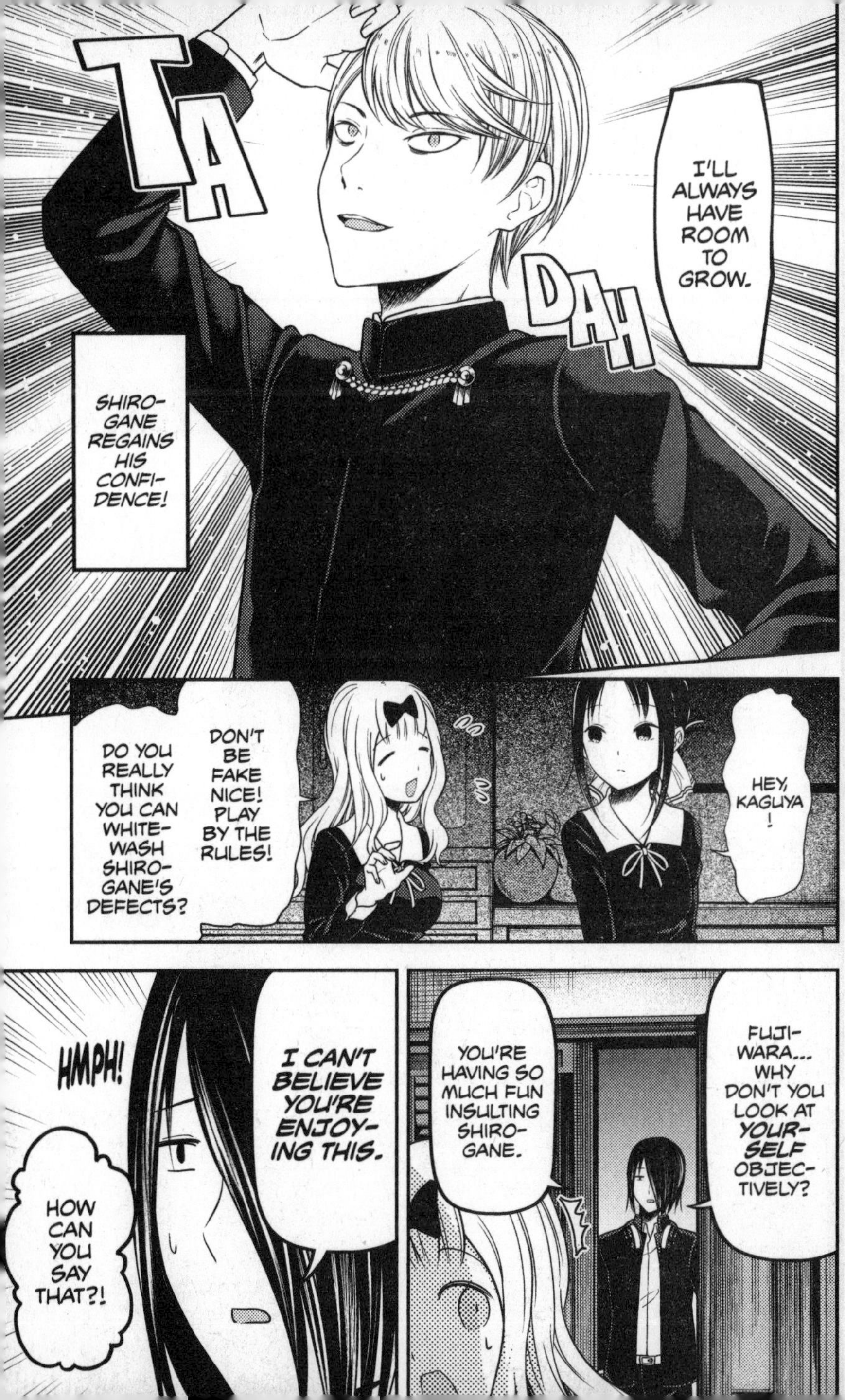
I'LL ALWAYS HAVE ROOM TO GROW.
TA DAH
SHIROGANE REGAINS HIS CONFIDENCE!
HEY, KAGUYA!
DON'T BE FAKE NICE! PLAY BY THE RULES!
DO YOU REALLY THINK YOU CAN WHITEWASH SHIROGANE'S DEFECTS?
FUJIWARA... WHY DON'T YOU LOOK AT YOURSELF OBJECTIVELY?
YOU'RE HAVING SO MUCH FUN INSULTING SHIROGANE.
I CAN'T BELIEVE YOU'RE ENJOYING THIS.
HMPH!
HOW CAN YOU SAY THAT?!

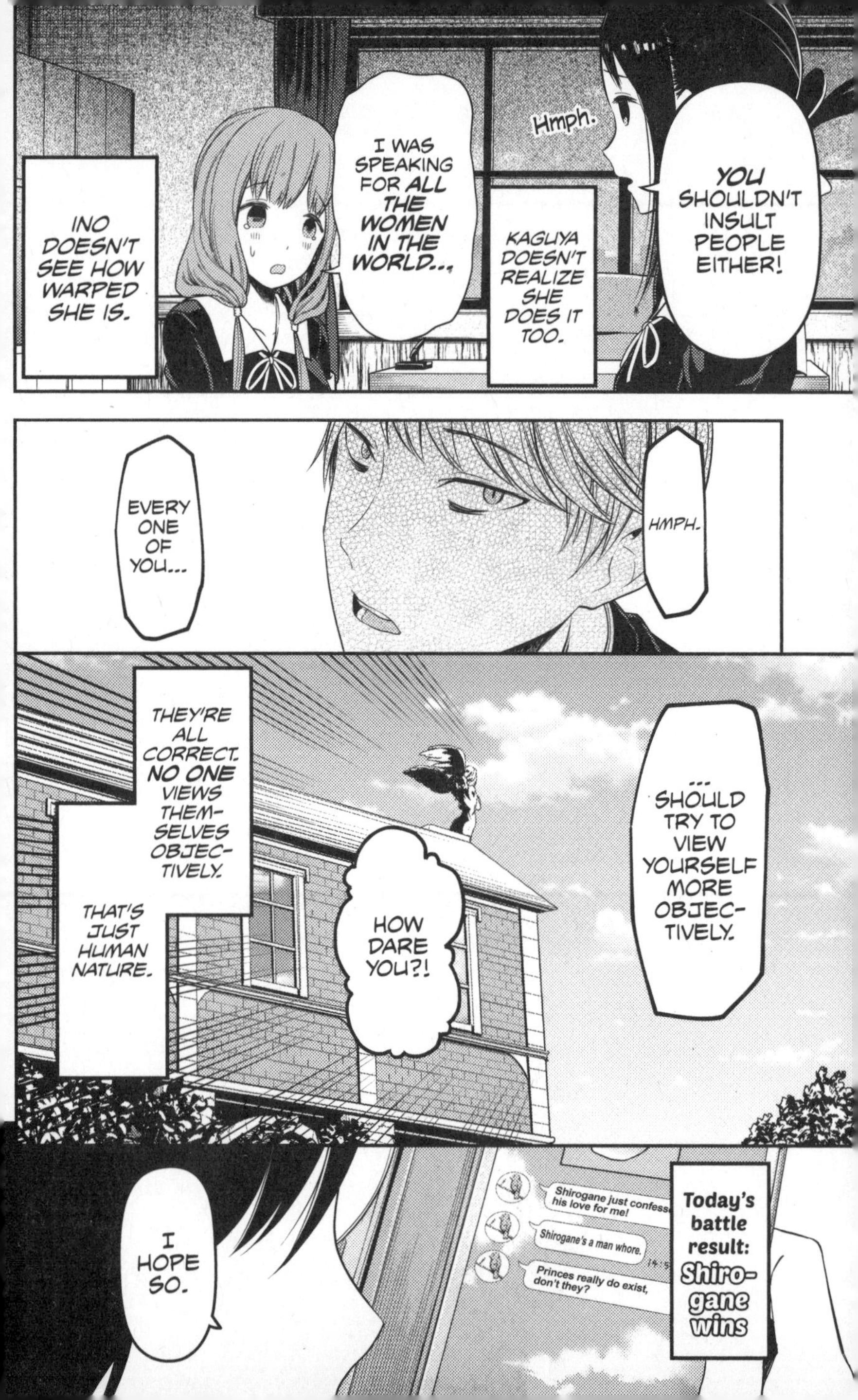
YOU SHOULDN'T INSULT PEOPLE EITHER!
Hmph.
KAGUYA DOESN'T REALIZE SHE DOES IT TOO.
I WAS SPEAKING FOR ALL THE WOMEN IN THE WORLD...
INO DOESN'T SEE HOW WARPED SHE IS.
HMPH.
EVERY ONE OF YOU...
...SHOULD TRY TO VIEW YOURSELF MORE OBJECTIVELY.
HOW DARE YOU?!
THEY'RE ALL CORRECT. NO ONE VIEWS THEMSELVES OBJECTIVELY.
THAT'S JUST HUMAN NATURE.
Today's battle result: Shirogane wins
Shirogane just confess
his love for me!
Shirogane's a man whore.
Princes really do exist, don't they?
I HOPE SO.

Koba is leaving me hanging on "read"...

KAGUYA-SAMA

LOVE IS WAR

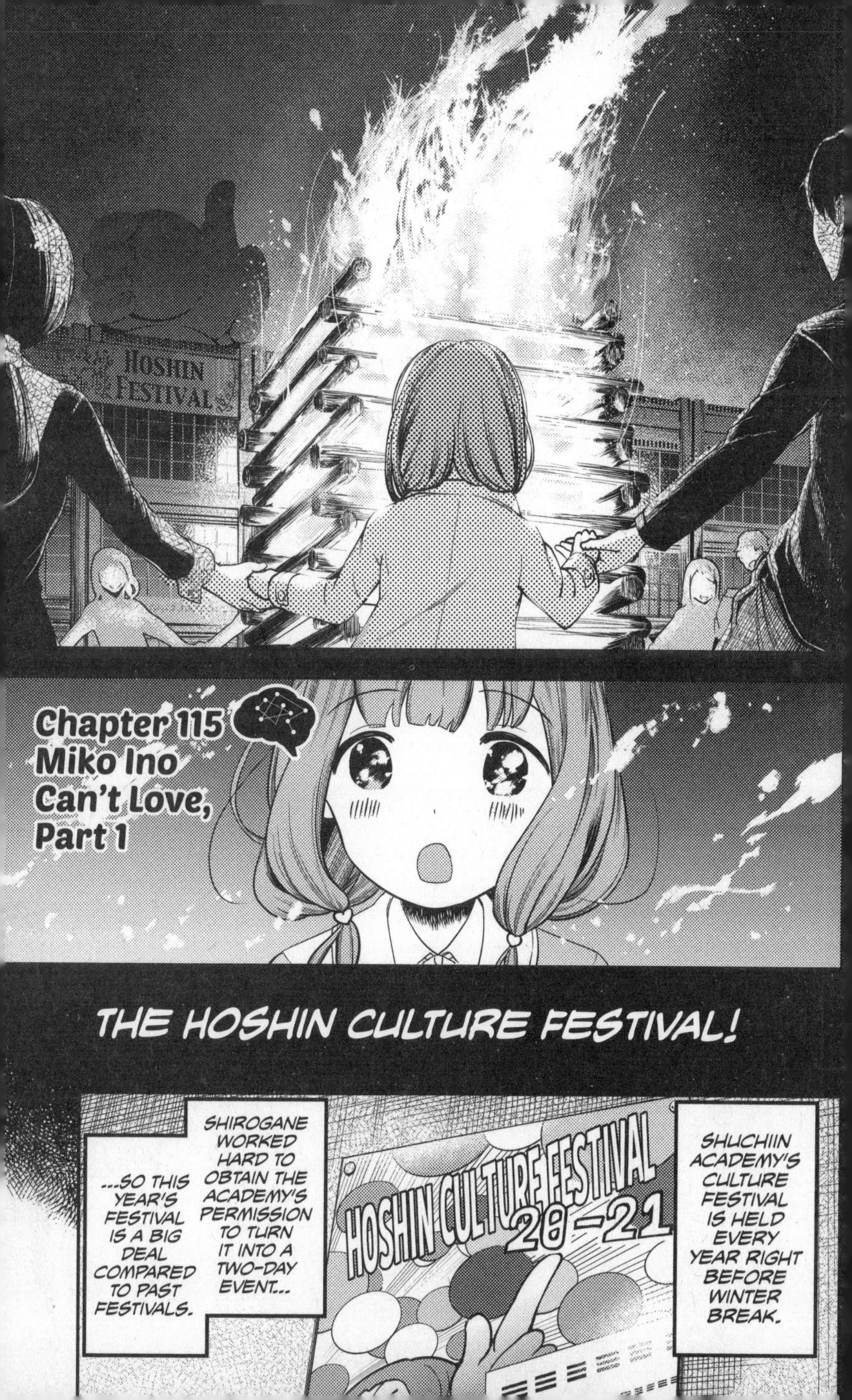
HOSHIN FESTIVAL
Chapter 115
Miko Ino Can't Love, Part 1
THE HOSHIN CULTURE FESTIVAL!
SHUCHIIN ACADEMY'S CULTURE FESTIVAL IS HELD EVERY YEAR RIGHT BEFORE WINTER BREAK.
HOSHIN CULTURE FESTIVAL 20-21
SHIROGANE WORKED HARD TO OBTAIN THE ACADEMY'S PERMISSION TO TURN IT INTO A TWO-DAY EVENT...
...SO THIS YEAR'S FESTIVAL IS A BIG DEAL COMPARED TO PAST FESTIVALS.

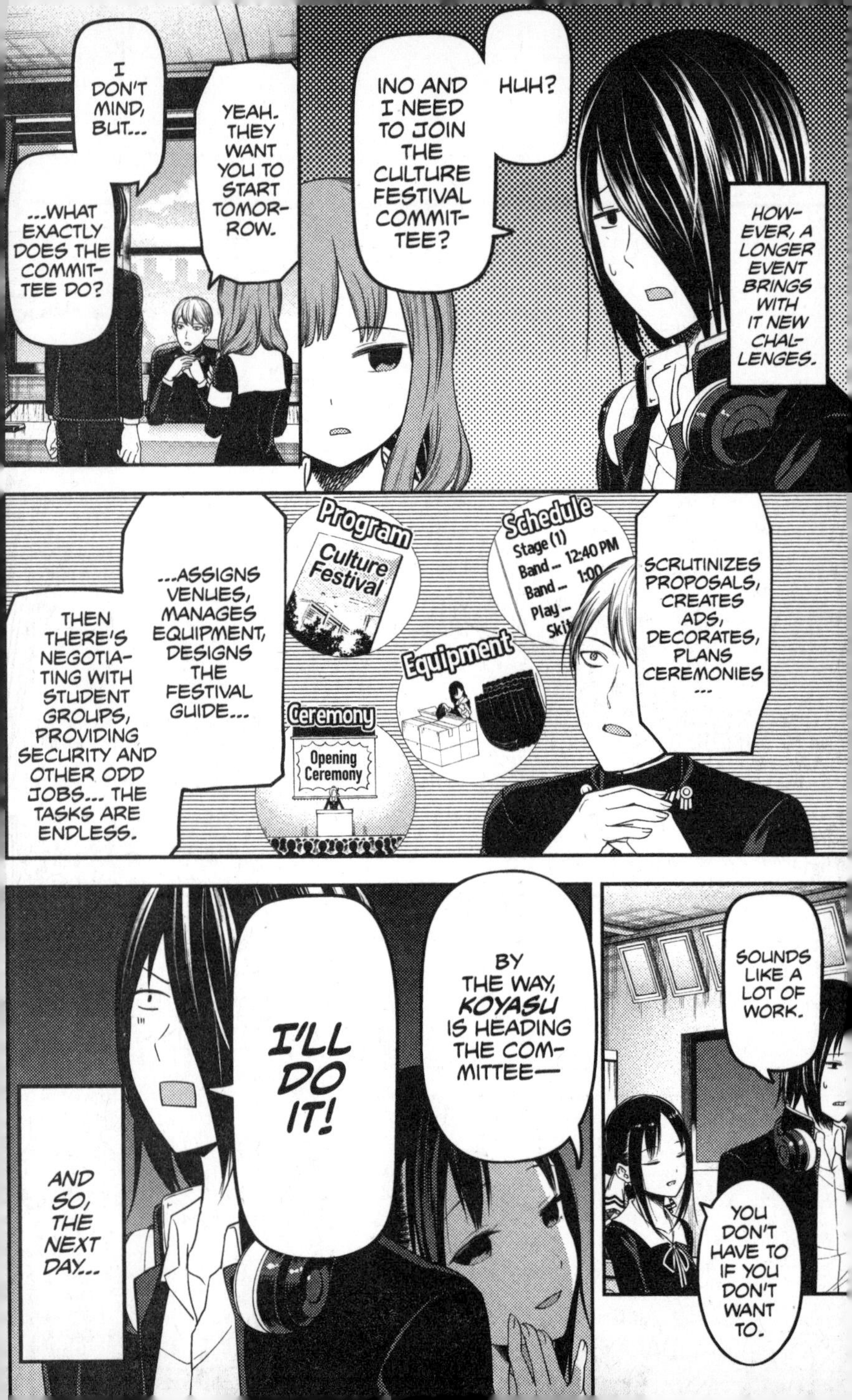
HOWEVER, A LONGER EVENT BRINGS WITH IT NEW CHALLENGES.
HUH?
INO AND I NEED TO JOIN THE CULTURE FESTIVAL COMMITTEE?
YEAH. THEY WANT YOU TO START TOMORROW.
I DON'T MIND, BUT...
...WHAT EXACTLY DOES THE COMMITTEE DO?
SCRUTINIZES PROPOSALS, CREATES ADS, DECORATES, PLANS CEREMONIES...
Schedule
Stage (1)
Band... 12:40 PM
Band... 1:00
Play...
Program
Culture Festival
Equipment
Ceremony
Opening Ceremony
...ASSIGNS VENUES, MANAGES EQUIPMENT, DESIGNS THE FESTIVAL GUIDE...
THEN THERE'S NEGOTIATING WITH STUDENT GROUPS, PROVIDING SECURITY AND OTHER ODD JOBS... THE TASKS ARE ENDLESS.
SOUNDS LIKE A LOT OF WORK.
YOU DON'T HAVE TO IF YOU DON'T WANT TO.
BY THE WAY, *KOYASU* IS HEADING THE COMMITTEE—
I'LL DO IT!
AND SO, THE NEXT DAY...

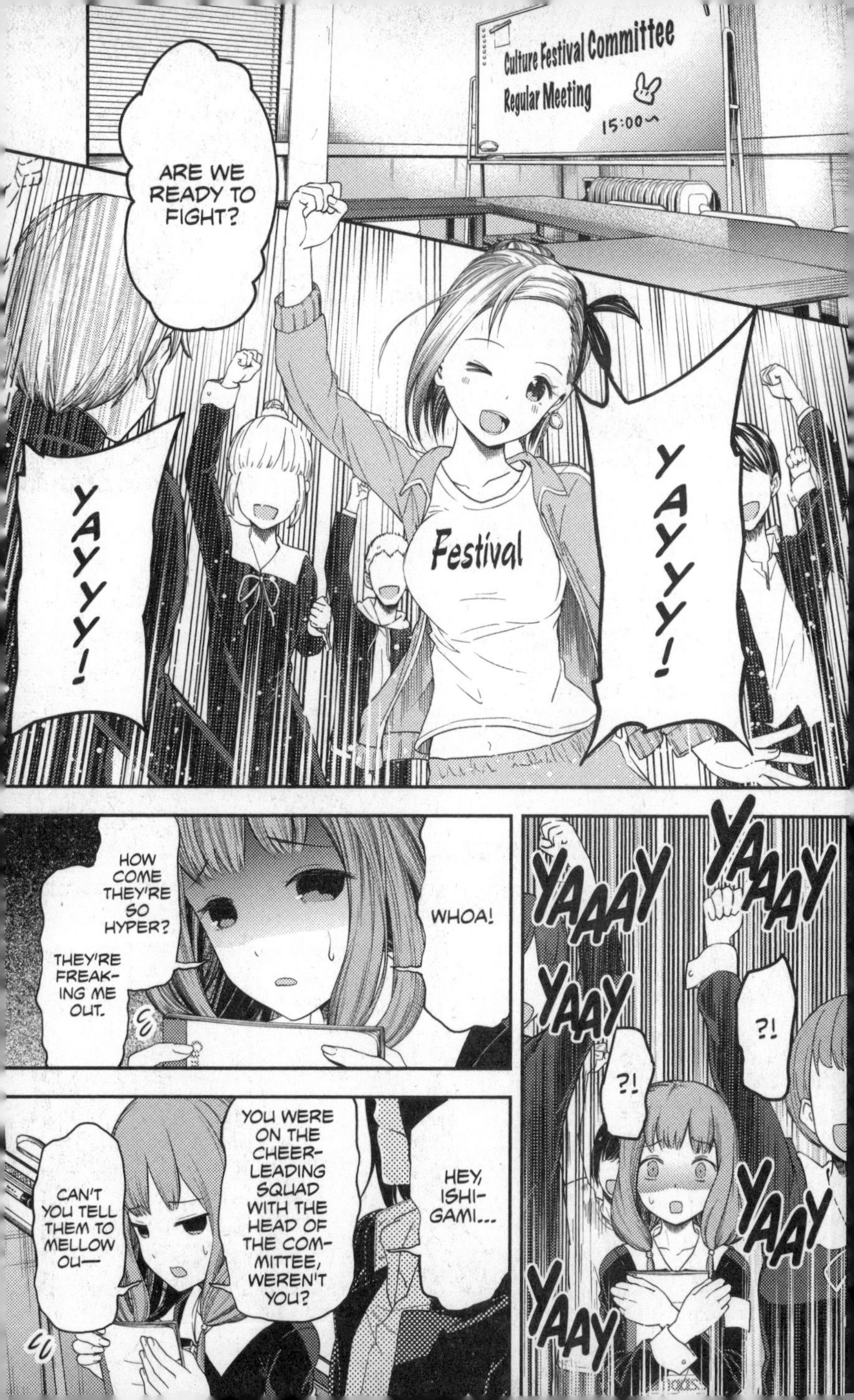
Culture Festival Committee
Regular Meeting
15:00~
ARE WE READY TO FIGHT?
YAYYY!
YAYYY!
Festival
YAAAAY
YAAAY
YAAY
?!
?!
YAAY
YAAY
WHOA!
HOW COME THEY'RE SO HYPER?
THEY'RE FREAK-ING ME OUT.
HEY, ISHI-GAMI...
YOU WERE ON THE CHEER-LEADING SQUAD WITH THE HEAD OF THE COM-MITTEE, WEREN'T YOU?
CAN'T YOU TELL THEM TO MELLOW OU—

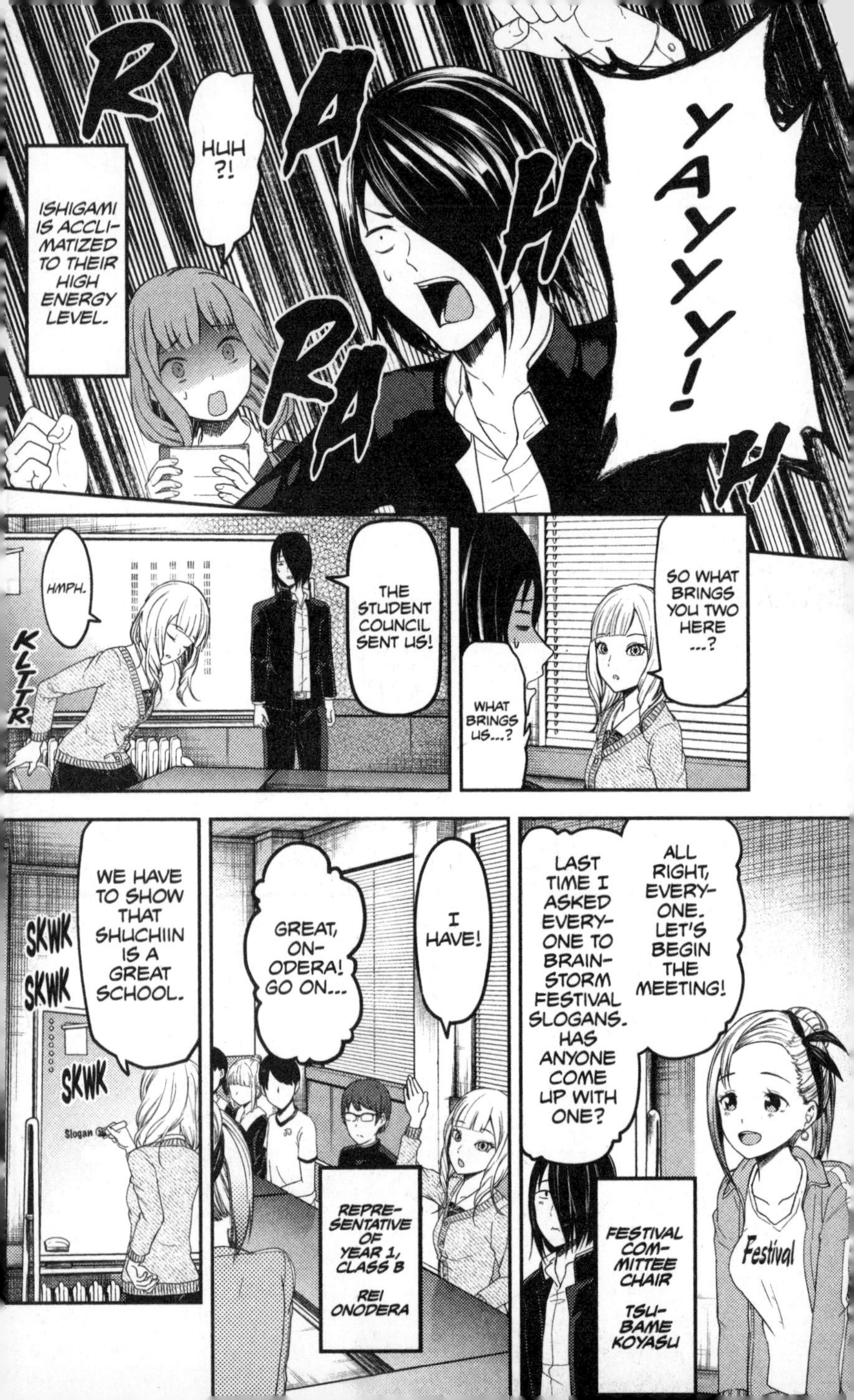
YAYYY!
RAH RAH
HUH?!
ISHIGAMI IS ACCLIMATIZED TO THEIR HIGH ENERGY LEVEL.
SO WHAT BRINGS YOU TWO HERE...?
WHAT BRINGS US...?
THE STUDENT COUNCIL SENT US!
HMPH.
KLTTR
ALL RIGHT, EVERYONE. LET'S BEGIN THE MEETING!
LAST TIME I ASKED EVERYONE TO BRAINSTORM FESTIVAL SLOGANS. HAS ANYONE COME UP WITH ONE?
FESTIVAL COMMITTEE CHAIR TSUBAME KOYASU
Festival
I HAVE!
GREAT, ONODERA! GO ON...
REPRESENTATIVE OF YEAR 1, CLASS B REI ONODERA
WE HAVE TO SHOW THAT SHUCHIIN IS A GREAT SCHOOL.
SKWK
SKWK
SKWK
Slogan

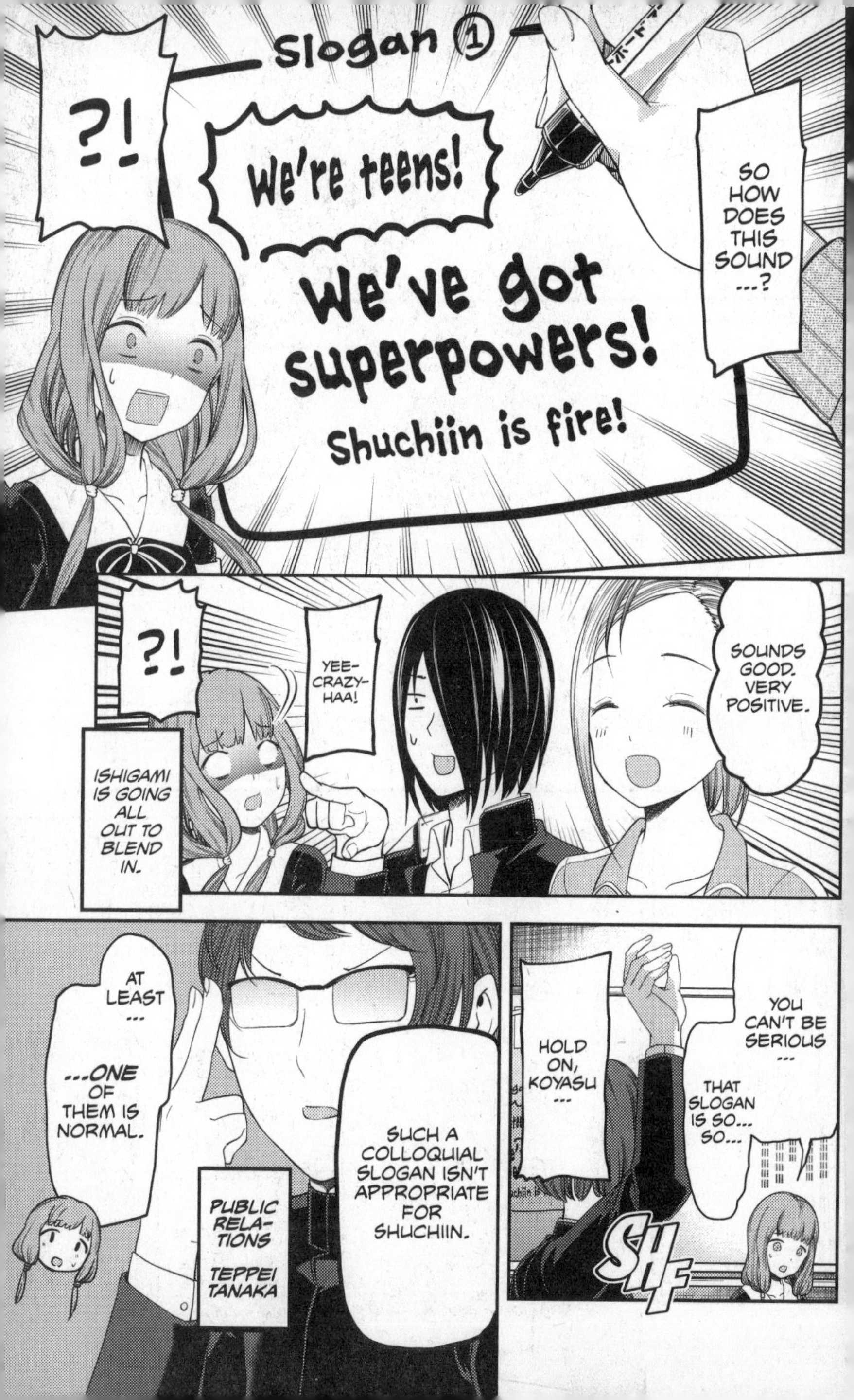
SO HOW DOES THIS SOUND...?
Slogan ①
We're teens!
We've got superpowers!
Shuchiin is fire!
?!
SOUNDS GOOD. VERY POSITIVE.
YEE-CRAZY-HAA!
?!
ISHIGAMI IS GOING ALL OUT TO BLEND IN.
YOU CAN'T BE SERIOUS...
THAT SLOGAN IS SO... SO...
HOLD ON, KOYASU...
SHF
SUCH A COLLOQUIAL SLOGAN ISN'T APPROPRIATE FOR SHUCHIIN.
PUBLIC RELATIONS TEPPEI TANAKA
AT LEAST...
...ONE OF THEM IS NORMAL.

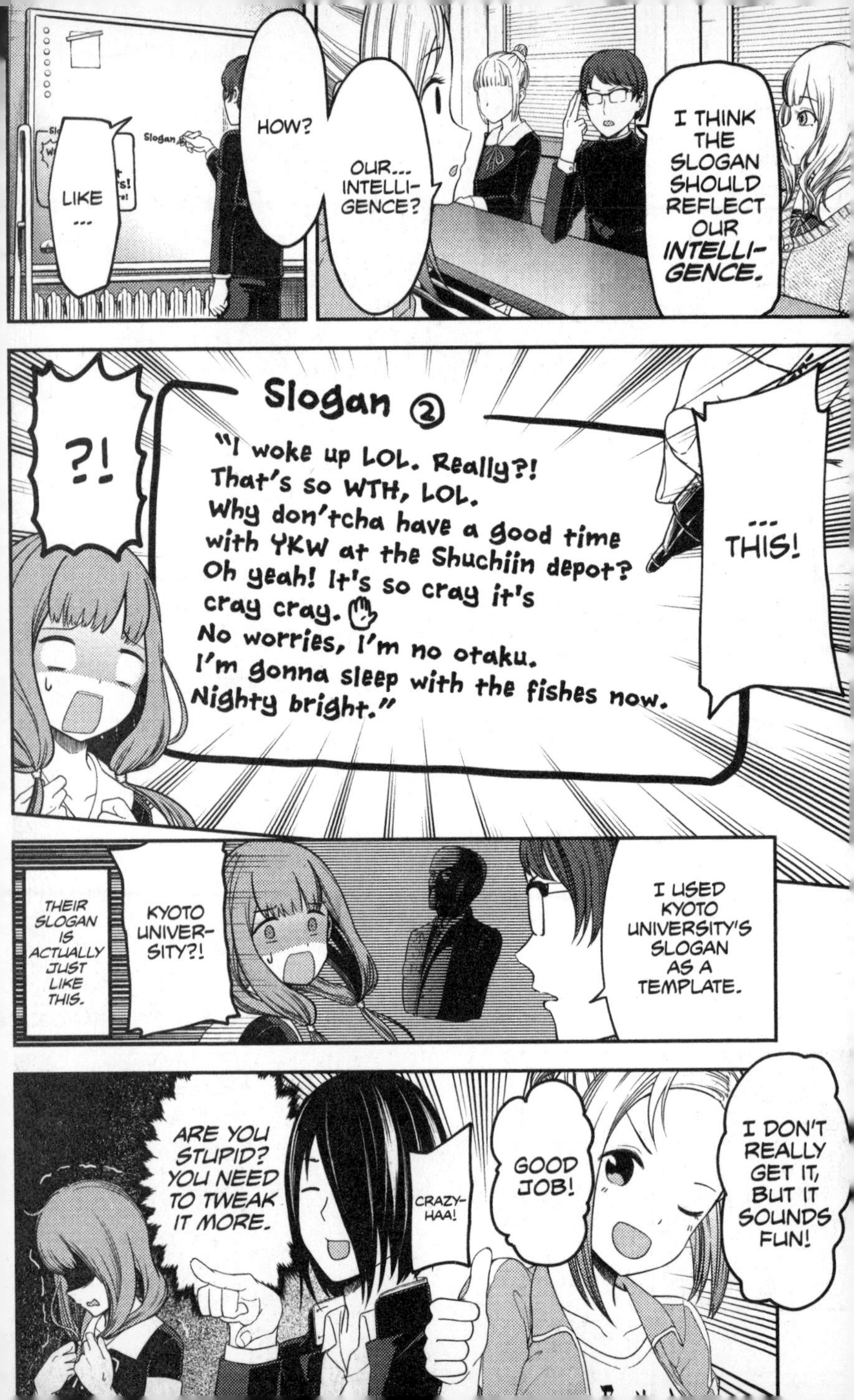
I THINK THE SLOGAN SHOULD REFLECT OUR INTELLIGENCE.
OUR... INTELLIGENCE?
HOW?
LIKE ...
... THIS!
Slogan ②
"I woke up LOL. Really?! That's so WTH, LOL. Why don'tcha have a good time with YKW at the Shuchiin depot? Oh yeah! It's so cray it's cray cray. No worries, I'm no otaku. I'm gonna sleep with the fishes now. Nighty bright."
?!
I USED KYOTO UNIVERSITY'S SLOGAN AS A TEMPLATE.
KYOTO UNIVERSITY?!
THEIR SLOGAN IS ACTUALLY JUST LIKE THIS.
I DON'T REALLY GET IT, BUT IT SOUNDS FUN!
GOOD JOB!
CRAZY-HAA!
ARE YOU STUPID? YOU NEED TO TWEAK IT MORE.

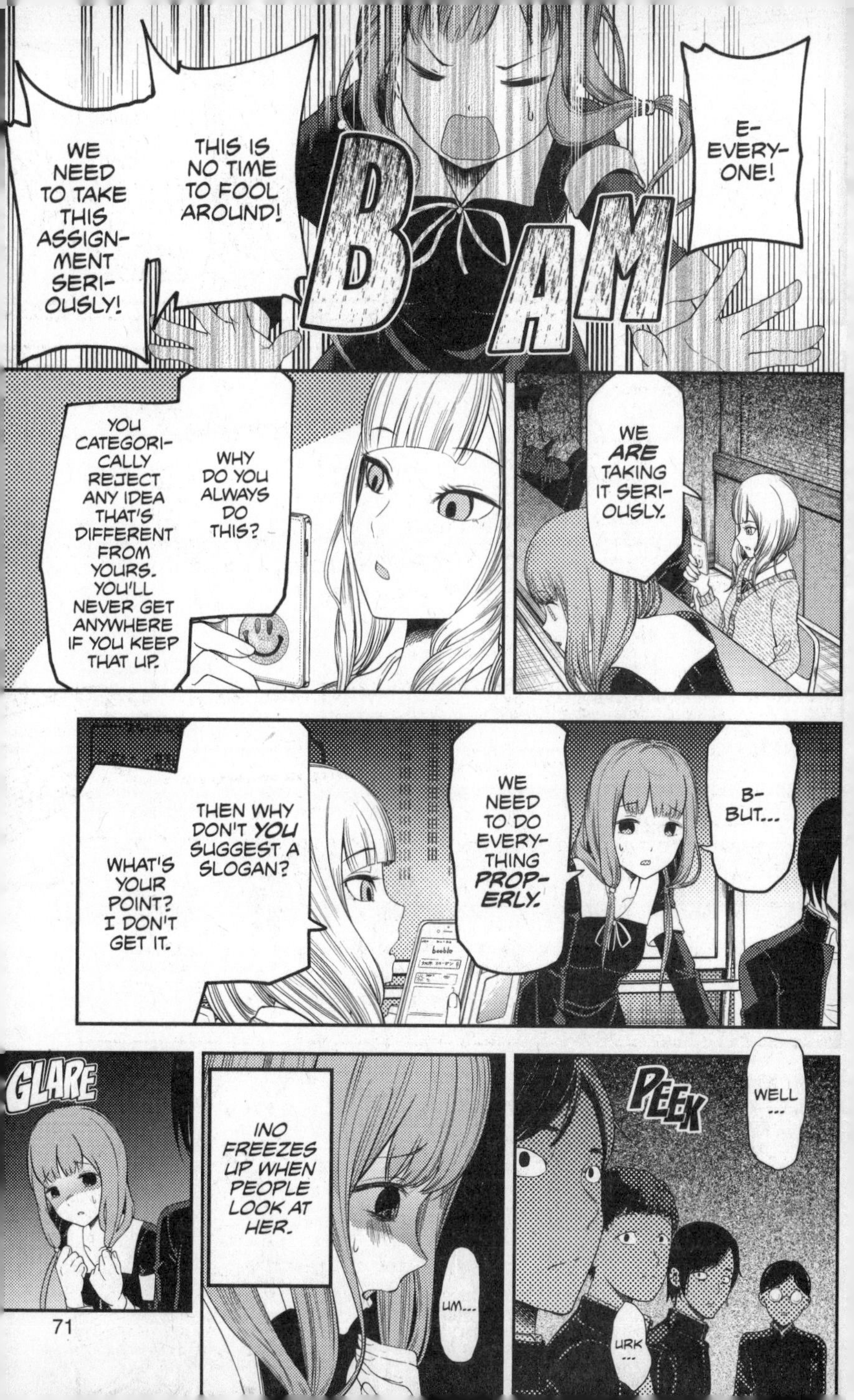
E-EVERYONE!
BAM
THIS IS NO TIME TO FOOL AROUND!
WE NEED TO TAKE THIS ASSIGNMENT SERIOUSLY!
WE *ARE* TAKING IT SERIOUSLY.
WHY DO YOU ALWAYS DO THIS?
YOU CATEGORICALLY REJECT ANY IDEA THAT'S DIFFERENT FROM YOURS. YOU'LL NEVER GET ANYWHERE IF YOU KEEP THAT UP.
B-BUT...
WE NEED TO DO EVERYTHING *PROPERLY.*
THEN WHY DON'T *YOU* SUGGEST A SLOGAN?
WHAT'S YOUR POINT? I DON'T GET IT.
beeble
WELL...
PEEK
URK...
INO FREEZES UP WHEN PEOPLE LOOK AT HER.
UM...
GLARE

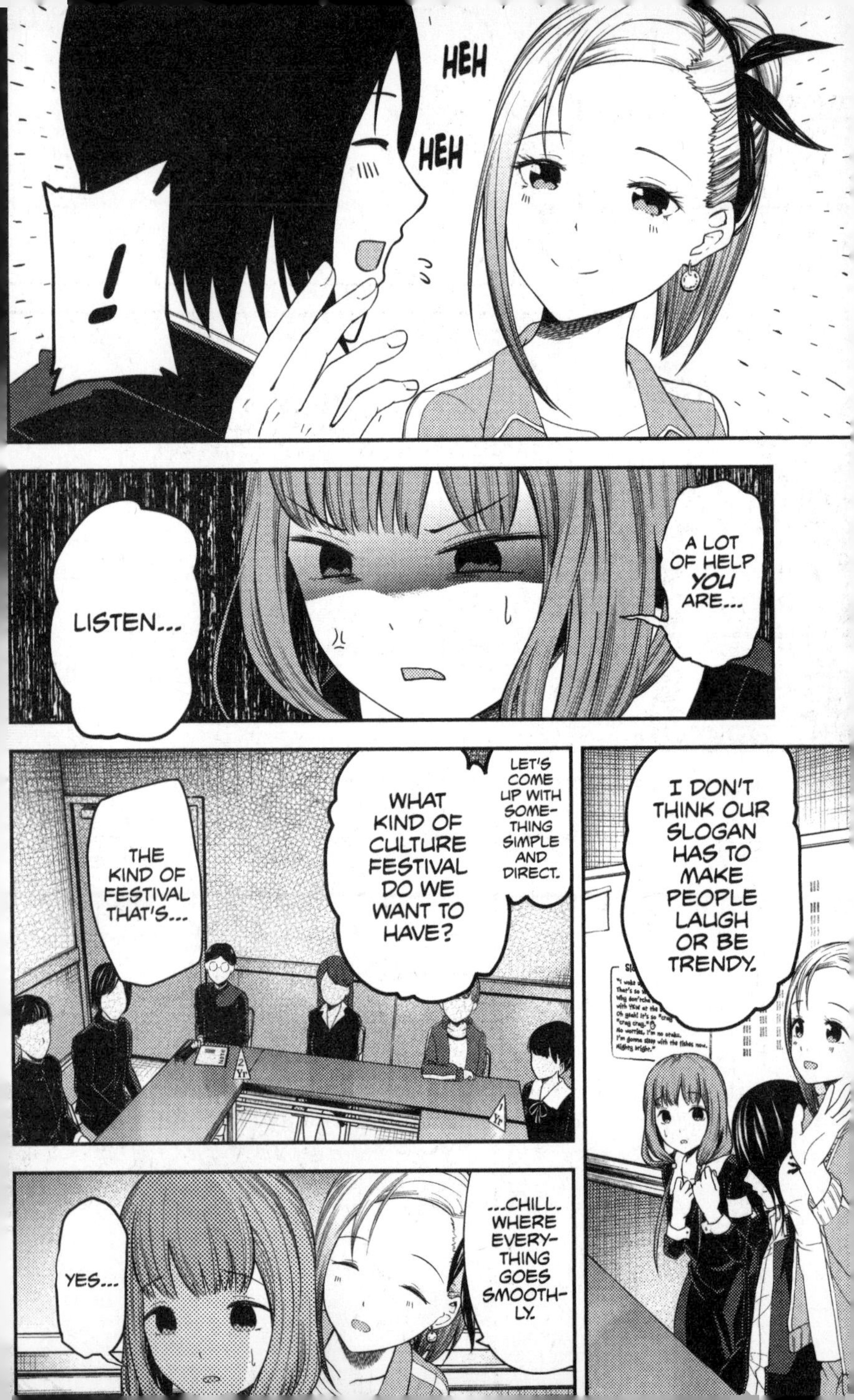
HEH
HEH
!
A LOT OF HELP YOU ARE...
LISTEN...
I DON'T THINK OUR SLOGAN HAS TO MAKE PEOPLE LAUGH OR BE TRENDY.
LET'S COME UP WITH SOMETHING SIMPLE AND DIRECT.
WHAT KIND OF CULTURE FESTIVAL DO WE WANT TO HAVE?
THE KIND OF FESTIVAL THAT'S...
...CHILL. WHERE EVERYTHING GOES SMOOTHLY.
YES...

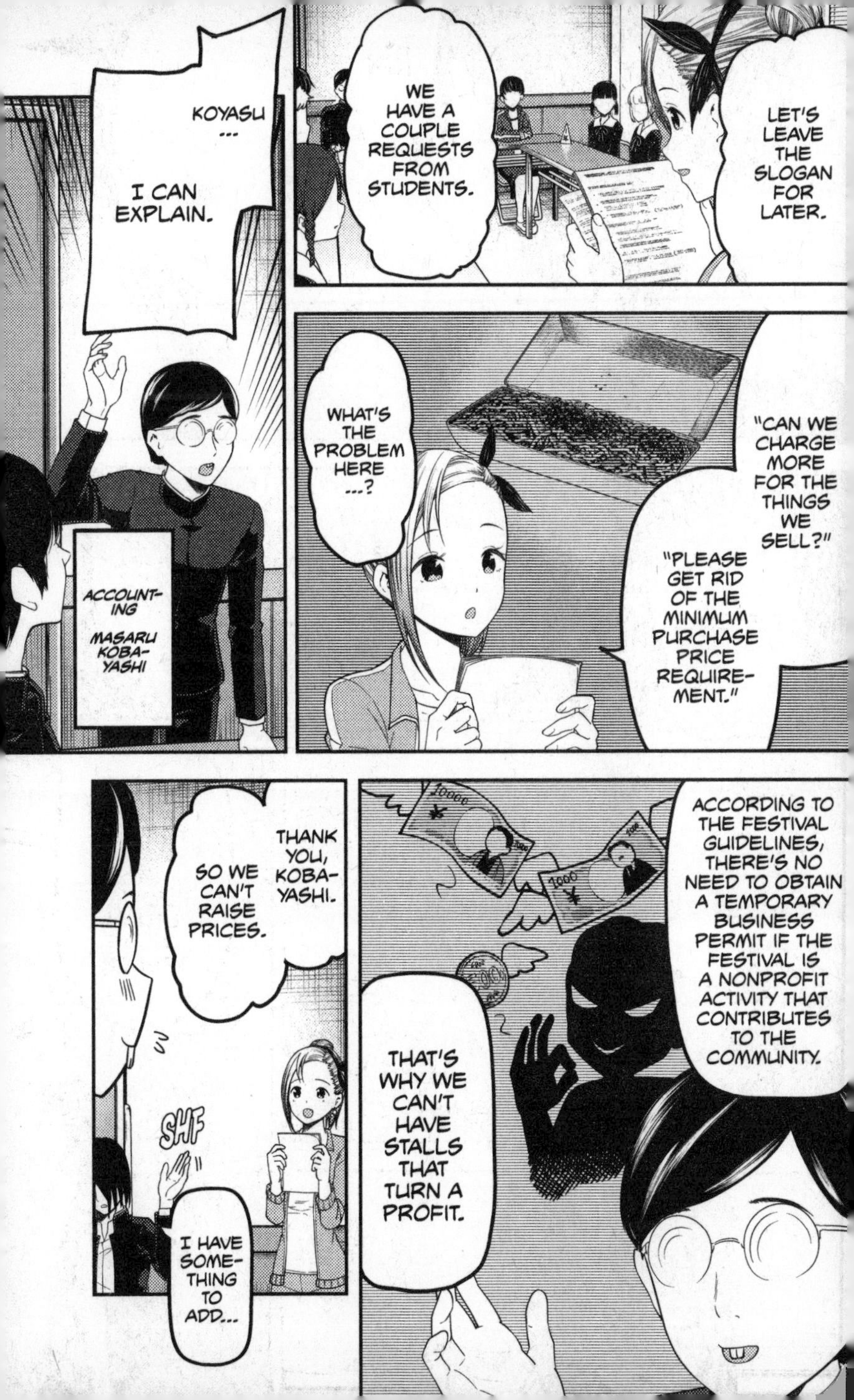
LET'S LEAVE THE SLOGAN FOR LATER.
WE HAVE A COUPLE REQUESTS FROM STUDENTS.
"CAN WE CHARGE MORE FOR THE THINGS WE SELL?"
"PLEASE GET RID OF THE MINIMUM PURCHASE PRICE REQUIREMENT."
WHAT'S THE PROBLEM HERE...?
KOYASU...
I CAN EXPLAIN.
ACCOUNTING
MASARU KOBAYASHI
ACCORDING TO THE FESTIVAL GUIDELINES, THERE'S NO NEED TO OBTAIN A TEMPORARY BUSINESS PERMIT IF THE FESTIVAL IS A NONPROFIT ACTIVITY THAT CONTRIBUTES TO THE COMMUNITY.
THAT'S WHY WE CAN'T HAVE STALLS THAT TURN A PROFIT.
THANK YOU, KOBAYASHI.
SO WE CAN'T RAISE PRICES.
SHF
I HAVE SOMETHING TO ADD...

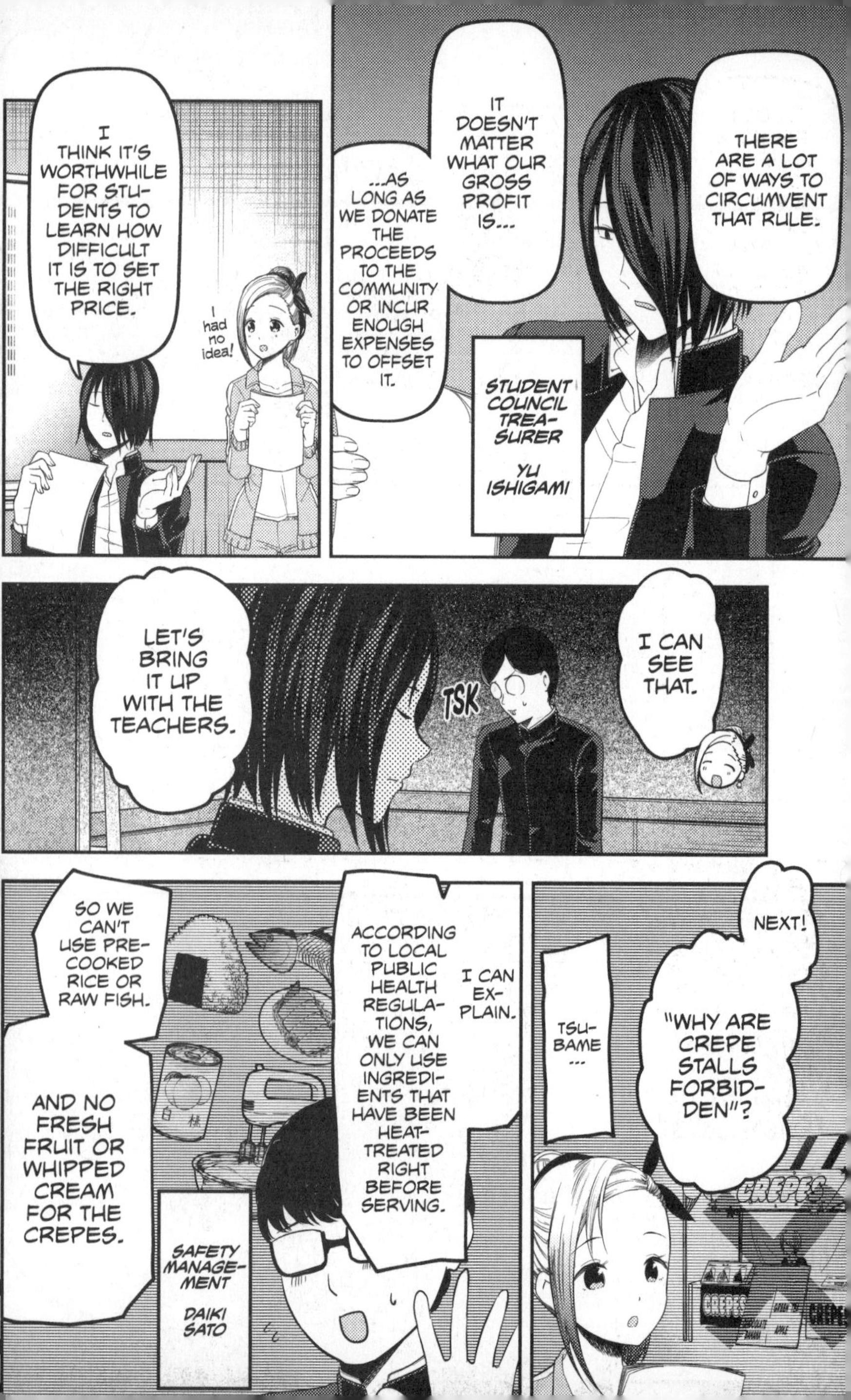
THERE ARE A LOT OF WAYS TO CIRCUMVENT THAT RULE.
IT DOESN'T MATTER WHAT OUR GROSS PROFIT IS...
...AS LONG AS WE DONATE THE PROCEEDS TO THE COMMUNITY OR INCUR ENOUGH EXPENSES TO OFFSET IT.
STUDENT COUNCIL TREASURER
YU ISHIGAMI
I THINK IT'S WORTHWHILE FOR STUDENTS TO LEARN HOW DIFFICULT IT IS TO SET THE RIGHT PRICE.
I had no idea!
I CAN SEE THAT.
TSK
LET'S BRING IT UP WITH THE TEACHERS.
NEXT!
"WHY ARE CREPE STALLS FORBIDDEN"?
TSUBAME...
CREPES
I CAN EXPLAIN.
ACCORDING TO LOCAL PUBLIC HEALTH REGULATIONS, WE CAN ONLY USE INGREDIENTS THAT HAVE BEEN HEAT-TREATED RIGHT BEFORE SERVING.
SAFETY MANAGEMENT
DAIKI SATO
SO WE CAN'T USE PRE-COOKED RICE OR RAW FISH.
AND NO FRESH FRUIT OR WHIPPED CREAM FOR THE CREPES.

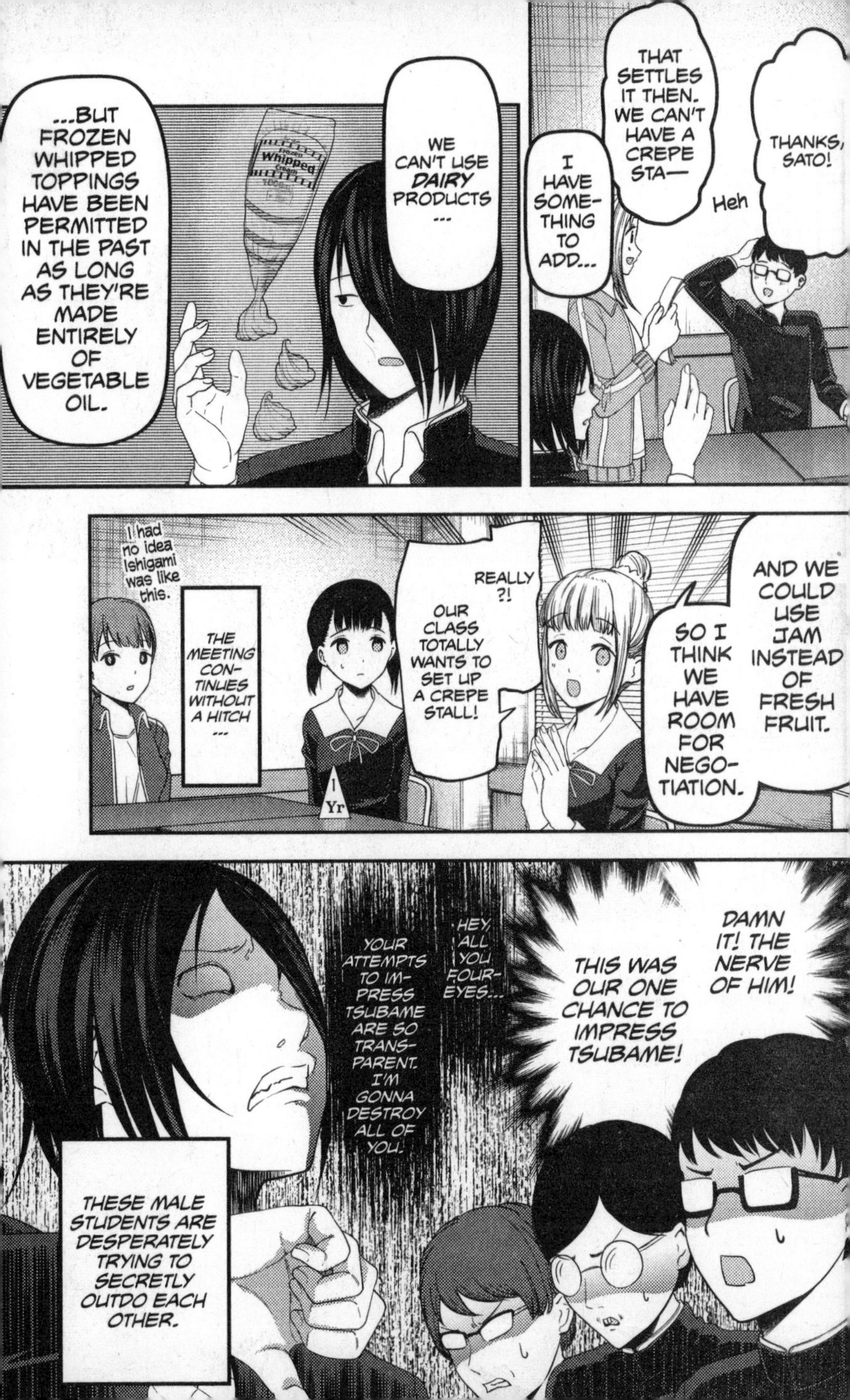
THANKS, SATO!
Heh
THAT SETTLES IT THEN. WE CAN'T HAVE A CREPE STA—
I HAVE SOMETHING TO ADD...
WE CAN'T USE DAIRY PRODUCTS...
...BUT FROZEN WHIPPED TOPPINGS HAVE BEEN PERMITTED IN THE PAST AS LONG AS THEY'RE MADE ENTIRELY OF VEGETABLE OIL.
AND WE COULD USE JAM INSTEAD OF FRESH FRUIT.
SO I THINK WE HAVE ROOM FOR NEGOTIATION.
REALLY?!
OUR CLASS TOTALLY WANTS TO SET UP A CREPE STALL!
THE MEETING CONTINUES WITHOUT A HITCH...
I had no idea Ishigami was like this.
1 Yr
DAMN IT! THE NERVE OF HIM!
THIS WAS OUR ONE CHANCE TO IMPRESS TSUBAME!
HEY, ALL YOU FOUR-EYES...
YOUR ATTEMPTS TO IMPRESS TSUBAME ARE SO TRANSPARENT. I'M GONNA DESTROY ALL OF YOU.
THESE MALE STUDENTS ARE DESPERATELY TRYING TO SECRETLY OUTDO EACH OTHER.

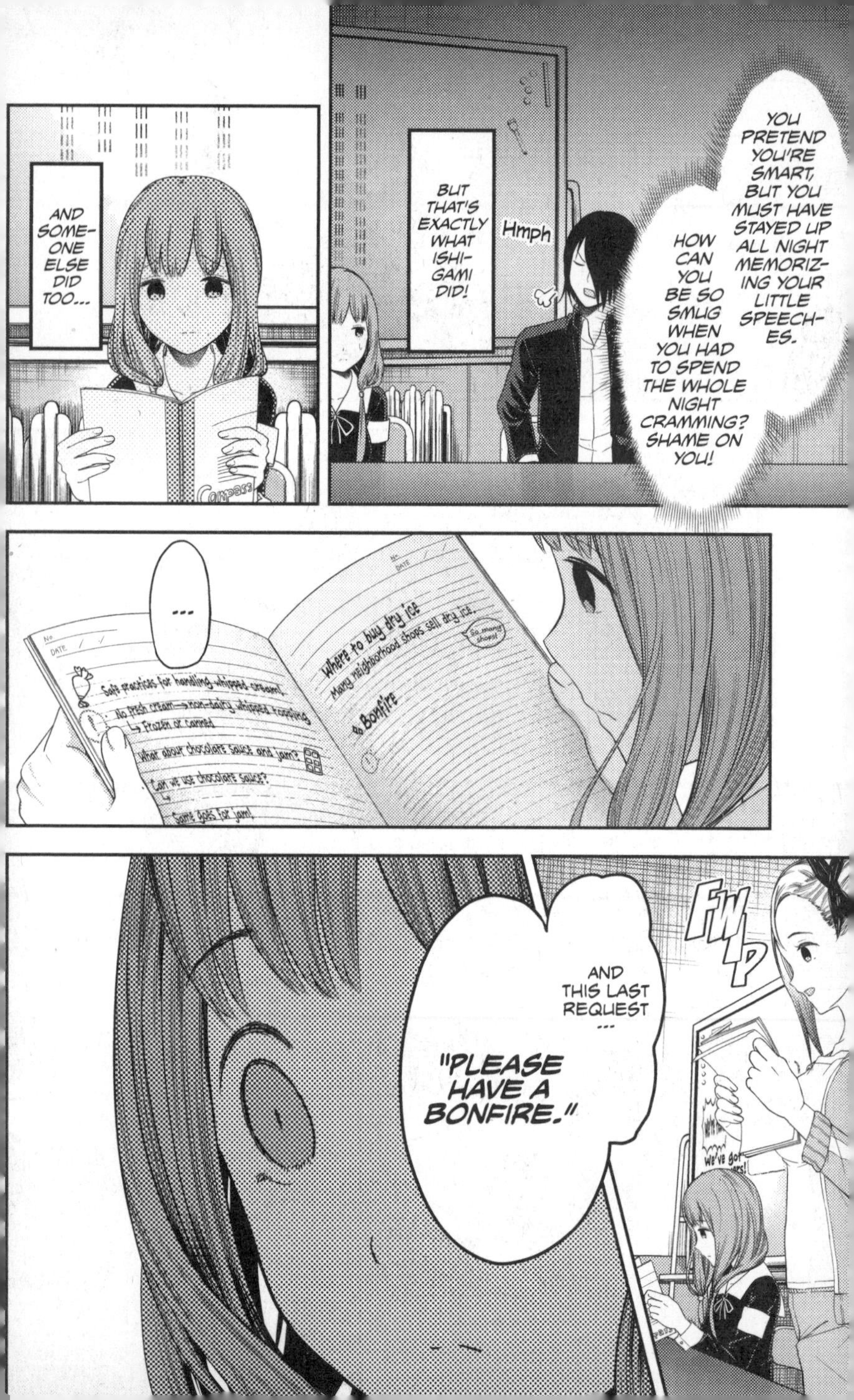
YOU PRETEND YOU'RE SMART, BUT YOU MUST HAVE STAYED UP ALL NIGHT MEMORIZING YOUR LITTLE SPEECHES.
HOW CAN YOU BE SO SMUG WHEN YOU HAD TO SPEND THE WHOLE NIGHT CRAMMING? SHAME ON YOU!
Hmph
BUT THAT'S EXACTLY WHAT ISHIGAMI DID!
AND SOMEONE ELSE DID TOO...
Compass
...
Where to buy dry ice
Many neighborhood shops sell dry ice.
So many shops!
Bonfire
Safe practices for handling whipped cream!
No fresh cream → non-dairy whipped topping
↳ Frozen or canned
What about chocolate sauce and jam?
Can we use chocolate sauce?
Same goes for jam!
FWIP
AND THIS LAST REQUEST...
"PLEASE HAVE A BONFIRE."

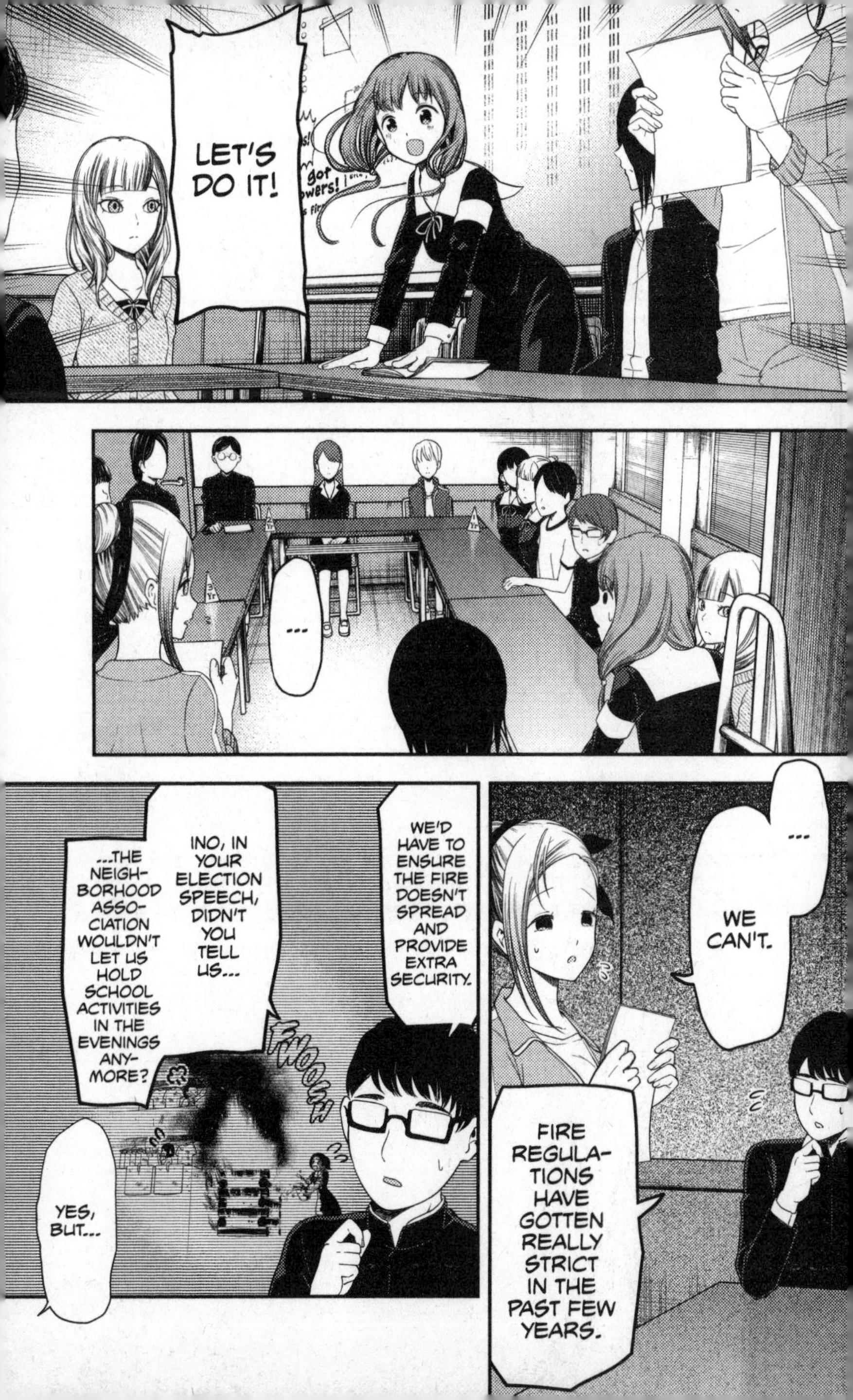
LET'S DO IT!
...
...
WE CAN'T.
FIRE REGULATIONS HAVE GOTTEN REALLY STRICT IN THE PAST FEW YEARS.
WE'D HAVE TO ENSURE THE FIRE DOESN'T SPREAD AND PROVIDE EXTRA SECURITY.
INO, IN YOUR ELECTION SPEECH, DIDN'T YOU TELL US...
...THE NEIGHBORHOOD ASSOCIATION WOULDN'T LET US HOLD SCHOOL ACTIVITIES IN THE EVENINGS ANYMORE?
FWOOSH
YES, BUT...

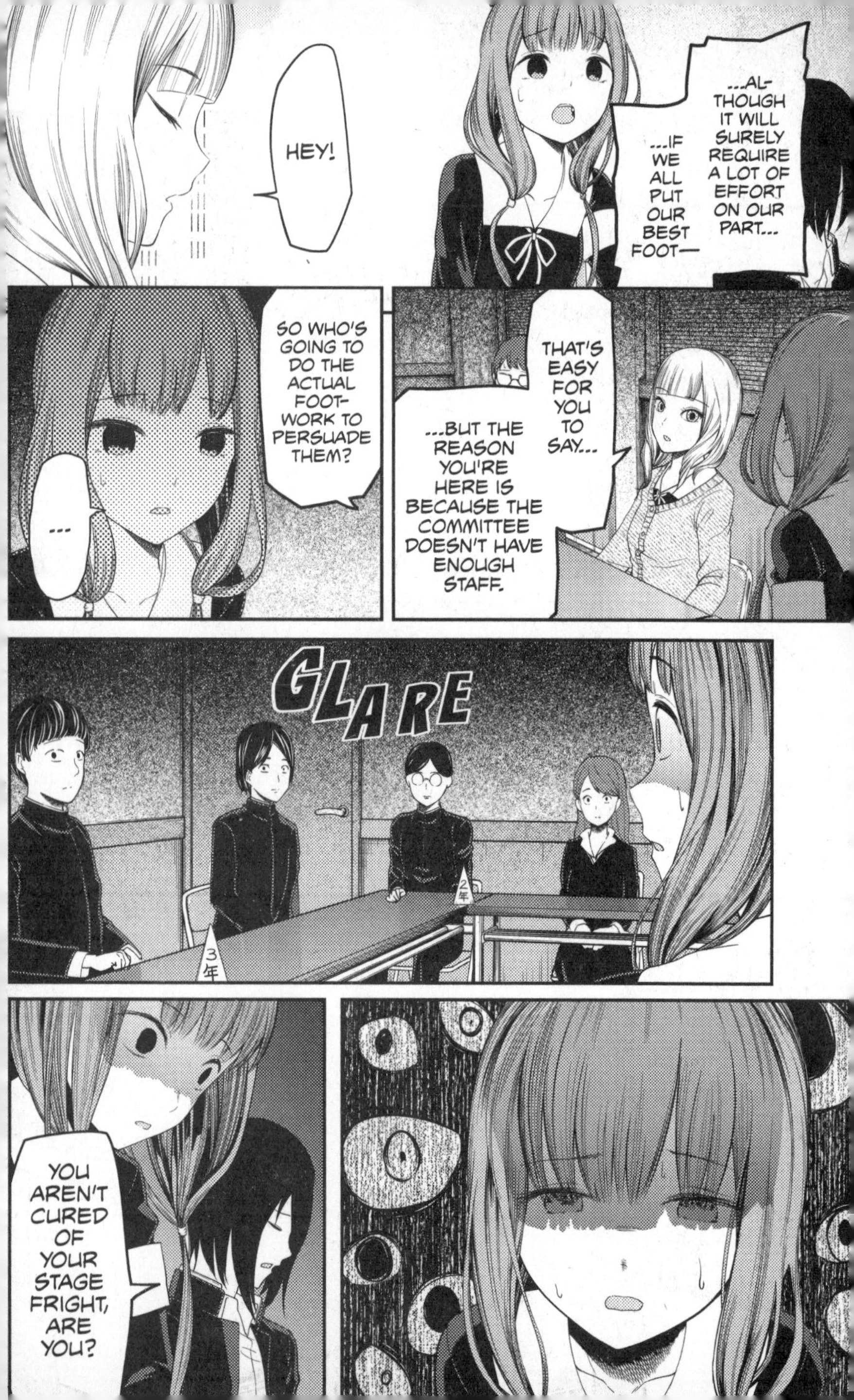
...ALTHOUGH IT WILL SURELY REQUIRE A LOT OF EFFORT ON OUR PART...
...IF WE ALL PUT OUR BEST FOOT—
HEY!
THAT'S EASY FOR YOU TO SAY...
...BUT THE REASON YOU'RE HERE IS BECAUSE THE COMMITTEE DOESN'T HAVE ENOUGH STAFF.
SO WHO'S GOING TO DO THE ACTUAL FOOTWORK TO PERSUADE THEM?
...
GLARE
2年
3年
YOU AREN'T CURED OF YOUR STAGE FRIGHT, ARE YOU?

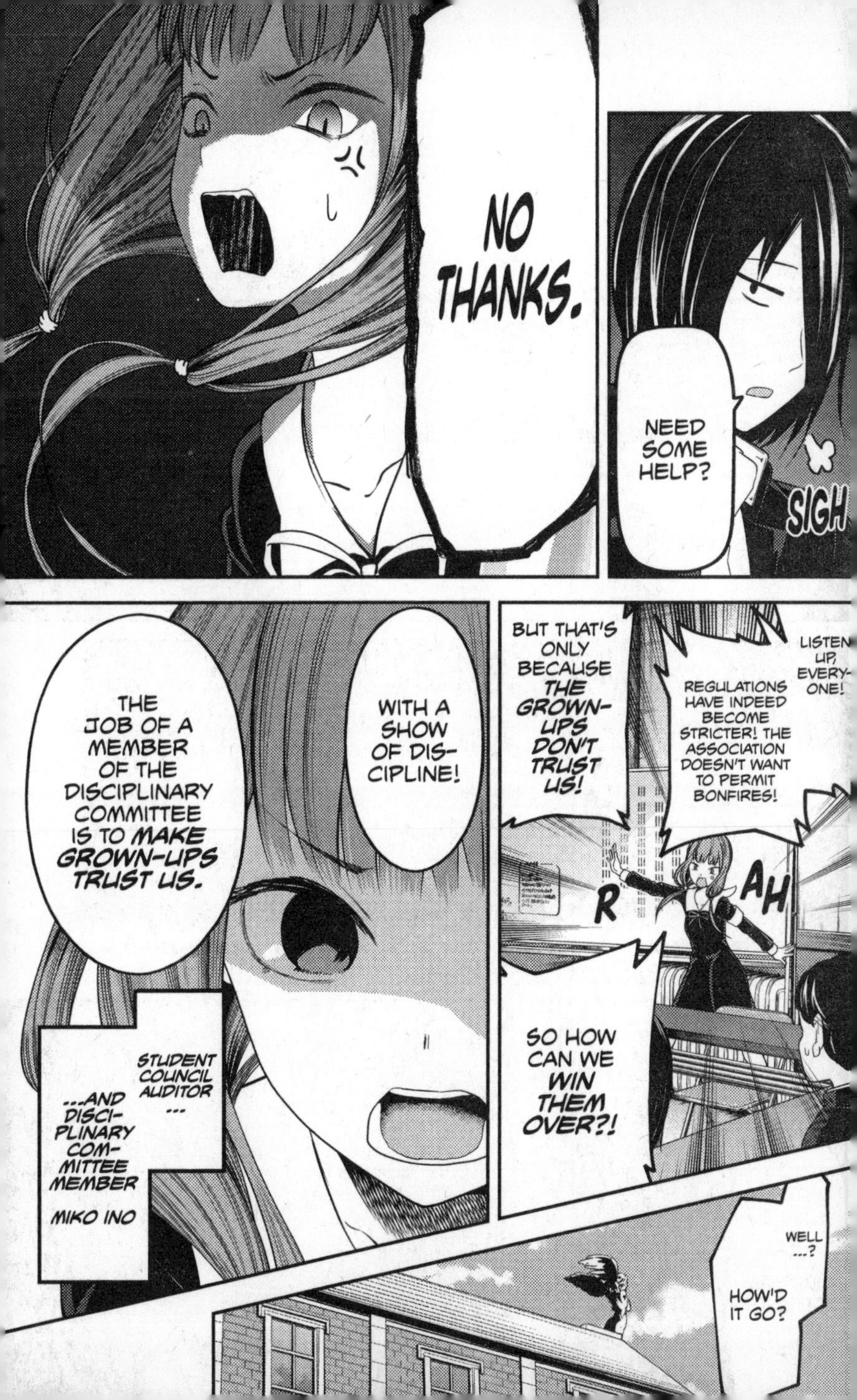
NEED SOME HELP?
SIGH
NO THANKS.
LISTEN UP, EVERY-ONE!
REGULATIONS HAVE INDEED BECOME STRICTER! THE ASSOCIATION DOESN'T WANT TO PERMIT BONFIRES!
BUT THAT'S ONLY BECAUSE THE GROWN-UPS DON'T TRUST US!
RAH
SO HOW CAN WE WIN THEM OVER?!
WITH A SHOW OF DIS-CIPLINE!
THE JOB OF A MEMBER OF THE DISCIPLINARY COMMITTEE IS TO MAKE GROWN-UPS TRUST US.
STUDENT COUNCIL AUDITOR ...
...AND DISCI-PLINARY COM-MITTEE MEMBER
MIKO INO
WELL ...?
HOW'D IT GO?

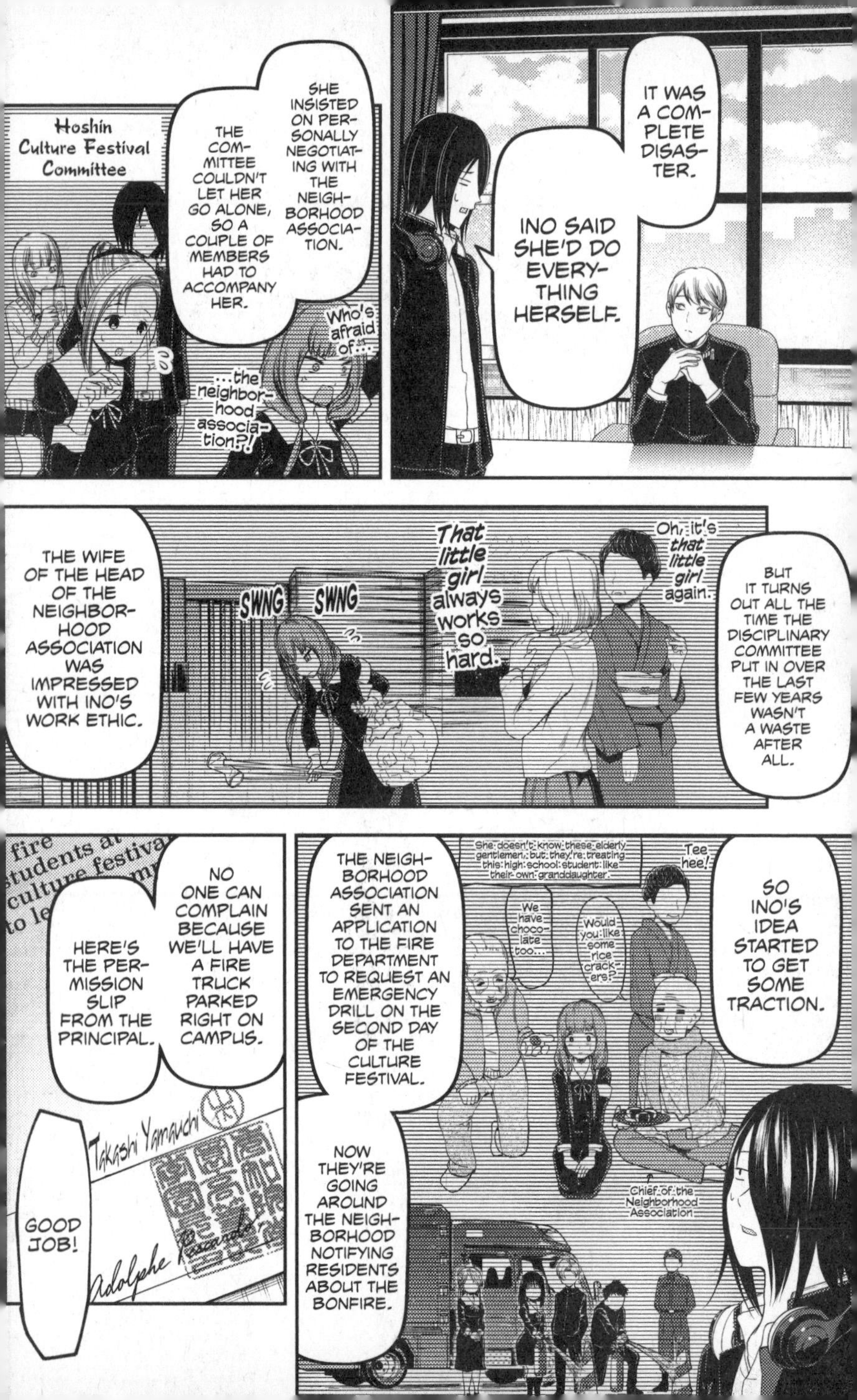
IT WAS A COMPLETE DISASTER.
INO SAID SHE'D DO EVERYTHING HERSELF.
SHE INSISTED ON PERSONALLY NEGOTIATING WITH THE NEIGHBORHOOD ASSOCIATION.
THE COMMITTEE COULDN'T LET HER GO ALONE, SO A COUPLE OF MEMBERS HAD TO ACCOMPANY HER.
Hoshin Culture Festival Committee
Who's afraid of...
...the neighborhood association?!
BUT IT TURNS OUT ALL THE TIME THE DISCIPLINARY COMMITTEE PUT IN OVER THE LAST FEW YEARS WASN'T A WASTE AFTER ALL.
Oh, it's *that little girl* again.
That little girl always works so hard.
SWNG
SWNG
THE WIFE OF THE HEAD OF THE NEIGHBORHOOD ASSOCIATION WAS IMPRESSED WITH INO'S WORK ETHIC.
SO INO'S IDEA STARTED TO GET SOME TRACTION.
Tee hee!
She doesn't know these elderly gentlemen, but they're treating this high school student like their own granddaughter.
Would you like some rice crackers?
We have chocolate too...
THE NEIGHBORHOOD ASSOCIATION SENT AN APPLICATION TO THE FIRE DEPARTMENT TO REQUEST AN EMERGENCY DRILL ON THE SECOND DAY OF THE CULTURE FESTIVAL.
Chief of the Neighborhood Association
NOW THEY'RE GOING AROUND THE NEIGHBORHOOD NOTIFYING RESIDENTS ABOUT THE BONFIRE.
NO ONE CAN COMPLAIN BECAUSE WE'LL HAVE A FIRE TRUCK PARKED RIGHT ON CAMPUS.
HERE'S THE PERMISSION SLIP FROM THE PRINCIPAL.
Takashi Yamauchi
Adolphe Pescarolo
GOOD JOB!

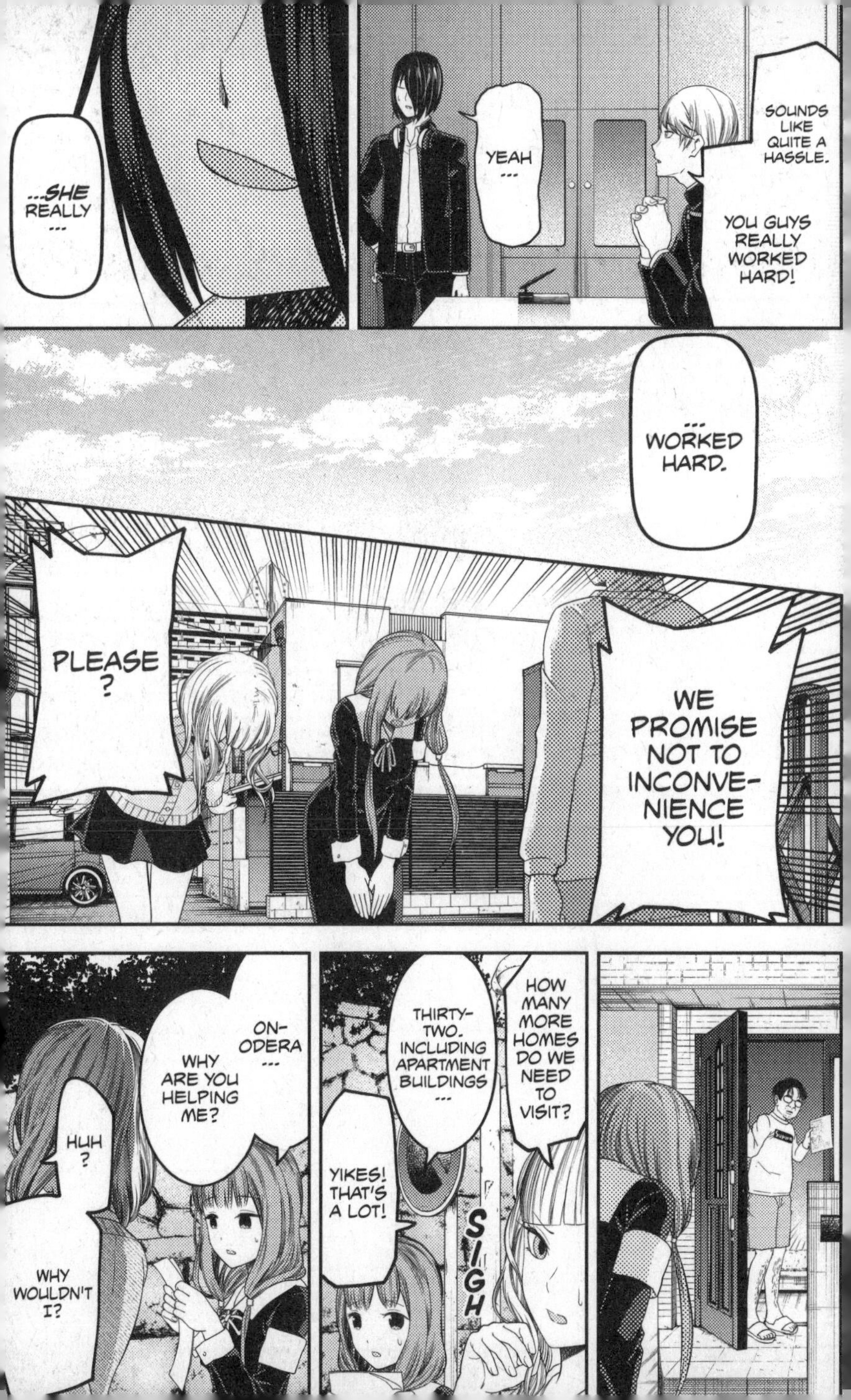
SOUNDS LIKE QUITE A HASSLE.
YOU GUYS REALLY WORKED HARD!
YEAH ---
...SHE REALLY ---
... WORKED HARD.
WE PROMISE NOT TO INCONVE-NIENCE YOU!
PLEASE?
HOW MANY MORE HOMES DO WE NEED TO VISIT?
THIRTY-TWO. INCLUDING APARTMENT BUILDINGS ---
SIGH
YIKES! THAT'S A LOT!
ON-ODERA ---
WHY ARE YOU HELPING ME?
HUH?
WHY WOULDN'T I?

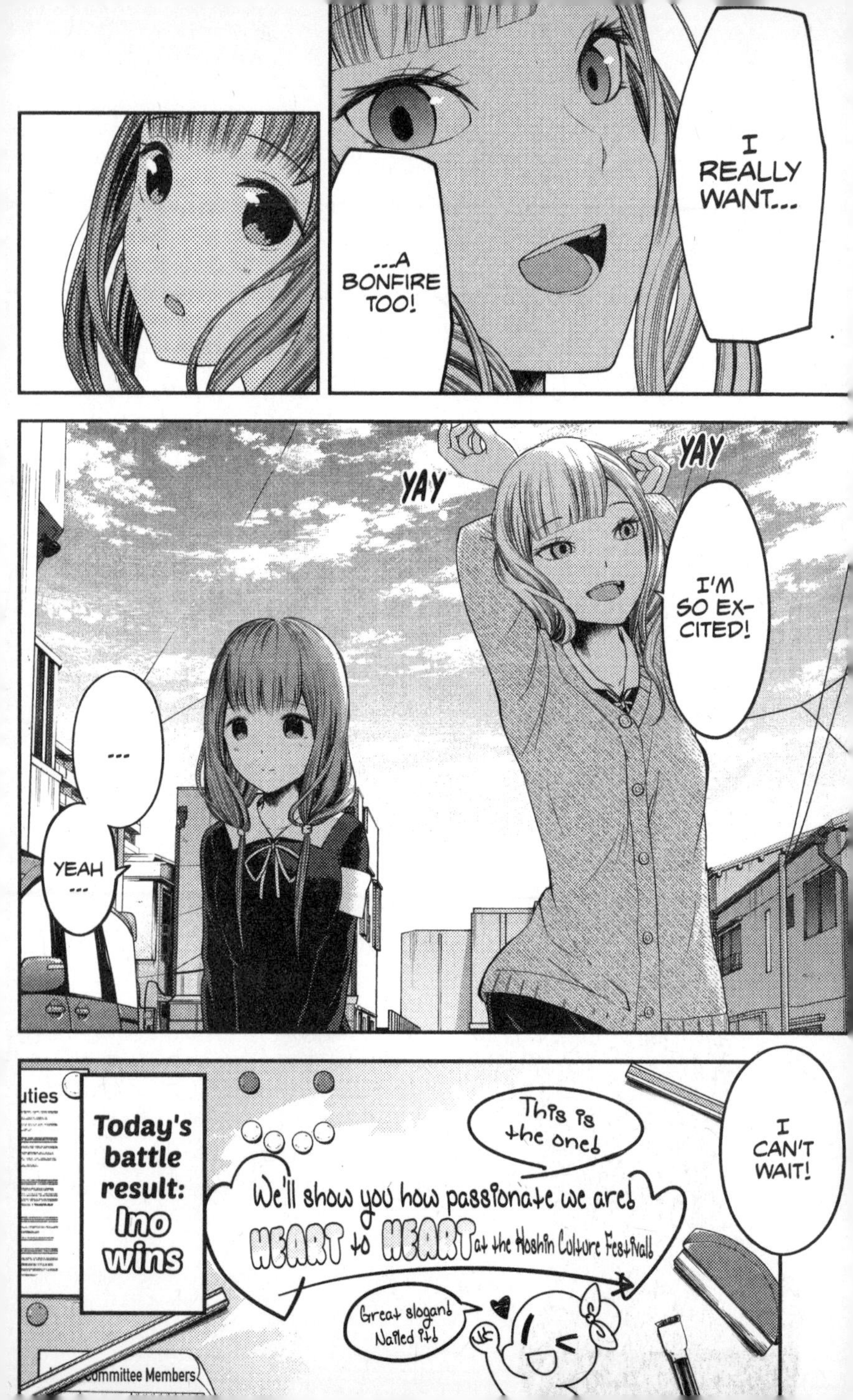
I REALLY WANT...
...A BONFIRE TOO!
YAY
I'M SO EX-CITED!
YAY
...
YEAH...
I CAN'T WAIT!
This is the one!
We'll show you how passionate we are! HEART to HEART at the Hoshin Culture Festival!
Great slogan! Nailed it!
Today's battle result: Ino wins
uties
Committee Members

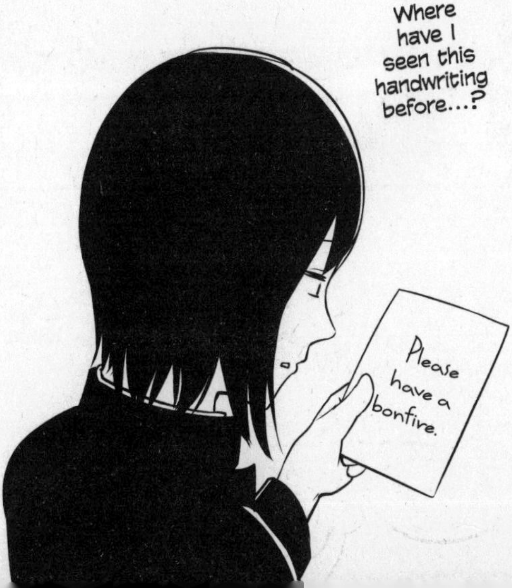
Where have I seen this handwriting before...?
Please have a bonfire.

KAGUYA-SAMA
LOVE IS WAR

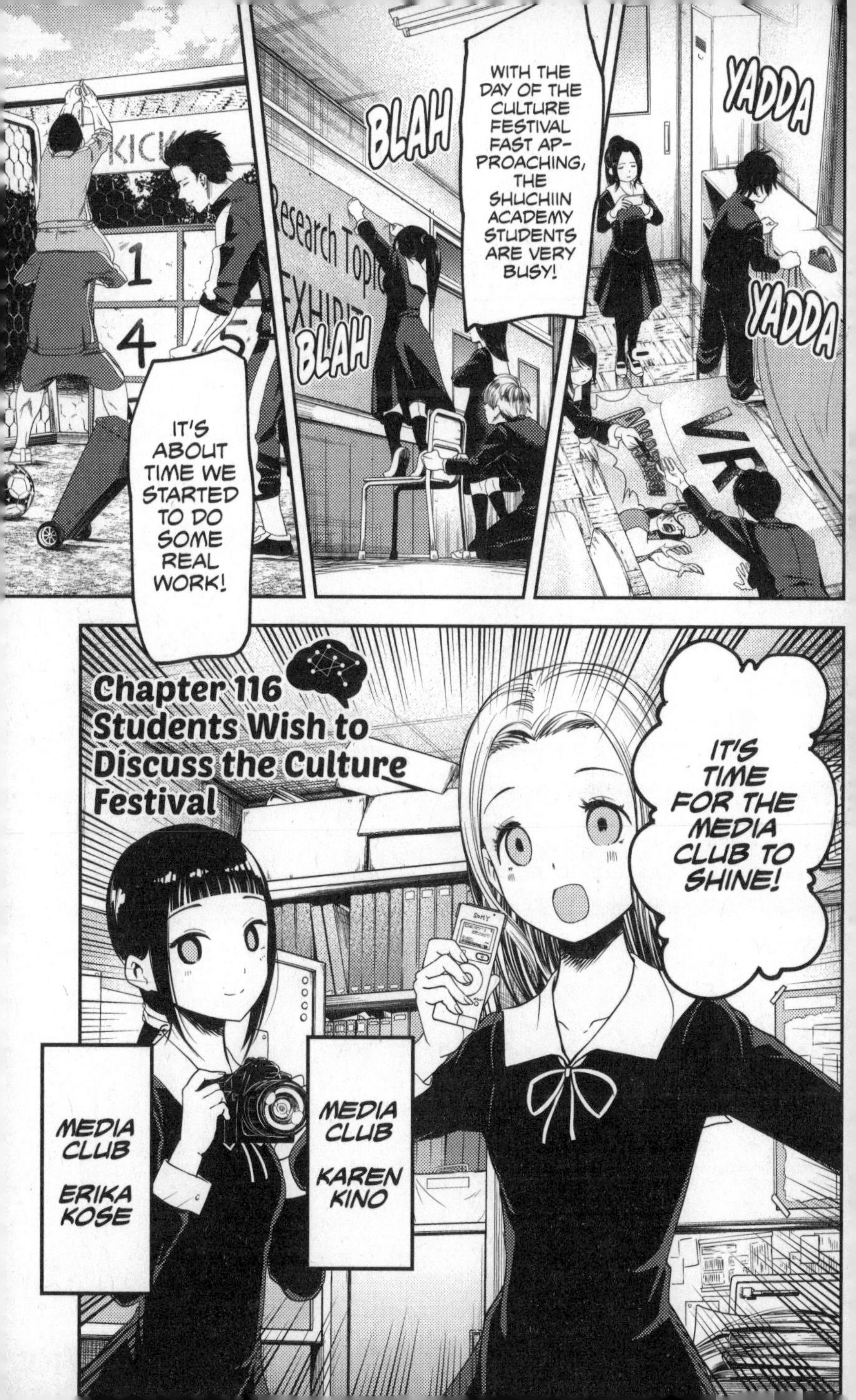
YADDA
YADDA
WITH THE DAY OF THE CULTURE FESTIVAL FAST AP-PROACHING, THE SHUCHIIN ACADEMY STUDENTS ARE VERY BUSY!
BLAH
BLAH
IT'S ABOUT TIME WE STARTED TO DO SOME REAL WORK!
Chapter 116 Students Wish to Discuss the Culture Festival
IT'S TIME FOR THE MEDIA CLUB TO SHINE!
MEDIA CLUB KAREN KINO
MEDIA CLUB ERIKA KOSE

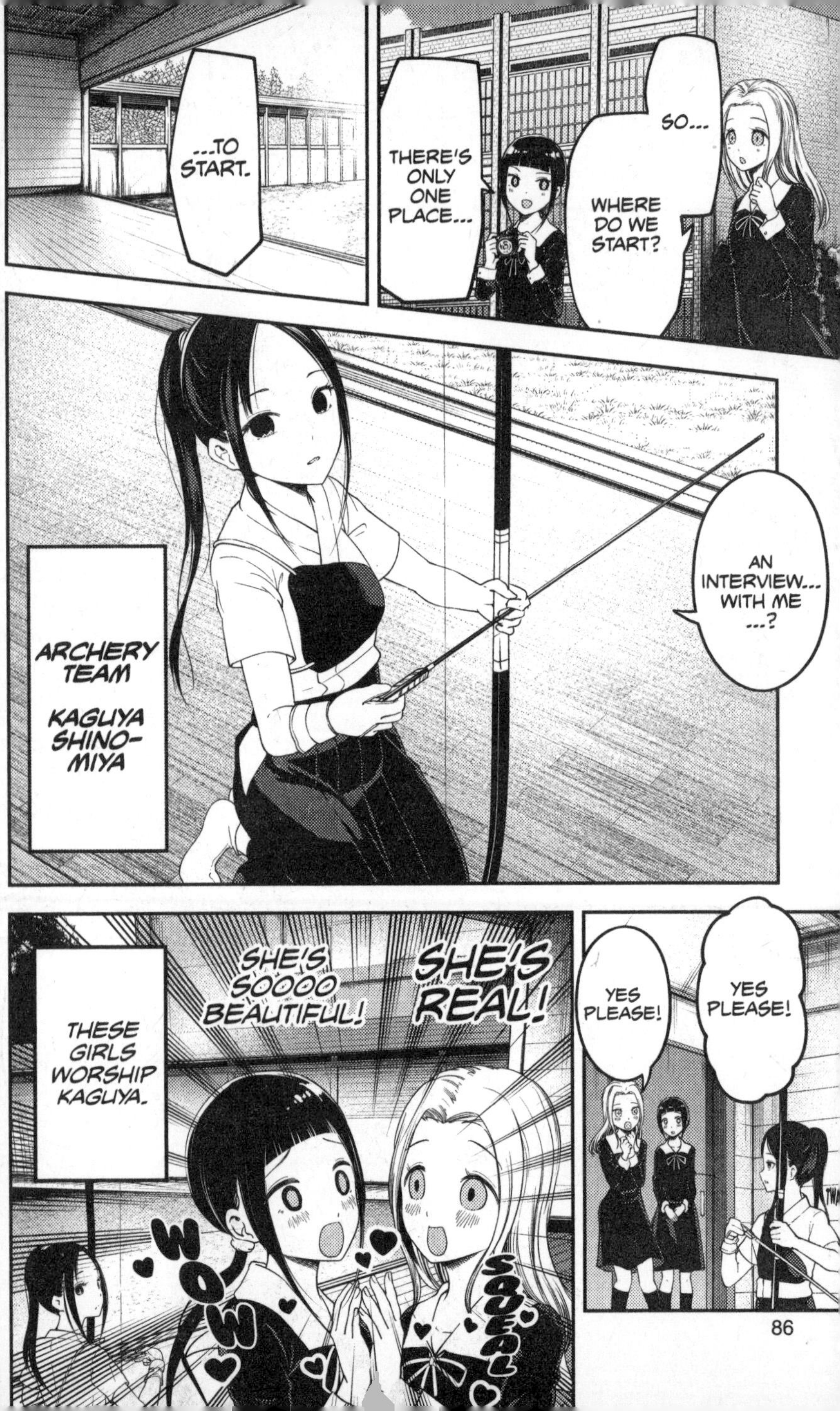
SO...
WHERE DO WE START?
THERE'S ONLY ONE PLACE...
...TO START.
AN INTERVIEW... WITH ME ...?
ARCHERY TEAM
KAGUYA SHINO-MIYA
YES PLEASE!
YES PLEASE!
SHE'S REAL!
SHE'S SOOOO BEAUTIFUL!
THESE GIRLS WORSHIP KAGUYA.
SQUEAL
WOW

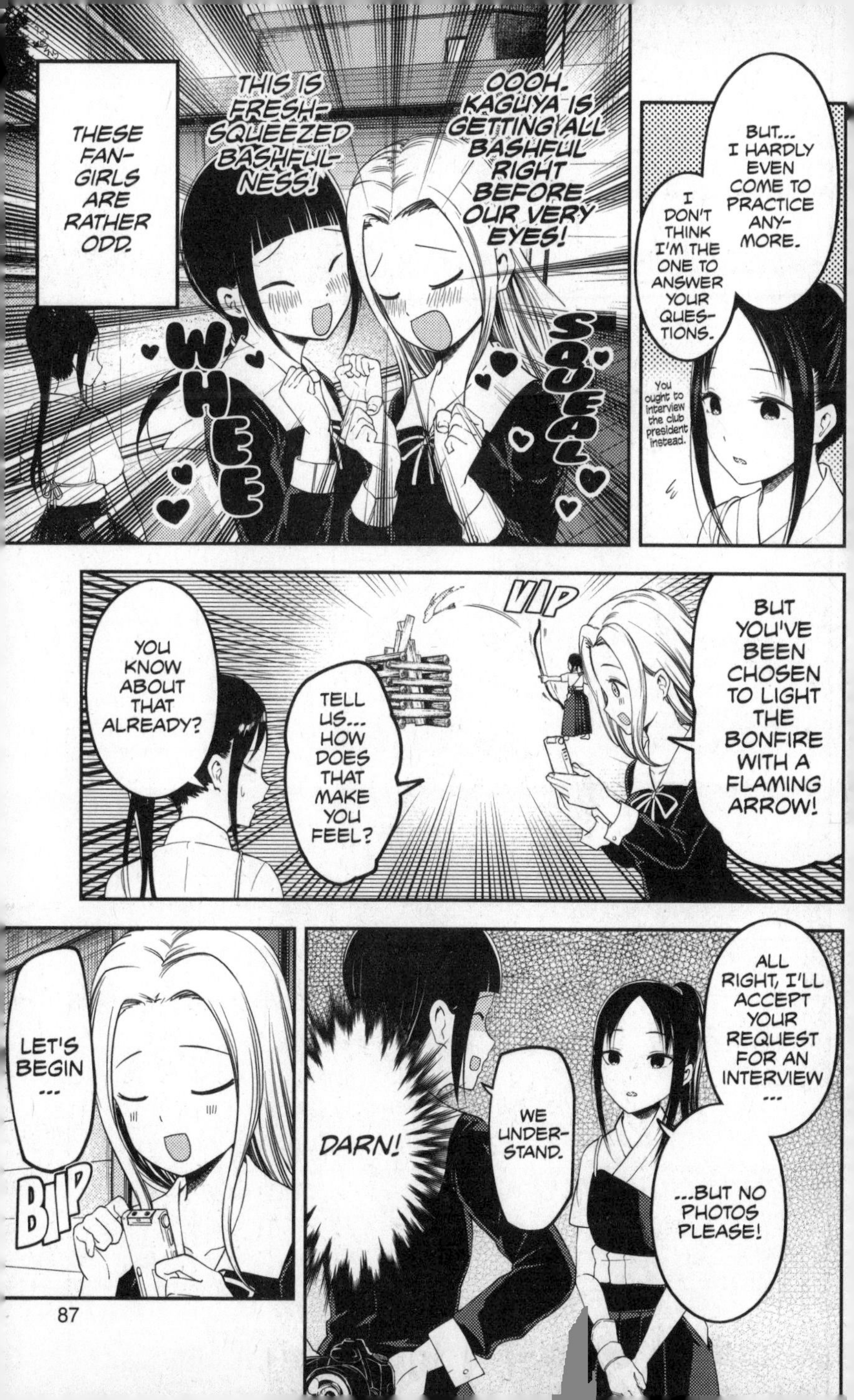

BUT... I HARDLY EVEN COME TO PRACTICE ANYMORE.
I DON'T THINK I'M THE ONE TO ANSWER YOUR QUESTIONS.
You ought to interview the club president instead.
OOOH. KAGUYA IS GETTING ALL BASHFUL RIGHT BEFORE OUR VERY EYES!
THIS IS FRESH-SQUEEZED BASHFULNESS!
SQUEAL
WHEE
THESE FAN-GIRLS ARE RATHER ODD.
BUT YOU'VE BEEN CHOSEN TO LIGHT THE BONFIRE WITH A FLAMING ARROW!
VIP
TELL US... HOW DOES THAT MAKE YOU FEEL?
YOU KNOW ABOUT THAT ALREADY?
ALL RIGHT, I'LL ACCEPT YOUR REQUEST FOR AN INTERVIEW...
...BUT NO PHOTOS PLEASE!
WE UNDERSTAND.
DARN!
LET'S BEGIN...
BIIP

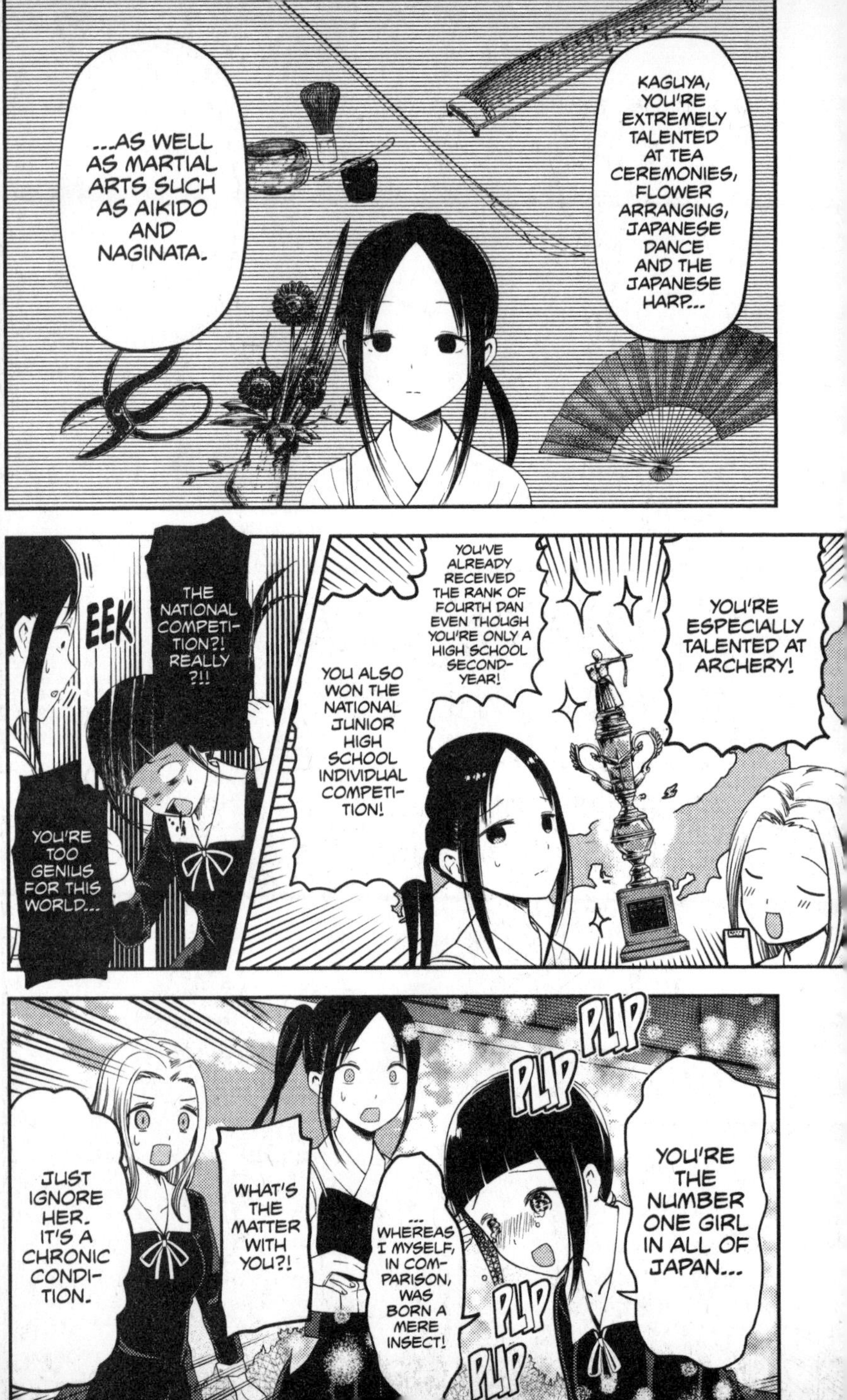
KAGUYA, YOU'RE EXTREMELY TALENTED AT TEA CEREMONIES, FLOWER ARRANGING, JAPANESE DANCE AND THE JAPANESE HARP...
...AS WELL AS MARTIAL ARTS SUCH AS AIKIDO AND NAGINATA.
YOU'RE ESPECIALLY TALENTED AT ARCHERY!
YOU'VE ALREADY RECEIVED THE RANK OF FOURTH DAN EVEN THOUGH YOU'RE ONLY A HIGH SCHOOL SECOND-YEAR!
YOU ALSO WON THE NATIONAL JUNIOR HIGH SCHOOL INDIVIDUAL COMPETITION!
THE NATIONAL COMPETITION?! REALLY?!!
EEK
YOU'RE TOO GENIUS FOR THIS WORLD...
PLIP
PLIP
YOU'RE THE NUMBER ONE GIRL IN ALL OF JAPAN...
...WHEREAS I MYSELF, IN COMPARISON, WAS BORN A MERE INSECT!
PLIP
PLIP
WHAT'S THE MATTER WITH YOU?!
JUST IGNORE HER. IT'S A CHRONIC CONDITION.

KAGUYA, YOU HAVE A STELLAR RECORD, YET...

...YOU **HAVEN'T PARTICIPATED IN A SINGLE COMPETITION** SINCE YOU ENTERED HIGH SCHOOL. CAN YOU TELL US WHY?

Athlete Name	I				II				III		
Kaguya	O	O	O	O	O	O	O	O	O	O	×
Weed	O	O	×								
Pebble	×										
Caterpillar											
Toilet paper											

YOU HAVE TO HIT THE TARGET TEN TIMES IN A ROW IN THE FINAL MATCH. WHOEVER MISSES IS ELIMINATED.

YOUR RECORD EVEN EXCEEDS THE HIGH SCHOOL COMPETITION RECORD OF THE SAME YEAR!

What the hell? You're legendary!

IT WAS JUST A STROKE OF LUCK.

SHE LOOKS SO MELANCHOLY...

I HAVE MY REASONS.

?!

WHAT IS IT?

HM... I THINK I GET IT.

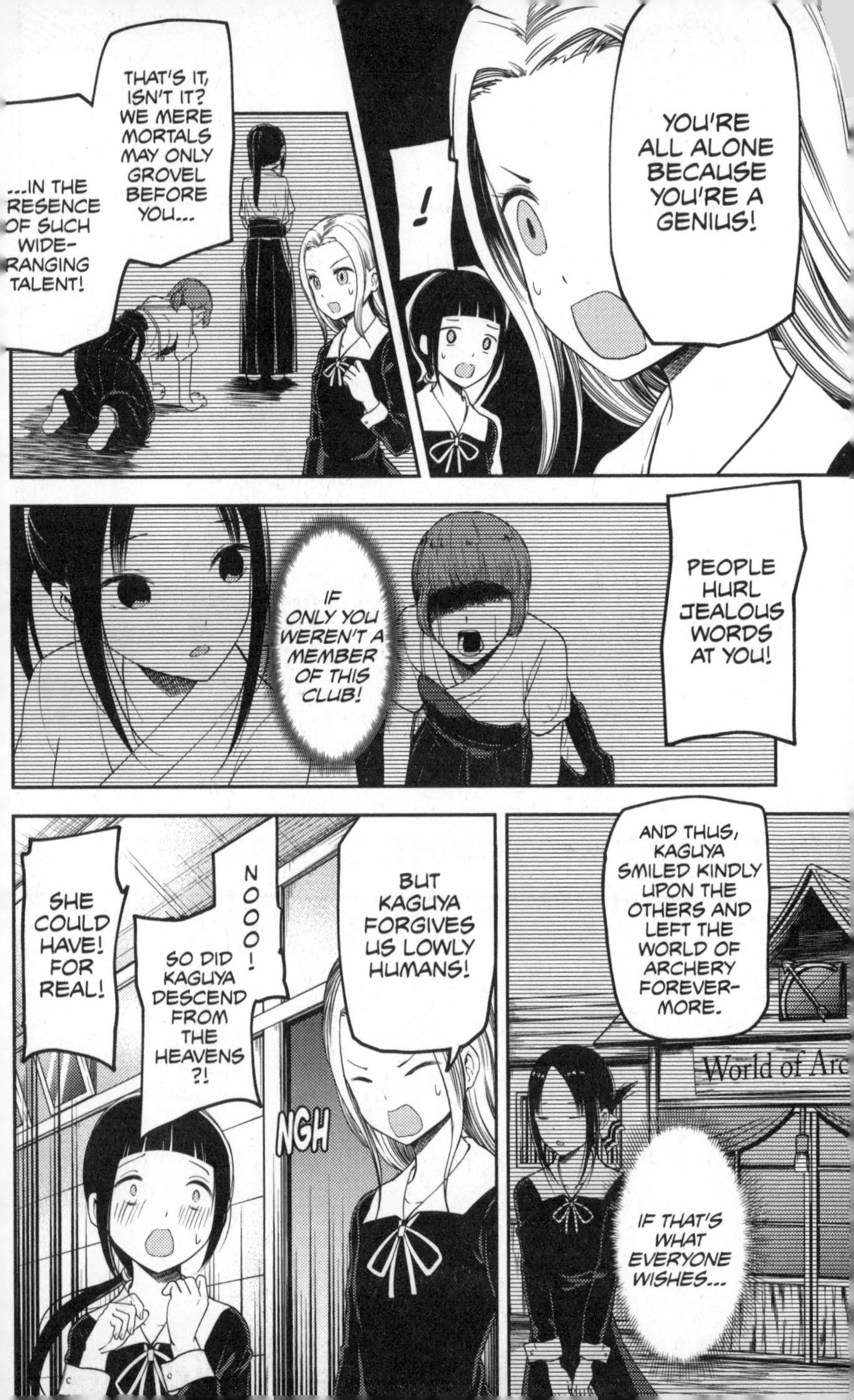
YOU'RE ALL ALONE BECAUSE YOU'RE A GENIUS!
!
THAT'S IT, ISN'T IT? WE MERE MORTALS MAY ONLY GROVEL BEFORE YOU...
...IN THE RESENCE OF SUCH WIDE-RANGING TALENT!
PEOPLE HURL JEALOUS WORDS AT YOU!
IF ONLY YOU WEREN'T A MEMBER OF THIS CLUB!
AND THUS, KAGUYA SMILED KINDLY UPON THE OTHERS AND LEFT THE WORLD OF ARCHERY FOREVER-MORE.
World of Arc
IF THAT'S WHAT EVERYONE WISHES...
BUT KAGUYA FORGIVES US LOWLY HUMANS!
NGH
NOOOO!
SO DID KAGUYA DESCEND FROM THE HEAVENS?!
SHE COULD HAVE! FOR REAL!

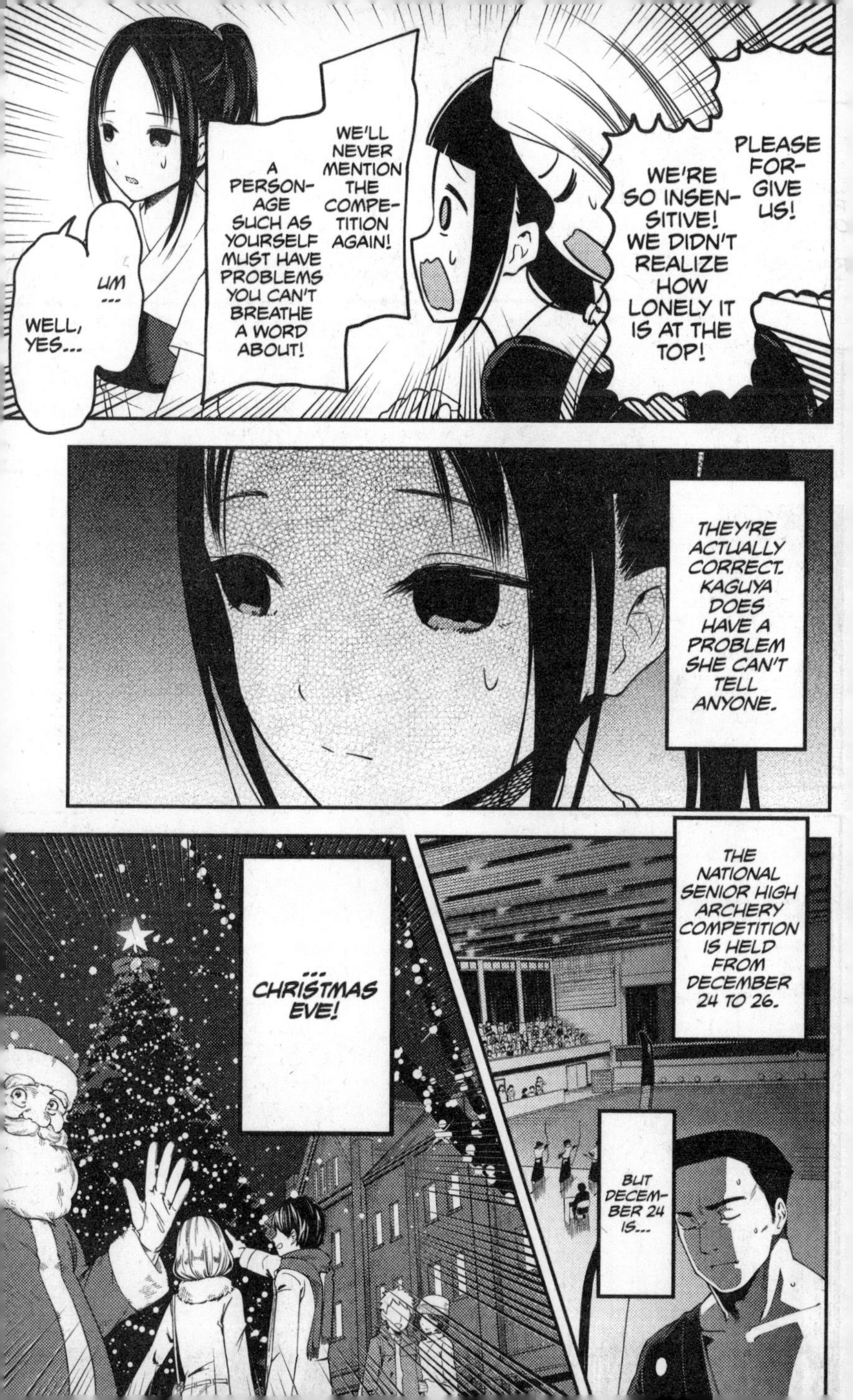
PLEASE FOR-GIVE US!
WE'RE SO INSEN-SITIVE! WE DIDN'T REALIZE HOW LONELY IT IS AT THE TOP!
WE'LL NEVER MENTION THE COMPE-TITION AGAIN!
A PERSON-AGE SUCH AS YOURSELF MUST HAVE PROBLEMS YOU CAN'T BREATHE A WORD ABOUT!
UM ... WELL, YES...
THEY'RE ACTUALLY CORRECT. KAGUYA DOES HAVE A PROBLEM SHE CAN'T TELL ANYONE.
THE NATIONAL SENIOR HIGH ARCHERY COMPETITION IS HELD FROM DECEMBER 24 TO 26.
BUT DECEM-BER 24 IS...
...CHRISTMAS EVE!

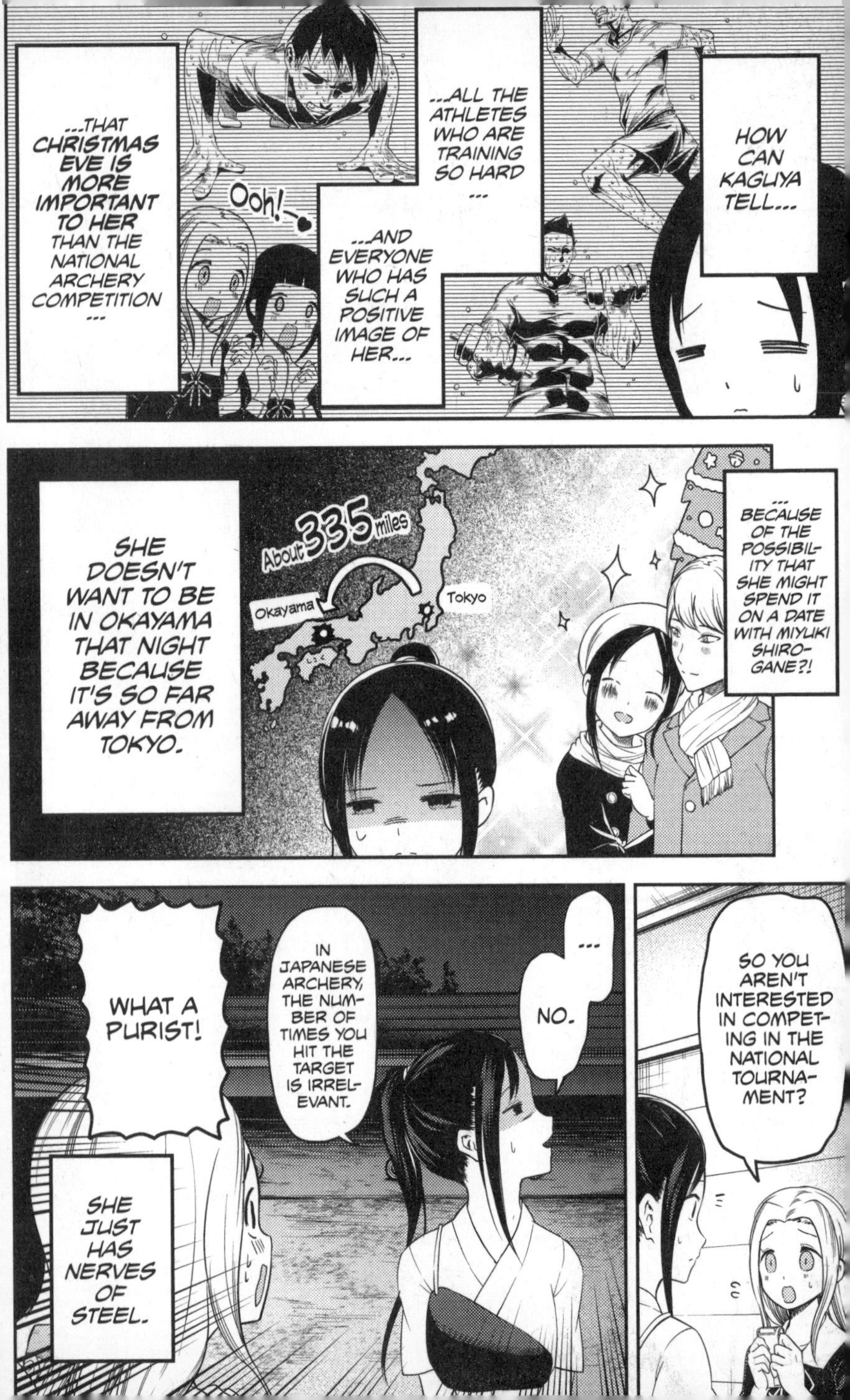
HOW CAN KAGUYA TELL...
...ALL THE ATHLETES WHO ARE TRAINING SO HARD...
...AND EVERYONE WHO HAS SUCH A POSITIVE IMAGE OF HER...
...THAT CHRISTMAS EVE IS MORE IMPORTANT TO HER THAN THE NATIONAL ARCHERY COMPETITION...
Ooh!
...BECAUSE OF THE POSSIBILITY THAT SHE MIGHT SPEND IT ON A DATE WITH MIYUKI SHIROGANE?!
About 335 miles
Tokyo
Okayama
SHE DOESN'T WANT TO BE IN OKAYAMA THAT NIGHT BECAUSE IT'S SO FAR AWAY FROM TOKYO.
SO YOU AREN'T INTERESTED IN COMPETING IN THE NATIONAL TOURNAMENT?
...
NO.
IN JAPANESE ARCHERY, THE NUMBER OF TIMES YOU HIT THE TARGET IS IRRELEVANT.
WHAT A PURIST!
SHE JUST HAS NERVES OF STEEL.

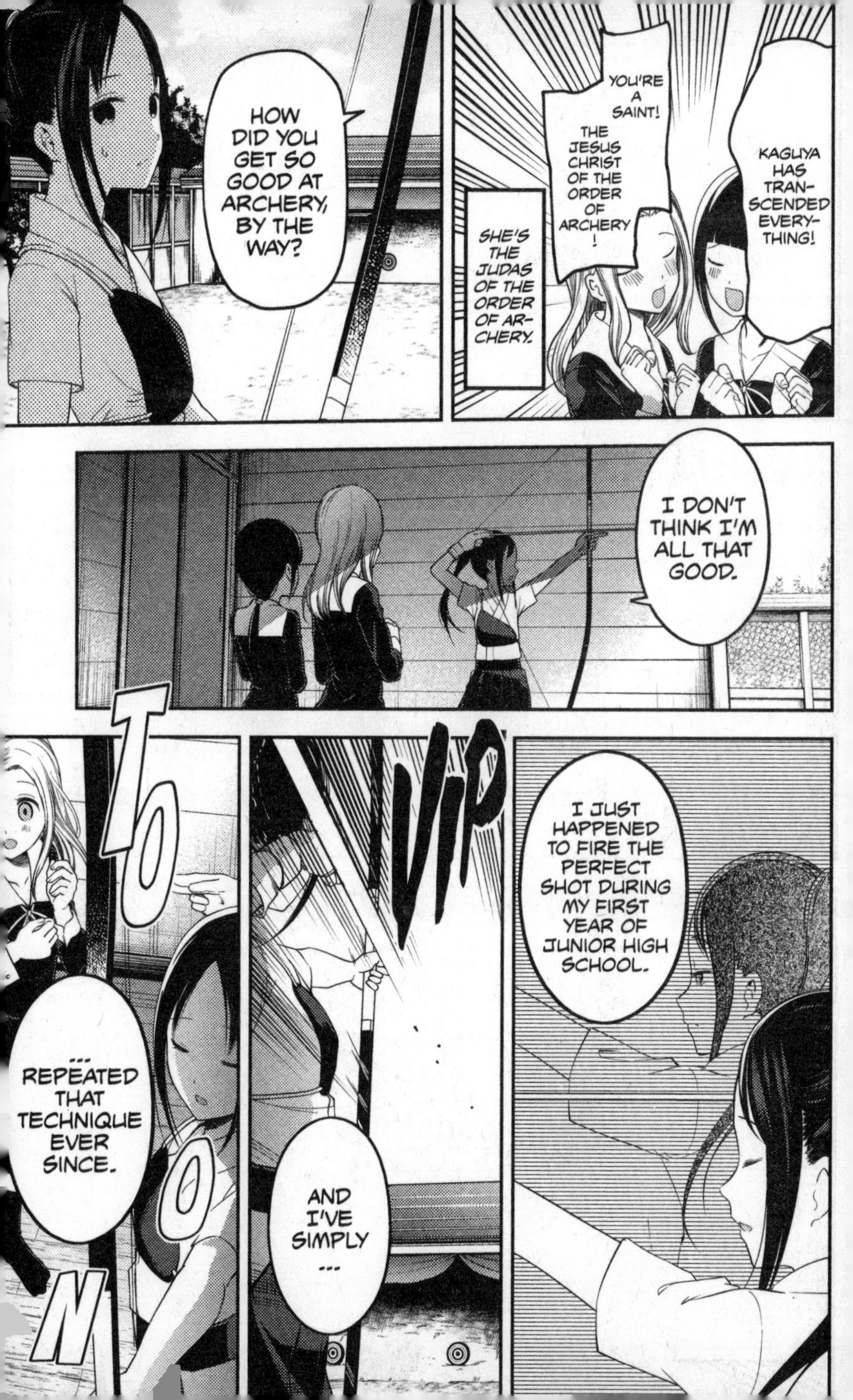
KAGUYA HAS TRAN-SCENDED EVERY-THING!
YOU'RE A SAINT! THE JESUS CHRIST OF THE ORDER OF ARCHERY!
SHE'S THE JUDAS OF THE ORDER OF AR-CHERY.
HOW DID YOU GET SO GOOD AT ARCHERY, BY THE WAY?
I DON'T THINK I'M ALL THAT GOOD.
I JUST HAPPENED TO FIRE THE PERFECT SHOT DURING MY FIRST YEAR OF JUNIOR HIGH SCHOOL.
VIP
AND I'VE SIMPLY ...
... REPEATED THAT TECHNIQUE EVER SINCE.
TOON

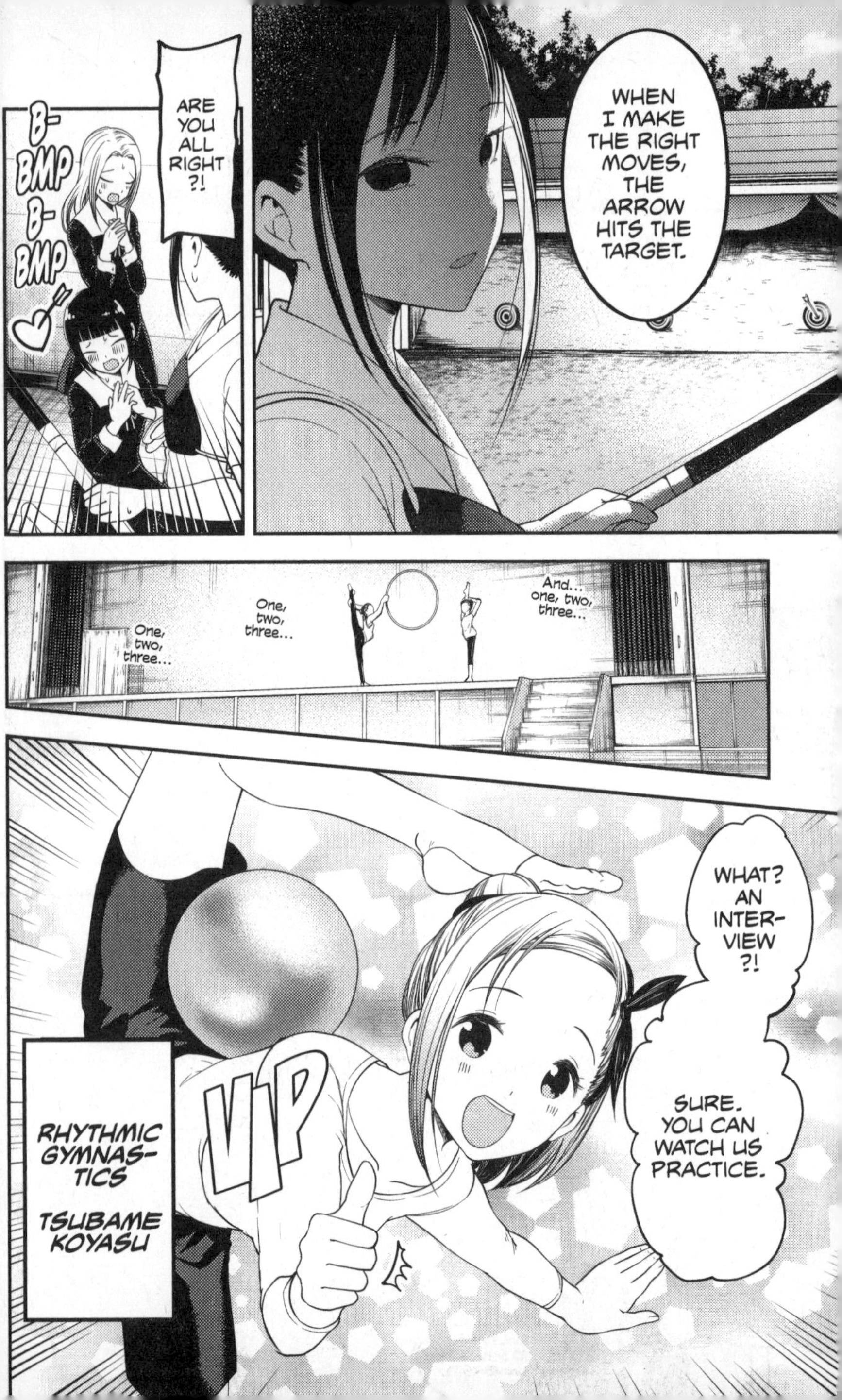
WHEN I MAKE THE RIGHT MOVES, THE ARROW HITS THE TARGET.
ARE YOU ALL RIGHT ?!
B-BMP B-BMP
And... one, two, three...
One, two, three...
One, two, three...
WHAT? AN INTER-VIEW ?!
SURE. YOU CAN WATCH US PRACTICE.
VIP
RHYTHMIC GYMNAS-TICS
TSUBAME KOYASU

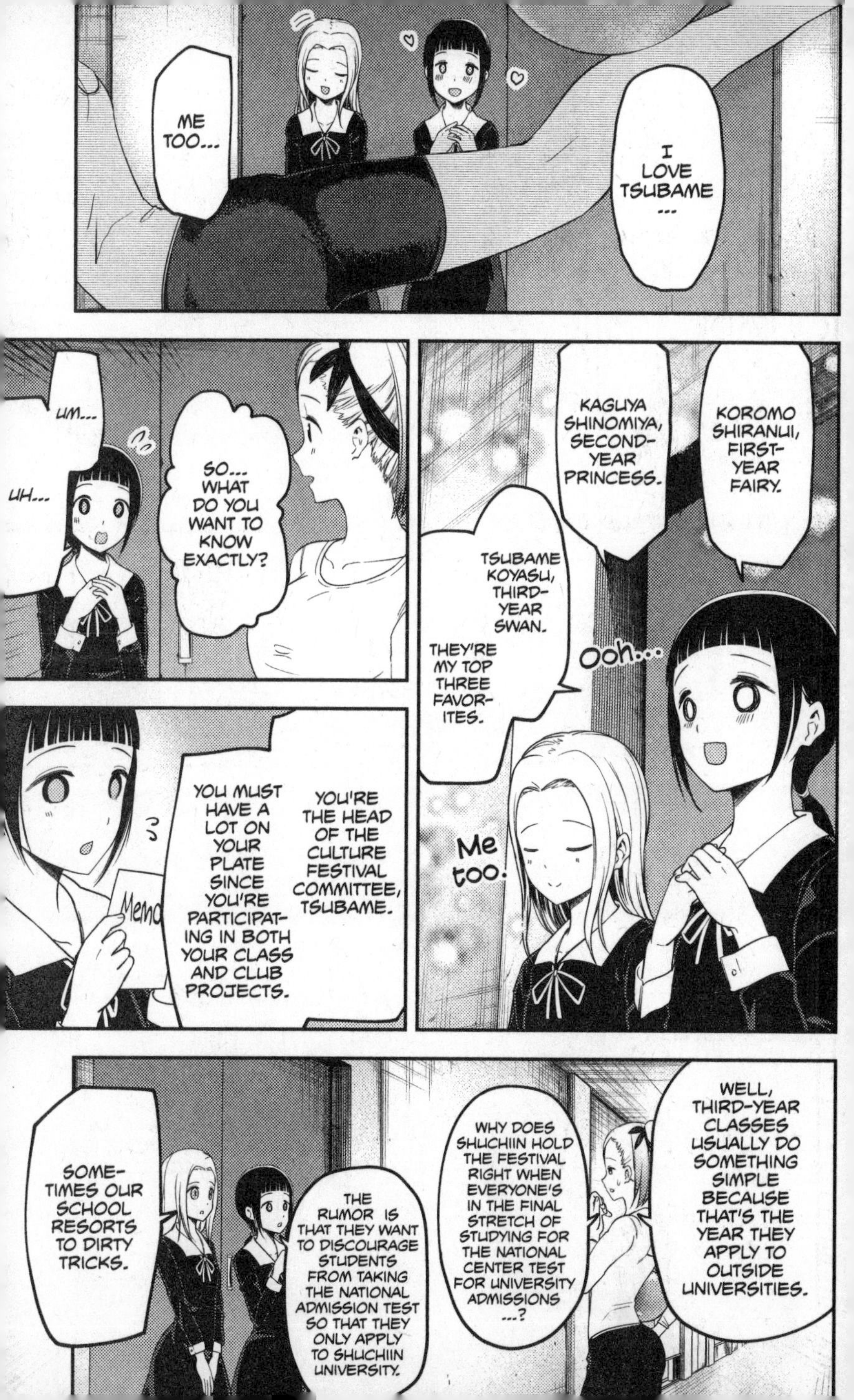
I LOVE TSUBAME...
ME TOO...
KOROMO SHIRANUI, FIRST-YEAR FAIRY.
KAGUYA SHINOMIYA, SECOND-YEAR PRINCESS.
TSUBAME KOYASU, THIRD-YEAR SWAN.
THEY'RE MY TOP THREE FAVORITES.
Ooh...
Me too.
SO... WHAT DO YOU WANT TO KNOW EXACTLY?
UM...
UH...
YOU'RE THE HEAD OF THE CULTURE FESTIVAL COMMITTEE, TSUBAME.
YOU MUST HAVE A LOT ON YOUR PLATE SINCE YOU'RE PARTICIPATING IN BOTH YOUR CLASS AND CLUB PROJECTS.
Memo
WELL, THIRD-YEAR CLASSES USUALLY DO SOMETHING SIMPLE BECAUSE THAT'S THE YEAR THEY APPLY TO OUTSIDE UNIVERSITIES.
WHY DOES SHUCHIIN HOLD THE FESTIVAL RIGHT WHEN EVERYONE'S IN THE FINAL STRETCH OF STUDYING FOR THE NATIONAL CENTER TEST FOR UNIVERSITY ADMISSIONS...?
THE RUMOR IS THAT THEY WANT TO DISCOURAGE STUDENTS FROM TAKING THE NATIONAL ADMISSION TEST SO THAT THEY ONLY APPLY TO SHUCHIIN UNIVERSITY.
SOMETIMES OUR SCHOOL RESORTS TO DIRTY TRICKS.

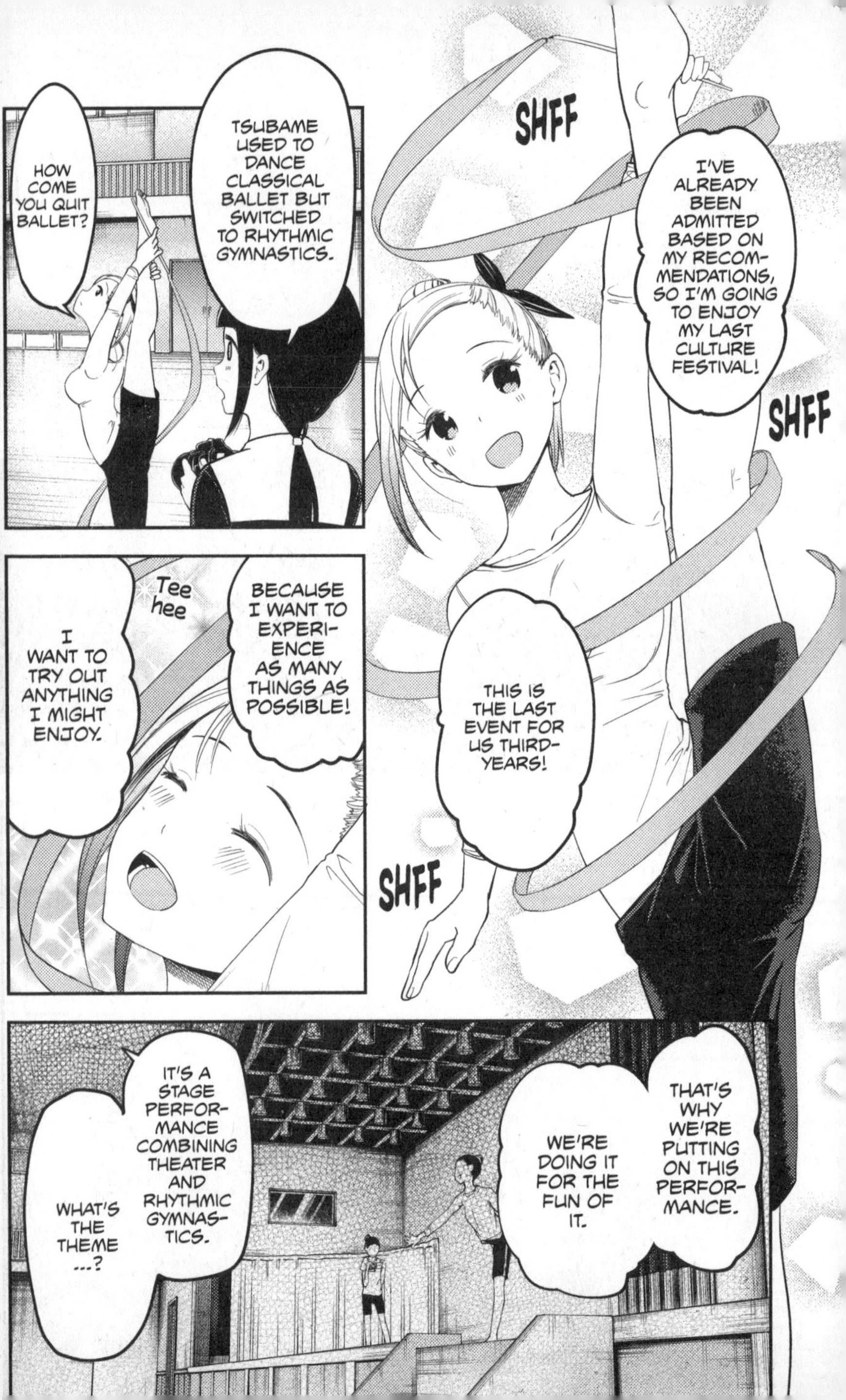
SHFF
I'VE ALREADY BEEN ADMITTED BASED ON MY RECOMMENDATIONS, SO I'M GOING TO ENJOY MY LAST CULTURE FESTIVAL!
SHFF
THIS IS THE LAST EVENT FOR US THIRD-YEARS!
SHFF
TSUBAME USED TO DANCE CLASSICAL BALLET BUT SWITCHED TO RHYTHMIC GYMNASTICS.
HOW COME YOU QUIT BALLET?
BECAUSE I WANT TO EXPERIENCE AS MANY THINGS AS POSSIBLE!
Tee hee
I WANT TO TRY OUT ANYTHING I MIGHT ENJOY.
THAT'S WHY WE'RE PUTTING ON THIS PERFORMANCE.
WE'RE DOING IT FOR THE FUN OF IT.
IT'S A STAGE PERFORMANCE COMBINING THEATER AND RHYTHMIC GYMNASTICS.
WHAT'S THE THEME ...?

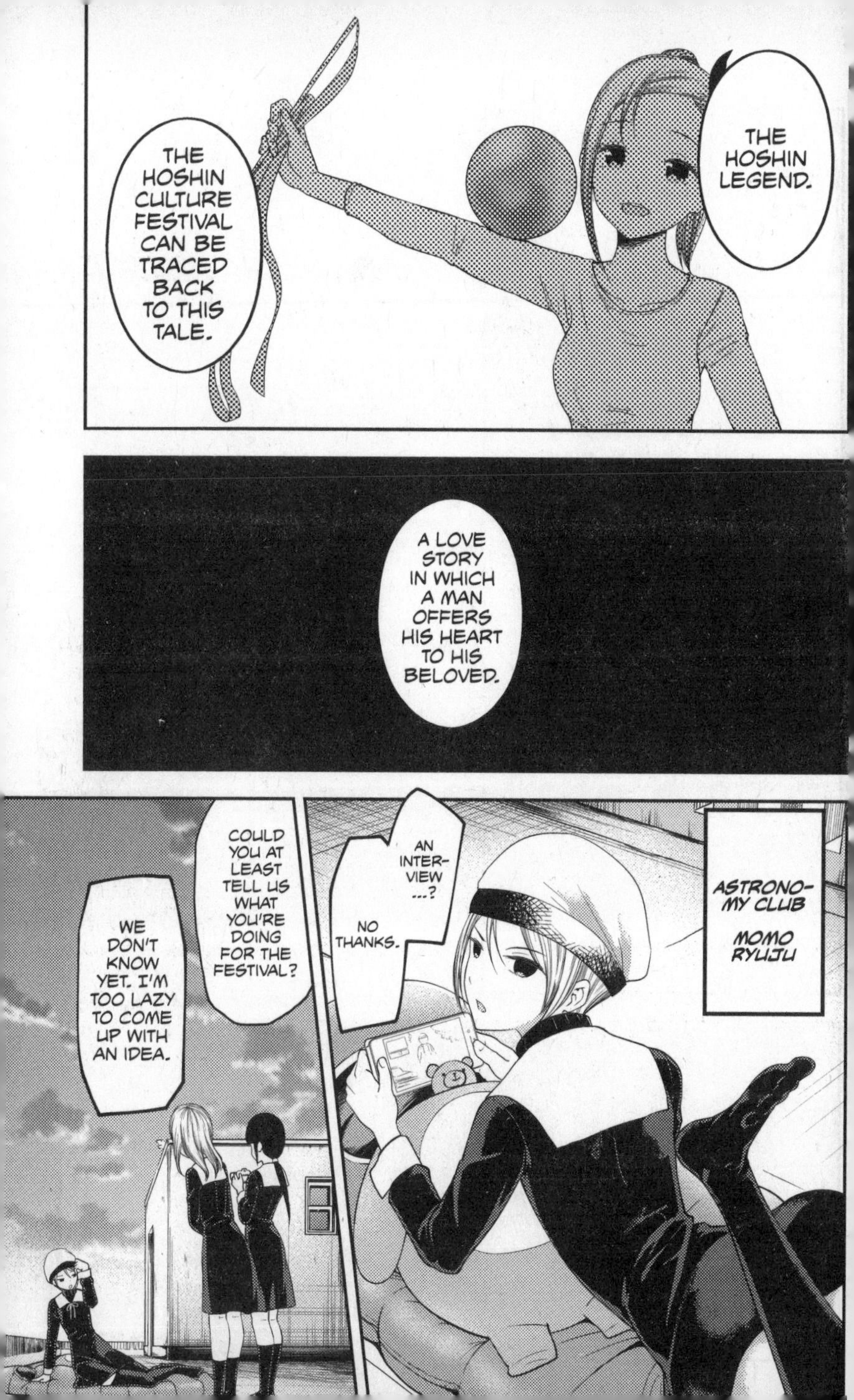
THE HOSHIN LEGEND.
THE HOSHIN CULTURE FESTIVAL CAN BE TRACED BACK TO THIS TALE.
A LOVE STORY IN WHICH A MAN OFFERS HIS HEART TO HIS BELOVED.
ASTRONO-MY CLUB MOMO RYUJU
AN INTER-VIEW ...?
NO THANKS.
COULD YOU AT LEAST TELL US WHAT YOU'RE DOING FOR THE FESTIVAL?
WE DON'T KNOW YET. I'M TOO LAZY TO COME UP WITH AN IDEA.

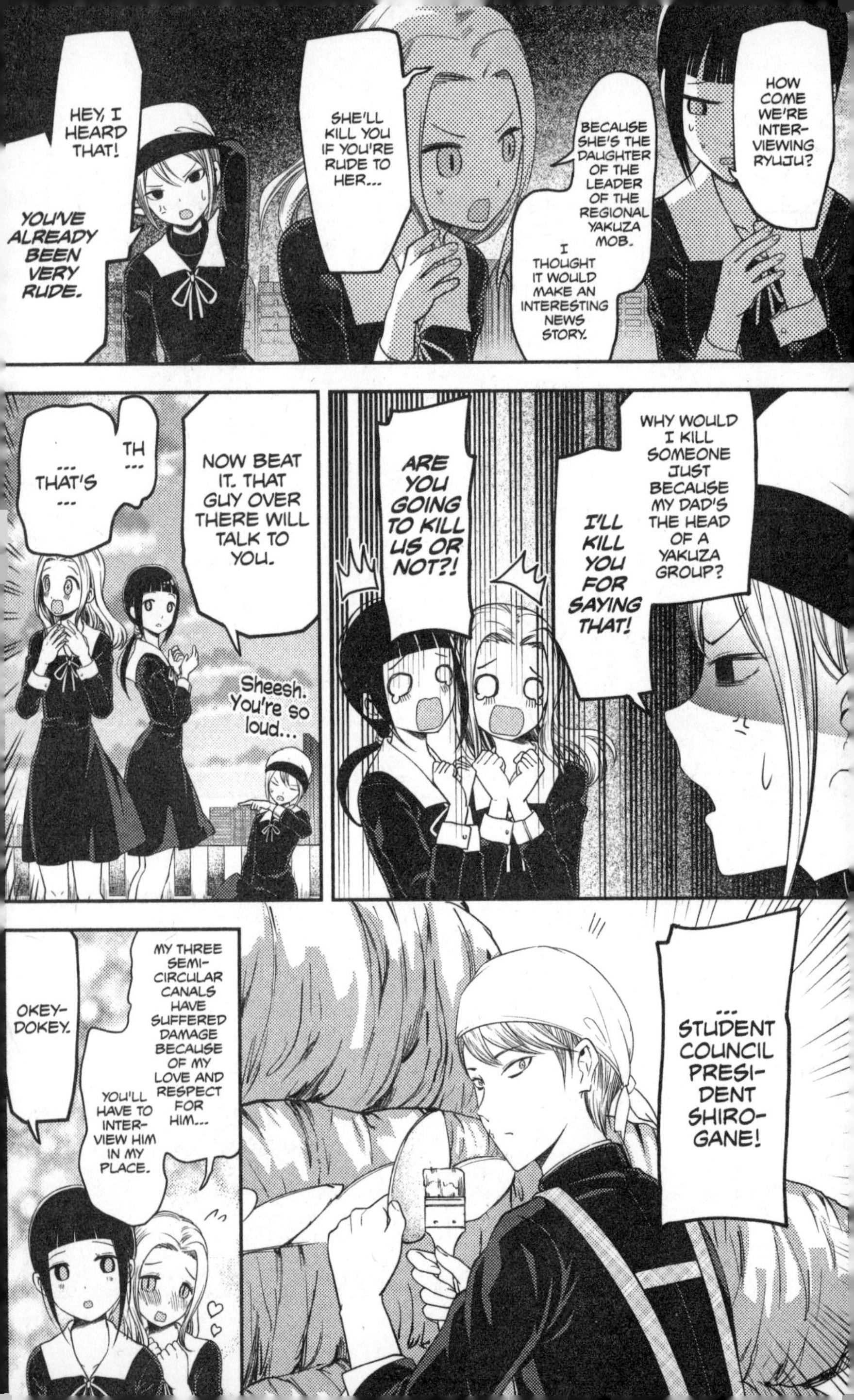
HOW COME WE'RE INTERVIEWING RYUJU?
BECAUSE SHE'S THE DAUGHTER OF THE LEADER OF THE REGIONAL YAKUZA MOB.
I THOUGHT IT WOULD MAKE AN INTERESTING NEWS STORY.
SHE'LL KILL YOU IF YOU'RE RUDE TO HER...
HEY, I HEARD THAT!
YOU'VE ALREADY BEEN VERY RUDE.
WHY WOULD I KILL SOMEONE JUST BECAUSE MY DAD'S THE HEAD OF A YAKUZA GROUP?
I'LL KILL YOU FOR SAYING THAT!
ARE YOU GOING TO KILL US OR NOT?!
NOW BEAT IT. THAT GUY OVER THERE WILL TALK TO YOU.
TH--- ...THAT'S---
Sheesh. You're so loud...
...STUDENT COUNCIL PRESIDENT SHIROGANE!
MY THREE SEMICIRCULAR CANALS HAVE SUFFERED DAMAGE BECAUSE OF MY LOVE AND RESPECT FOR HIM...
YOU'LL HAVE TO INTERVIEW HIM IN MY PLACE.
OKEY-DOKEY.

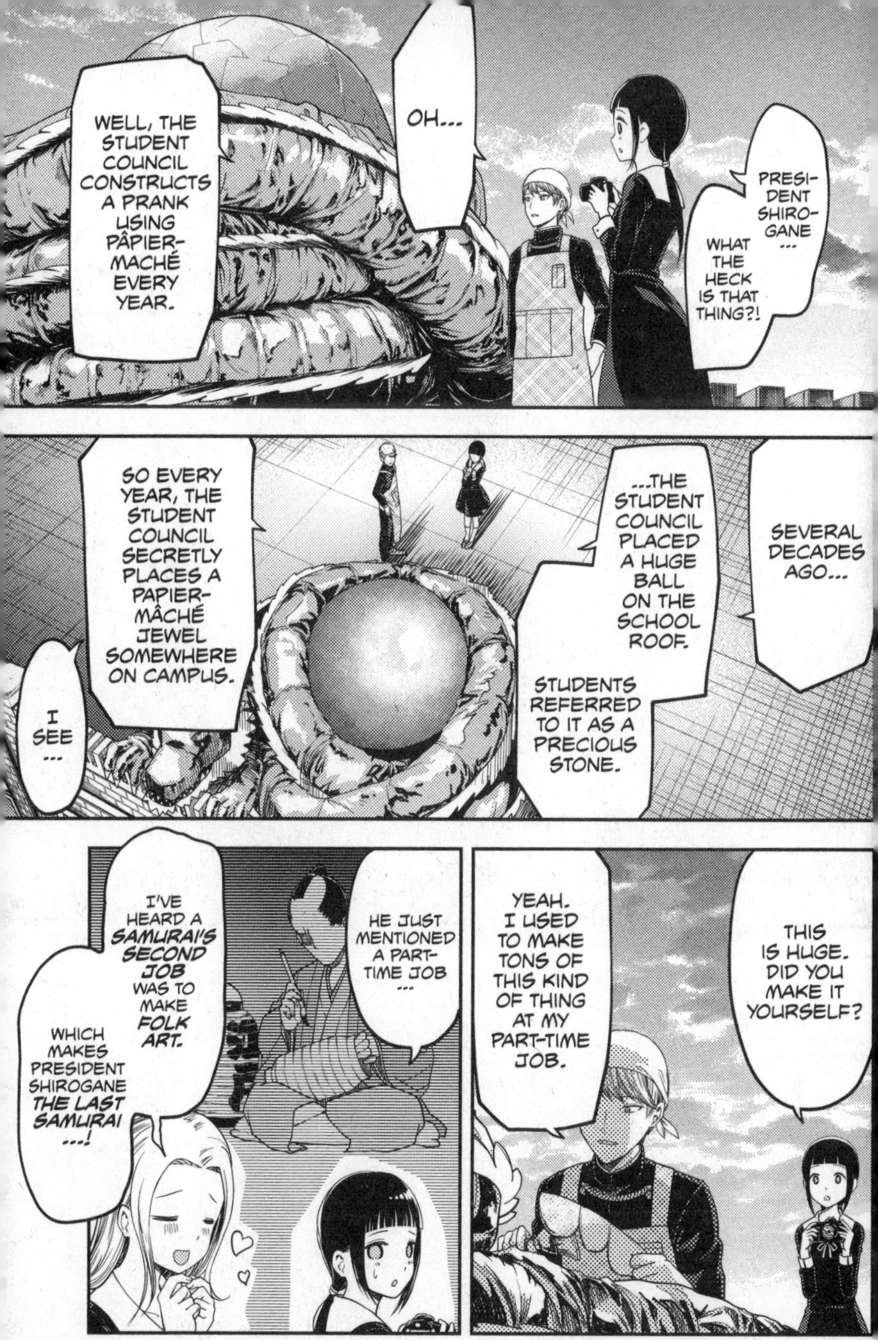
PRESIDENT SHIROGANE...
WHAT THE HECK IS THAT THING?!
OH...
WELL, THE STUDENT COUNCIL CONSTRUCTS A PRANK USING PÂPIER-MACHÉ EVERY YEAR.
SEVERAL DECADES AGO...
...THE STUDENT COUNCIL PLACED A HUGE BALL ON THE SCHOOL ROOF.
STUDENTS REFERRED TO IT AS A PRECIOUS STONE.
SO EVERY YEAR, THE STUDENT COUNCIL SECRETLY PLACES A PAPIER-MÂCHÉ JEWEL SOMEWHERE ON CAMPUS.
I SEE...
THIS IS HUGE. DID YOU MAKE IT YOURSELF?
YEAH. I USED TO MAKE TONS OF THIS KIND OF THING AT MY PART-TIME JOB.
HE JUST MENTIONED A PART-TIME JOB...
I'VE HEARD A SAMURAI'S SECOND JOB WAS TO MAKE FOLK ART.
WHICH MAKES PRESIDENT SHIROGANE THE LAST SAMURAI...!

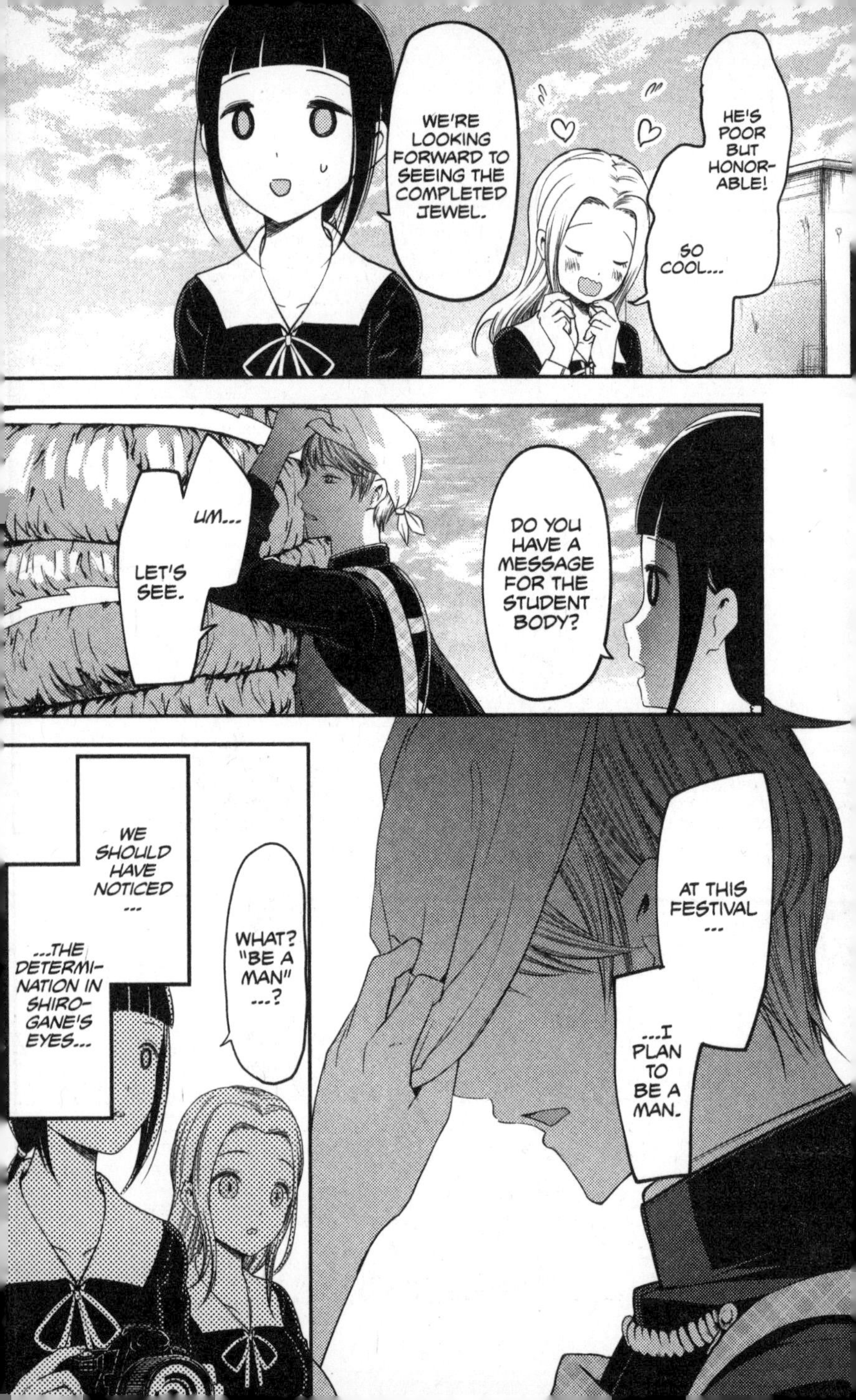
HE'S POOR BUT HONORABLE!
SO COOL...
WE'RE LOOKING FORWARD TO SEEING THE COMPLETED JEWEL.
DO YOU HAVE A MESSAGE FOR THE STUDENT BODY?
UM... LET'S SEE.
AT THIS FESTIVAL...
...I PLAN TO BE A MAN.
WHAT? "BE A MAN"...?
WE SHOULD HAVE NOTICED...
...THE DETERMINATION IN SHIROGANE'S EYES...

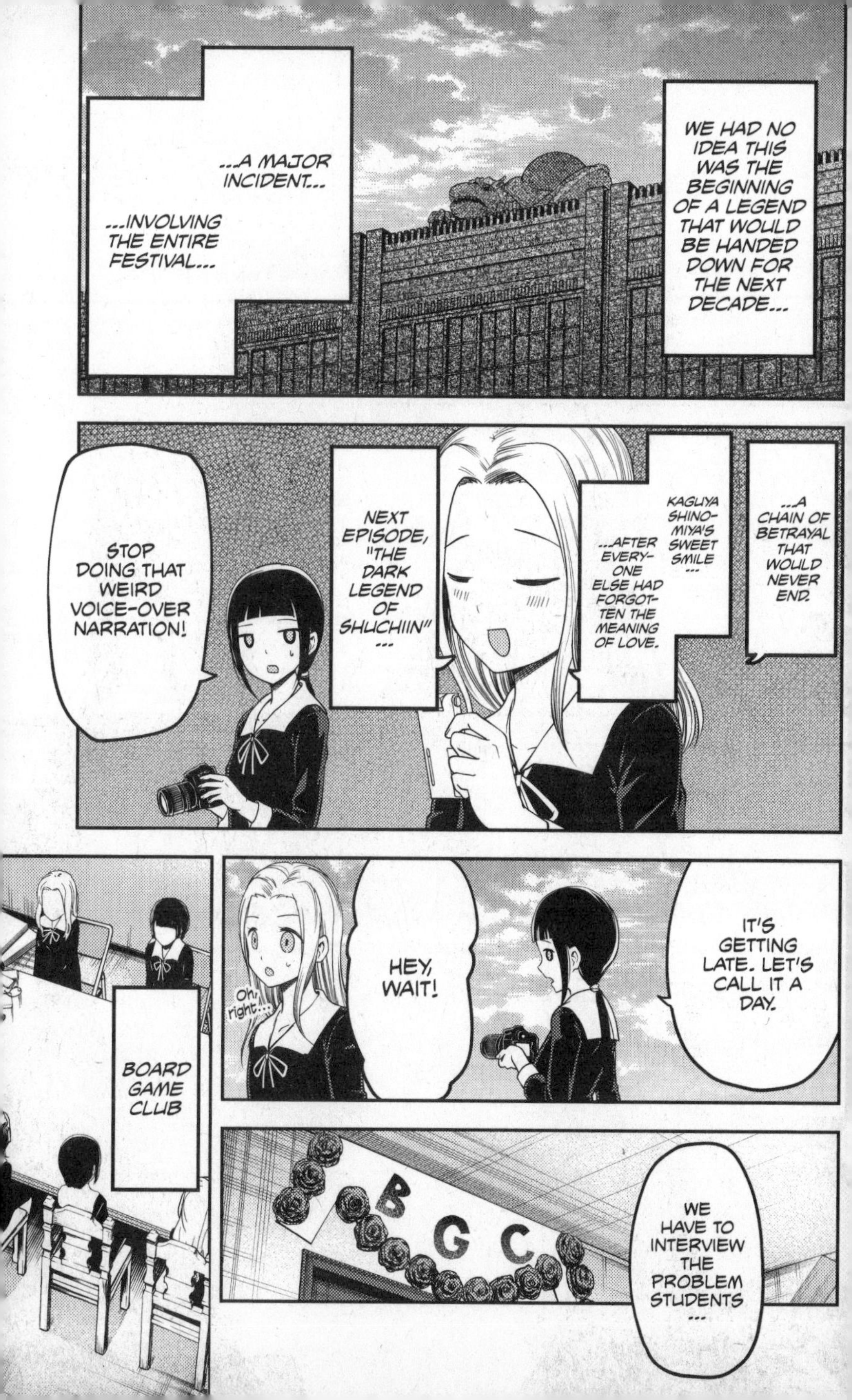
WE HAD NO IDEA THIS WAS THE BEGINNING OF A LEGEND THAT WOULD BE HANDED DOWN FOR THE NEXT DECADE...
...A MAJOR INCIDENT...
...INVOLVING THE ENTIRE FESTIVAL...
...A CHAIN OF BETRAYAL THAT WOULD NEVER END.
KAGUYA SHINOMIYA'S SWEET SMILE...
...AFTER EVERYONE ELSE HAD FORGOTTEN THE MEANING OF LOVE.
NEXT EPISODE, "THE DARK LEGEND OF SHUCHIIN"...
STOP DOING THAT WEIRD VOICE-OVER NARRATION!
IT'S GETTING LATE. LET'S CALL IT A DAY.
HEY, WAIT!
Oh, right...
WE HAVE TO INTERVIEW THE PROBLEM STUDENTS...
B G C
BOARD GAME CLUB

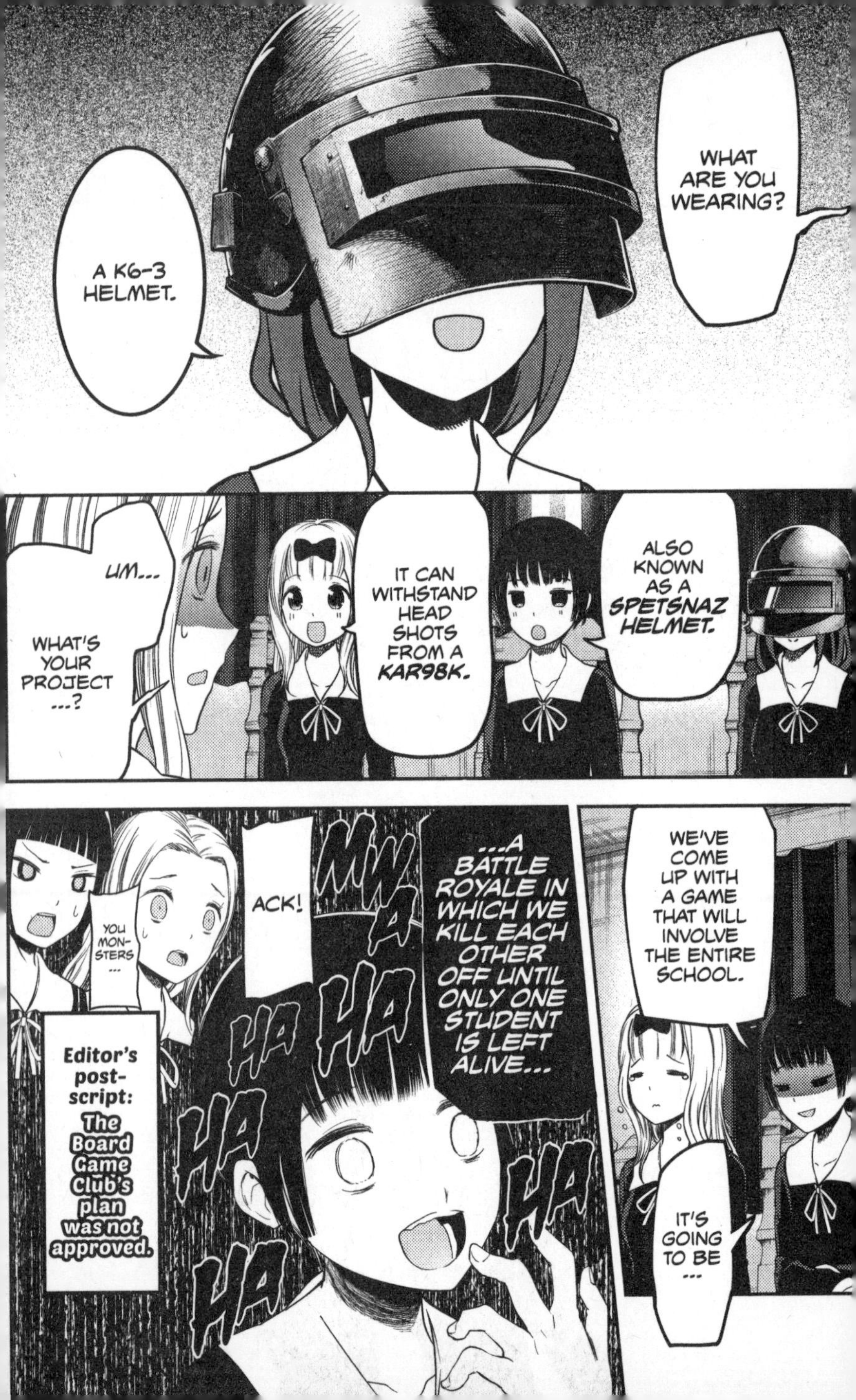
WHAT ARE YOU WEARING?
A K6-3 HELMET.
ALSO KNOWN AS A SPETSNAZ HELMET.
IT CAN WITHSTAND HEAD SHOTS FROM A KAR98K.
UM...
WHAT'S YOUR PROJECT ...?
WE'VE COME UP WITH A GAME THAT WILL INVOLVE THE ENTIRE SCHOOL.
IT'S GOING TO BE ...
...A BATTLE ROYALE IN WHICH WE KILL EACH OTHER OFF UNTIL ONLY ONE STUDENT IS LEFT ALIVE...
MWAHAHAHAHAHA
ACK!
YOU MONSTERS ...
Editor's post-script: The Board Game Club's plan was not approved.

And we're the stars!

KAGUYA-SAMA
LOVE IS WAR

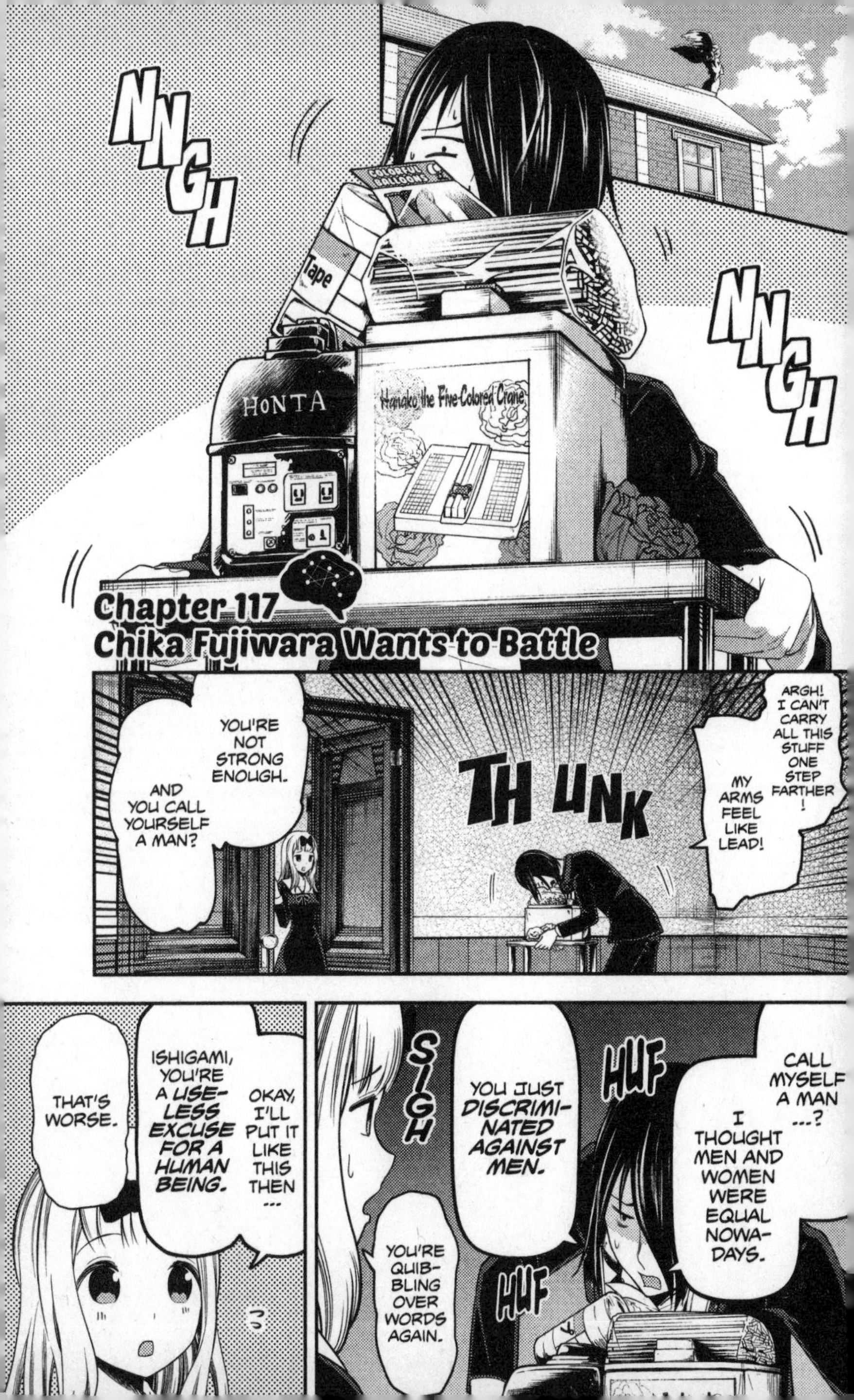
NNGH
NNGH
COLORFUL BALLOONS
Tape
Hanako the Five-Colored Crane
HONTA
Chapter 117
Chika Fujiwara Wants to Battle
ARGH! I CAN'T CARRY ALL THIS STUFF ONE STEP FARTHER!
MY ARMS FEEL LIKE LEAD!
THUNK
YOU'RE NOT STRONG ENOUGH.
AND YOU CALL YOURSELF A MAN?
CALL MYSELF A MAN...?
I THOUGHT MEN AND WOMEN WERE EQUAL NOWADAYS.
HUF
HUF
YOU JUST DISCRIMINATED AGAINST MEN.
SIGH
YOU'RE QUIBBLING OVER WORDS AGAIN.
OKAY, I'LL PUT IT LIKE THIS THEN...
ISHIGAMI, YOU'RE A USELESS EXCUSE FOR A HUMAN BEING.
THAT'S WORSE.

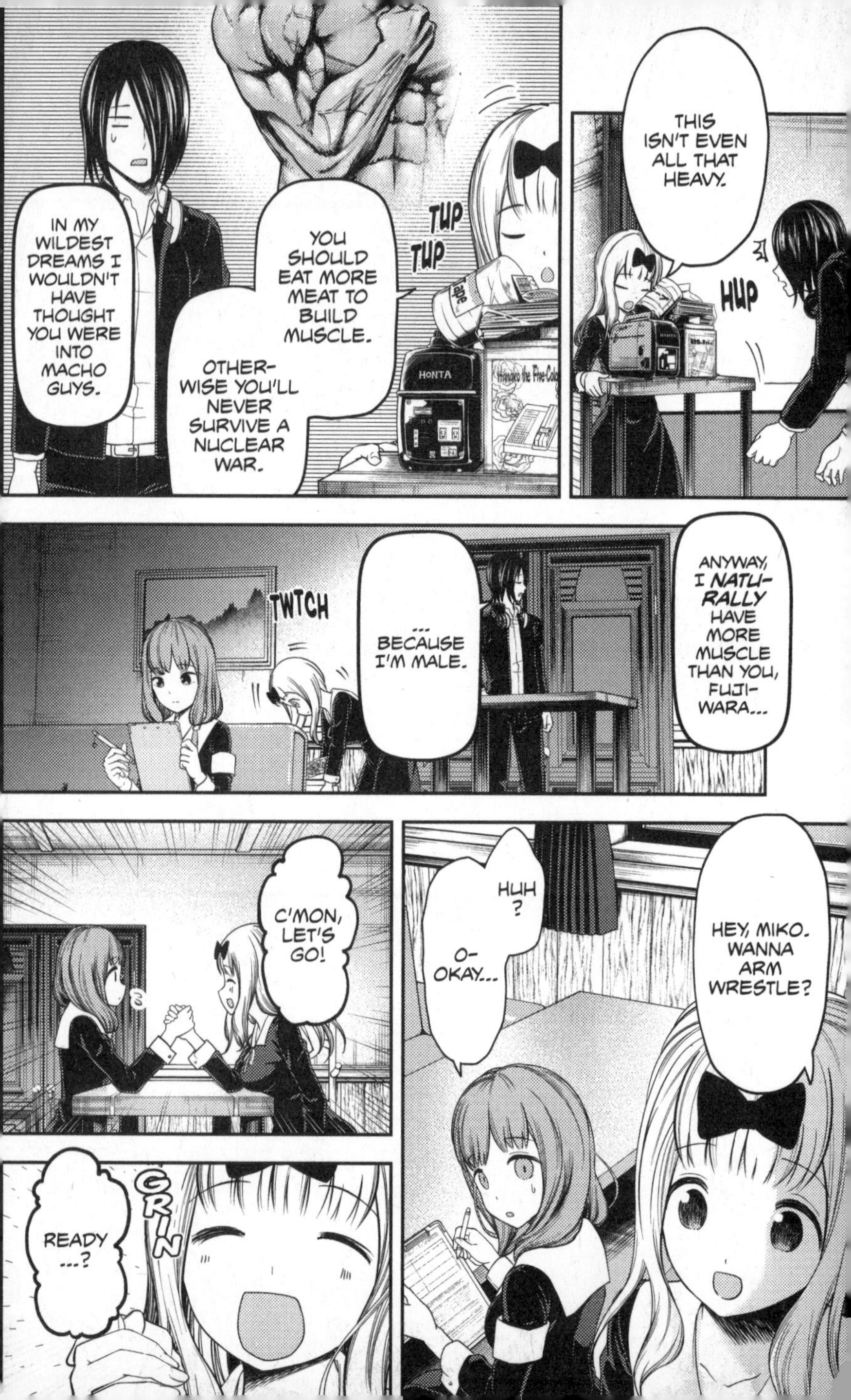
THIS ISN'T EVEN ALL THAT HEAVY.
HUP
TUP TUP
YOU SHOULD EAT MORE MEAT TO BUILD MUSCLE.
OTHERWISE YOU'LL NEVER SURVIVE A NUCLEAR WAR.
IN MY WILDEST DREAMS I WOULDN'T HAVE THOUGHT YOU WERE INTO MACHO GUYS.
ANYWAY, I *NATURALLY* HAVE MORE MUSCLE THAN YOU, FUJIWARA...
...BECAUSE I'M MALE.
TWTCH
HEY, MIKO. WANNA ARM WRESTLE?
HUH?
O-OKAY...
C'MON, LET'S GO!
GRIN
READY...?

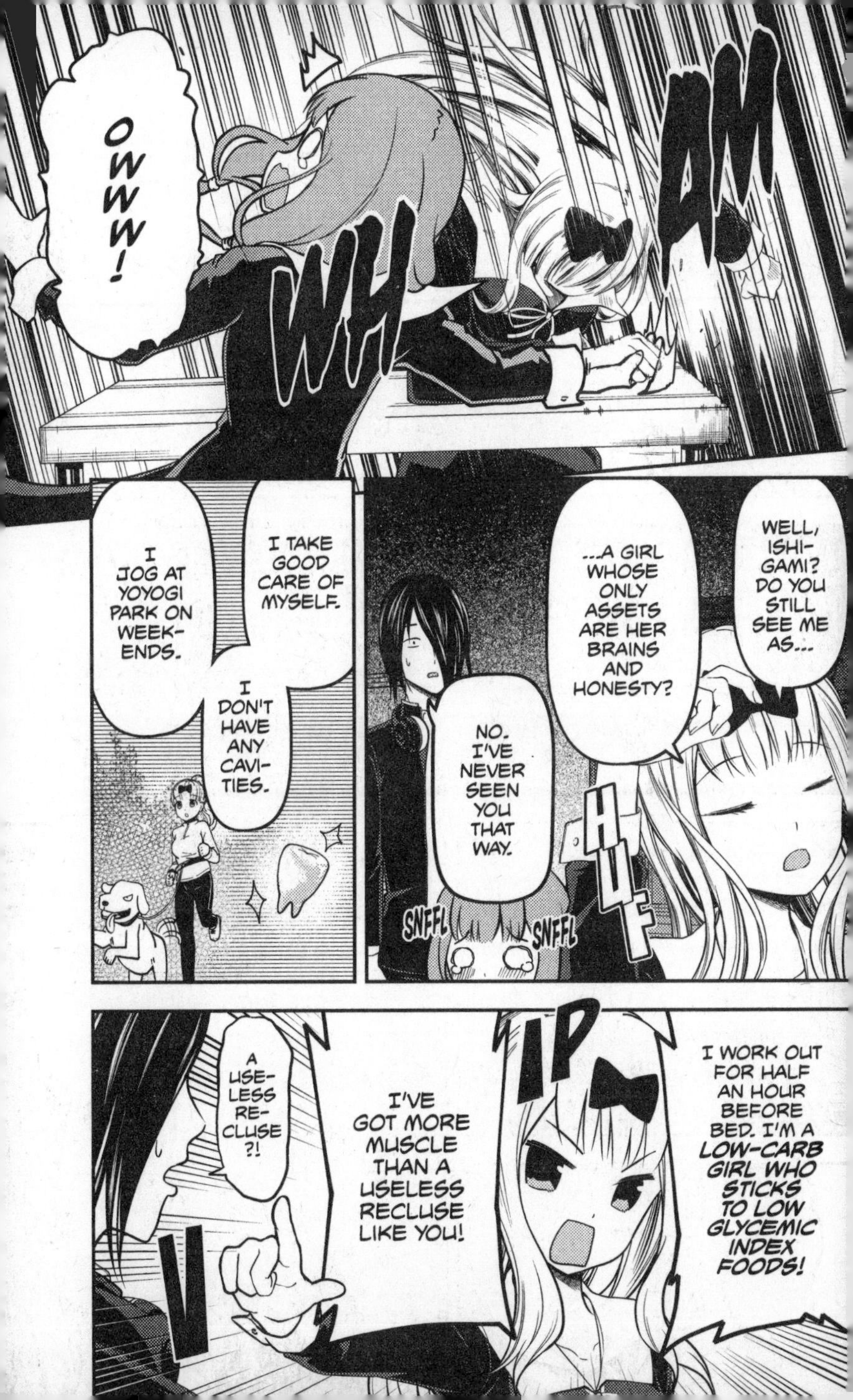

OWWW!
WHAM
WELL, ISHIGAMI? DO YOU STILL SEE ME AS...
...A GIRL WHOSE ONLY ASSETS ARE HER BRAINS AND HONESTY?
NO. I'VE NEVER SEEN YOU THAT WAY.
HUFF
SNFFL
SNFFL
I TAKE GOOD CARE OF MYSELF.
I JOG AT YOYOGI PARK ON WEEKENDS.
I DON'T HAVE ANY CAVITIES.
I WORK OUT FOR HALF AN HOUR BEFORE BED. I'M A LOW-CARB GIRL WHO STICKS TO LOW GLYCEMIC INDEX FOODS!
I'VE GOT MORE MUSCLE THAN A USELESS RECLUSE LIKE YOU!
A USELESS RECLUSE?!

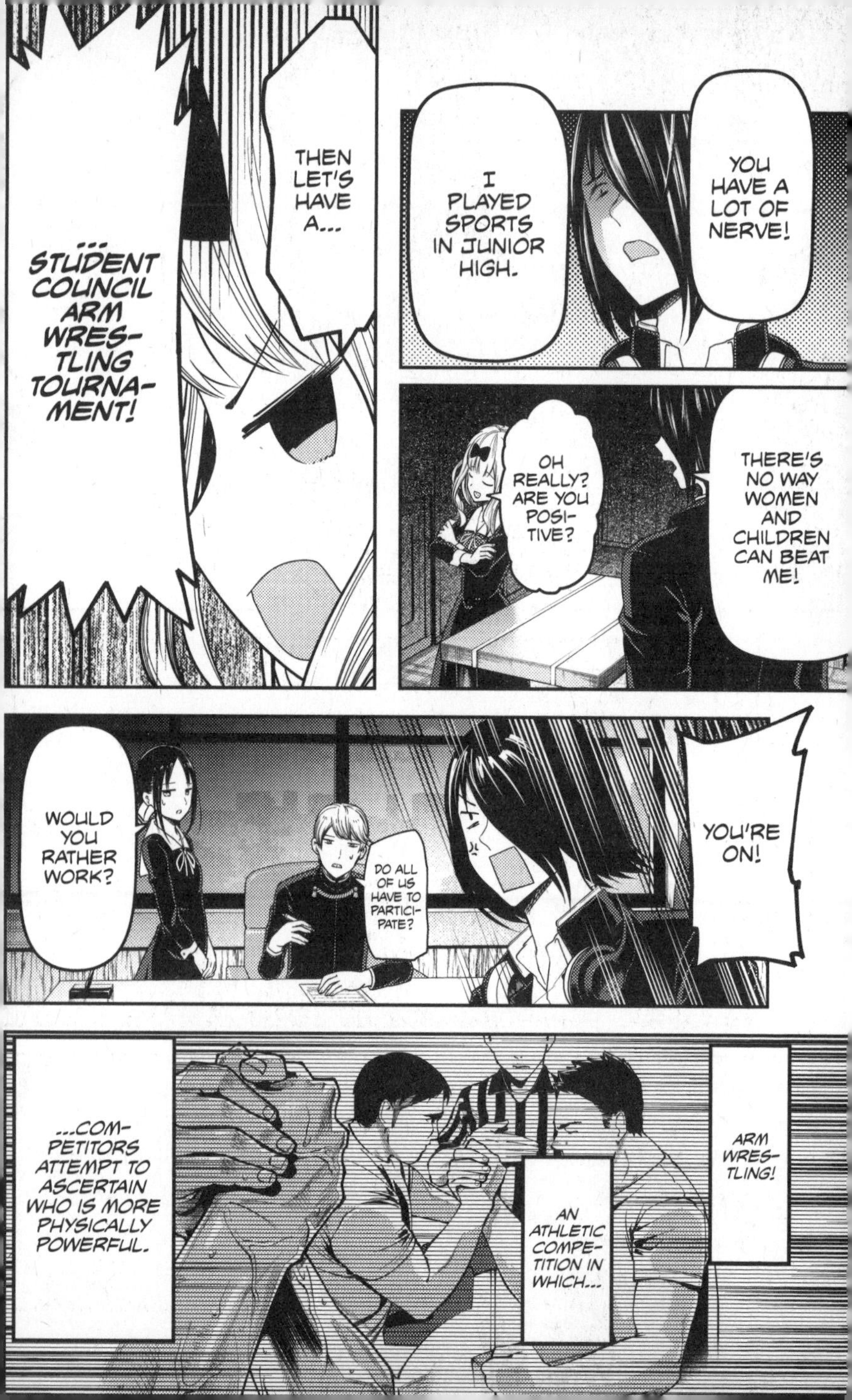
YOU HAVE A LOT OF NERVE!
I PLAYED SPORTS IN JUNIOR HIGH.
THERE'S NO WAY WOMEN AND CHILDREN CAN BEAT ME!
OH REALLY? ARE YOU POSITIVE?
THEN LET'S HAVE A...
...STUDENT COUNCIL ARM WRESTLING TOURNAMENT!
YOU'RE ON!
DO ALL OF US HAVE TO PARTICIPATE?
WOULD YOU RATHER WORK?
ARM WRESTLING!
AN ATHLETIC COMPETITION IN WHICH...
...COMPETITORS ATTEMPT TO ASCERTAIN WHO IS MORE PHYSICALLY POWERFUL.

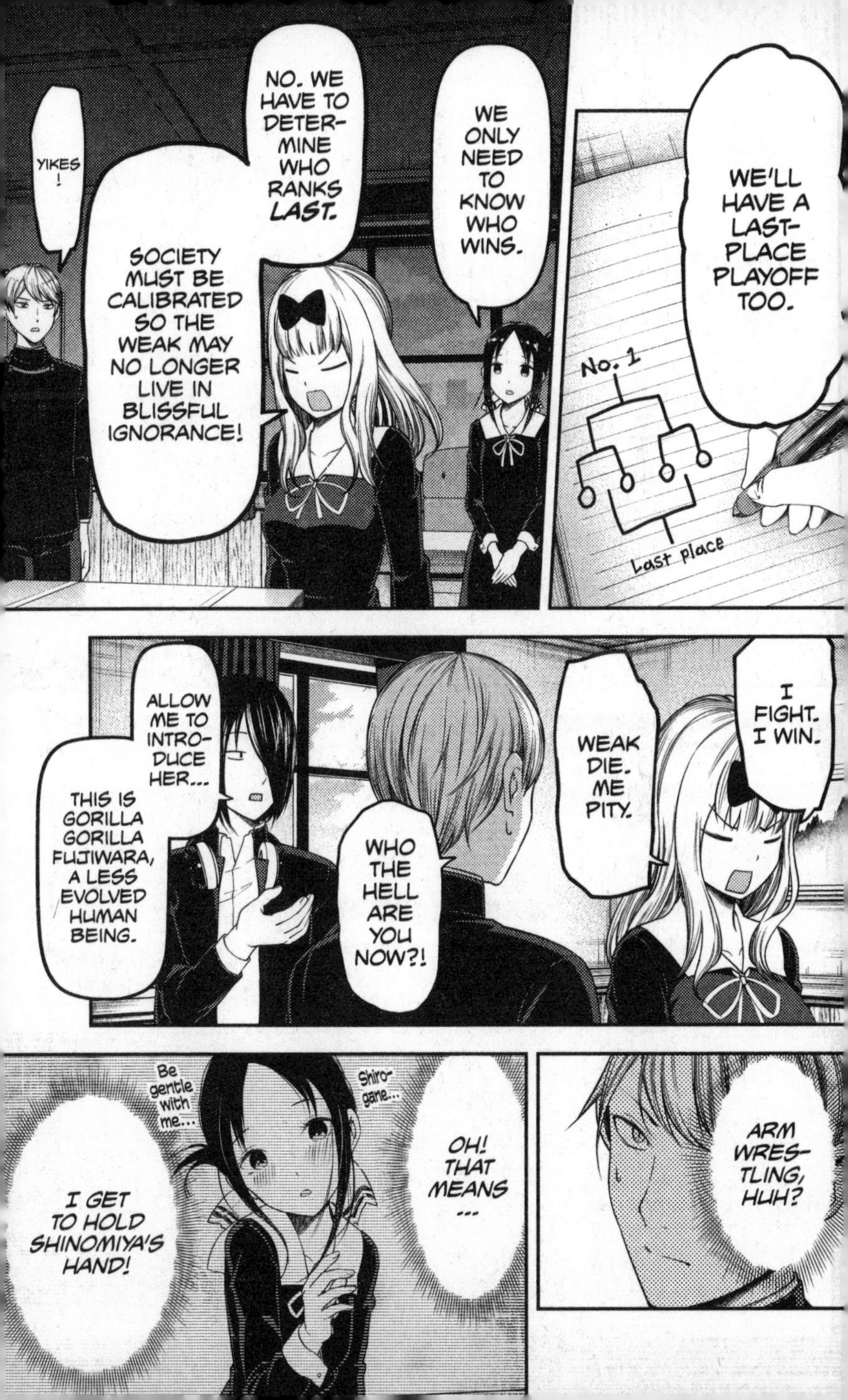
WE'LL HAVE A LAST-PLACE PLAYOFF TOO.
No. 1
Last place
WE ONLY NEED TO KNOW WHO WINS.
NO. WE HAVE TO DETERMINE WHO RANKS LAST.
SOCIETY MUST BE CALIBRATED SO THE WEAK MAY NO LONGER LIVE IN BLISSFUL IGNORANCE!
YIKES!
I FIGHT. I WIN.
WEAK DIE. ME PITY.
WHO THE HELL ARE YOU NOW?!
ALLOW ME TO INTRODUCE HER...
THIS IS GORILLA GORILLA FUJIWARA, A LESS EVOLVED HUMAN BEING.
ARM WRESTLING, HUH?
OH! THAT MEANS...
Shirogane...
Be gentle with me...
I GET TO HOLD SHINOMIYA'S HAND!

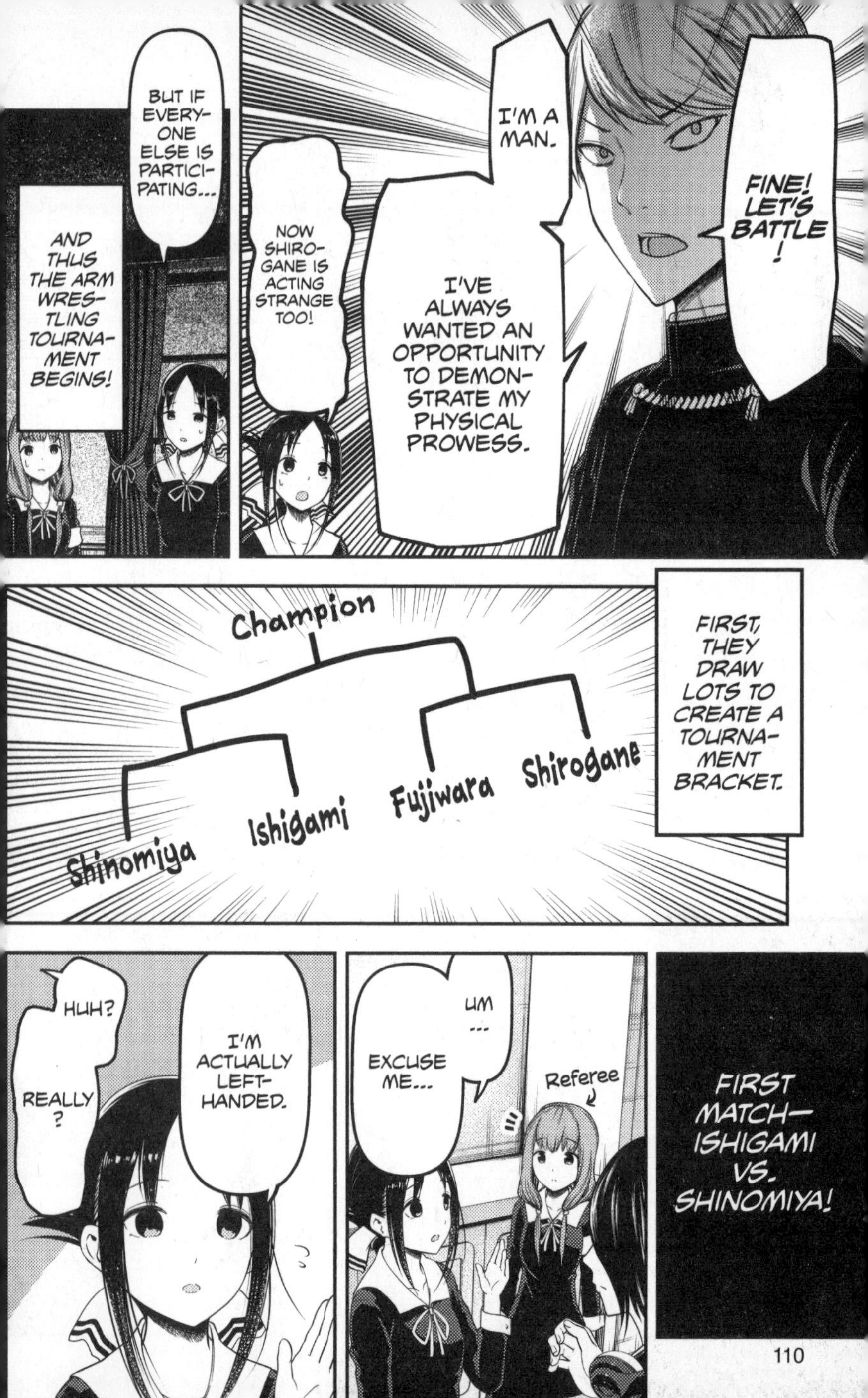
FINE! LET'S BATTLE!
I'M A MAN.
I'VE ALWAYS WANTED AN OPPORTUNITY TO DEMONSTRATE MY PHYSICAL PROWESS.
NOW SHIROGANE IS ACTING STRANGE TOO!
BUT IF EVERYONE ELSE IS PARTICIPATING...
AND THUS THE ARM WRESTLING TOURNAMENT BEGINS!
FIRST, THEY DRAW LOTS TO CREATE A TOURNAMENT BRACKET.
Champion
Shinomiya
Ishigami
Fujiwara
Shirogane
FIRST MATCH—ISHIGAMI VS. SHINOMIYA!
UM...
EXCUSE ME...
Referee
I'M ACTUALLY LEFT-HANDED.
HUH?
REALLY?

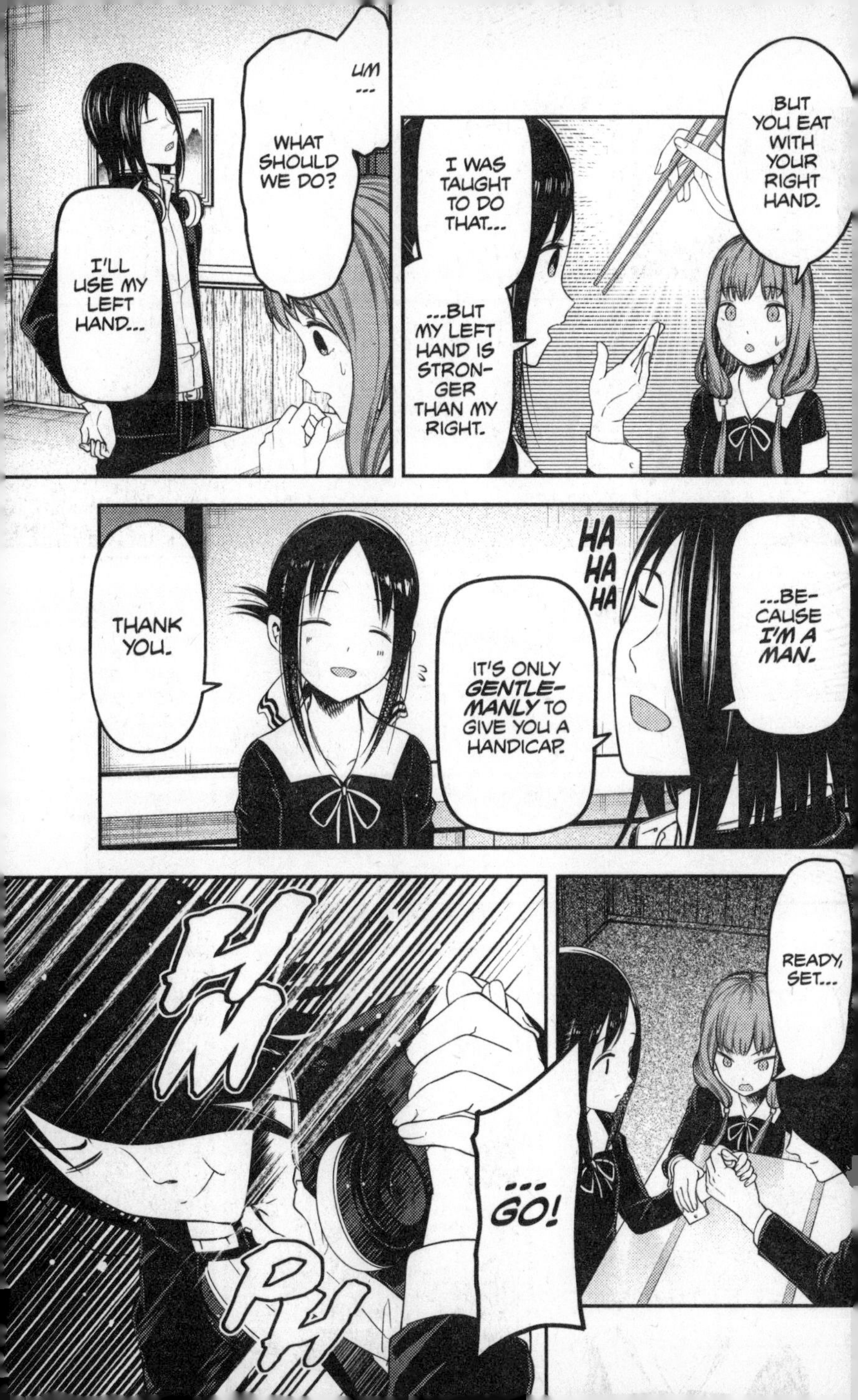
BUT YOU EAT WITH YOUR RIGHT HAND.
I WAS TAUGHT TO DO THAT...
...BUT MY LEFT HAND IS STRON-GER THAN MY RIGHT.
UM ...
WHAT SHOULD WE DO?
I'LL USE MY LEFT HAND...
...BE-CAUSE *I'M A MAN.*
HA HA HA
IT'S ONLY *GENTLE-MANLY* TO GIVE YOU A HANDICAP.
THANK YOU.
READY, SET...
...GO!
HMPH

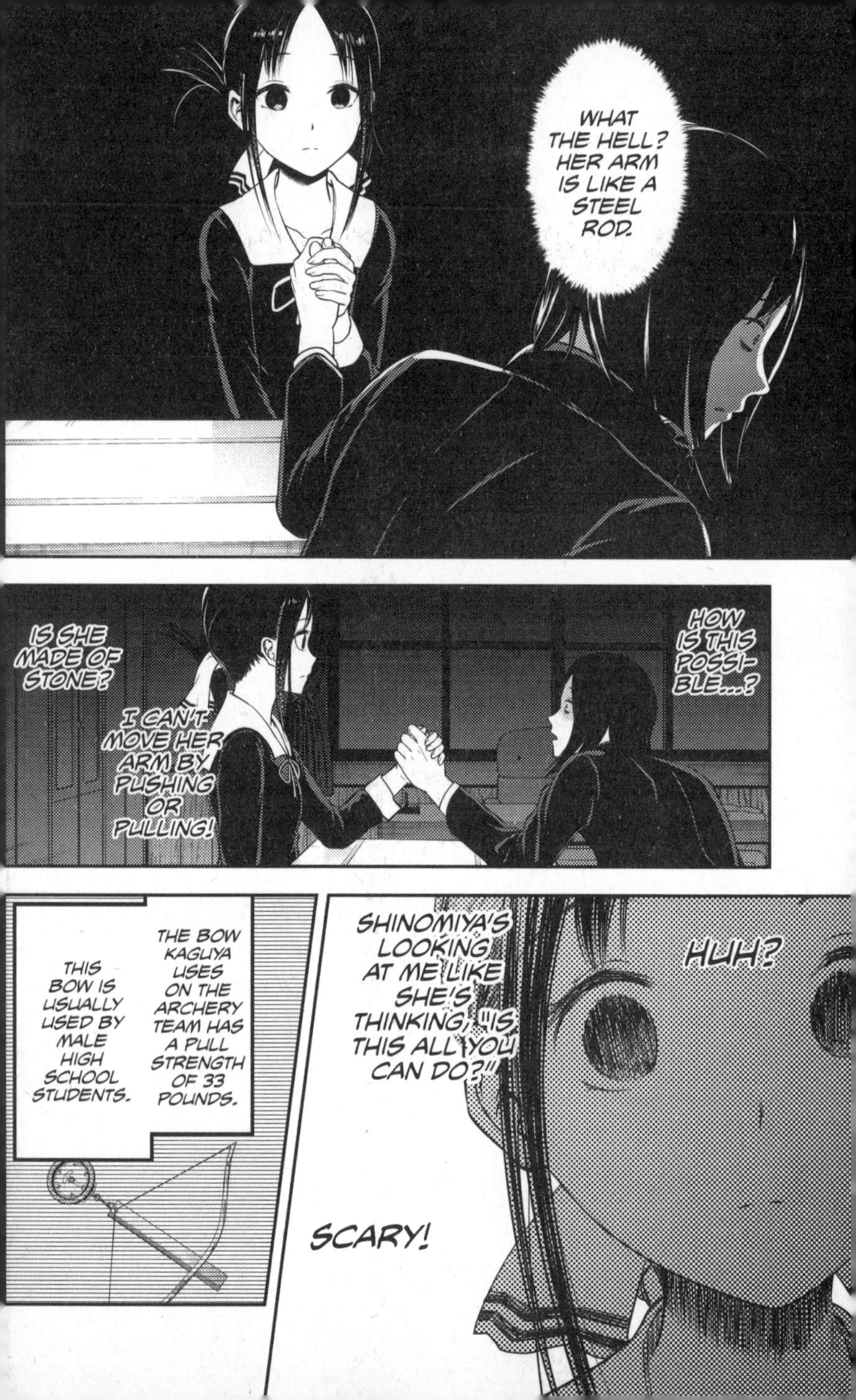
WHAT THE HELL? HER ARM IS LIKE A STEEL ROD.
HOW IS THIS POSSI-BLE...?
IS SHE MADE OF STONE?
I CAN'T MOVE HER ARM BY PUSHING OR PULLING!
HUH?
SHINOMIYA'S LOOKING AT ME LIKE SHE'S THINKING, "IS THIS ALL YOU CAN DO?"
SCARY!
THE BOW KAGUYA USES ON THE ARCHERY TEAM HAS A PULL STRENGTH OF 33 POUNDS.
THIS BOW IS USUALLY USED BY MALE HIGH SCHOOL STUDENTS.

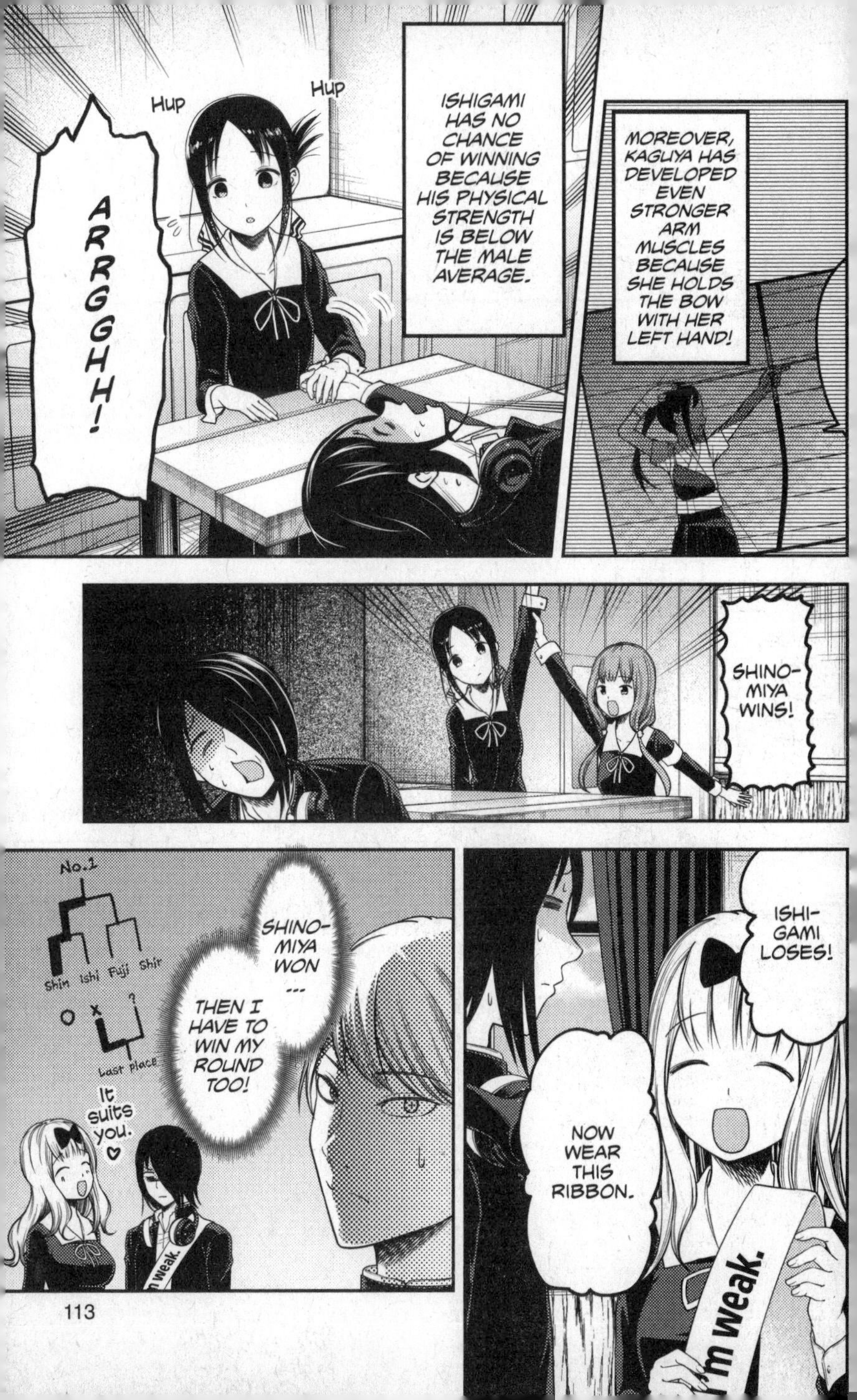
ISHIGAMI HAS NO CHANCE OF WINNING BECAUSE HIS PHYSICAL STRENGTH IS BELOW THE MALE AVERAGE.
MOREOVER, KAGUYA HAS DEVELOPED EVEN STRONGER ARM MUSCLES BECAUSE SHE HOLDS THE BOW WITH HER LEFT HAND!
Hup
Hup
ARRGGHH!
SHINO-MIYA WINS!
ISHI-GAMI LOSES!
NOW WEAR THIS RIBBON.
I'm weak.
SHINO-MIYA WON...
THEN I HAVE TO WIN MY ROUND TOO!
No.1
Shin Ishi Fuji Shir
○ x ?
Last place
It suits you. ♡
m weak.

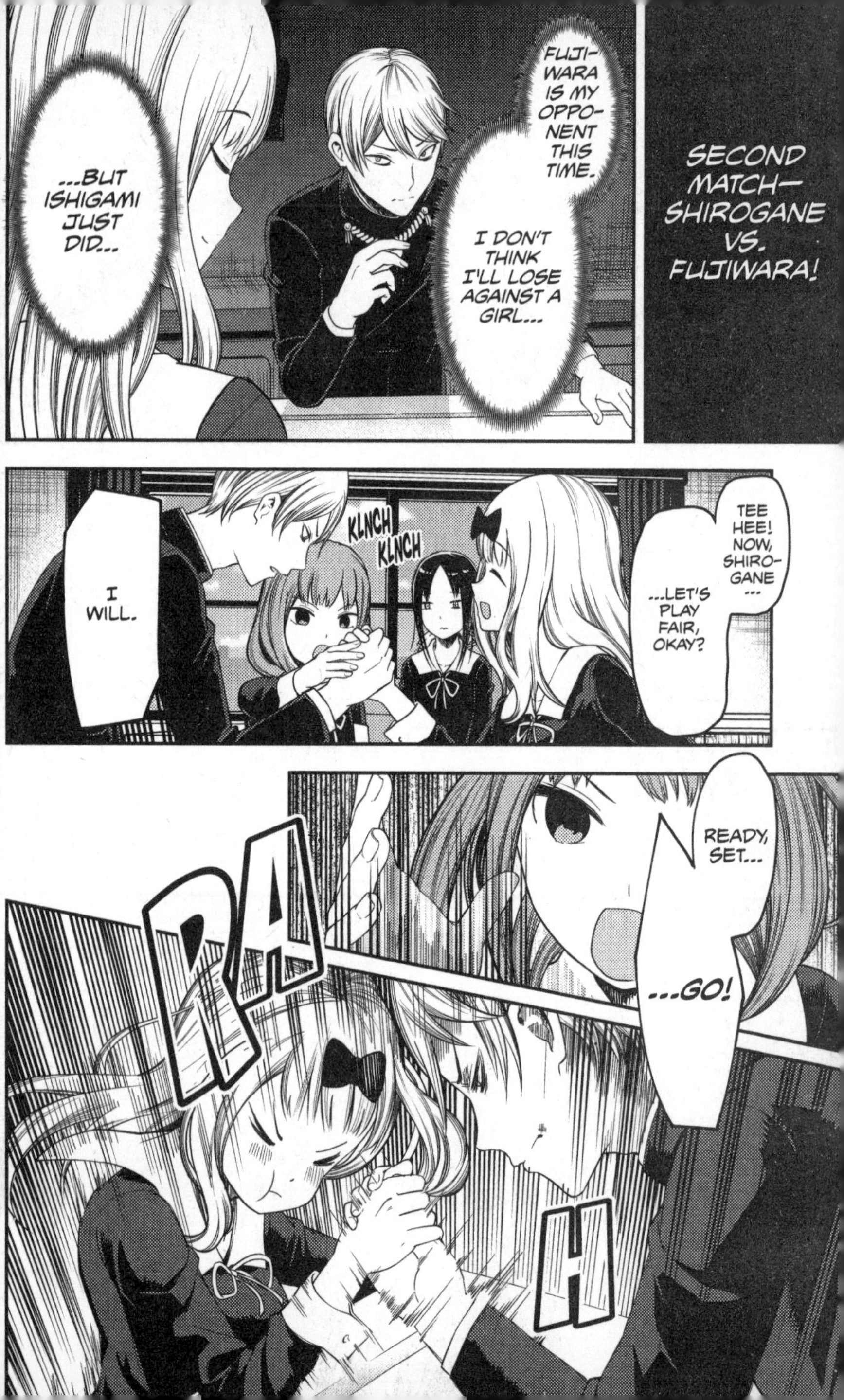

SECOND MATCH—SHIROGANE VS. FUJIWARA!
FUJI-WARA IS MY OPPO-NENT THIS TIME.
I DON'T THINK I'LL LOSE AGAINST A GIRL...
...BUT ISHIGAMI JUST DID...
TEE HEE! NOW, SHIRO-GANE...
...LET'S PLAY FAIR, OKAY?
KLNCH KLNCH
I WILL.
READY, SET...
...GO!
RAH

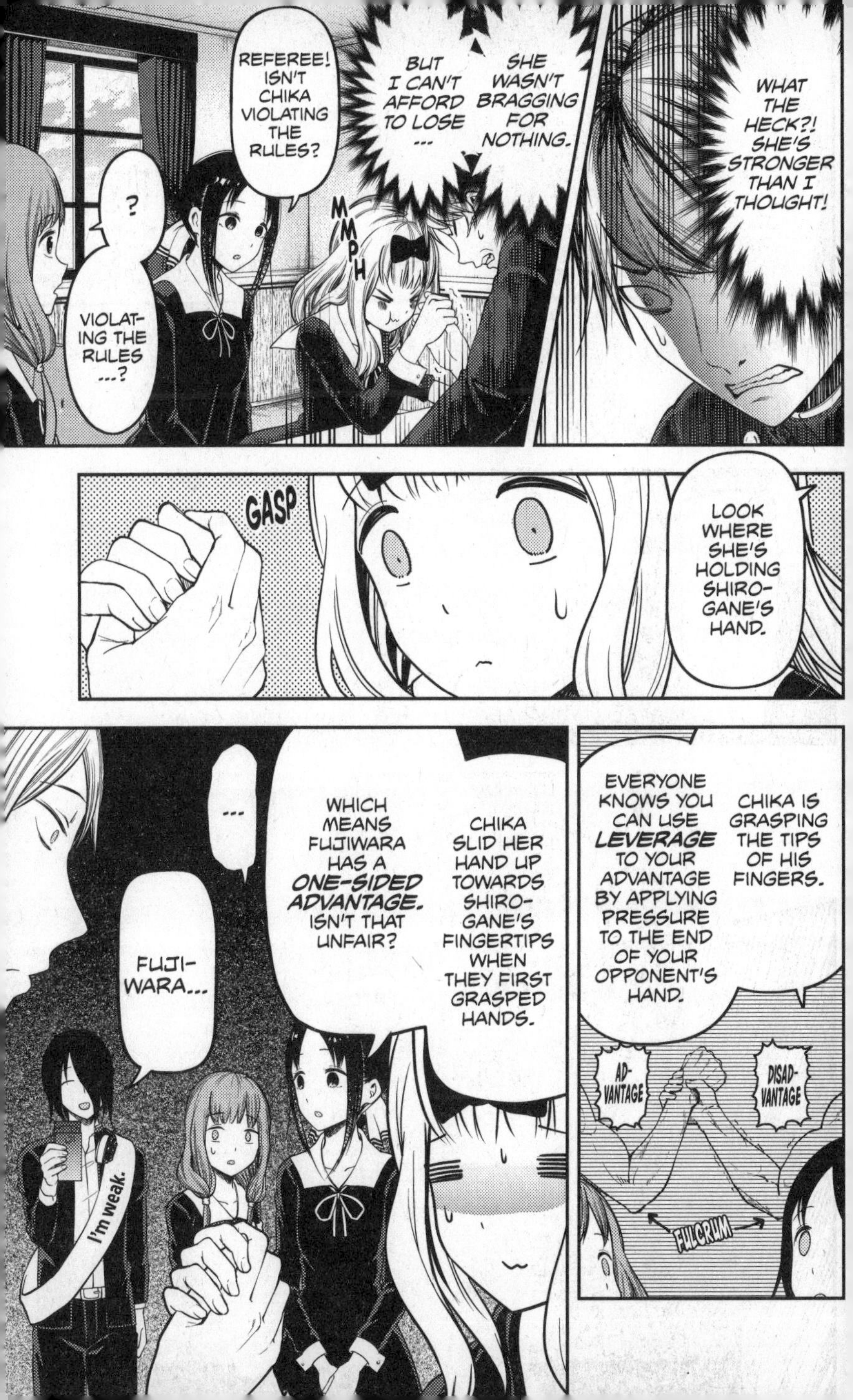
WHAT THE HECK?! SHE'S STRONGER THAN I THOUGHT!
SHE WASN'T BRAGGING FOR NOTHING.
BUT I CAN'T AFFORD TO LOSE ---
MMPH
REFEREE! ISN'T CHIKA VIOLATING THE RULES?
?
VIOLATING THE RULES ...?
LOOK WHERE SHE'S HOLDING SHIROGANE'S HAND.
GASP
CHIKA IS GRASPING THE TIPS OF HIS FINGERS.
EVERYONE KNOWS YOU CAN USE LEVERAGE TO YOUR ADVANTAGE BY APPLYING PRESSURE TO THE END OF YOUR OPPONENT'S HAND.
DISADVANTAGE
ADVANTAGE
FULCRUM
CHIKA SLID HER HAND UP TOWARDS SHIROGANE'S FINGERTIPS WHEN THEY FIRST GRASPED HANDS.
WHICH MEANS FUJIWARA HAS A ONE-SIDED ADVANTAGE. ISN'T THAT UNFAIR?
...
FUJIWARA...
I'm weak.

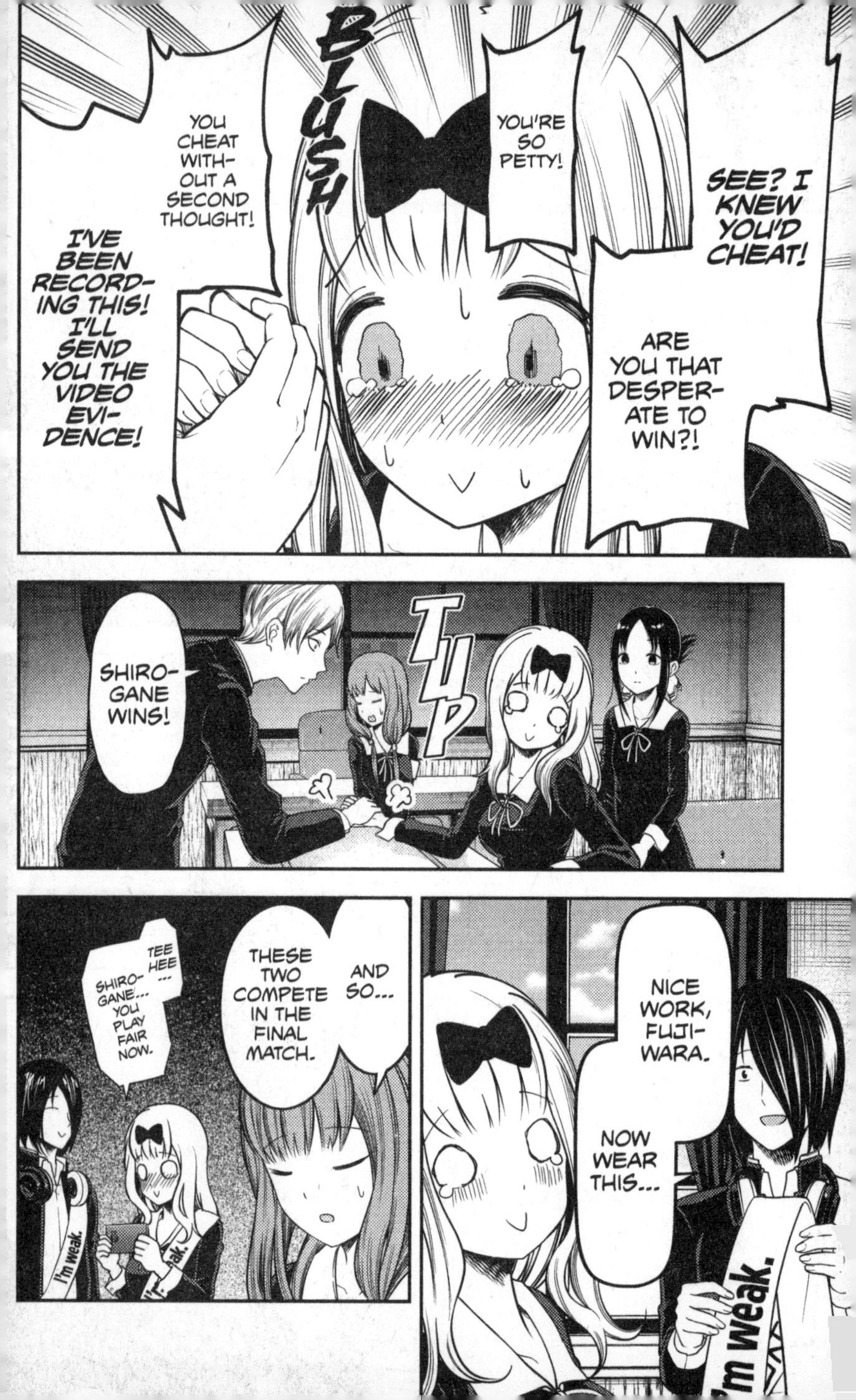
SEE? I KNEW YOU'D CHEAT!
ARE YOU THAT DESPERATE TO WIN?!
YOU'RE SO PETTY!
BLUSH
YOU CHEAT WITHOUT A SECOND THOUGHT!
I'VE BEEN RECORDING THIS! I'LL SEND YOU THE VIDEO EVIDENCE!
THUD
SHIROGANE WINS!
NICE WORK, FUJIWARA.
NOW WEAR THIS...
I'm weak.
AND SO...
THESE TWO COMPETE IN THE FINAL MATCH.
TEE HEE...
SHIROGANE... YOU PLAY FAIR NOW.
I'm weak.

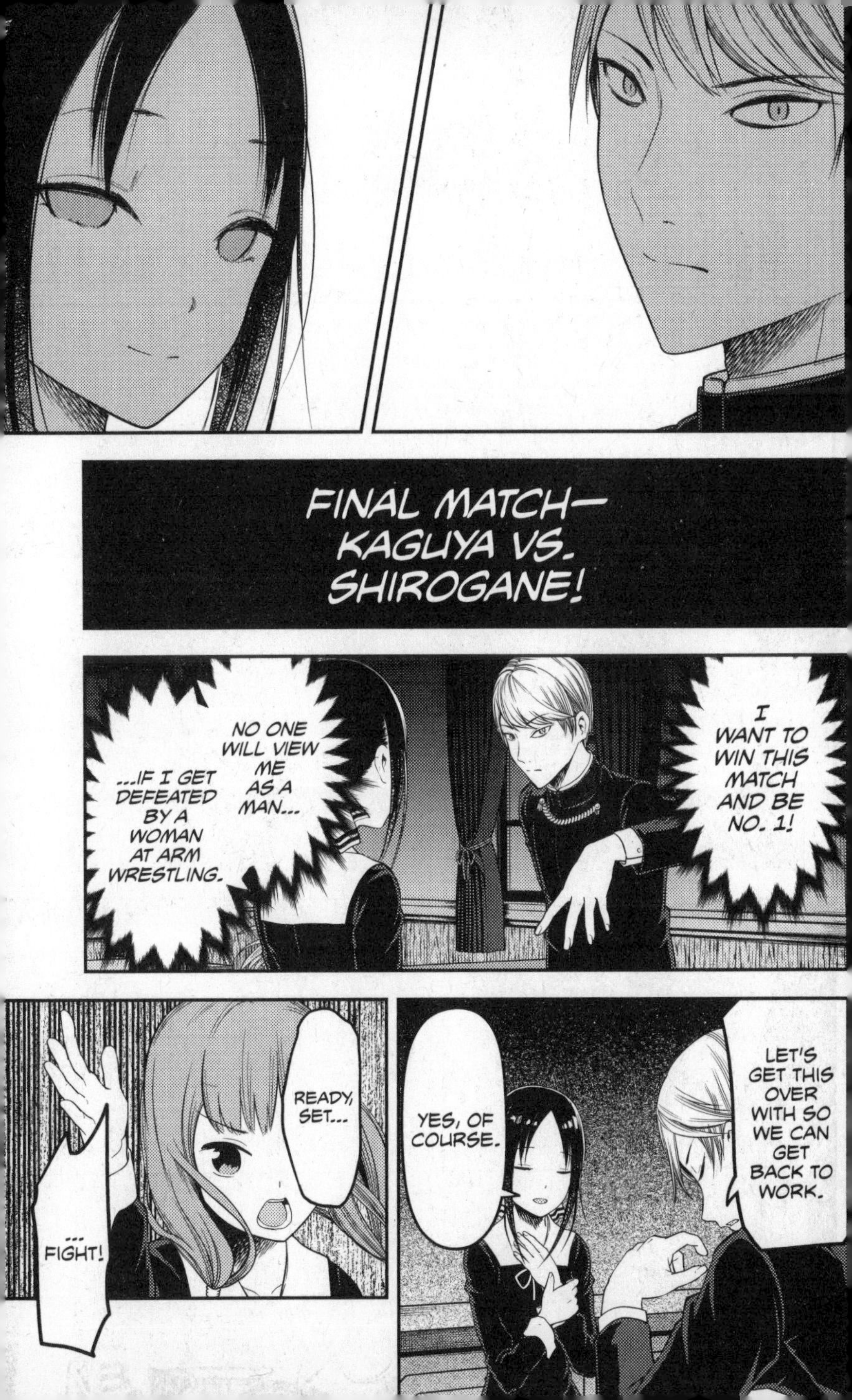
FINAL MATCH— KAGUYA VS. SHIROGANE!
I WANT TO WIN THIS MATCH AND BE NO. 1!
NO ONE WILL VIEW ME AS A MAN...
...IF I GET DEFEATED BY A WOMAN AT ARM WRESTLING.
LET'S GET THIS OVER WITH SO WE CAN GET BACK TO WORK.
YES, OF COURSE.
READY, SET...
...FIGHT!

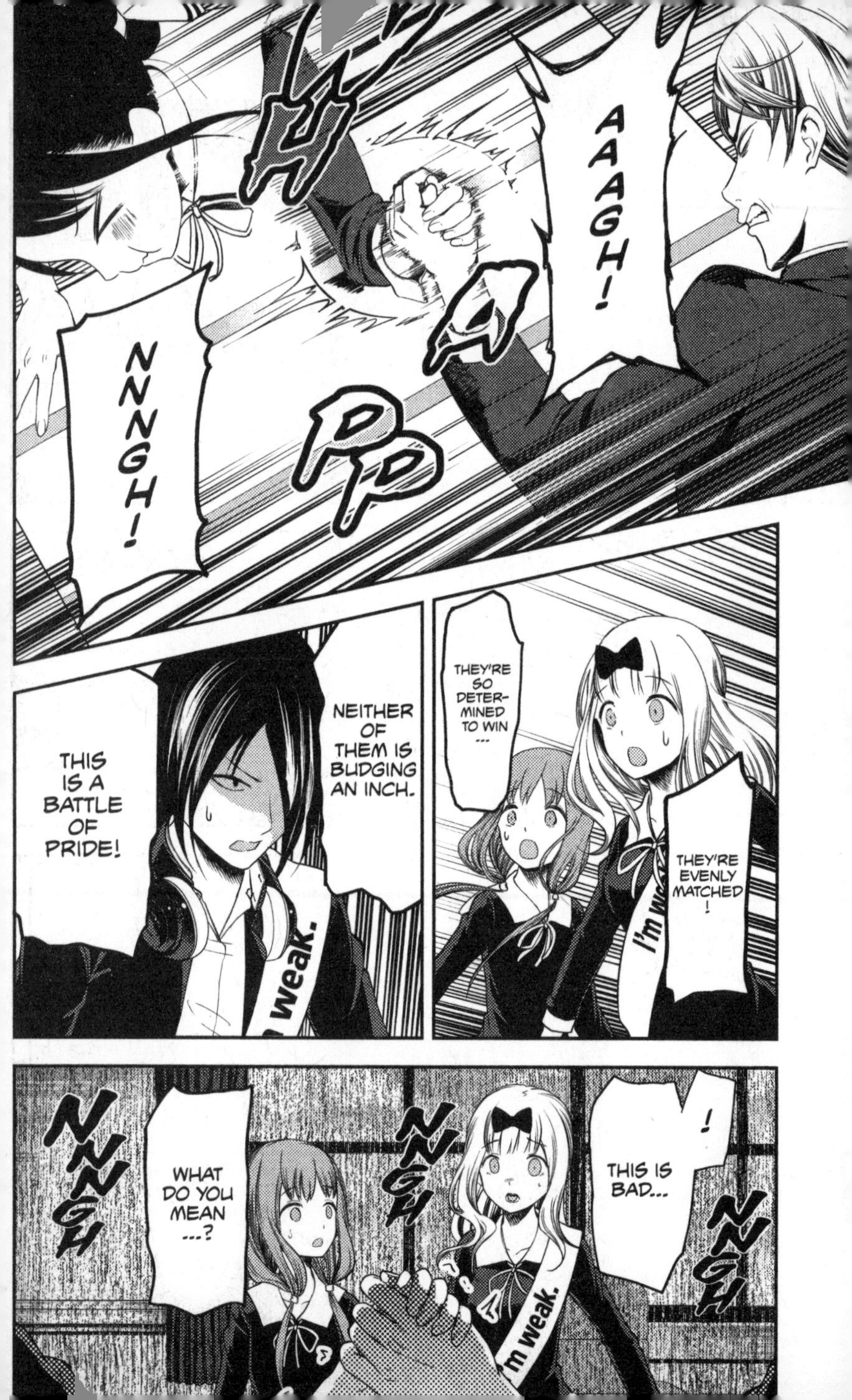
AAAGH!
NNNGH!
THEY'RE SO DETERMINED TO WIN ...
THEY'RE EVENLY MATCHED!
NEITHER OF THEM IS BUDGING AN INCH.
THIS IS A BATTLE OF PRIDE!
!
THIS IS BAD...
NNNGH
NNGH
WHAT DO YOU MEAN ...?
NNNGH

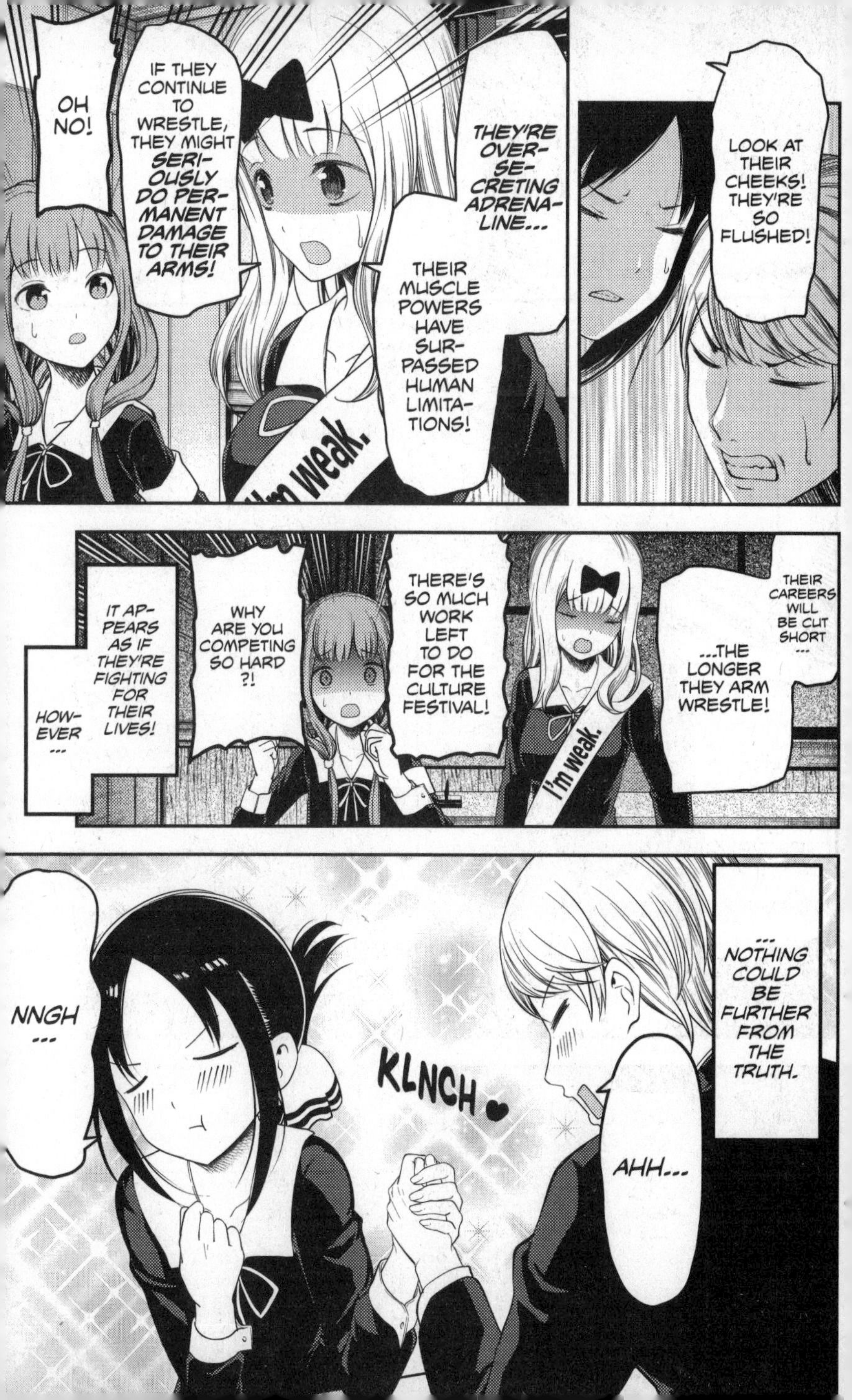
LOOK AT THEIR CHEEKS! THEY'RE SO FLUSHED!
THEY'RE OVER-SECRETING ADRENALINE...
THEIR MUSCLE POWERS HAVE SURPASSED HUMAN LIMITATIONS!
I'm weak.
IF THEY CONTINUE TO WRESTLE, THEY MIGHT SERIOUSLY DO PERMANENT DAMAGE TO THEIR ARMS!
OH NO!
THEIR CAREERS WILL BE CUT SHORT...
...THE LONGER THEY ARM WRESTLE!
I'm weak.
THERE'S SO MUCH WORK LEFT TO DO FOR THE CULTURE FESTIVAL!
WHY ARE YOU COMPETING SO HARD?!
IT APPEARS AS IF THEY'RE FIGHTING FOR THEIR LIVES!
HOWEVER...
...NOTHING COULD BE FURTHER FROM THE TRUTH.
AHH...
KLNCH
NNGH...

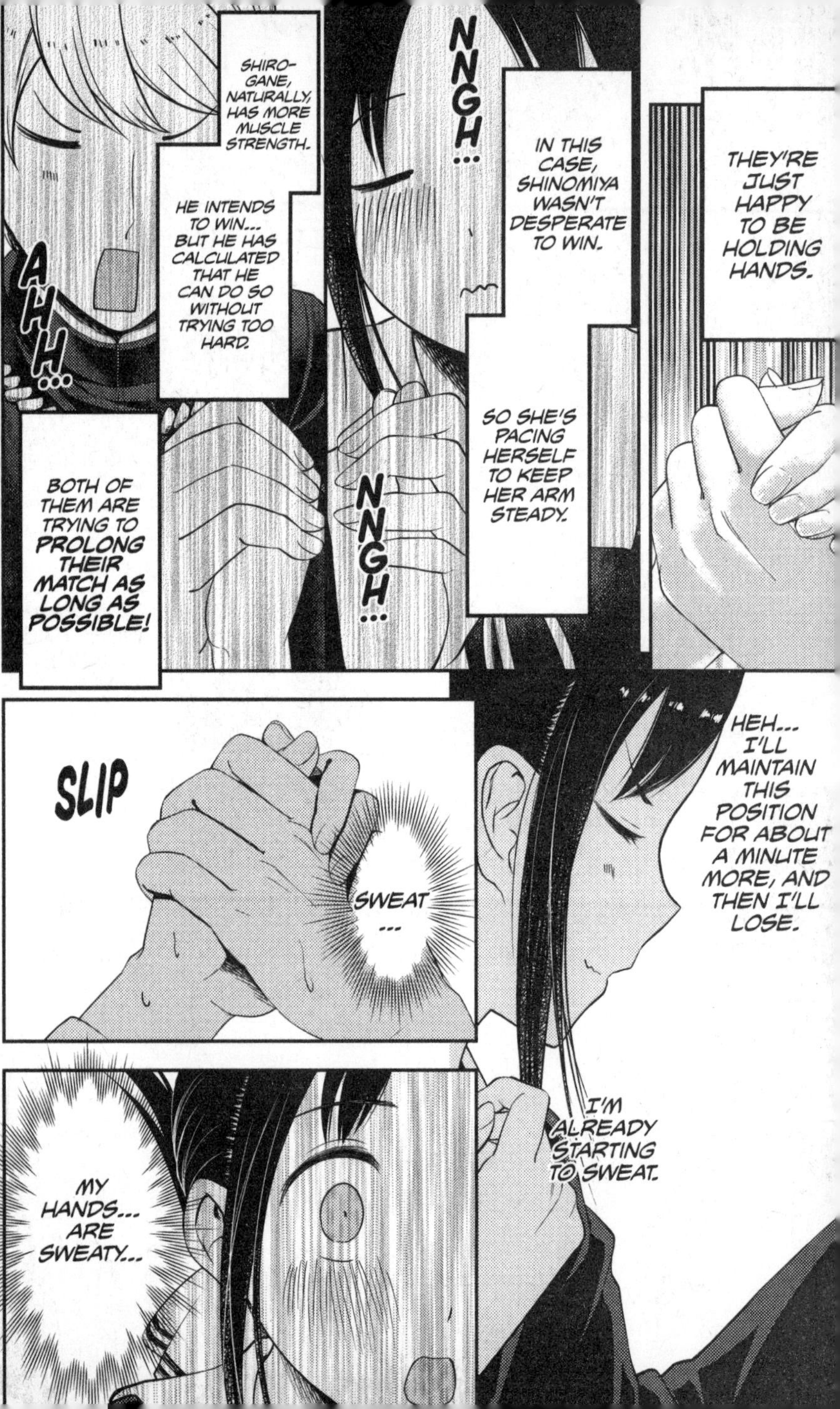
THEY'RE JUST HAPPY TO BE HOLDING HANDS.
NNGH...
IN THIS CASE, SHINOMIYA WASN'T DESPERATE TO WIN.
SO SHE'S PACING HERSELF TO KEEP HER ARM STEADY.
NNGH...
SHIRO-GANE, NATURALLY, HAS MORE MUSCLE STRENGTH.
HE INTENDS TO WIN... BUT HE HAS CALCULATED THAT HE CAN DO SO WITHOUT TRYING TOO HARD.
AHH...
BOTH OF THEM ARE TRYING TO PROLONG THEIR MATCH AS LONG AS POSSIBLE!
HEH... I'LL MAINTAIN THIS POSITION FOR ABOUT A MINUTE MORE, AND THEN I'LL LOSE.
I'M ALREADY STARTING TO SWEAT.
SLIP
SWEAT...
MY HANDS... ARE SWEATY...

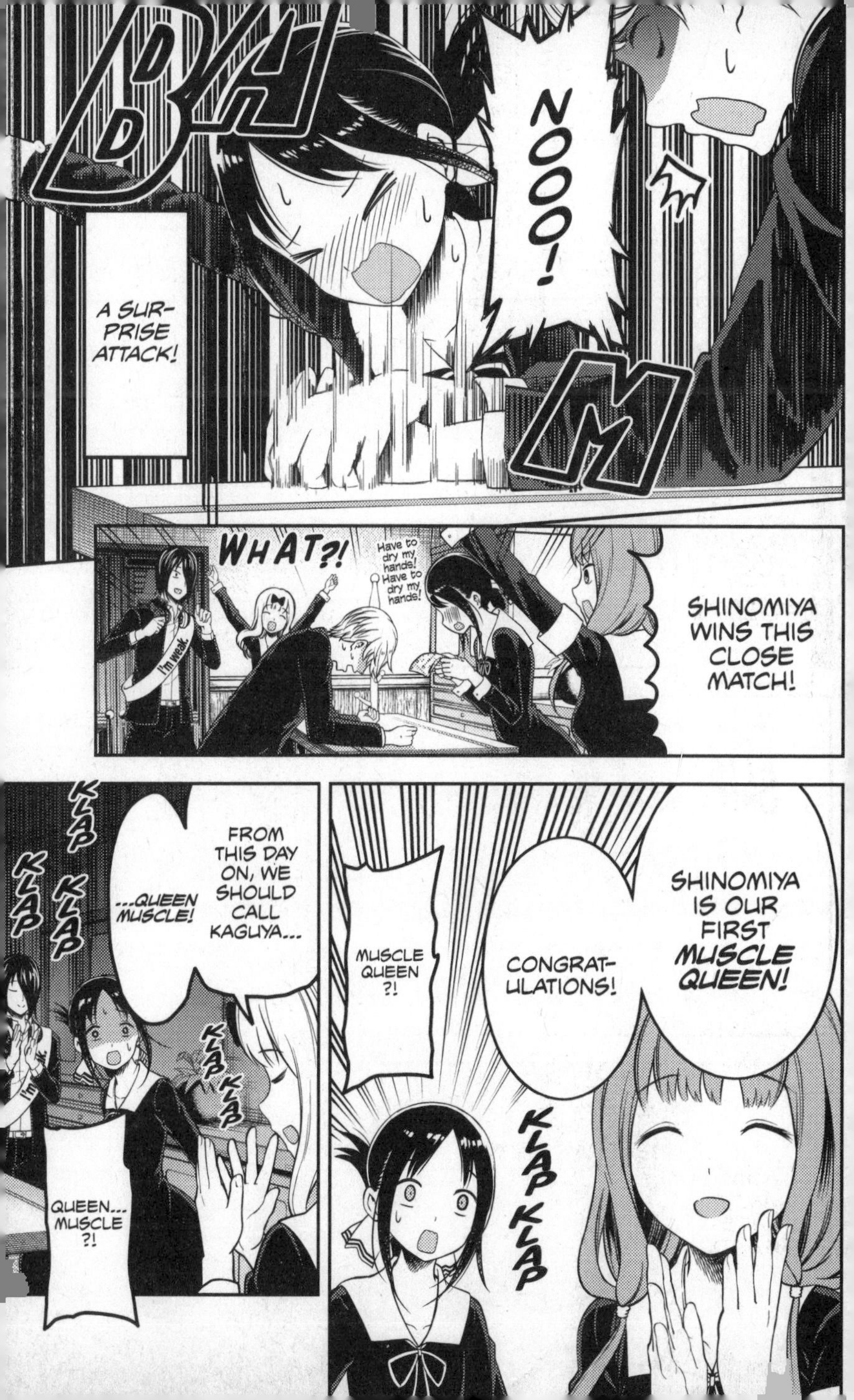

BADDA
NOOOO!
M
A SUR-PRISE ATTACK!
SHINOMIYA WINS THIS CLOSE MATCH!
Have to dry my hands! Have to dry my hands!
WHAT?!
I'm weak.
SHINOMIYA IS OUR FIRST MUSCLE QUEEN!
CONGRAT-ULATIONS!
MUSCLE QUEEN?!
KLAP KLAP
FROM THIS DAY ON, WE SHOULD CALL KAGUYA...
...QUEEN MUSCLE!
KLAP KLAP
KLAP KLAP KLAP
QUEEN... MUSCLE?!

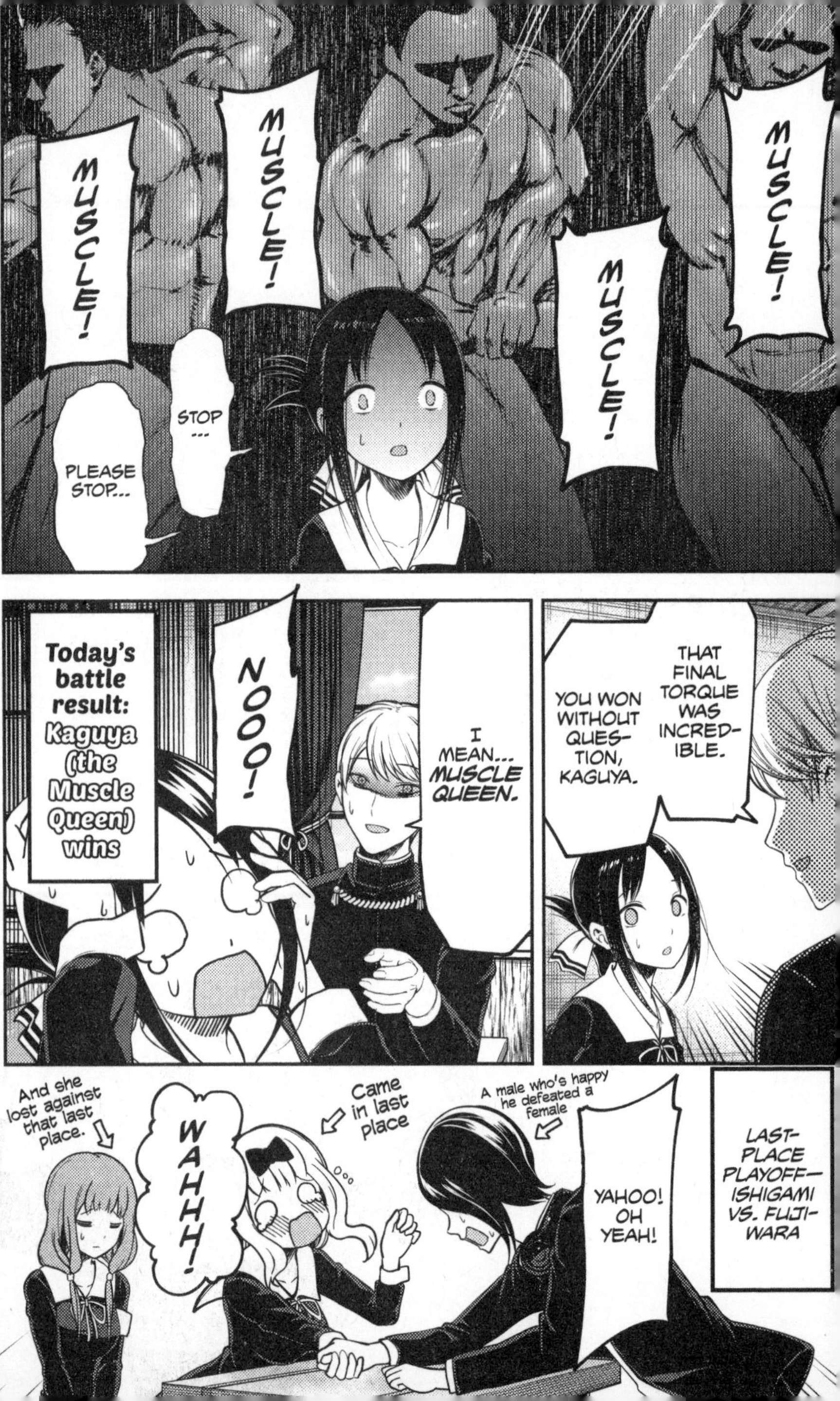
MUSCLE!
MUSCLE!
MUSCLE!
MUSCLE!
STOP...
PLEASE STOP...
THAT FINAL TORQUE WAS INCREDIBLE.
YOU WON WITHOUT QUESTION, KAGUYA.
I MEAN... MUSCLE QUEEN.
NOOO!
Today's battle result: Kaguya (the Muscle Queen) wins
LAST-PLACE PLAYOFF—ISHIGAMI VS. FUJIWARA
YAHOO! OH YEAH!
A male who's happy he defeated a female
Came in last place
WAHHH!
And she lost against that last place.

Student Council
MP
(Muscle Points) List

Men's average	60 MP
Women's average	40 MP
Shirogane	64 MP
Kaguya	62 MP
Ishigami	55 MP
Fujiwara	54 MP
Ino	21 MP

RRGH

KAGUYA-SAMA
LOVE IS WAR

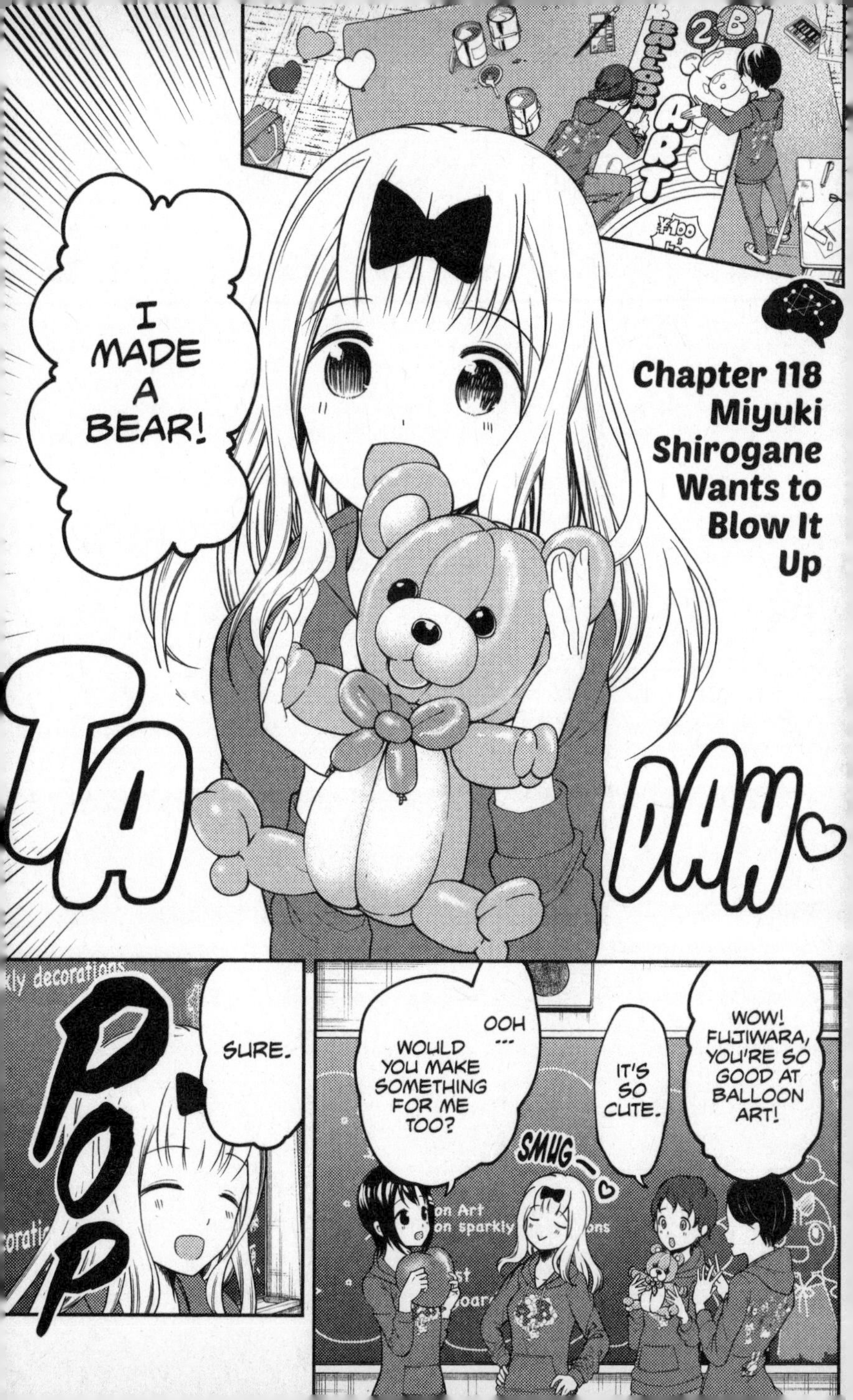
Chapter 118 Miyuki Shirogane Wants to Blow It Up
I MADE A BEAR!
TA DAH♡
WOW! FUJIWARA, YOU'RE SO GOOD AT BALLOON ART!
IT'S SO CUTE.
SMUG♡
OOH...
WOULD YOU MAKE SOMETHING FOR ME TOO?
SURE.
POP

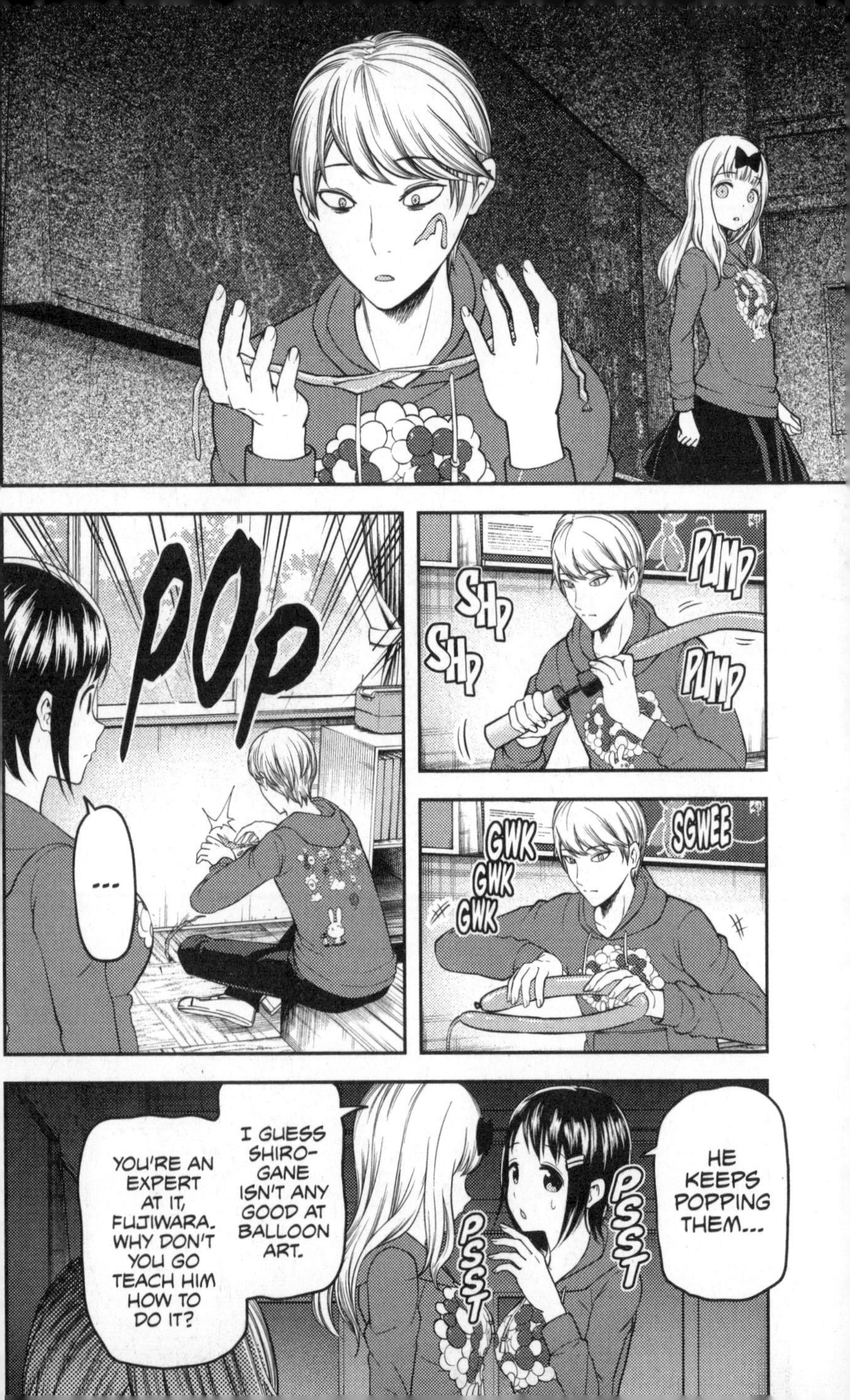
PUMP
PUMP
SHP
SHP
SGWEE
GWK
GWK
GWK
POP
...
HE KEEPS POPPING THEM...
PSST
PSST
I GUESS SHIRO-GANE ISN'T ANY GOOD AT BALLOON ART.
YOU'RE AN EXPERT AT IT, FUJIWARA. WHY DON'T YOU GO TEACH HIM HOW TO DO IT?

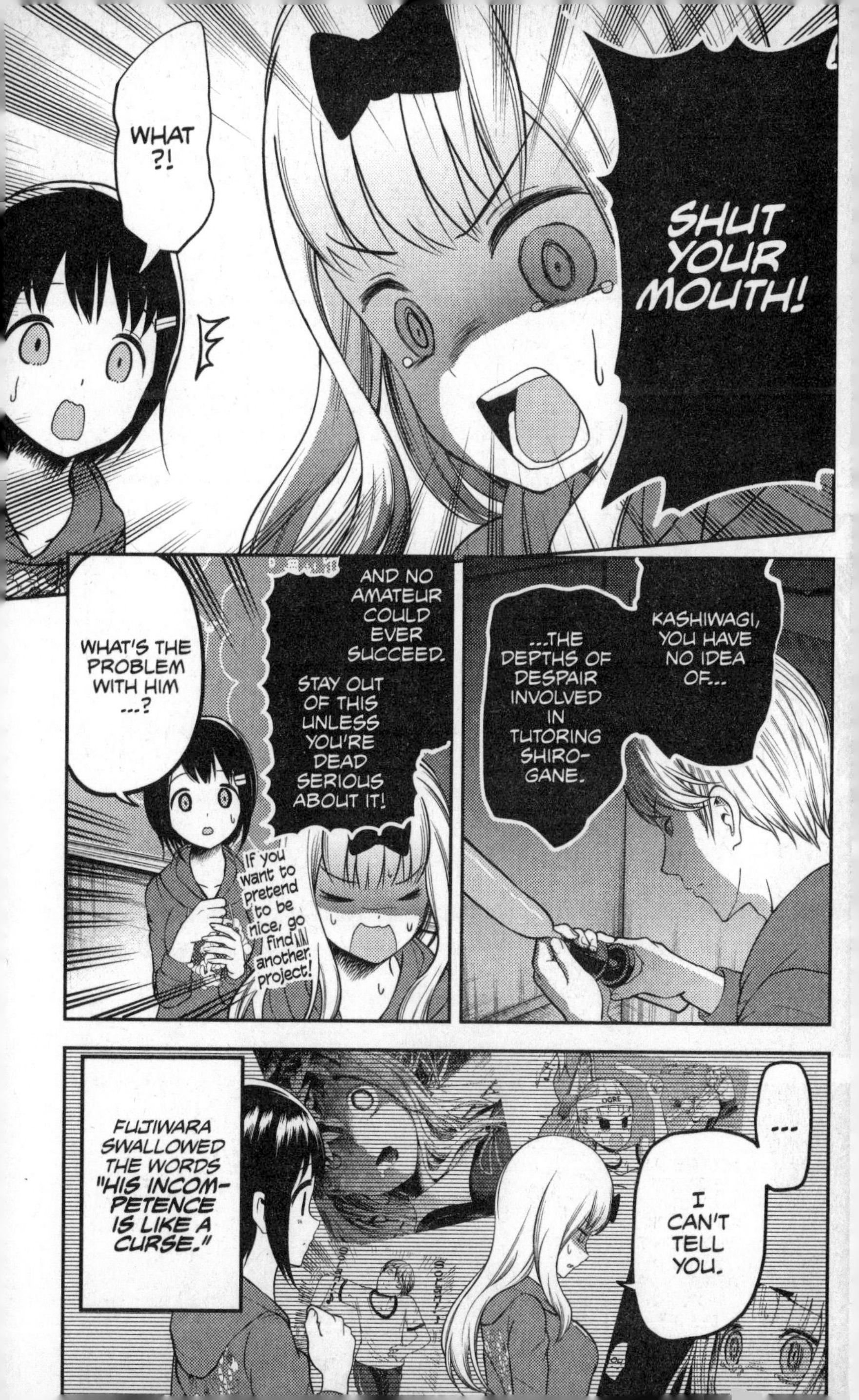
SHUT YOUR MOUTH!
WHAT?!
KASHIWAGI, YOU HAVE NO IDEA OF...
...THE DEPTHS OF DESPAIR INVOLVED IN TUTORING SHIROGANE.
AND NO AMATEUR COULD EVER SUCCEED.
STAY OUT OF THIS UNLESS YOU'RE DEAD SERIOUS ABOUT IT!
If you want to pretend to be nice, go find another project!
WHAT'S THE PROBLEM WITH HIM...?
... I CAN'T TELL YOU.
FUJIWARA SWALLOWED THE WORDS "HIS INCOMPETENCE IS LIKE A CURSE."

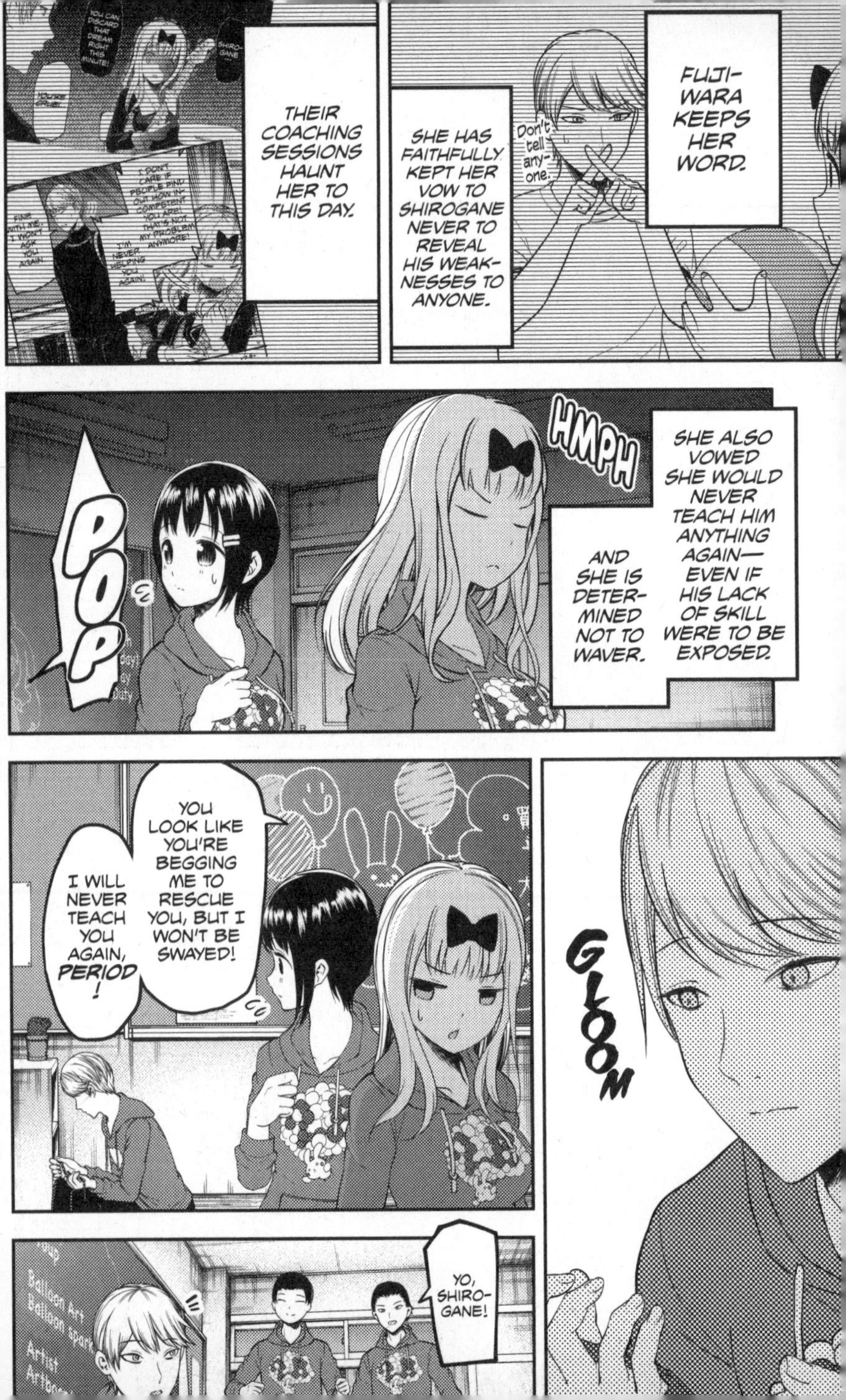

FUJIWARA KEEPS HER WORD.
Don't tell anyone.
SHE HAS FAITHFULLY KEPT HER VOW TO SHIROGANE NEVER TO REVEAL HIS WEAKNESSES TO ANYONE.
THEIR COACHING SESSIONS HAUNT HER TO THIS DAY.
SHIROGANE...
YOU CAN DISCARD THAT DREAM RIGHT THIS MINUTE!
YOU'RE CRUEL.
I DON'T CARE IF PEOPLE FIND OUT HOW INCOMPETENT YOU ARE! THAT'S NOT MY PROBLEM ANYMORE!
I'M NEVER HELPING YOU AGAIN!
FINE WITH ME. I WON'T ASK YOU AGAIN.
SHE ALSO VOWED SHE WOULD NEVER TEACH HIM ANYTHING AGAIN—EVEN IF HIS LACK OF SKILL WERE TO BE EXPOSED.
AND SHE IS DETERMINED NOT TO WAVER.
HMPH
POP
GLOOM
YOU LOOK LIKE YOU'RE BEGGING ME TO RESCUE YOU, BUT I WON'T BE SWAYED!
I WILL NEVER TEACH YOU AGAIN, PERIOD!
YO, SHIROGANE!

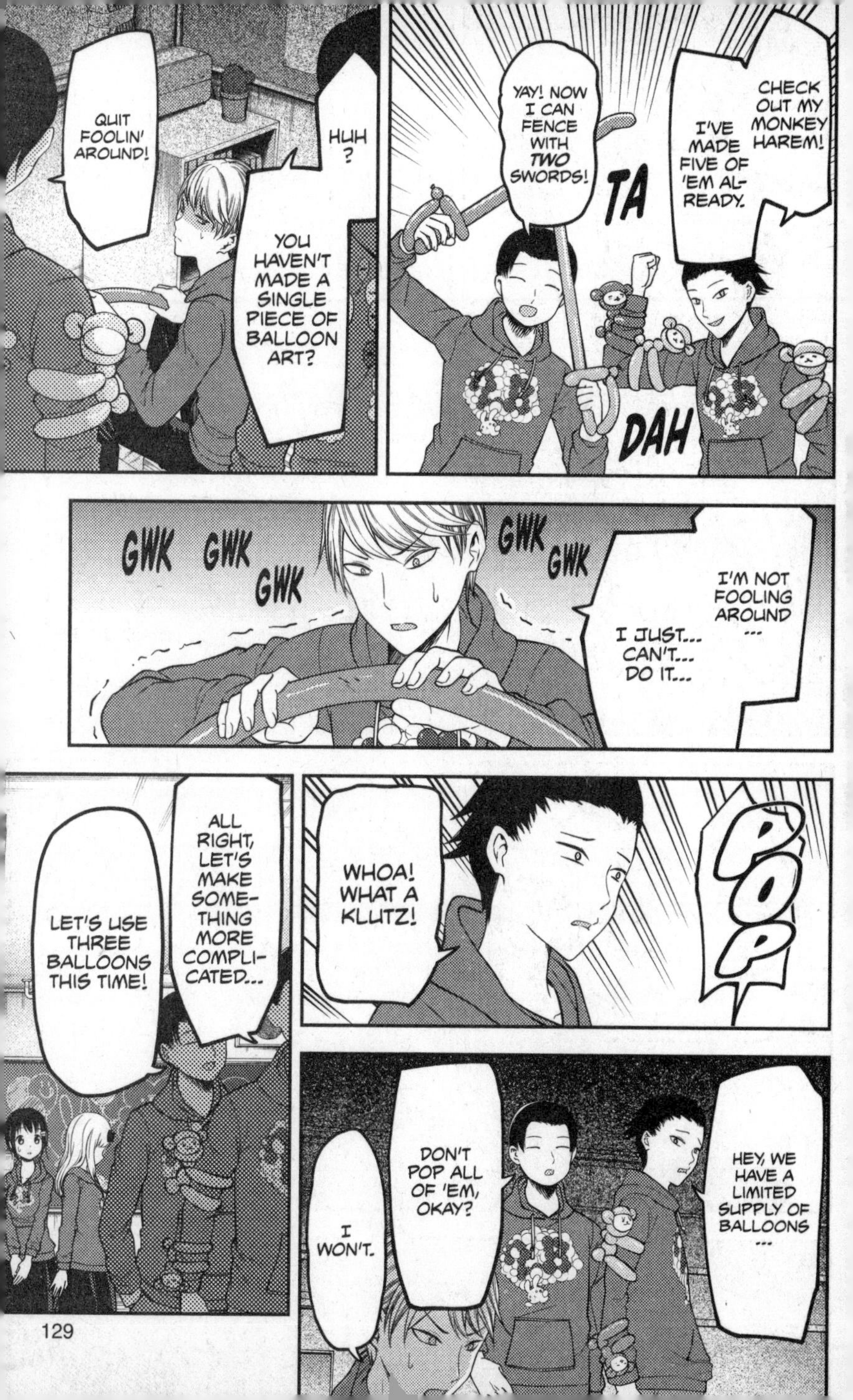
CHECK OUT MY MONKEY HAREM!
I'VE MADE FIVE OF 'EM AL-READY.
YAY! NOW I CAN FENCE WITH TWO SWORDS!
TA
DAH
HUH?
YOU HAVEN'T MADE A SINGLE PIECE OF BALLOON ART?
QUIT FOOLIN' AROUND!
GWK GWK
GWK
GWK GWK
I'M NOT FOOLING AROUND...
I JUST... CAN'T... DO IT...
POP
WHOA! WHAT A KLUTZ!
HEY, WE HAVE A LIMITED SUPPLY OF BALLOONS...
DON'T POP ALL OF 'EM, OKAY?
I WON'T.
ALL RIGHT, LET'S MAKE SOME-THING MORE COMPLI-CATED...
LET'S USE THREE BALLOONS THIS TIME!

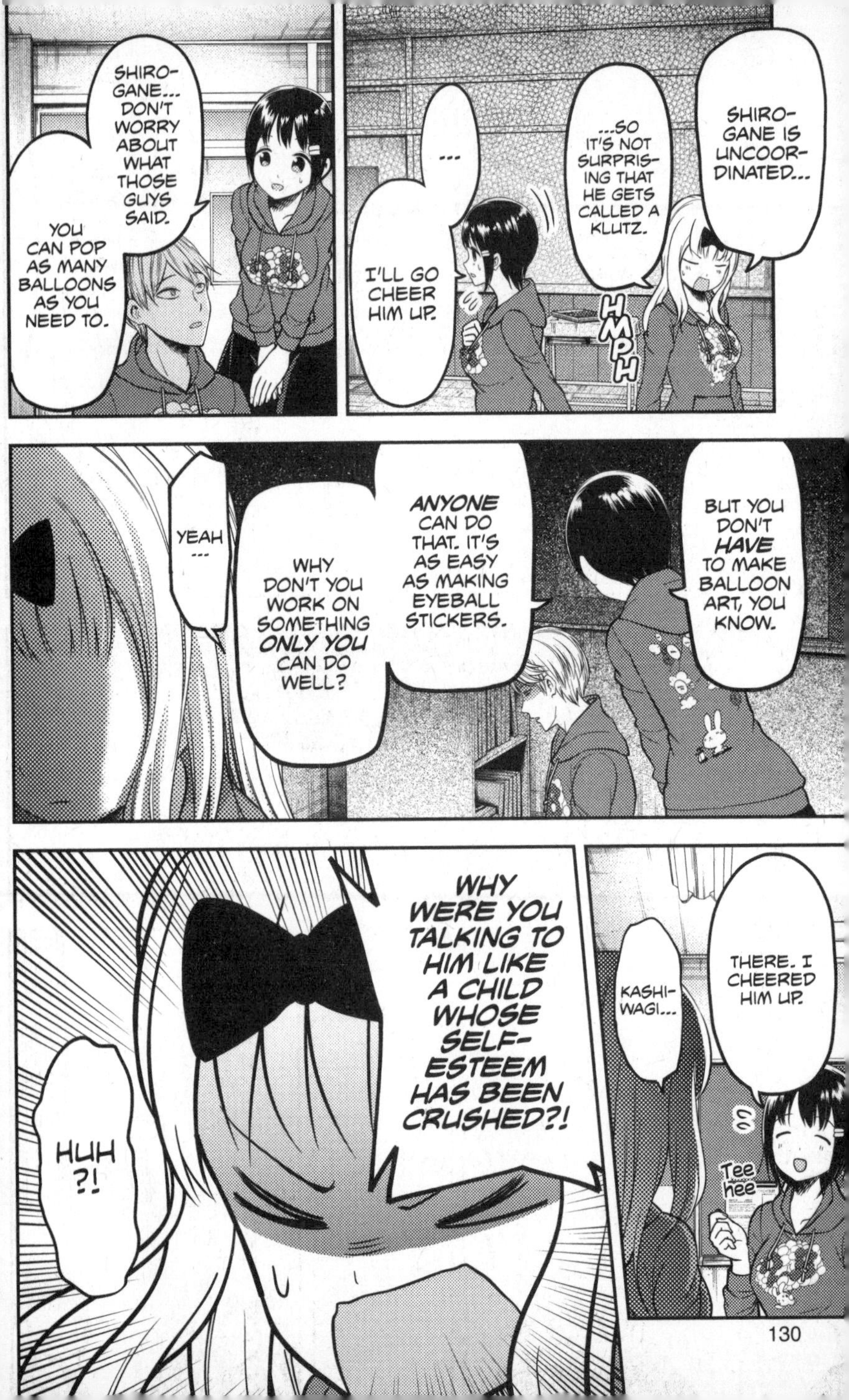
SHIROGANE IS UNCOORDINATED...
...SO IT'S NOT SURPRISING THAT HE GETS CALLED A KLUTZ.
HMPH
...
I'LL GO CHEER HIM UP.
SHIROGANE... DON'T WORRY ABOUT WHAT THOSE GUYS SAID.
YOU CAN POP AS MANY BALLOONS AS YOU NEED TO.
BUT YOU DON'T HAVE TO MAKE BALLOON ART, YOU KNOW.
ANYONE CAN DO THAT. IT'S AS EASY AS MAKING EYEBALL STICKERS.
WHY DON'T YOU WORK ON SOMETHING ONLY YOU CAN DO WELL?
YEAH...
THERE. I CHEERED HIM UP.
Tee hee
KASHIWAGI...
WHY WERE YOU TALKING TO HIM LIKE A CHILD WHOSE SELF-ESTEEM HAS BEEN CRUSHED?!
HUH?!

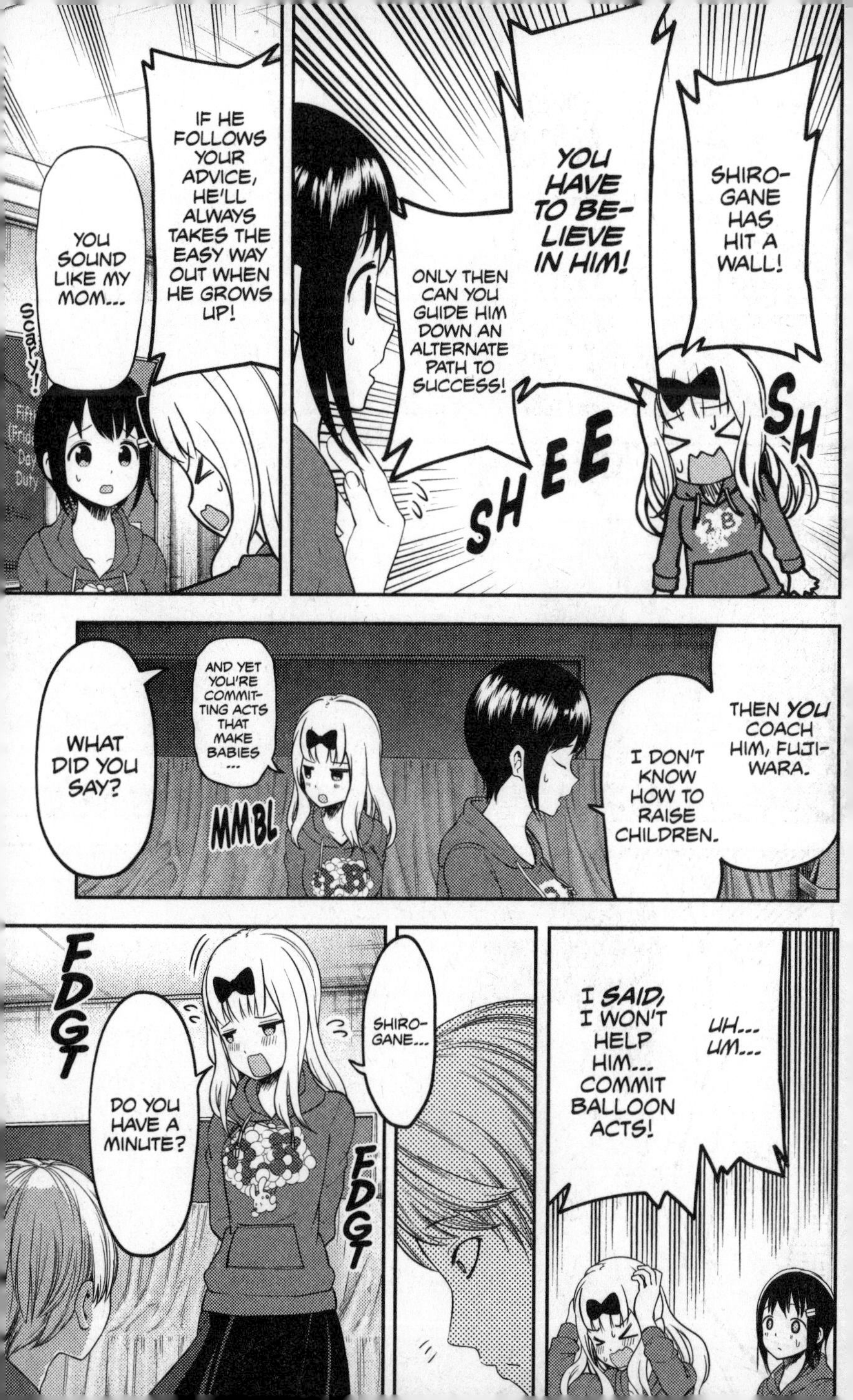

SHIRO-GANE HAS HIT A WALL!
YOU HAVE TO BE-LIEVE IN HIM!
ONLY THEN CAN YOU GUIDE HIM DOWN AN ALTERNATE PATH TO SUCCESS!
SH
SHEE
IF HE FOLLOWS YOUR ADVICE, HE'LL ALWAYS TAKES THE EASY WAY OUT WHEN HE GROWS UP!
YOU SOUND LIKE MY MOM...
Scary!
THEN YOU COACH HIM, FUJI-WARA.
I DON'T KNOW HOW TO RAISE CHILDREN.
AND YET YOU'RE COMMIT-TING ACTS THAT MAKE BABIES...
MMBL
WHAT DID YOU SAY?
UH... UM...
I SAID, I WON'T HELP HIM... COMMIT BALLOON ACTS!
SHIRO-GANE...
FDGT
DO YOU HAVE A MINUTE?
FDGT

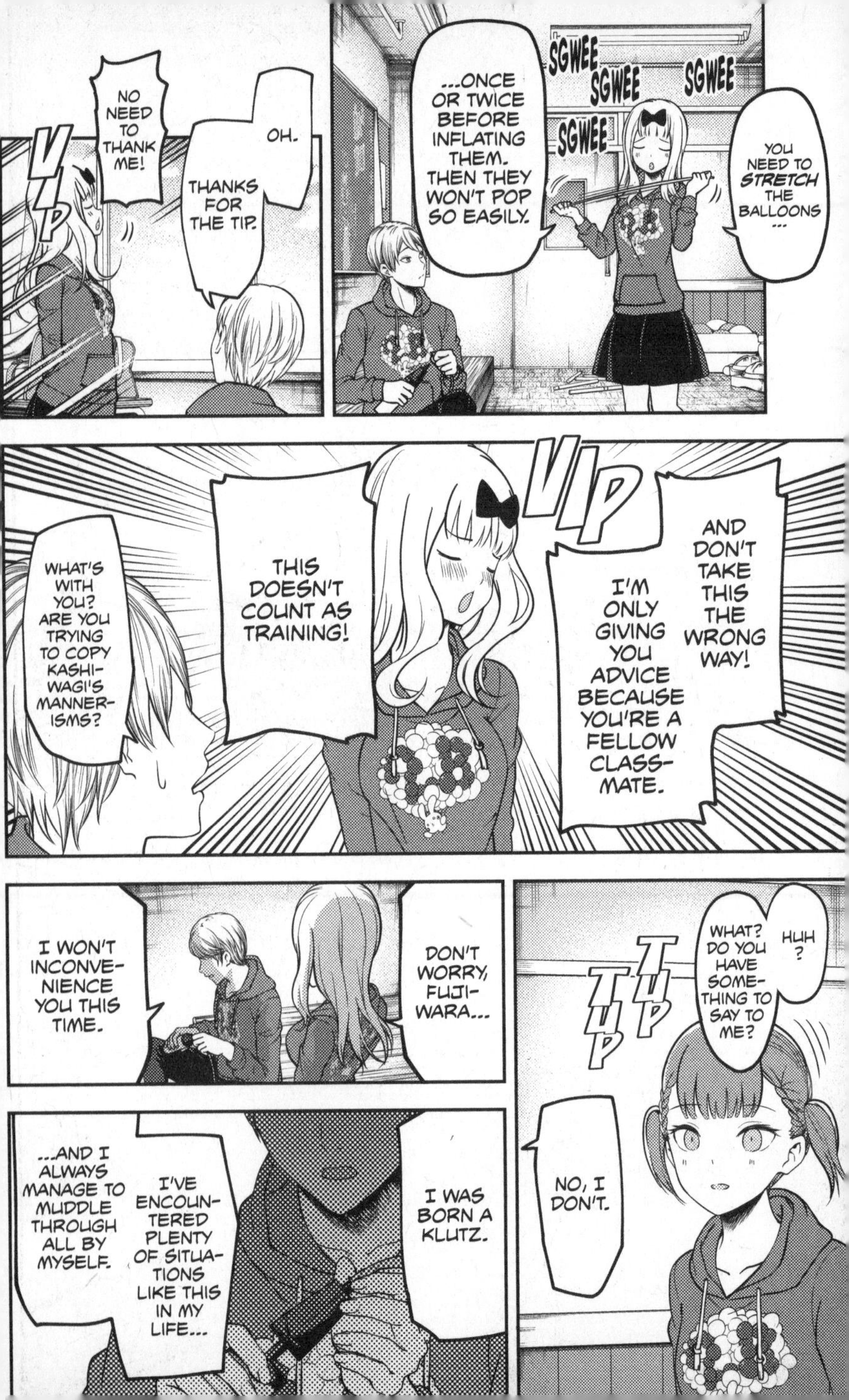
YOU NEED TO STRETCH THE BALLOONS...
SGWEE SGWEE SGWEE SGWEE
...ONCE OR TWICE BEFORE INFLATING THEM. THEN THEY WON'T POP SO EASILY.
OH.
THANKS FOR THE TIP.
NO NEED TO THANK ME!
VIP
VIP
AND DON'T TAKE THIS THE WRONG WAY!
I'M ONLY GIVING YOU ADVICE BECAUSE YOU'RE A FELLOW CLASSMATE.
THIS DOESN'T COUNT AS TRAINING!
WHAT'S WITH YOU? ARE YOU TRYING TO COPY KASHIWAGI'S MANNERISMS?
HUH?
WHAT? DO YOU HAVE SOMETHING TO SAY TO ME?
TUP TUP
NO, I DON'T.
DON'T WORRY, FUJIWARA...
I WON'T INCONVENIENCE YOU THIS TIME.
I WAS BORN A KLUTZ.
I'VE ENCOUNTERED PLENTY OF SITUATIONS LIKE THIS IN MY LIFE...
...AND I ALWAYS MANAGE TO MUDDLE THROUGH ALL BY MYSELF.

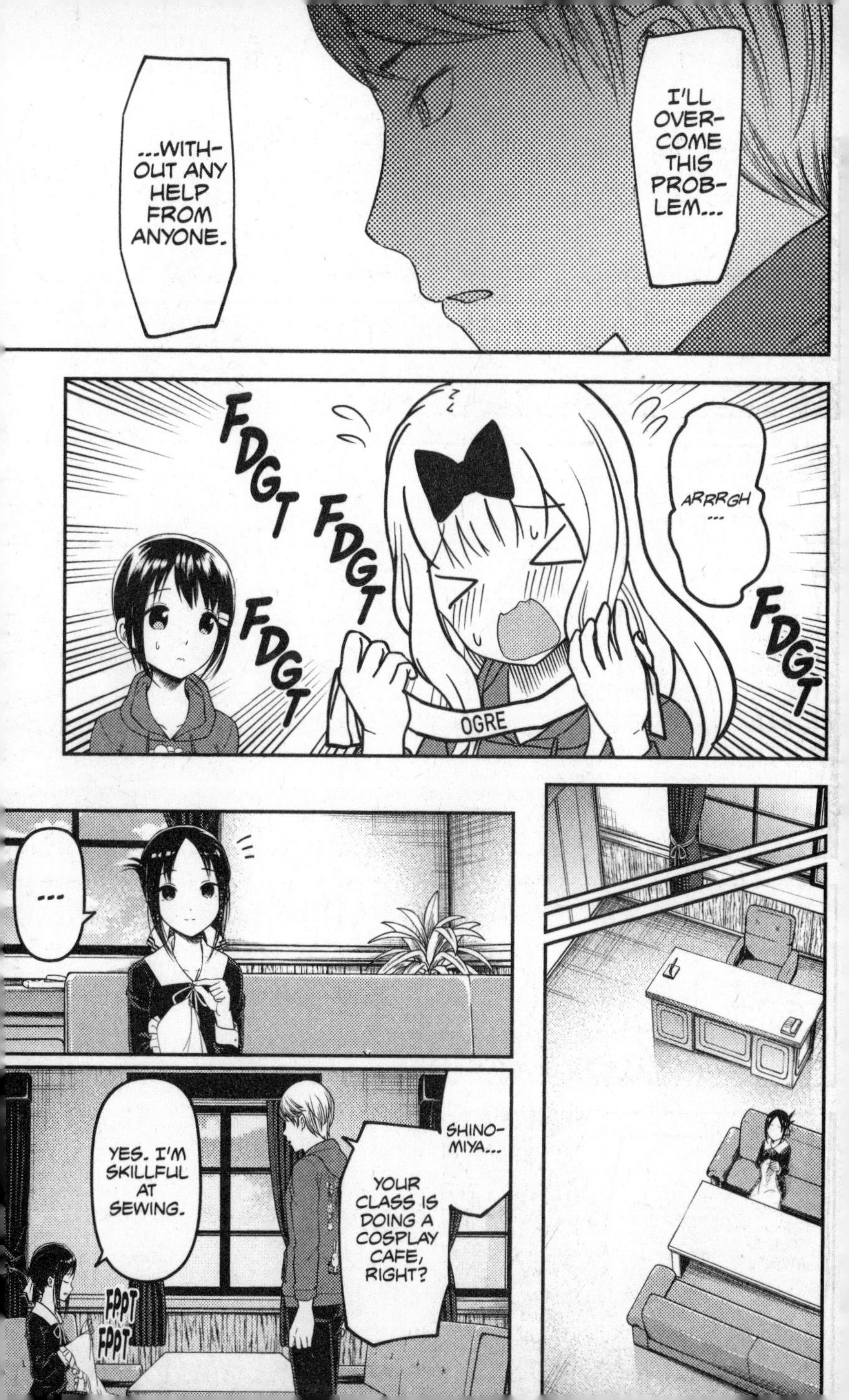
I'LL OVERCOME THIS PROBLEM...
...WITHOUT ANY HELP FROM ANYONE.
ARRRGH...
FDGT
OGRE
FDGT
FDGT
FDGT
...
SHINOMIYA...
YOUR CLASS IS DOING A COSPLAY CAFE, RIGHT?
YES. I'M SKILLFUL AT SEWING.
FPPT FPPT

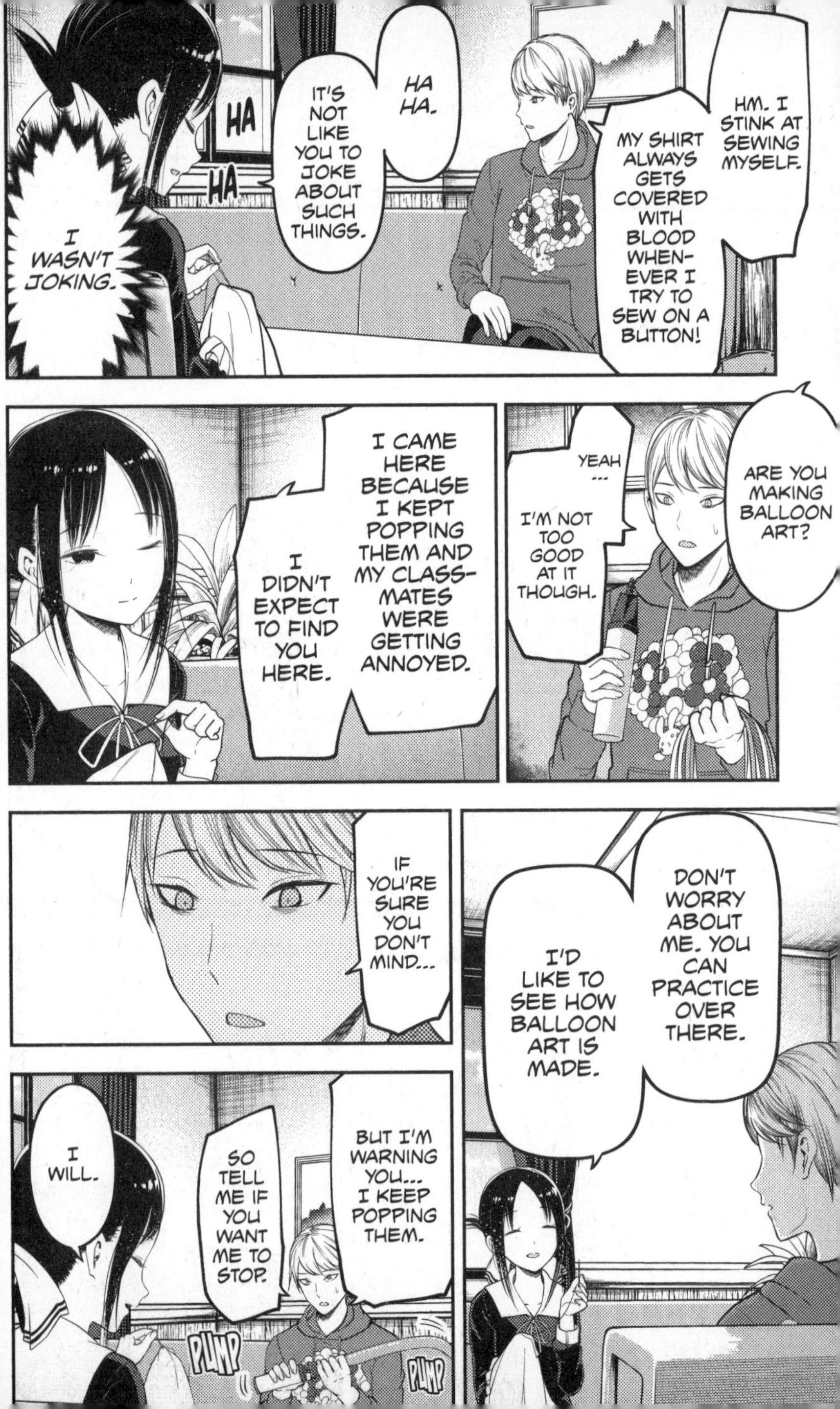
HM. I STINK AT SEWING MYSELF.
MY SHIRT ALWAYS GETS COVERED WITH BLOOD WHENEVER I TRY TO SEW ON A BUTTON!
HA HA.
HA
HA
IT'S NOT LIKE YOU TO JOKE ABOUT SUCH THINGS.
I WASN'T JOKING.
ARE YOU MAKING BALLOON ART?
YEAH...
I'M NOT TOO GOOD AT IT THOUGH.
I CAME HERE BECAUSE I KEPT POPPING THEM AND MY CLASSMATES WERE GETTING ANNOYED.
I DIDN'T EXPECT TO FIND YOU HERE.
DON'T WORRY ABOUT ME. YOU CAN PRACTICE OVER THERE.
I'D LIKE TO SEE HOW BALLOON ART IS MADE.
IF YOU'RE SURE YOU DON'T MIND...
BUT I'M WARNING YOU... I KEEP POPPING THEM.
SO TELL ME IF YOU WANT ME TO STOP.
I WILL.
PUMP
PUMP

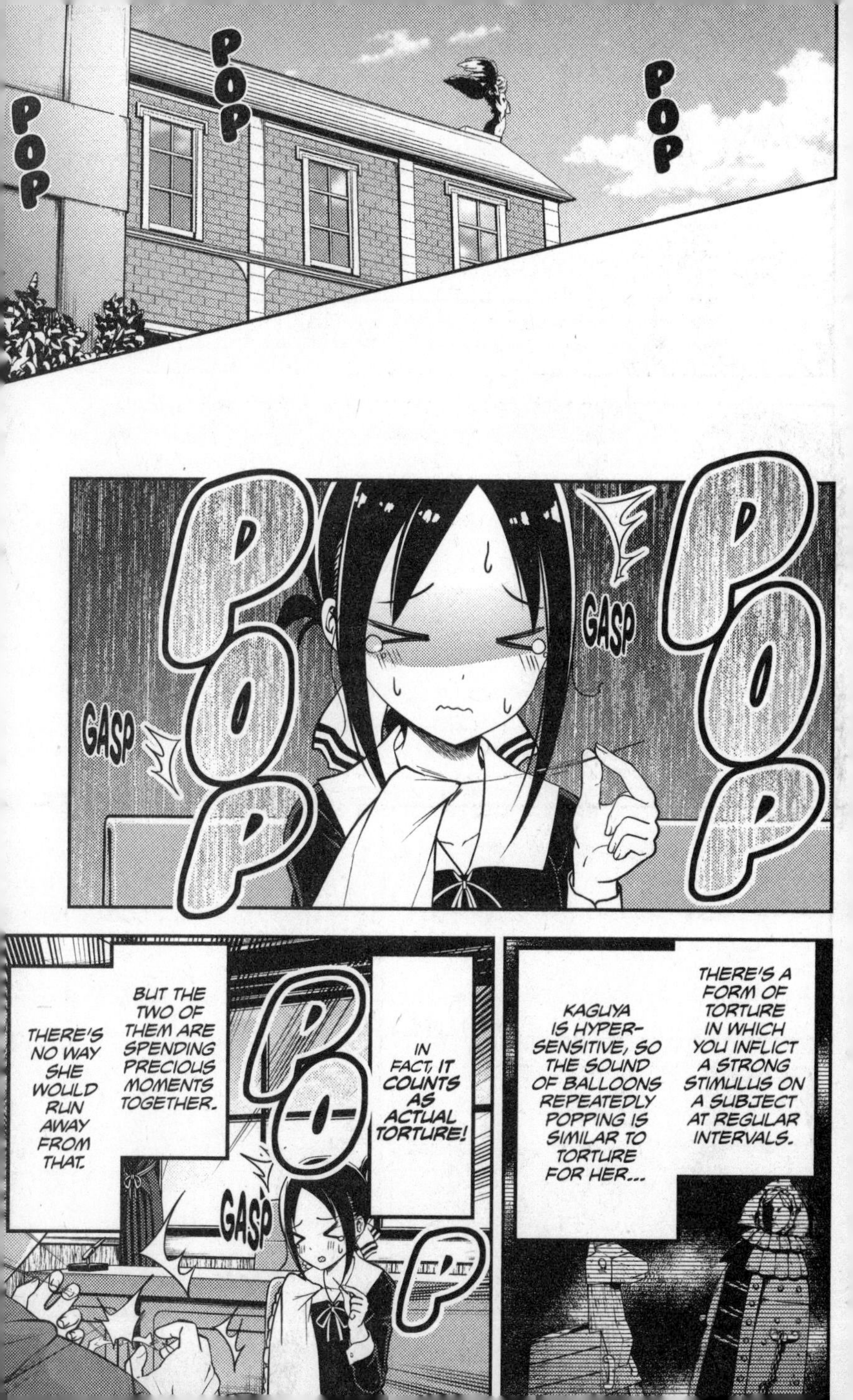
POP POP
POP POP
POP POP
POP POP
GASP
POP POP
GASP
THERE'S A FORM OF TORTURE IN WHICH YOU INFLICT A STRONG STIMULUS ON A SUBJECT AT REGULAR INTERVALS.
KAGUYA IS HYPER-SENSITIVE, SO THE SOUND OF BALLOONS REPEATEDLY POPPING IS SIMILAR TO TORTURE FOR HER...
IN FACT, IT COUNTS AS ACTUAL TORTURE!
POP
POP
GASP
BUT THE TWO OF THEM ARE SPENDING PRECIOUS MOMENTS TOGETHER.
THERE'S NO WAY SHE WOULD RUN AWAY FROM THAT.

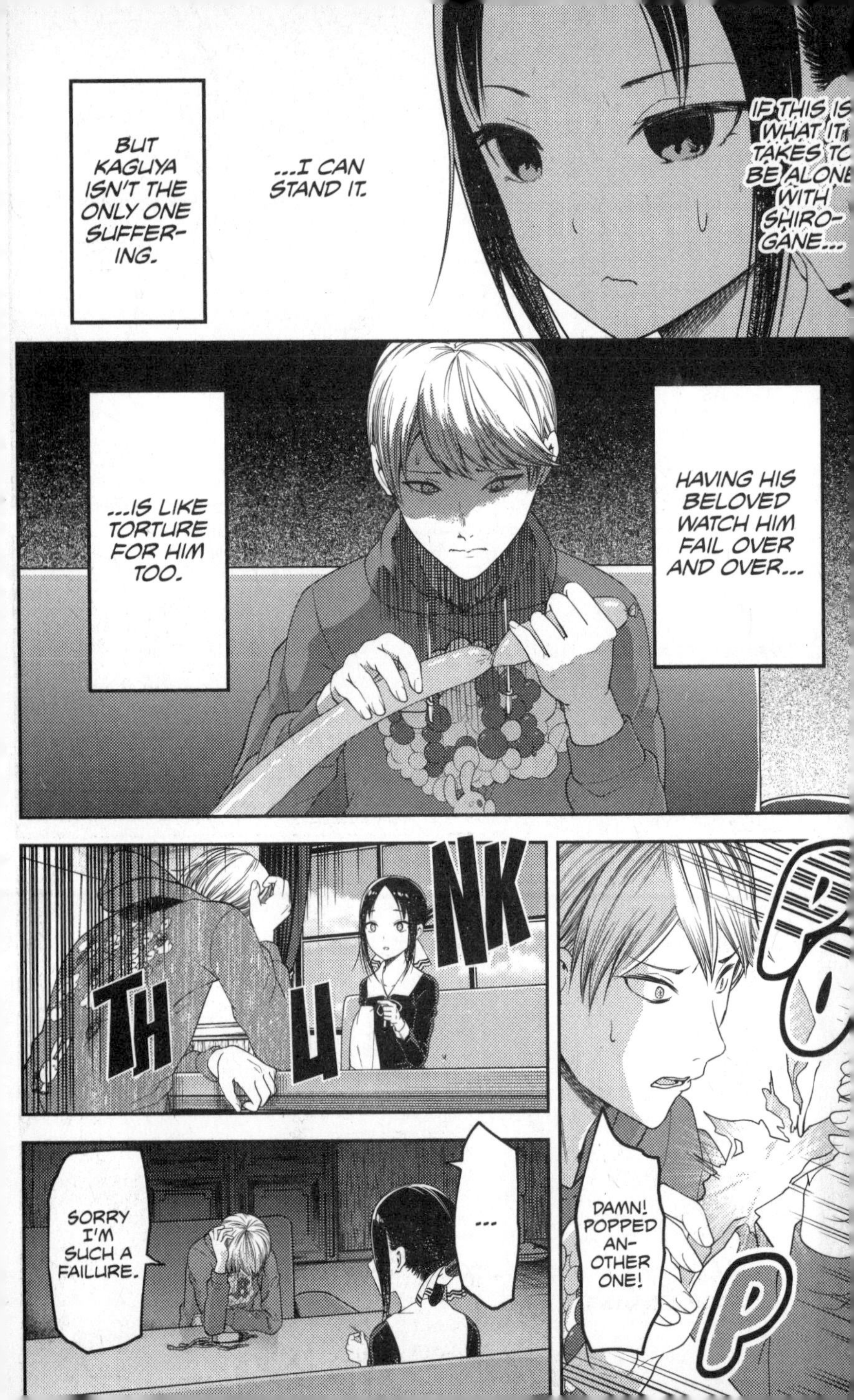

IF THIS IS WHAT IT TAKES TO BE ALONE WITH SHIROGANE...
...I CAN STAND IT.
BUT KAGUYA ISN'T THE ONLY ONE SUFFERING.
HAVING HIS BELOVED WATCH HIM FAIL OVER AND OVER...
...IS LIKE TORTURE FOR HIM TOO.
POP
DAMN! POPPED ANOTHER ONE!
THUNK
...
SORRY I'M SUCH A FAILURE.

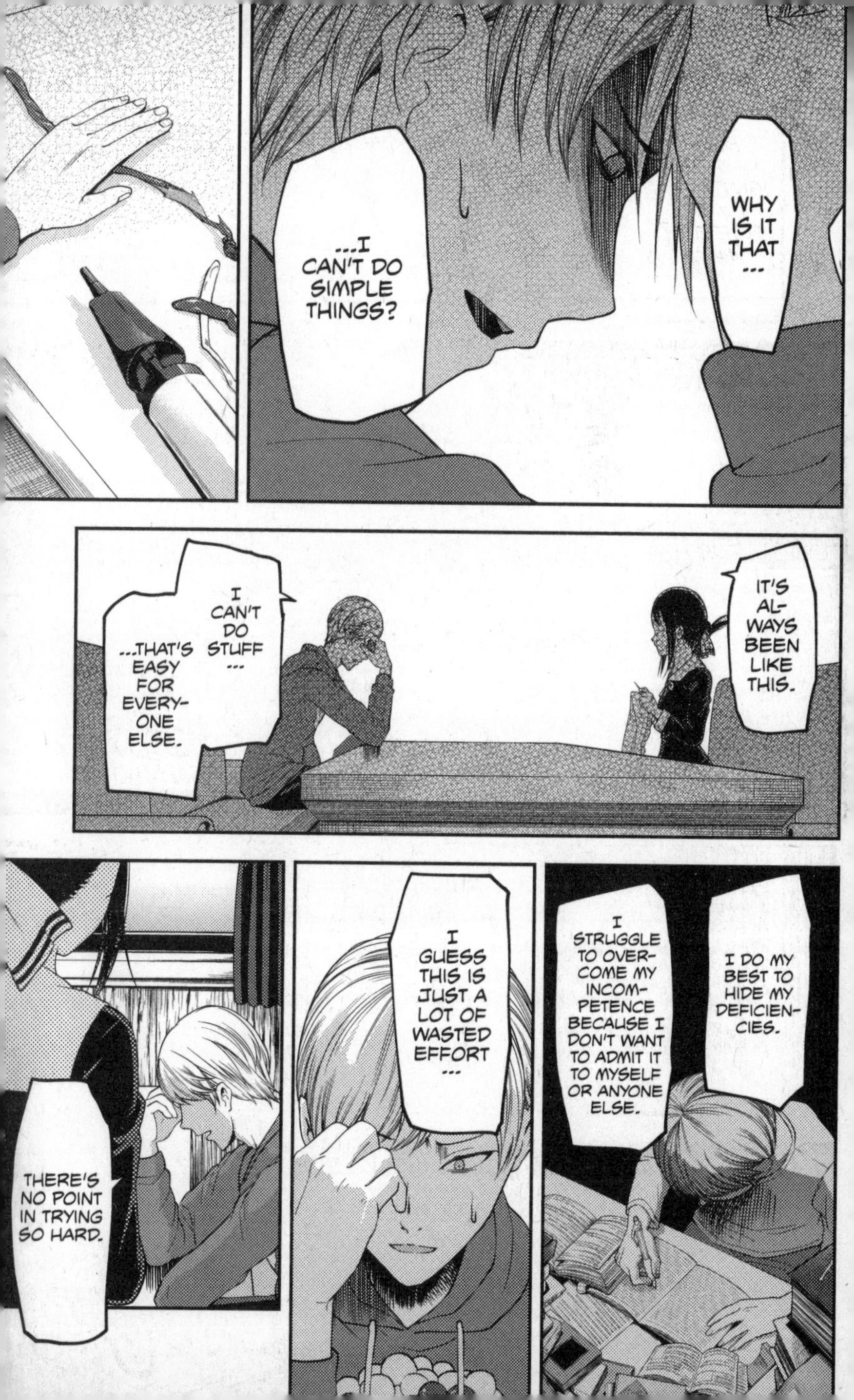

WHY IS IT THAT ...
...I CAN'T DO SIMPLE THINGS?
IT'S AL-WAYS BEEN LIKE THIS.
I CAN'T DO STUFF ...
...THAT'S EASY FOR EVERY-ONE ELSE.
I DO MY BEST TO HIDE MY DEFICIEN-CIES.
I STRUGGLE TO OVER-COME MY INCOM-PETENCE BECAUSE I DON'T WANT TO ADMIT IT TO MYSELF OR ANYONE ELSE.
I GUESS THIS IS JUST A LOT OF WASTED EFFORT ...
THERE'S NO POINT IN TRYING SO HARD.

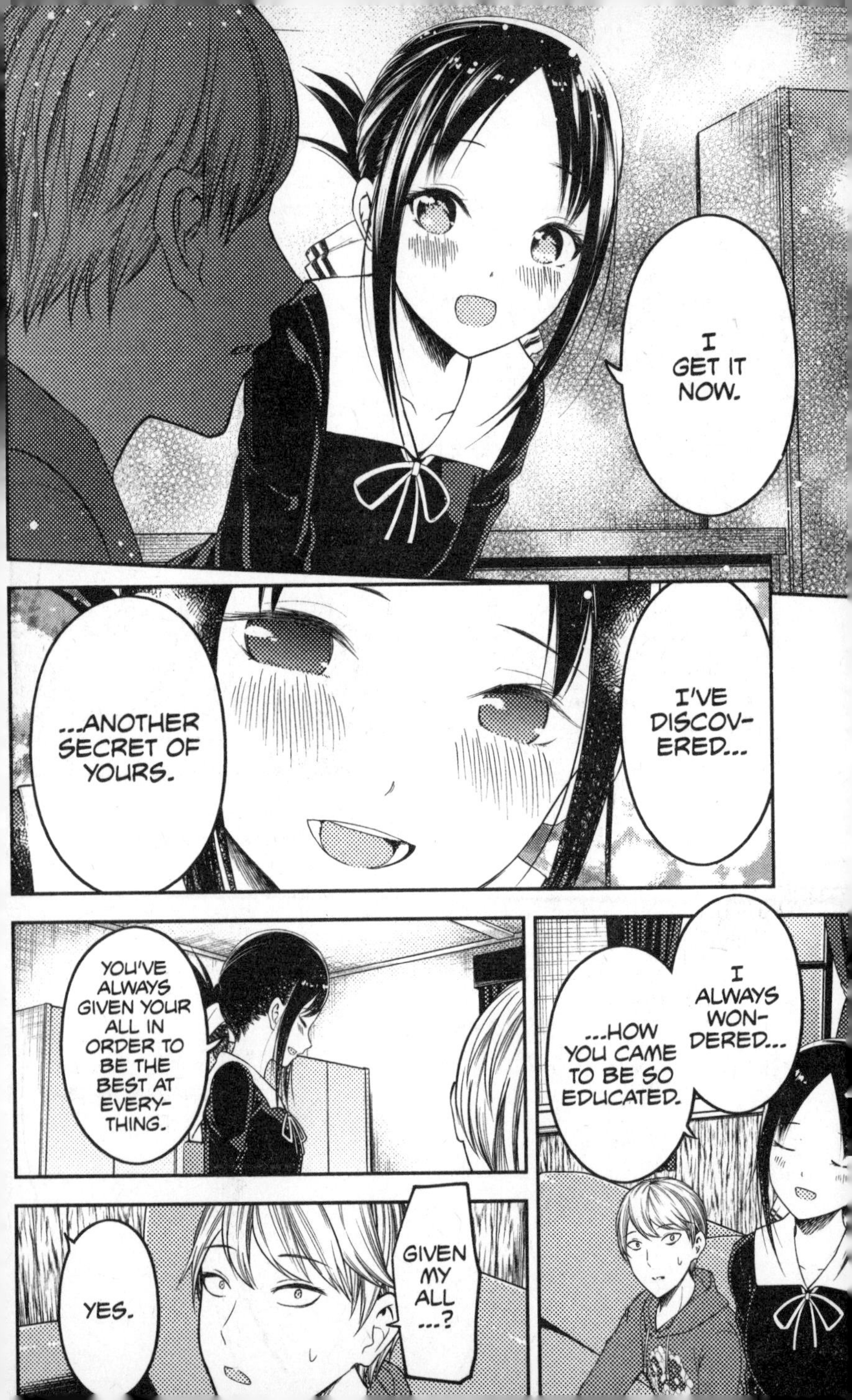
I GET IT NOW.
I'VE DISCOV-ERED...
...ANOTHER SECRET OF YOURS.
I ALWAYS WON-DERED...
...HOW YOU CAME TO BE SO EDUCATED.
YOU'VE ALWAYS GIVEN YOUR ALL IN ORDER TO BE THE BEST AT EVERY-THING.
GIVEN MY ALL...?
YES.

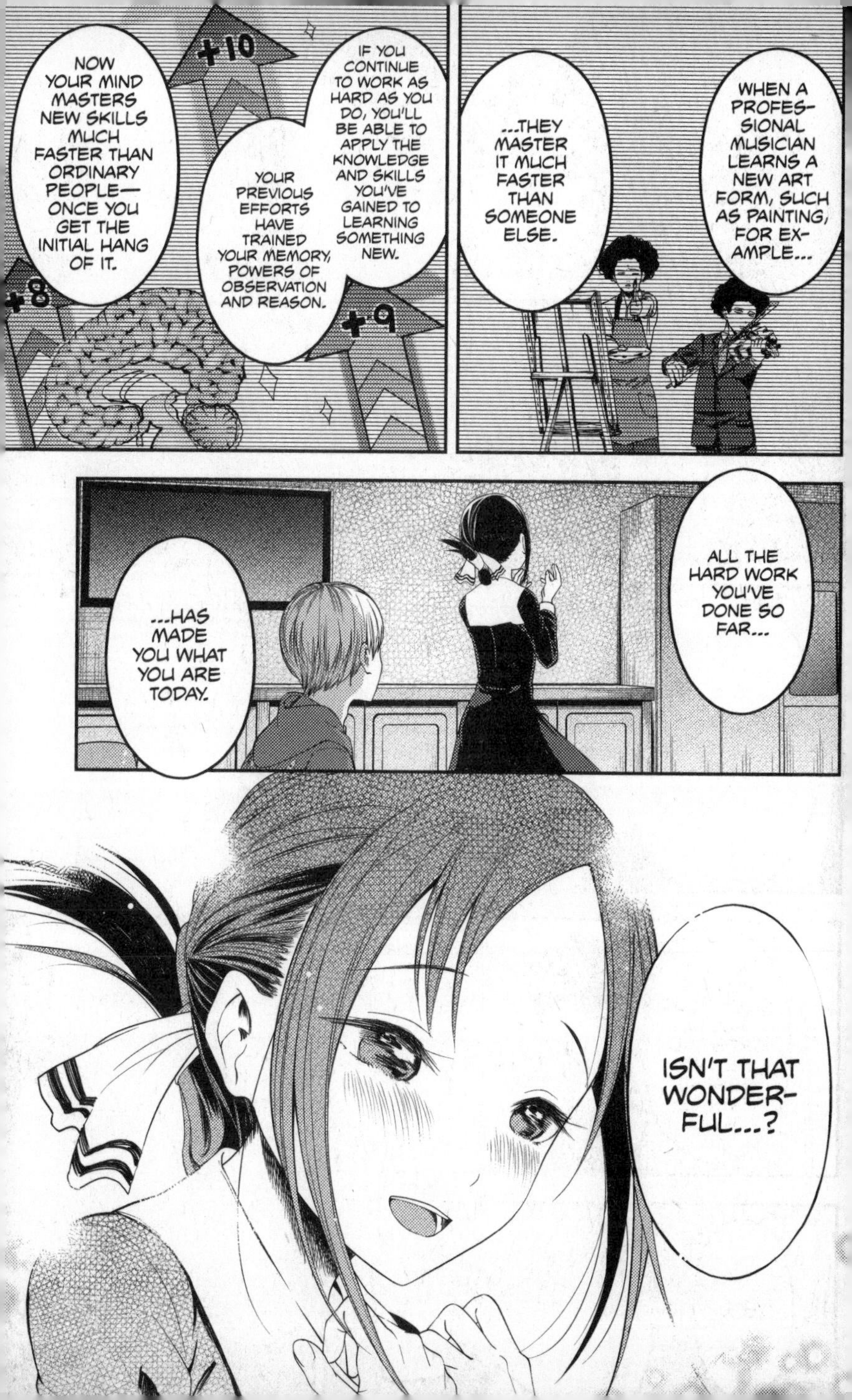
WHEN A PROFES-SIONAL MUSICIAN LEARNS A NEW ART FORM, SUCH AS PAINTING, FOR EX-AMPLE...
...THEY MASTER IT MUCH FASTER THAN SOMEONE ELSE.
+10
IF YOU CONTINUE TO WORK AS HARD AS YOU DO, YOU'LL BE ABLE TO APPLY THE KNOWLEDGE AND SKILLS YOU'VE GAINED TO LEARNING SOMETHING NEW.
YOUR PREVIOUS EFFORTS HAVE TRAINED YOUR MEMORY, POWERS OF OBSERVATION AND REASON.
NOW YOUR MIND MASTERS NEW SKILLS MUCH FASTER THAN ORDINARY PEOPLE—ONCE YOU GET THE INITIAL HANG OF IT.
+9
+8
ALL THE HARD WORK YOU'VE DONE SO FAR...
...HAS MADE YOU WHAT YOU ARE TODAY.
ISN'T THAT WONDER-FUL...?

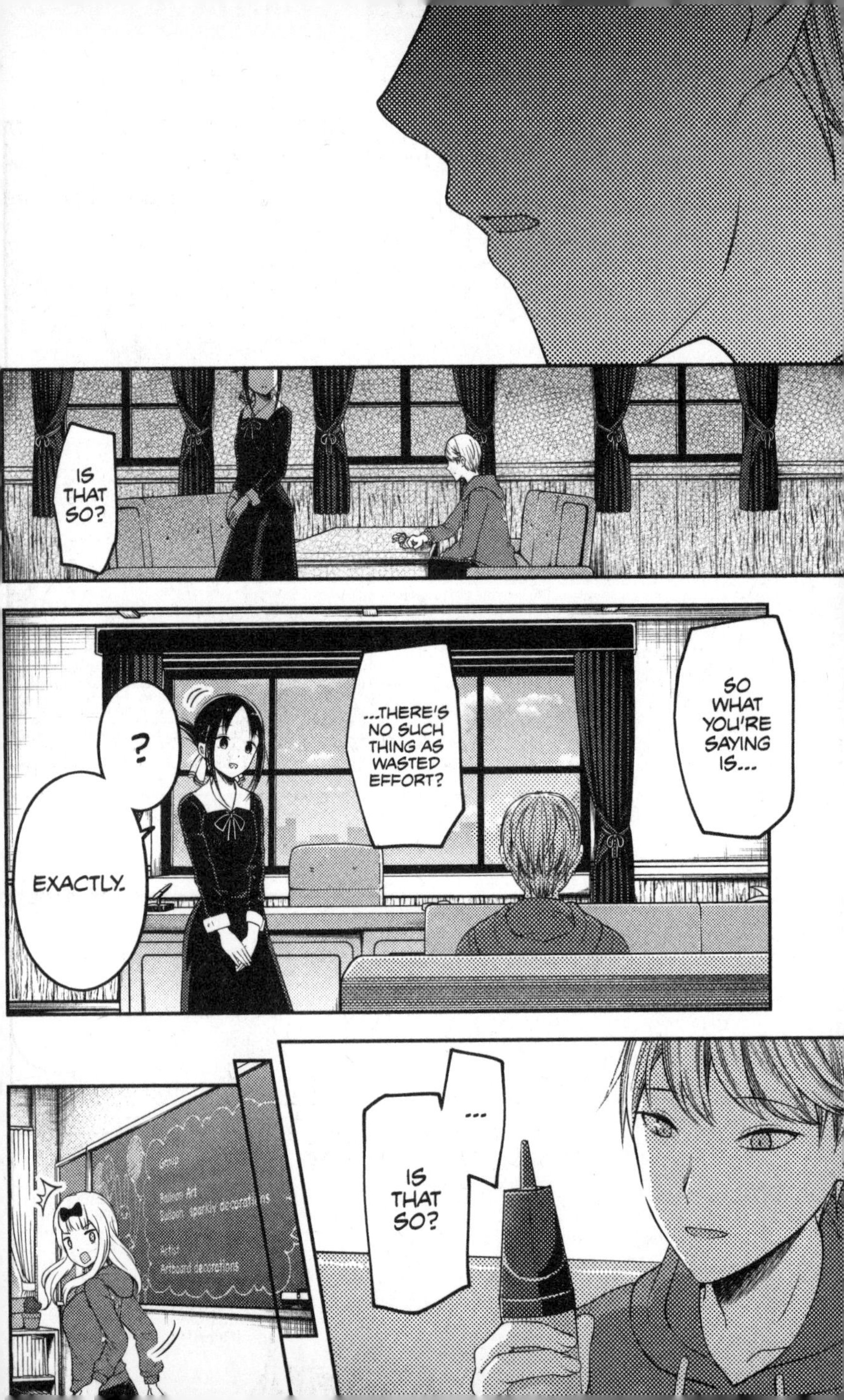
IS THAT SO?
SO WHAT YOU'RE SAYING IS...
...THERE'S NO SUCH THING AS WASTED EFFORT?
?
EXACTLY.
...
IS THAT SO?

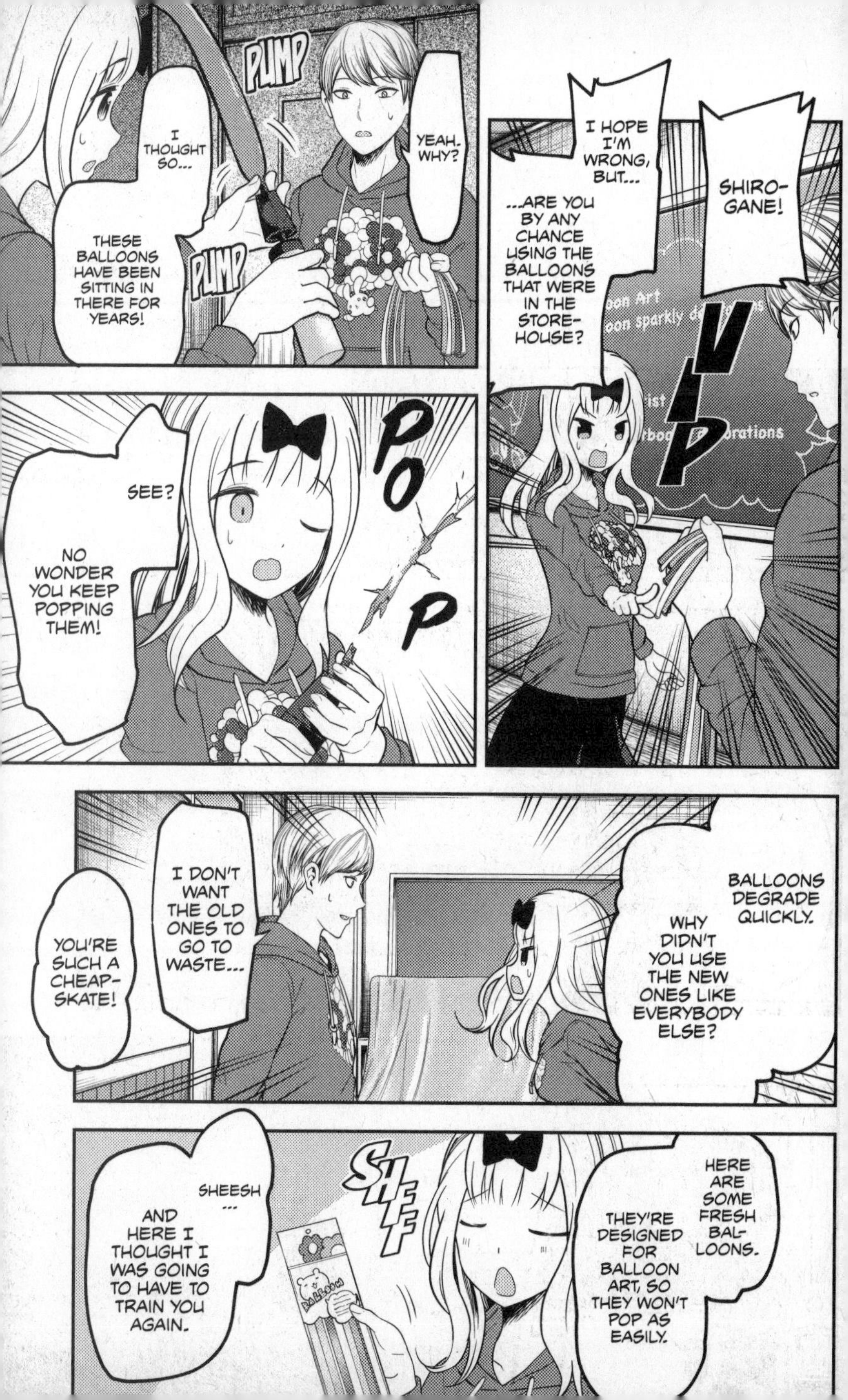
SHIRO-GANE!
I HOPE I'M WRONG, BUT...
...ARE YOU BY ANY CHANCE USING THE BALLOONS THAT WERE IN THE STORE-HOUSE?
VIP
PUMP
YEAH. WHY?
I THOUGHT SO...
THESE BALLOONS HAVE BEEN SITTING IN THERE FOR YEARS!
PUMP
POP
SEE?
NO WONDER YOU KEEP POPPING THEM!
BALLOONS DEGRADE QUICKLY.
WHY DIDN'T YOU USE THE NEW ONES LIKE EVERYBODY ELSE?
I DON'T WANT THE OLD ONES TO GO TO WASTE...
YOU'RE SUCH A CHEAP-SKATE!
HERE ARE SOME FRESH BAL-LOONS.
THEY'RE DESIGNED FOR BALLOON ART, SO THEY WON'T POP AS EASILY.
SHFF
SHEESH...
AND HERE I THOUGHT I WAS GOING TO HAVE TO TRAIN YOU AGAIN.

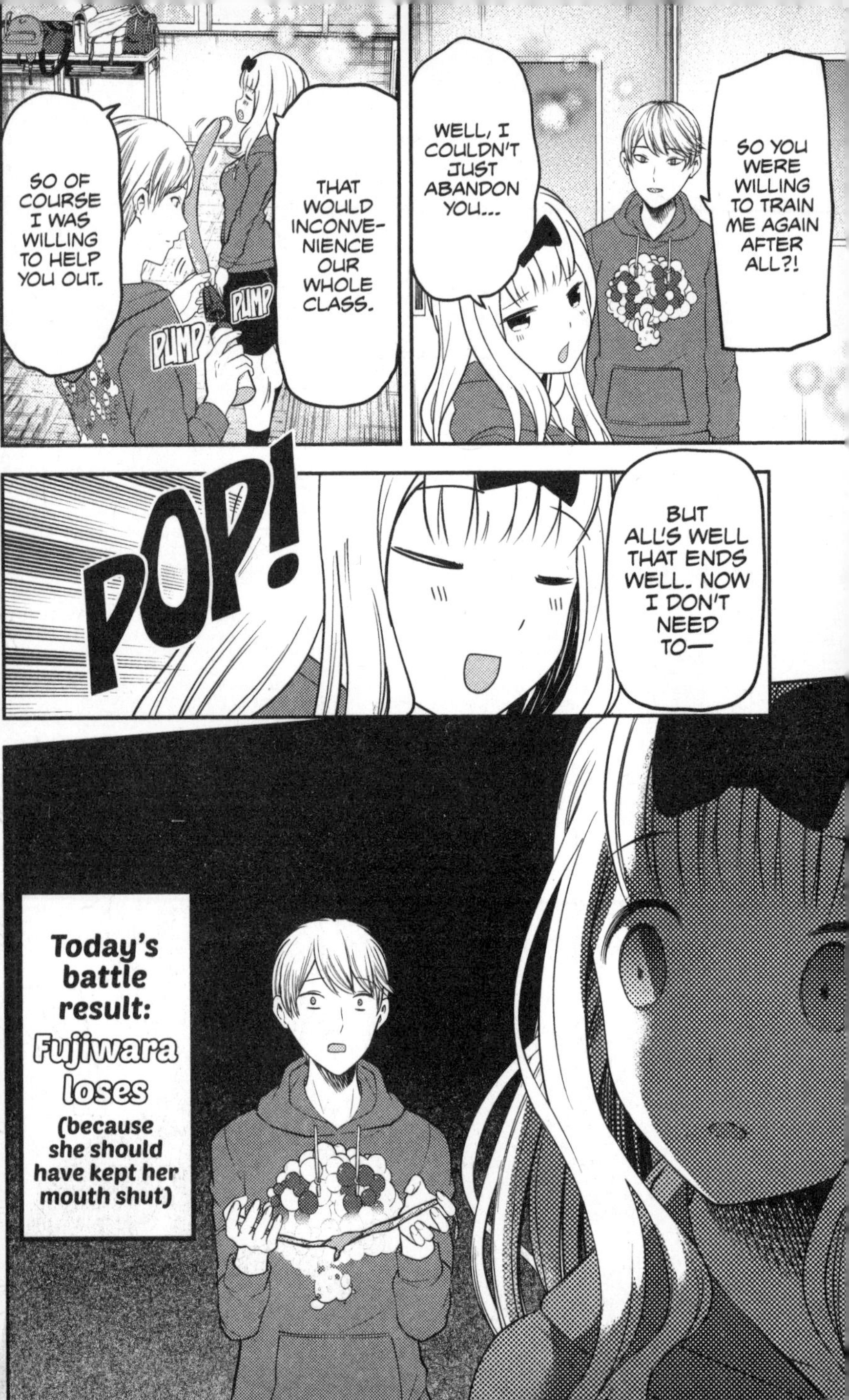
SO YOU WERE WILLING TO TRAIN ME AGAIN AFTER ALL?!
WELL, I COULDN'T JUST ABANDON YOU...
THAT WOULD INCONVENIENCE OUR WHOLE CLASS.
SO OF COURSE I WAS WILLING TO HELP YOU OUT.
PUMP
PUMP
BUT ALL'S WELL THAT ENDS WELL. NOW I DON'T NEED TO—
POP!
Today's battle result: Fujiwara loses (because she should have kept her mouth shut)

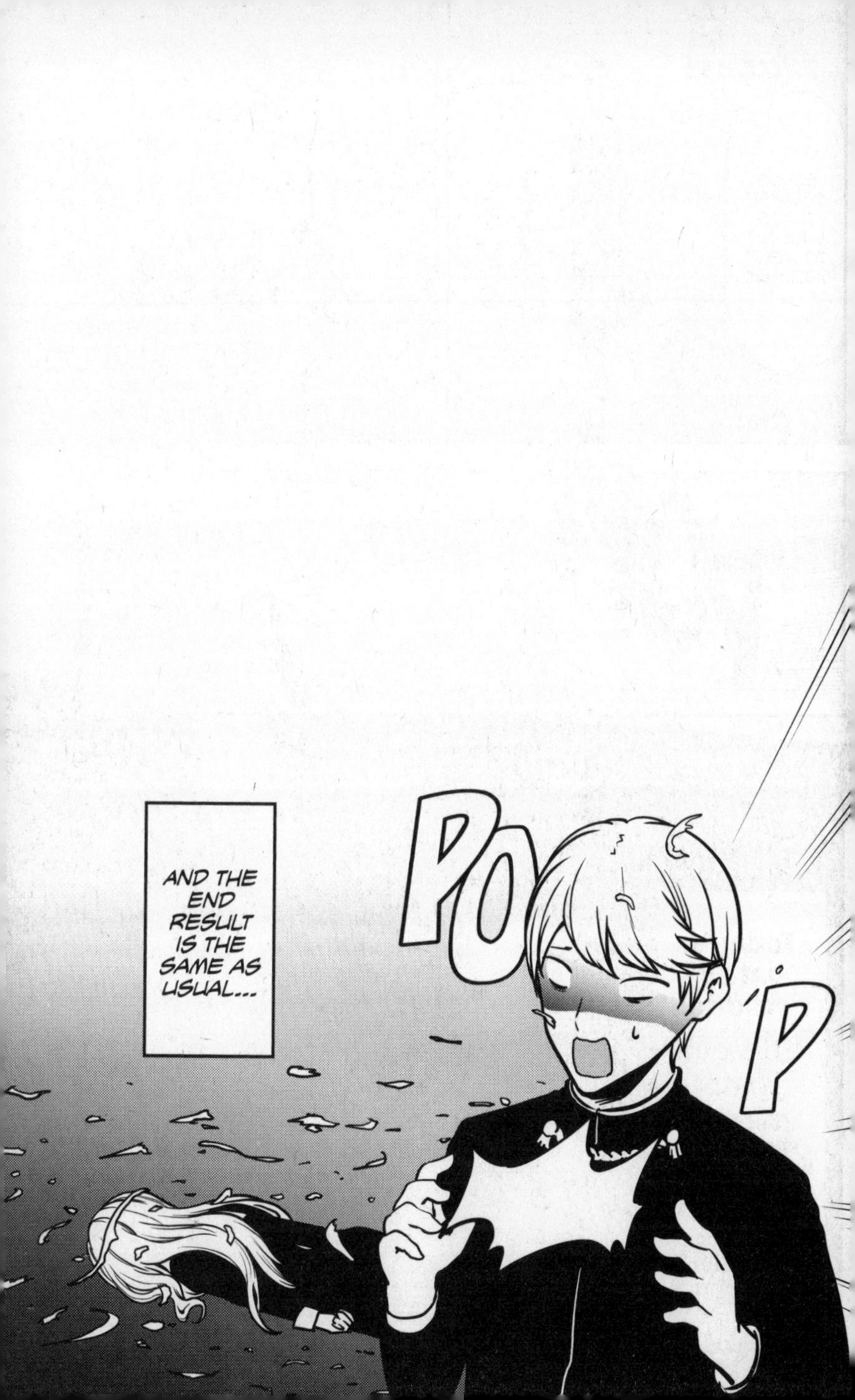
AND THE END RESULT IS THE SAME AS USUAL...
POP

KAGUYA-SAMA

LOVE IS WAR

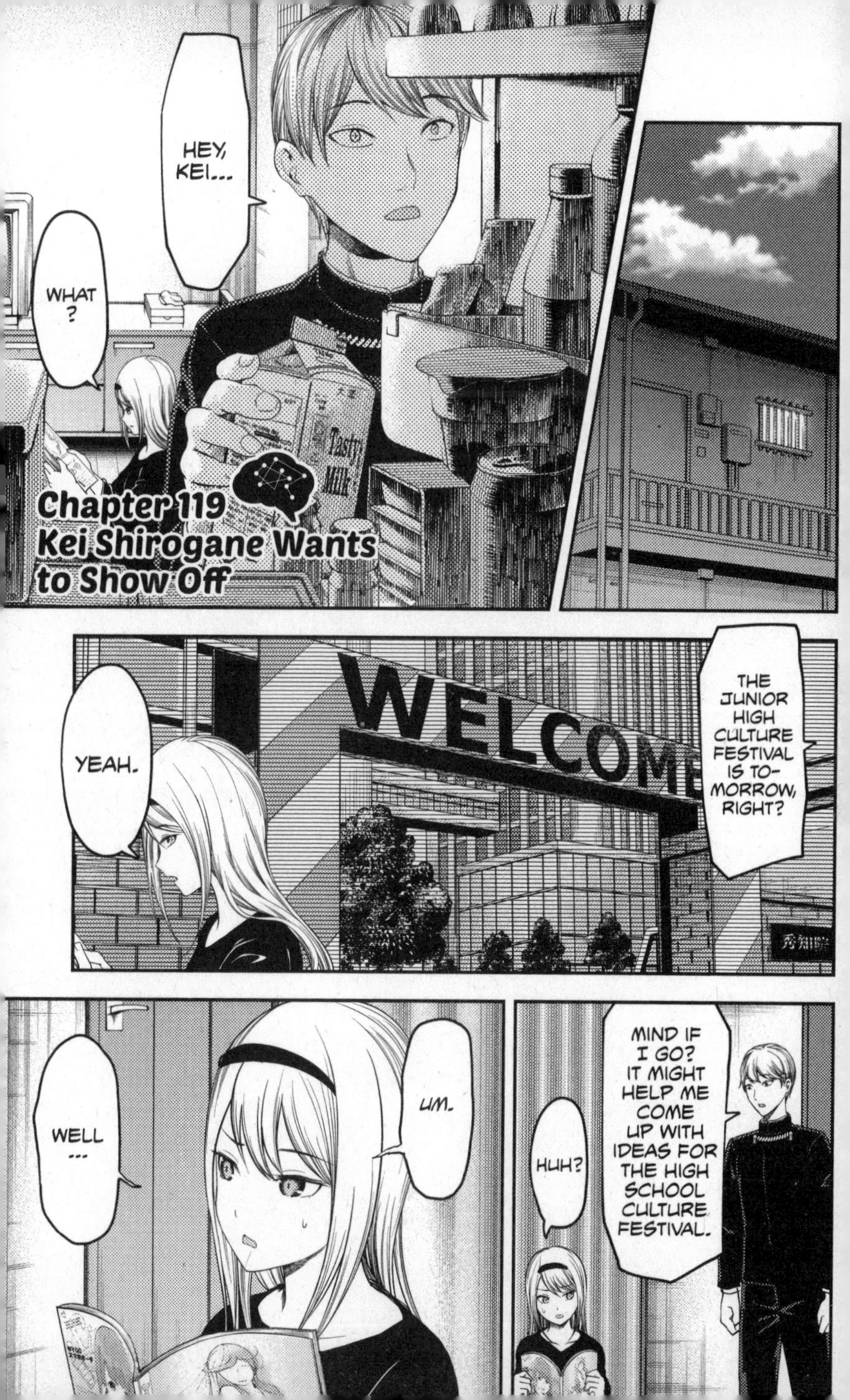
HEY, KEI...
WHAT?
Tasty Milk
Chapter 119
Kei Shirogane Wants to Show Off
THE JUNIOR HIGH CULTURE FESTIVAL IS TO-MORROW, RIGHT?
WELCOME
YEAH.
MIND IF I GO? IT MIGHT HELP ME COME UP WITH IDEAS FOR THE HIGH SCHOOL CULTURE FESTIVAL.
HUH?
UM.
WELL...

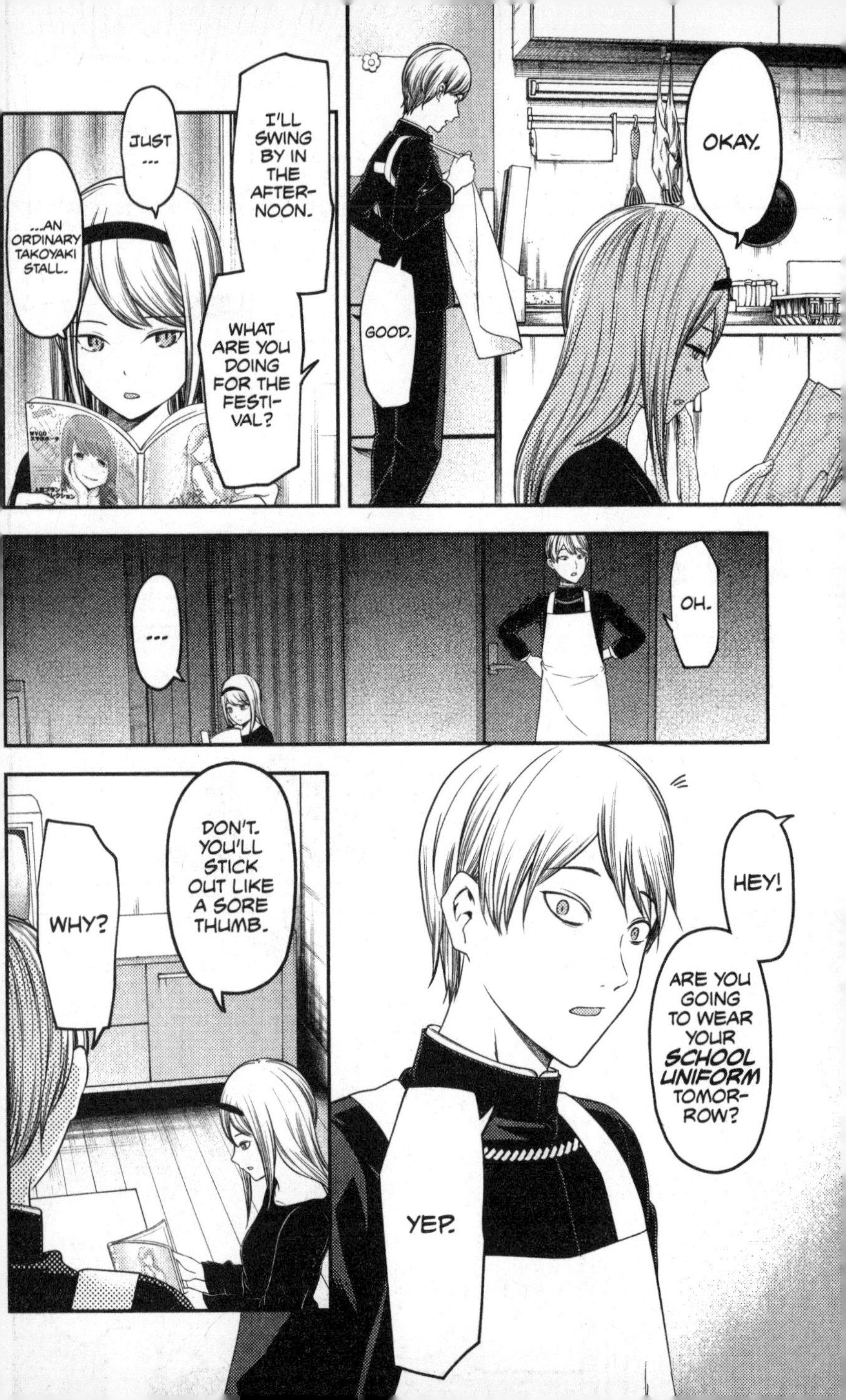

OKAY.
GOOD.
I'LL SWING BY IN THE AFTERNOON.
JUST ...
WHAT ARE YOU DOING FOR THE FESTIVAL?
...AN ORDINARY TAKOYAKI STALL.
OH.
...
HEY!
ARE YOU GOING TO WEAR YOUR SCHOOL UNIFORM TOMORROW?
YEP.
DON'T. YOU'LL STICK OUT LIKE A SORE THUMB.
WHY?

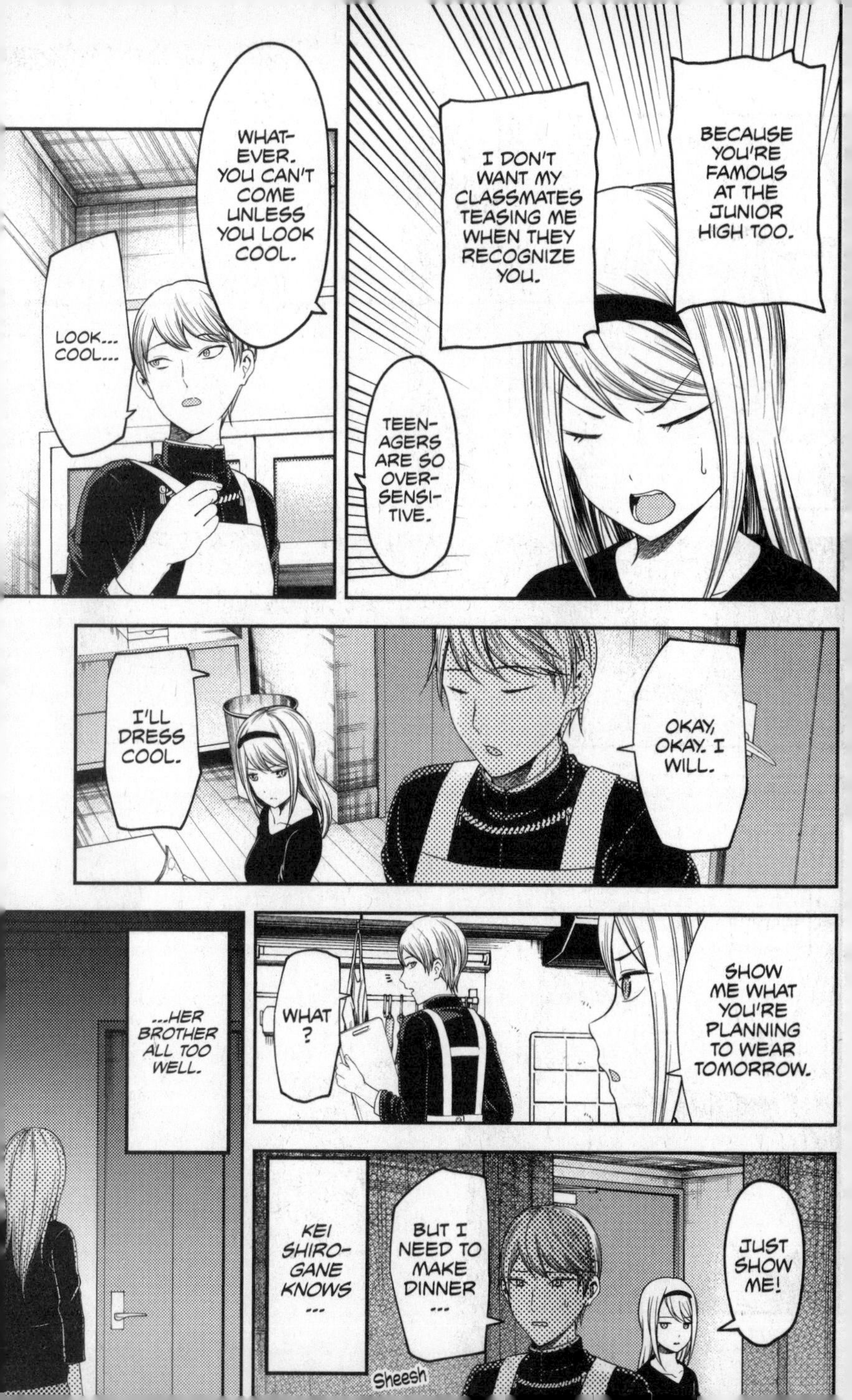
BECAUSE YOU'RE FAMOUS AT THE JUNIOR HIGH TOO.
I DON'T WANT MY CLASSMATES TEASING ME WHEN THEY RECOGNIZE YOU.
TEENAGERS ARE SO OVERSENSITIVE.
WHATEVER. YOU CAN'T COME UNLESS YOU LOOK COOL.
LOOK... COOL...
OKAY, OKAY. I WILL.
I'LL DRESS COOL.
SHOW ME WHAT YOU'RE PLANNING TO WEAR TOMORROW.
WHAT?
JUST SHOW ME!
BUT I NEED TO MAKE DINNER...
KEI SHIROGANE KNOWS...
Sheesh
...HER BROTHER ALL TOO WELL.

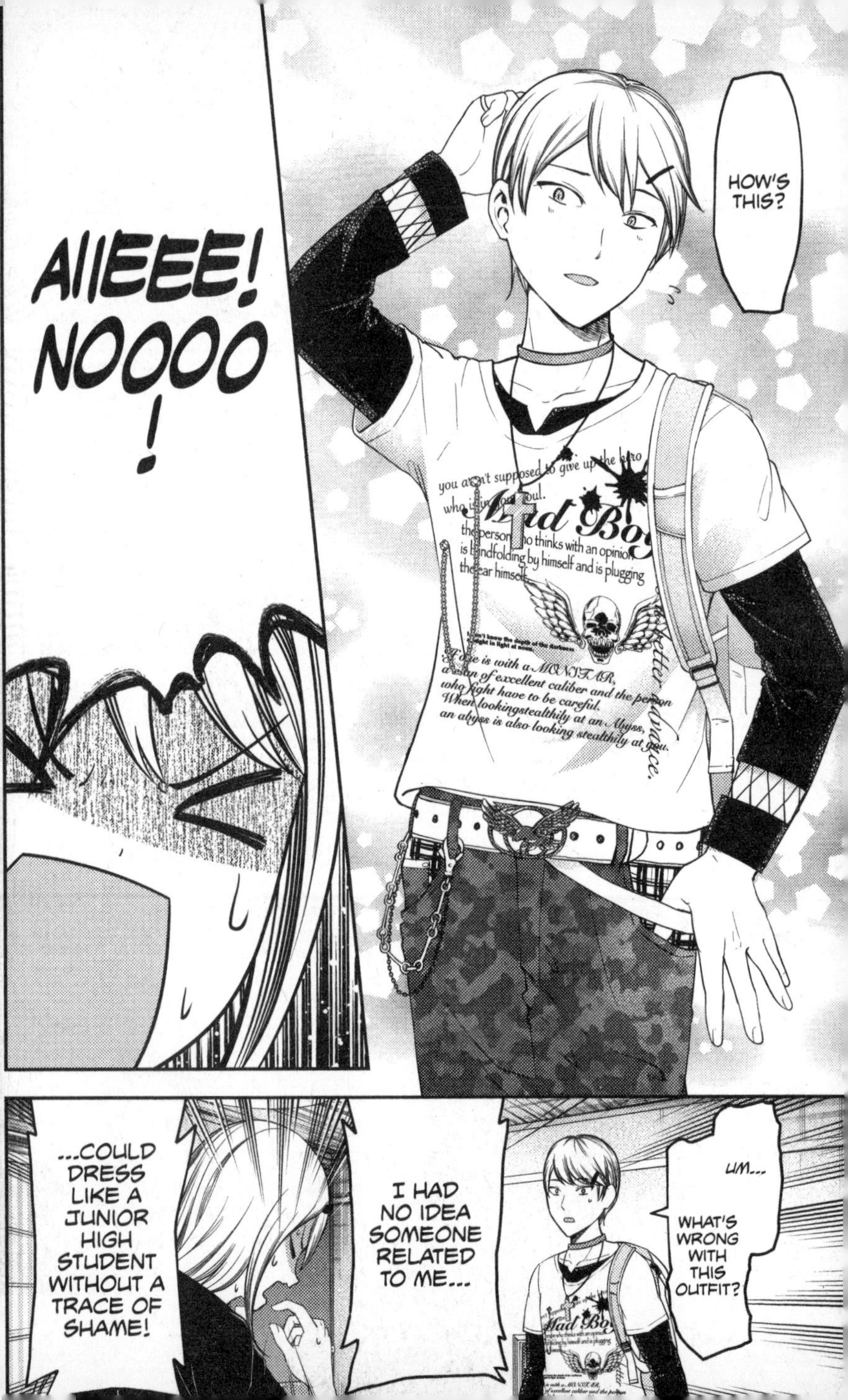
HOW'S THIS?
AIIEEE! NOOOO!
UM...
WHAT'S WRONG WITH THIS OUTFIT?
I HAD NO IDEA SOMEONE RELATED TO ME...
...COULD DRESS LIKE A JUNIOR HIGH STUDENT WITHOUT A TRACE OF SHAME!

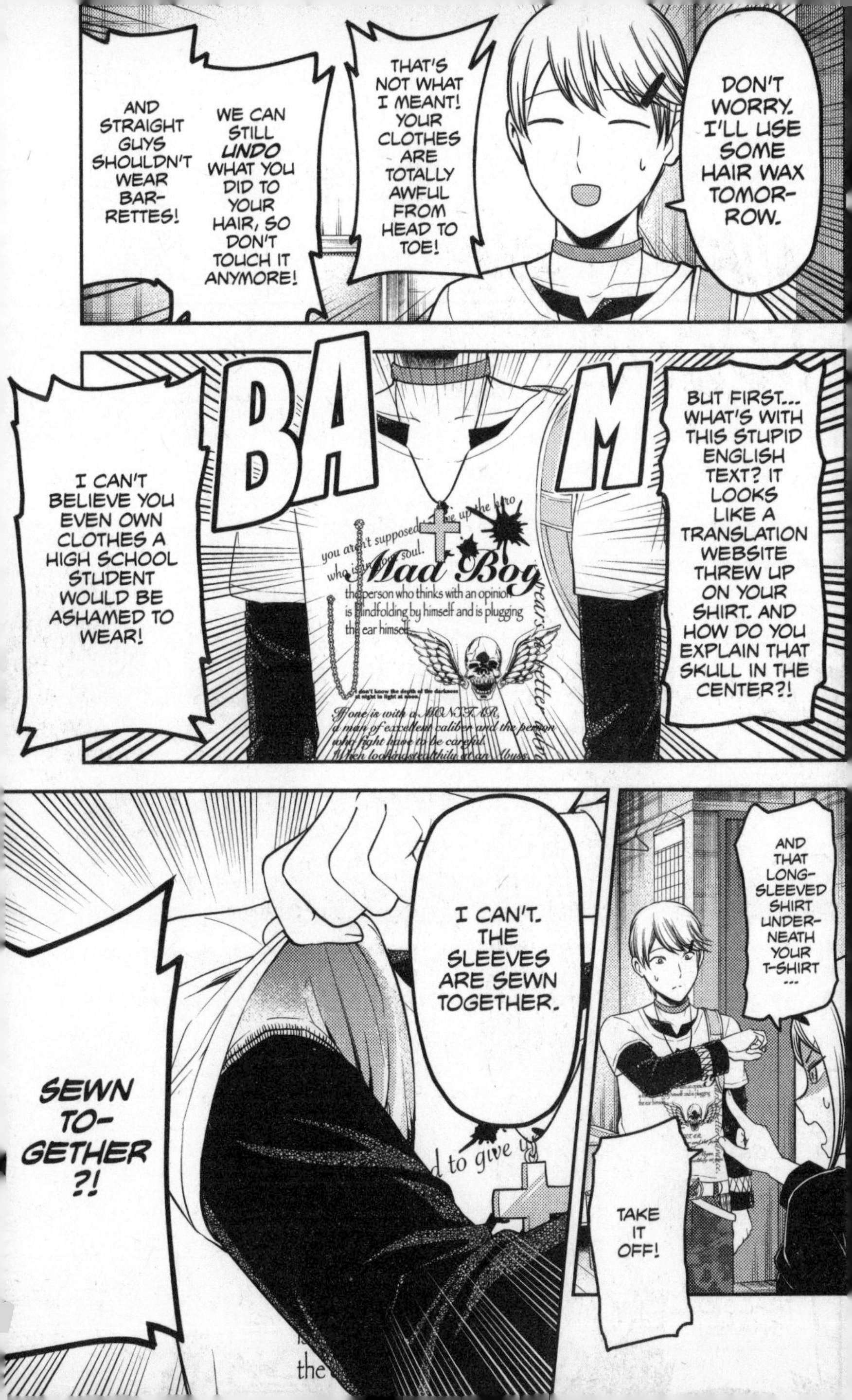
DON'T WORRY. I'LL USE SOME HAIR WAX TOMORROW.
THAT'S NOT WHAT I MEANT! YOUR CLOTHES ARE TOTALLY AWFUL FROM HEAD TO TOE!
WE CAN STILL *UNDO* WHAT YOU DID TO YOUR HAIR, SO DON'T TOUCH IT ANYMORE!
AND STRAIGHT GUYS SHOULDN'T WEAR BARRETTES!
BAM
Mad Bog
BUT FIRST... WHAT'S WITH THIS STUPID ENGLISH TEXT? IT LOOKS LIKE A TRANSLATION WEBSITE THREW UP ON YOUR SHIRT. AND HOW DO YOU EXPLAIN THAT SKULL IN THE CENTER?!
I CAN'T BELIEVE YOU EVEN OWN CLOTHES A HIGH SCHOOL STUDENT WOULD BE ASHAMED TO WEAR!
AND THAT LONG-SLEEVED SHIRT UNDERNEATH YOUR T-SHIRT...
TAKE IT OFF!
I CAN'T. THE SLEEVES ARE SEWN TOGETHER.
SEWN TOGETHER?!

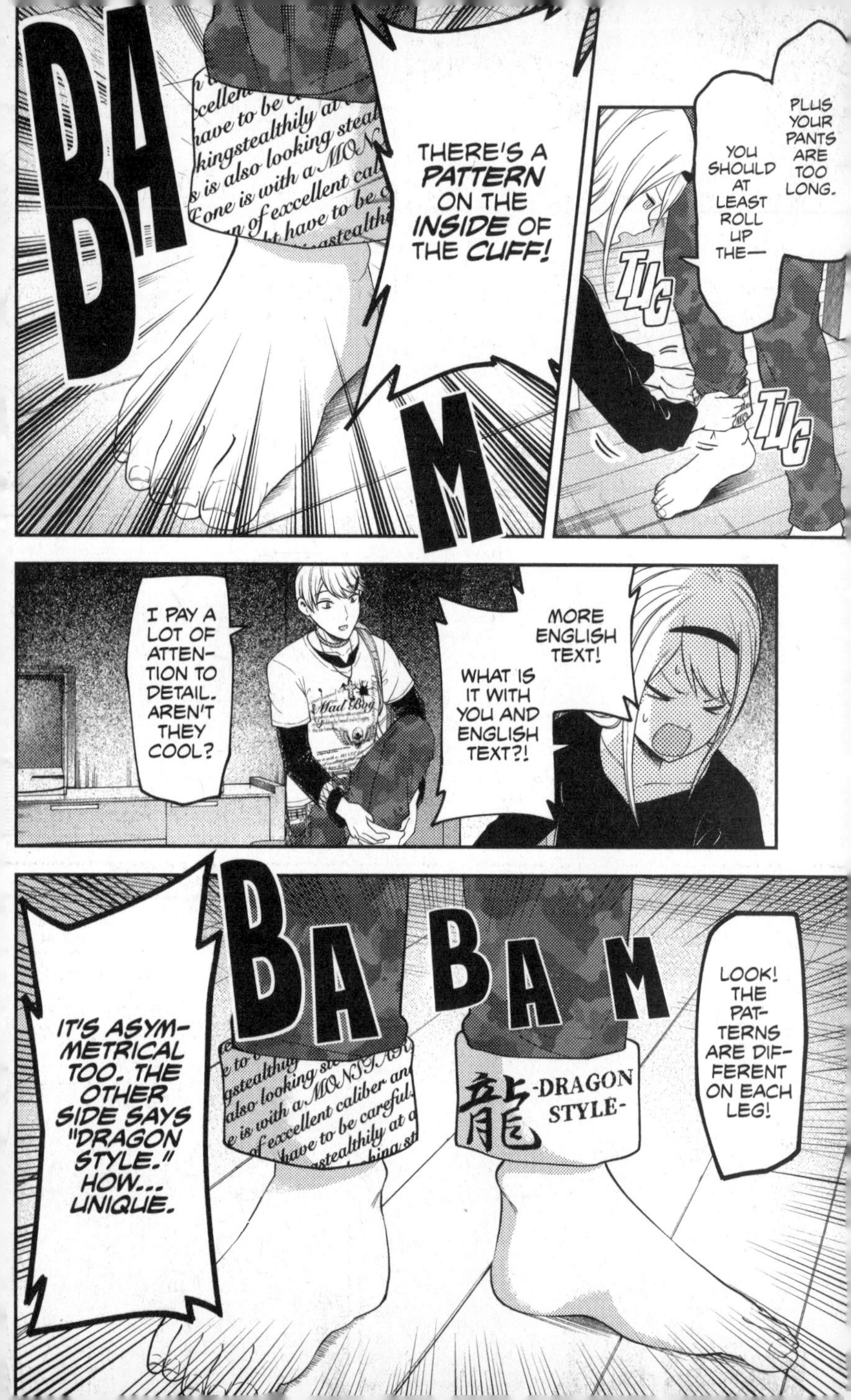
PLUS YOUR PANTS ARE TOO LONG.
YOU SHOULD AT LEAST ROLL UP THE—
TUG
TUG
THERE'S A *PATTERN* ON THE *INSIDE* OF THE *CUFF!*
BA... M
MORE ENGLISH TEXT!
WHAT IS IT WITH YOU AND ENGLISH TEXT?!
I PAY A LOT OF ATTENTION TO DETAIL. AREN'T THEY COOL?
LOOK! THE PATTERNS ARE DIFFERENT ON EACH LEG!
BA BA M
龍 -DRAGON STYLE-
IT'S ASYMMETRICAL TOO. THE OTHER SIDE SAYS "DRAGON STYLE." HOW... UNIQUE.

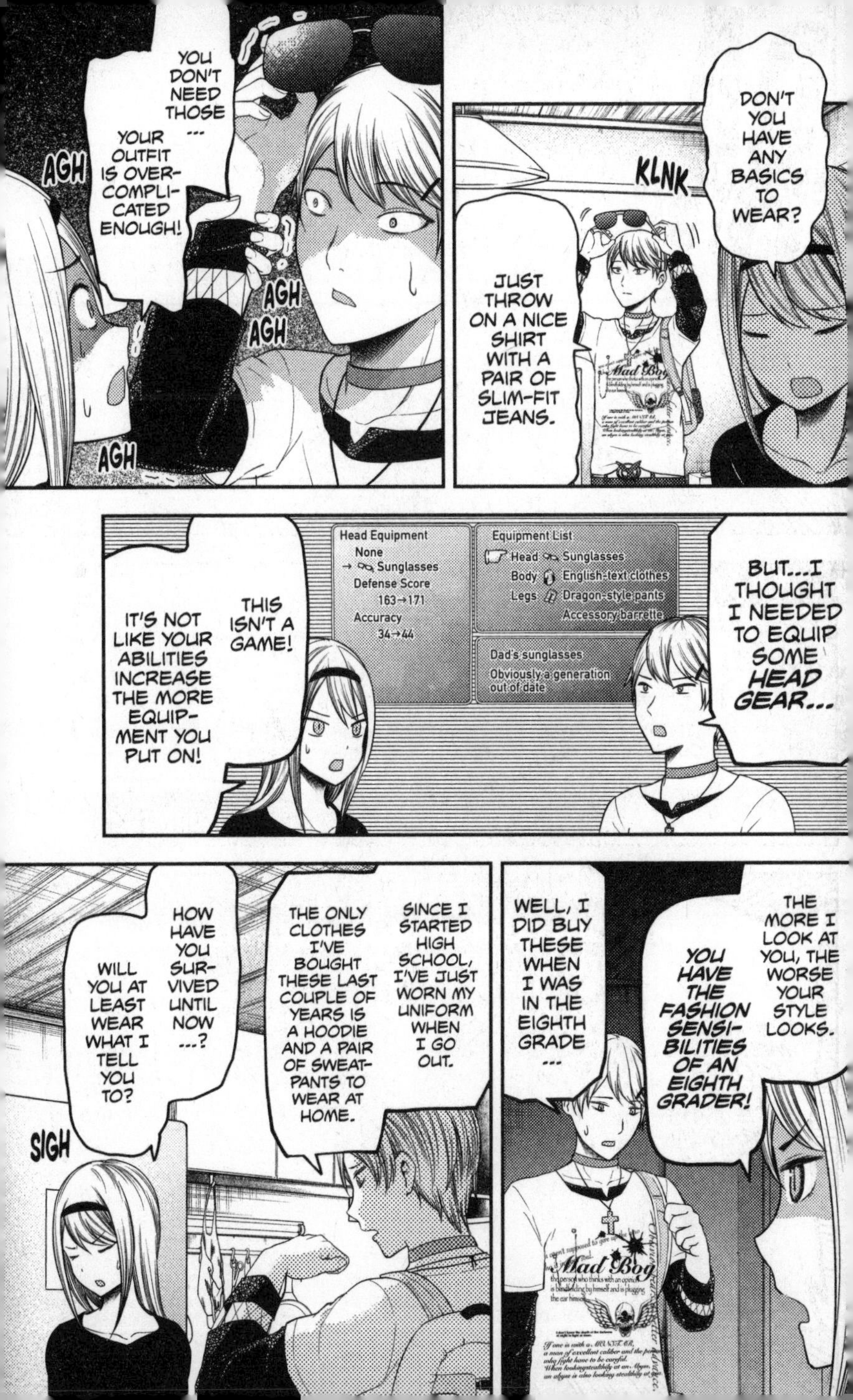
DON'T YOU HAVE ANY BASICS TO WEAR?
KLNK
JUST THROW ON A NICE SHIRT WITH A PAIR OF SLIM-FIT JEANS.
Mad Bog
YOU DON'T NEED THOSE ...
YOUR OUTFIT IS OVER-COMPLICATED ENOUGH!
AGH
AGH
AGH
AGH
BUT...I THOUGHT I NEEDED TO EQUIP SOME HEAD GEAR...
Equipment List
Head Sunglasses
Body English-text clothes
Legs Dragon-style pants
Accessory barrette
Dad's sunglasses
Obviously a generation out of date
Head Equipment
None
→ Sunglasses
Defense Score
163→171
Accuracy
34→44
THIS ISN'T A GAME!
IT'S NOT LIKE YOUR ABILITIES INCREASE THE MORE EQUIPMENT YOU PUT ON!
THE MORE I LOOK AT YOU, THE WORSE YOUR STYLE LOOKS.
YOU HAVE THE FASHION SENSIBILITIES OF AN EIGHTH GRADER!
WELL, I DID BUY THESE WHEN I WAS IN THE EIGHTH GRADE ...
Mad Bog
SINCE I STARTED HIGH SCHOOL, I'VE JUST WORN MY UNIFORM WHEN I GO OUT.
THE ONLY CLOTHES I'VE BOUGHT THESE LAST COUPLE OF YEARS IS A HOODIE AND A PAIR OF SWEATPANTS TO WEAR AT HOME.
HOW HAVE YOU SURVIVED UNTIL NOW ...?
WILL YOU AT LEAST WEAR WHAT I TELL YOU TO?
SIGH

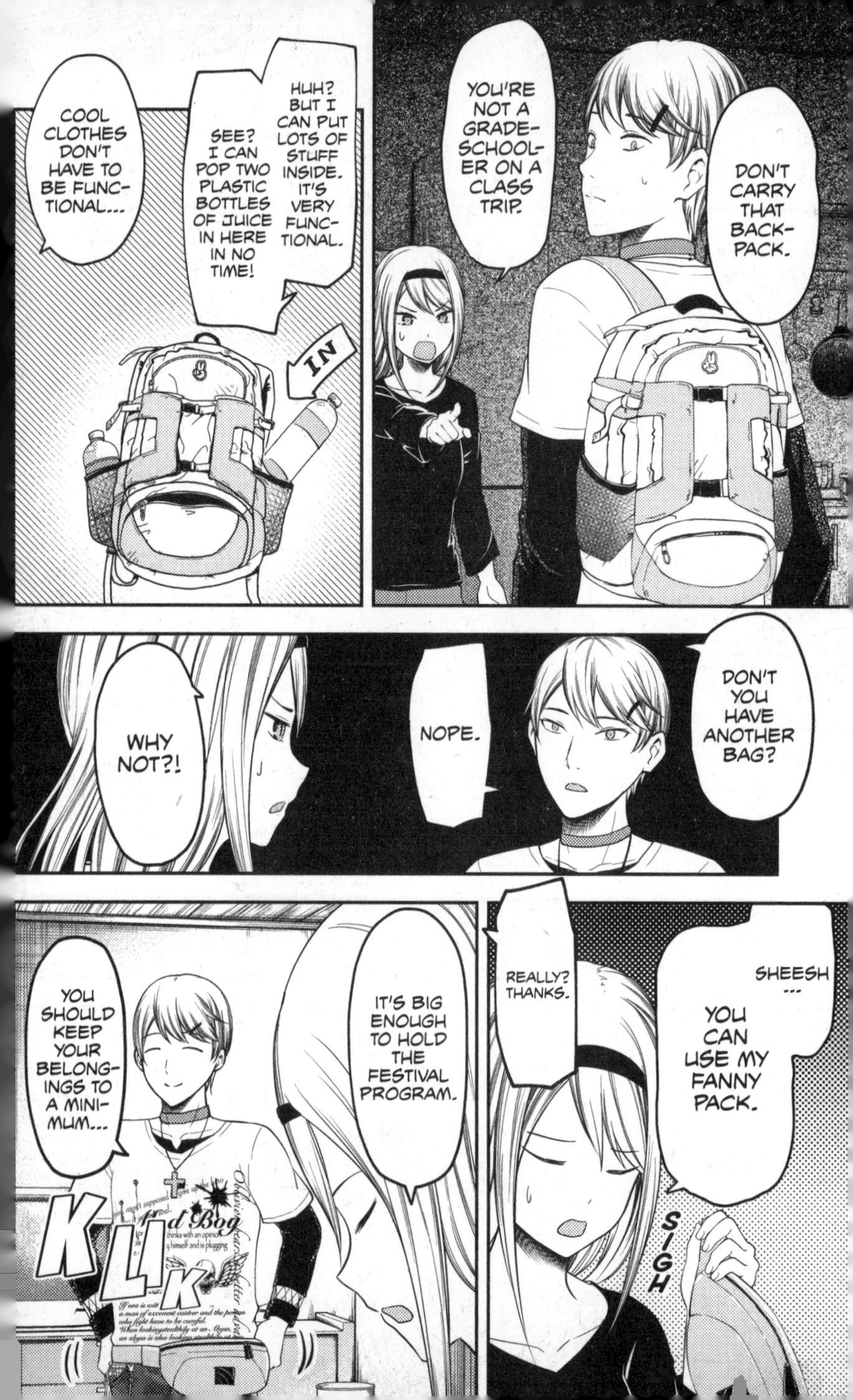
DON'T CARRY THAT BACK-PACK.
YOU'RE NOT A GRADE-SCHOOL-ER ON A CLASS TRIP.
HUH? BUT I CAN PUT LOTS OF STUFF INSIDE. IT'S VERY FUNC-TIONAL.
SEE? I CAN POP TWO PLASTIC BOTTLES OF JUICE IN HERE IN NO TIME!
IN
COOL CLOTHES DON'T HAVE TO BE FUNC-TIONAL...
DON'T YOU HAVE ANOTHER BAG?
NOPE.
WHY NOT?!
SHEESH...
YOU CAN USE MY FANNY PACK.
SIGH
REALLY? THANKS.
IT'S BIG ENOUGH TO HOLD THE FESTIVAL PROGRAM.
YOU SHOULD KEEP YOUR BELONG-INGS TO A MINI-MUM...
KLIK

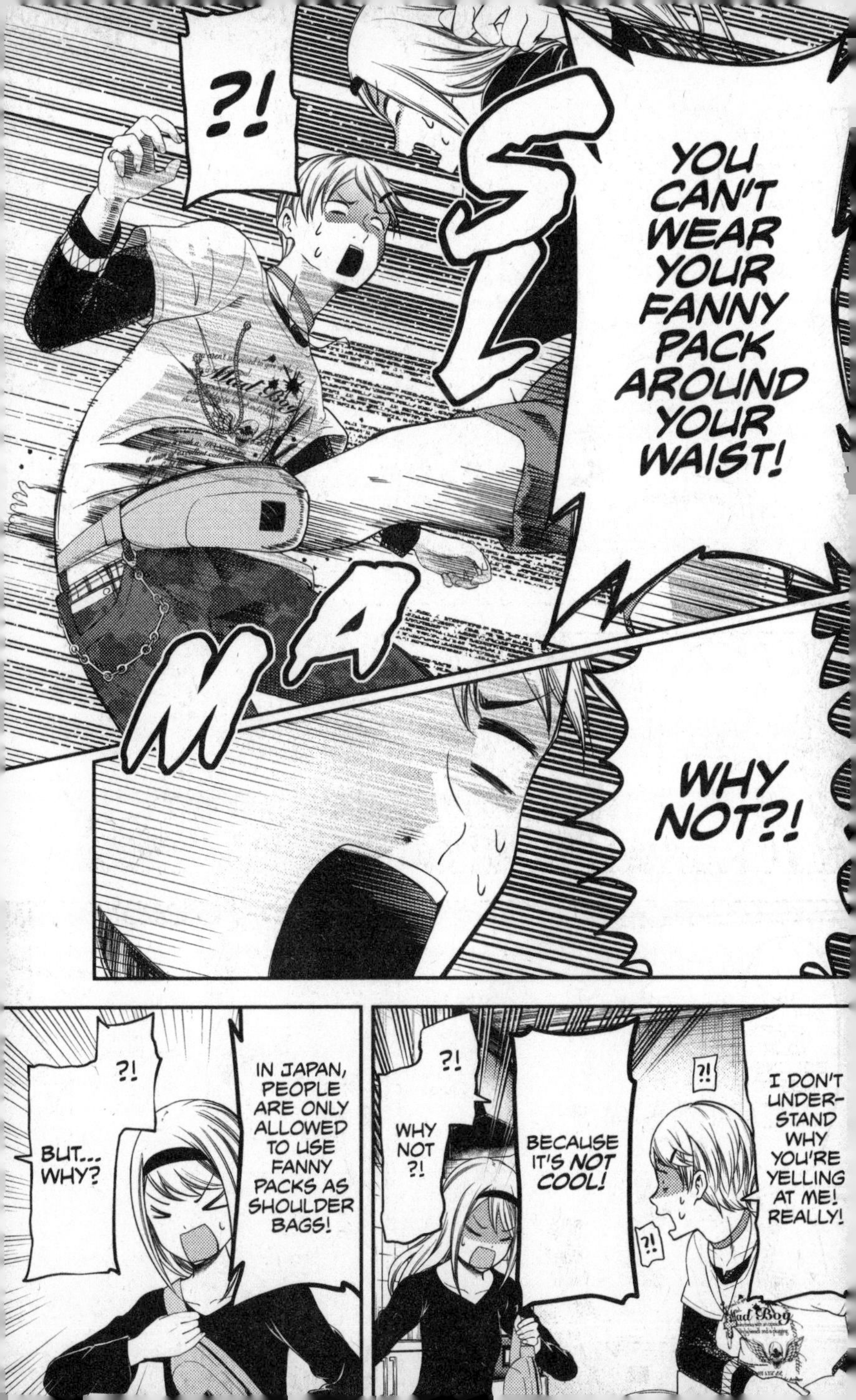
YOU CAN'T WEAR YOUR FANNY PACK AROUND YOUR WAIST!
?!
S
M
A
WHY NOT?!
?!
I DON'T UNDERSTAND WHY YOU'RE YELLING AT ME! REALLY!
BECAUSE IT'S *NOT COOL!*
?!
WHY NOT ?!
?!
IN JAPAN, PEOPLE ARE ONLY ALLOWED TO USE FANNY PACKS AS SHOULDER BAGS!
?!
BUT... WHY?

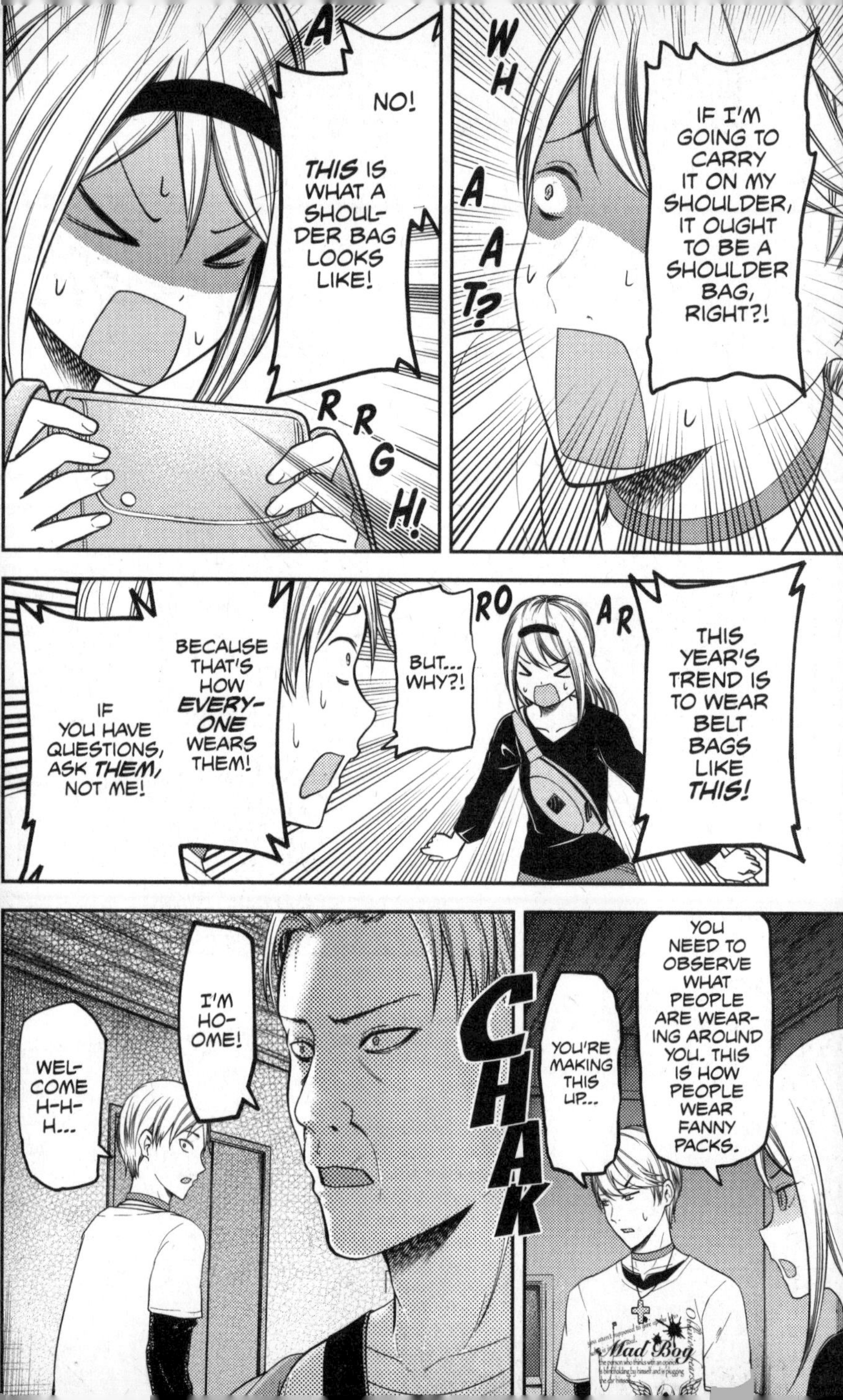
IF I'M GOING TO CARRY IT ON MY SHOULDER, IT OUGHT TO BE A SHOULDER BAG, RIGHT?!
WHAAAT?
A
NO!
THIS IS WHAT A SHOUL-DER BAG LOOKS LIKE!
RRRGH!
THIS YEAR'S TREND IS TO WEAR BELT BAGS LIKE THIS!
ROAR
BUT... WHY?!
BECAUSE THAT'S HOW EVERY-ONE WEARS THEM!
IF YOU HAVE QUESTIONS, ASK THEM, NOT ME!
YOU NEED TO OBSERVE WHAT PEOPLE ARE WEAR-ING AROUND YOU. THIS IS HOW PEOPLE WEAR FANNY PACKS.
YOU'RE MAKING THIS UP...
CHAK
Mad Bog
I'M HO-OME!
WEL-COME H-H-H-H...

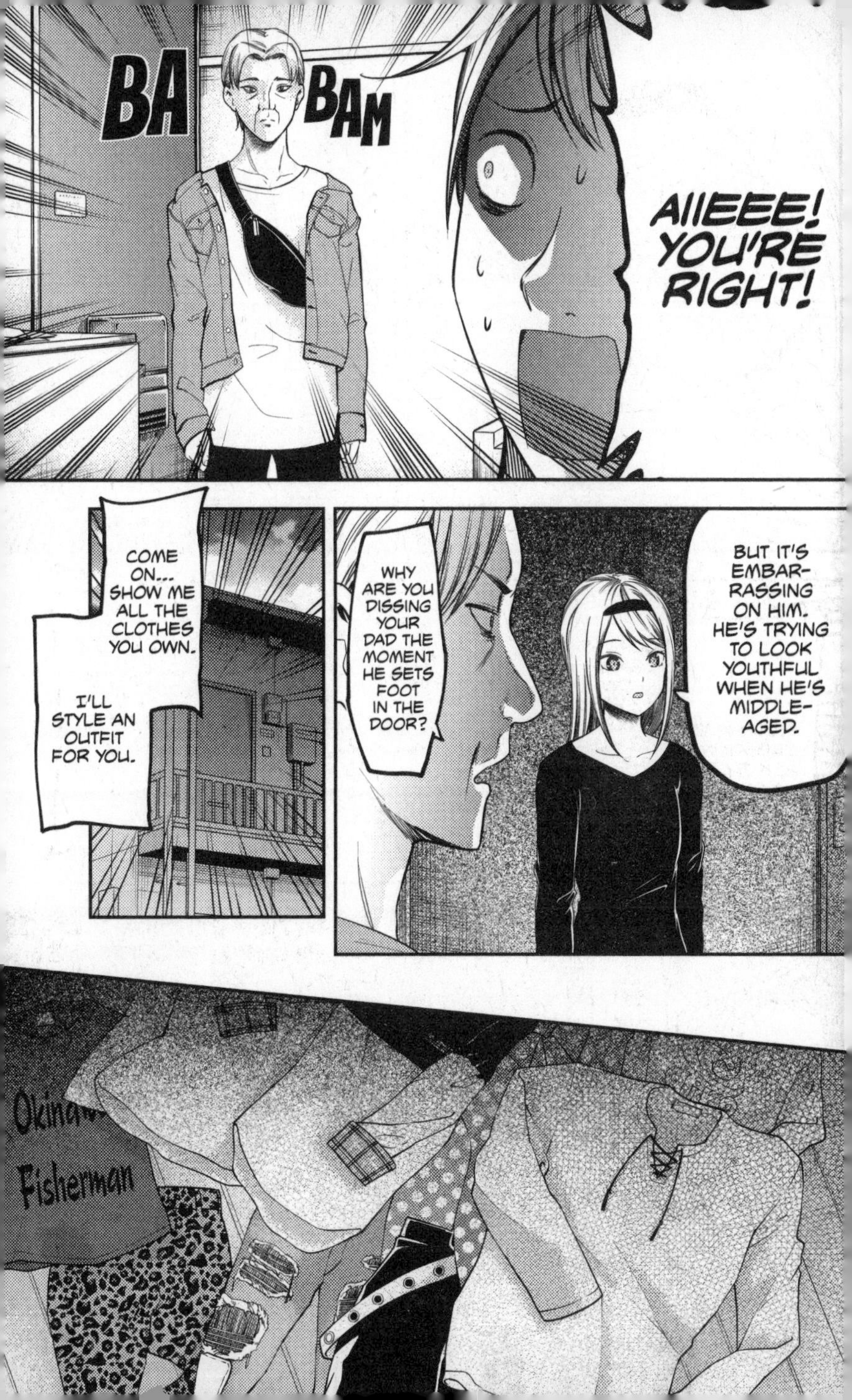
AIIEEE! YOU'RE RIGHT!
BA BAM
BUT IT'S EMBARRASSING ON HIM. HE'S TRYING TO LOOK YOUTHFUL WHEN HE'S MIDDLE-AGED.
WHY ARE YOU DISSING YOUR DAD THE MOMENT HE SETS FOOT IN THE DOOR?
COME ON... SHOW ME ALL THE CLOTHES YOU OWN.
I'LL STYLE AN OUTFIT FOR YOU.
Fisherman

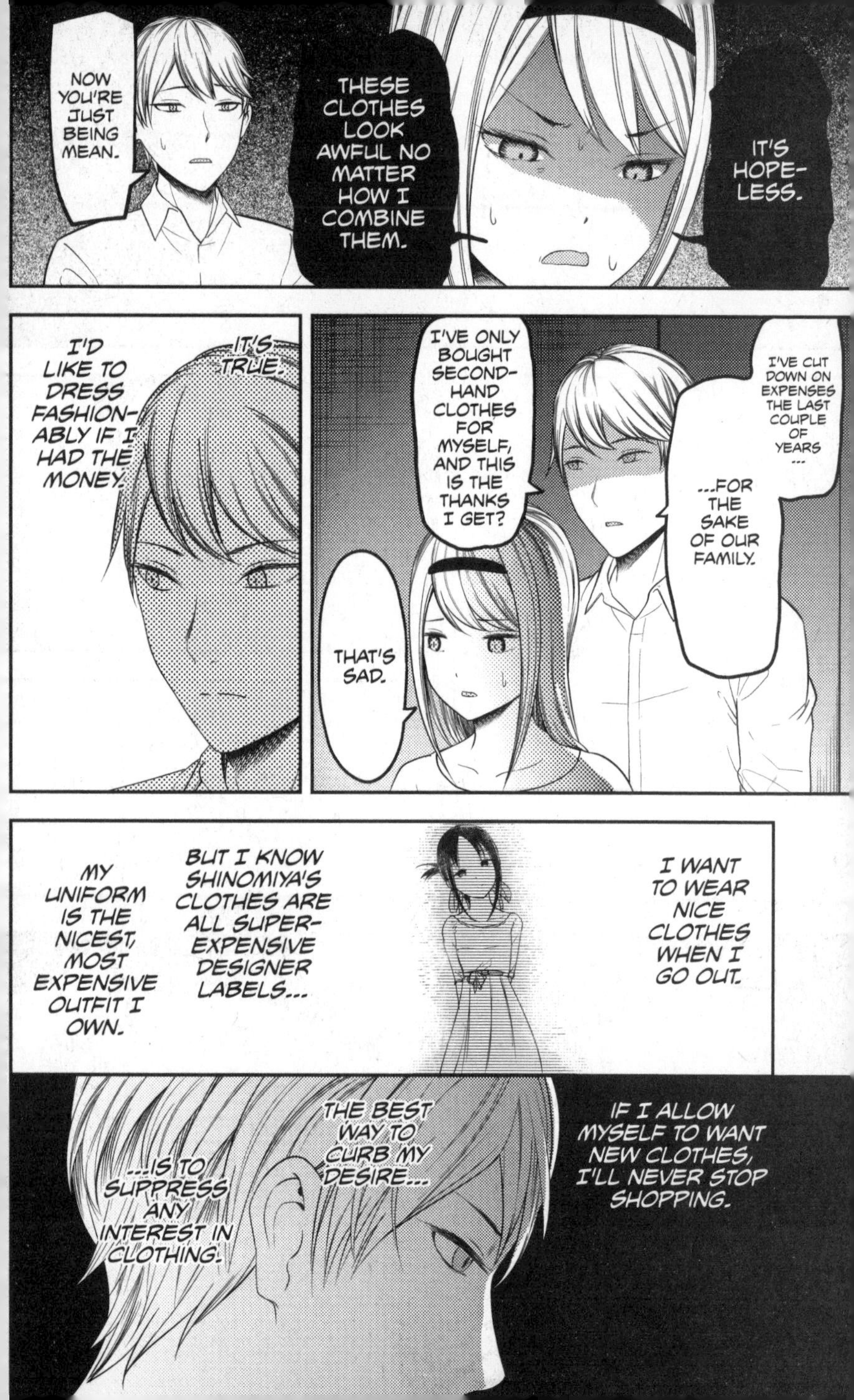
IT'S HOPE-LESS.
THESE CLOTHES LOOK AWFUL NO MATTER HOW I COMBINE THEM.
NOW YOU'RE JUST BEING MEAN.
I'VE CUT DOWN ON EXPENSES THE LAST COUPLE OF YEARS...
...FOR THE SAKE OF OUR FAMILY.
I'VE ONLY BOUGHT SECOND-HAND CLOTHES FOR MYSELF, AND THIS IS THE THANKS I GET?
THAT'S SAD.
IT'S TRUE.
I'D LIKE TO DRESS FASHION-ABLY IF I HAD THE MONEY.
I WANT TO WEAR NICE CLOTHES WHEN I GO OUT.
BUT I KNOW SHINOMIYA'S CLOTHES ARE ALL SUPER-EXPENSIVE DESIGNER LABELS...
MY UNIFORM IS THE NICEST, MOST EXPENSIVE OUTFIT I OWN.
IF I ALLOW MYSELF TO WANT NEW CLOTHES, I'LL NEVER STOP SHOPPING.
THE BEST WAY TO CURB MY DESIRE...
...IS TO SUPPRESS ANY INTEREST IN CLOTHING.

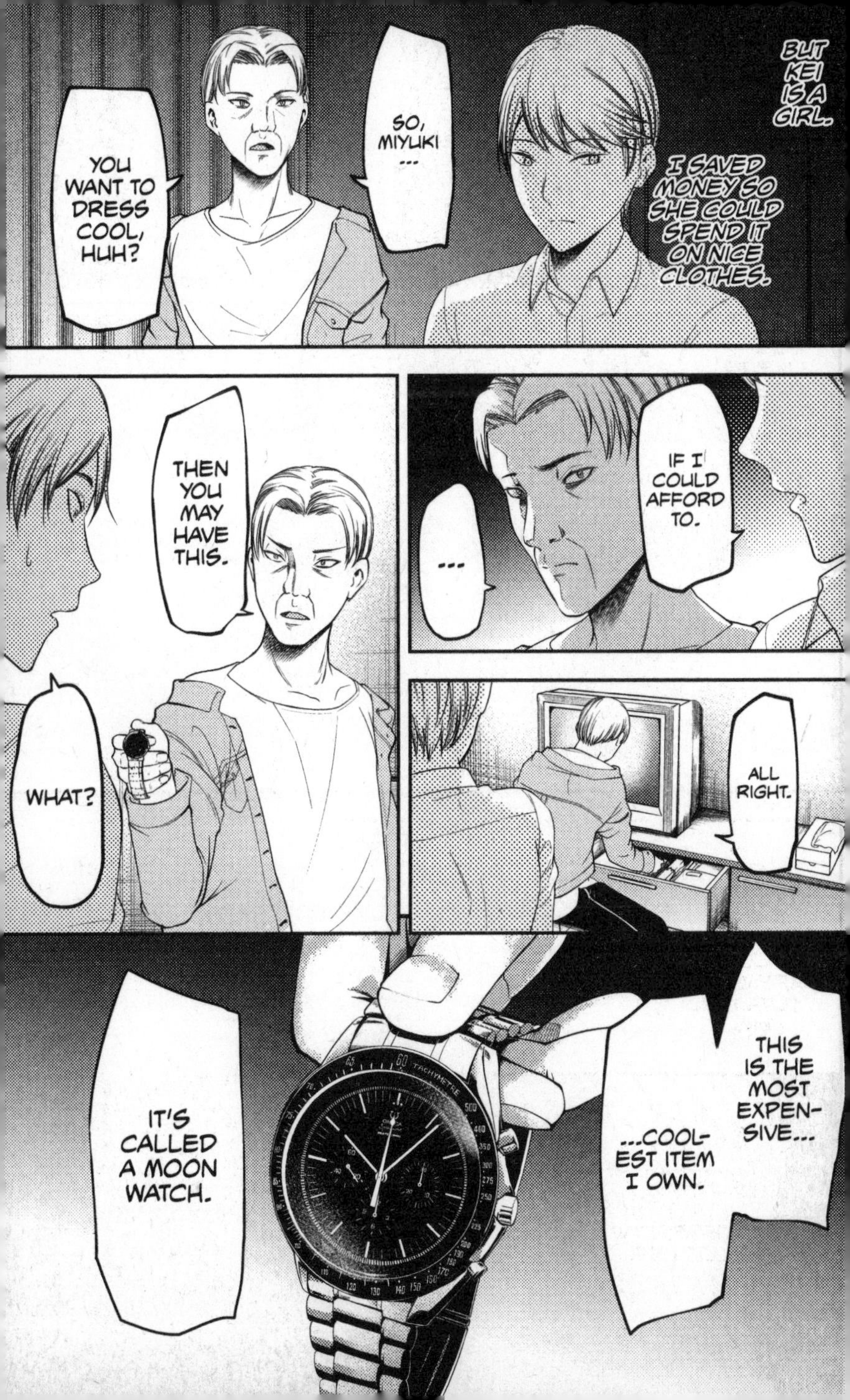
BUT KEI IS A GIRL.
I SAVED MONEY SO SHE COULD SPEND IT ON NICE CLOTHES.
SO, MIYUKI...
YOU WANT TO DRESS COOL, HUH?
IF I COULD AFFORD TO.
...
ALL RIGHT.
THEN YOU MAY HAVE THIS.
WHAT?
THIS IS THE MOST EXPEN-SIVE...
...COOL-EST ITEM I OWN.
IT'S CALLED A MOON WATCH.

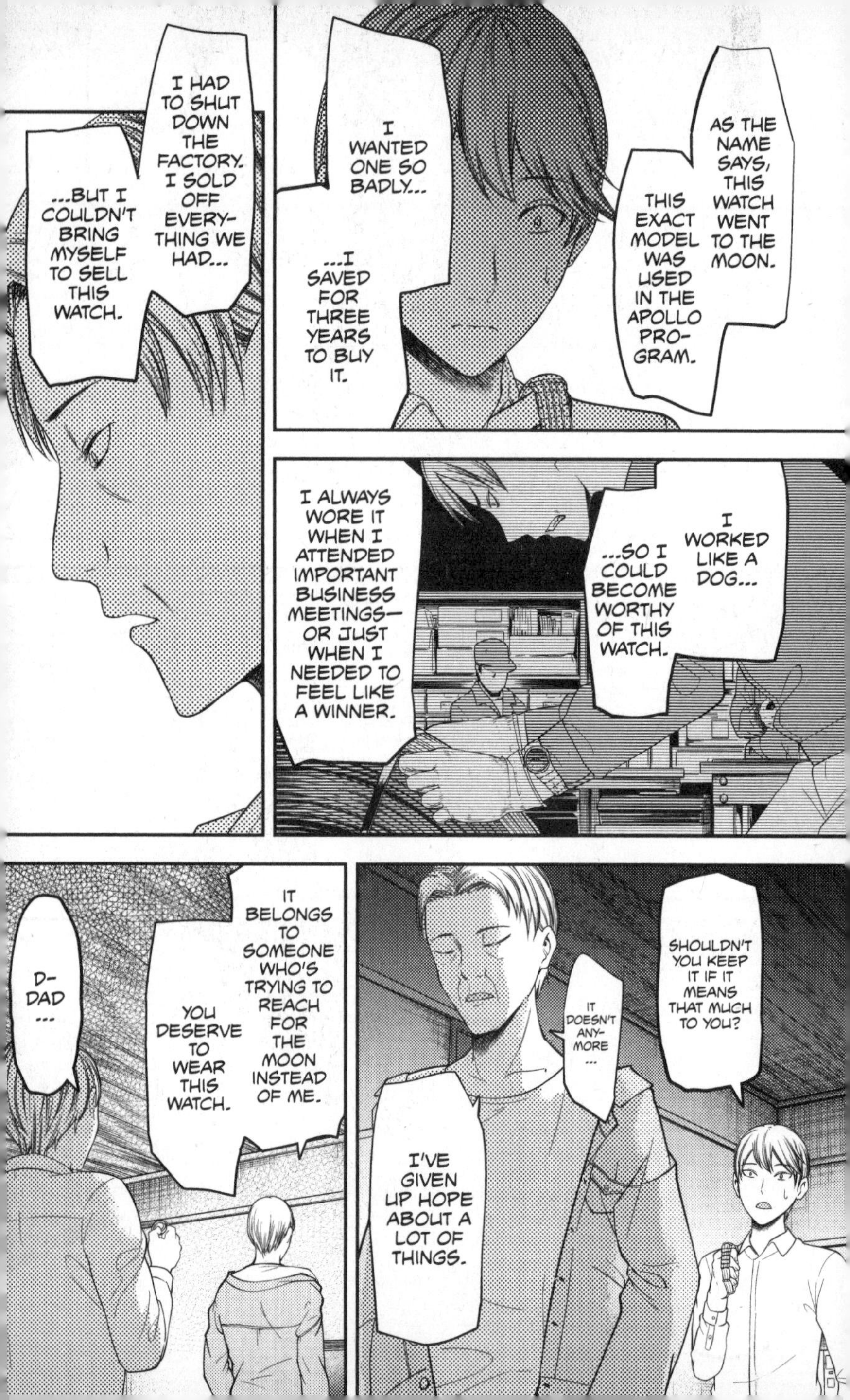
AS THE NAME SAYS, THIS WATCH WENT TO THE MOON.
THIS EXACT MODEL WAS USED IN THE APOLLO PROGRAM.
I WANTED ONE SO BADLY...
...I SAVED FOR THREE YEARS TO BUY IT.
I WORKED LIKE A DOG...
...SO I COULD BECOME WORTHY OF THIS WATCH.
I ALWAYS WORE IT WHEN I ATTENDED IMPORTANT BUSINESS MEETINGS—OR JUST WHEN I NEEDED TO FEEL LIKE A WINNER.
I HAD TO SHUT DOWN THE FACTORY. I SOLD OFF EVERYTHING WE HAD...
...BUT I COULDN'T BRING MYSELF TO SELL THIS WATCH.
SHOULDN'T YOU KEEP IT IF IT MEANS THAT MUCH TO YOU?
IT DOESN'T ANYMORE...
I'VE GIVEN UP HOPE ABOUT A LOT OF THINGS.
IT BELONGS TO SOMEONE WHO'S TRYING TO REACH FOR THE MOON INSTEAD OF ME.
YOU DESERVE TO WEAR THIS WATCH.
D-DAD...

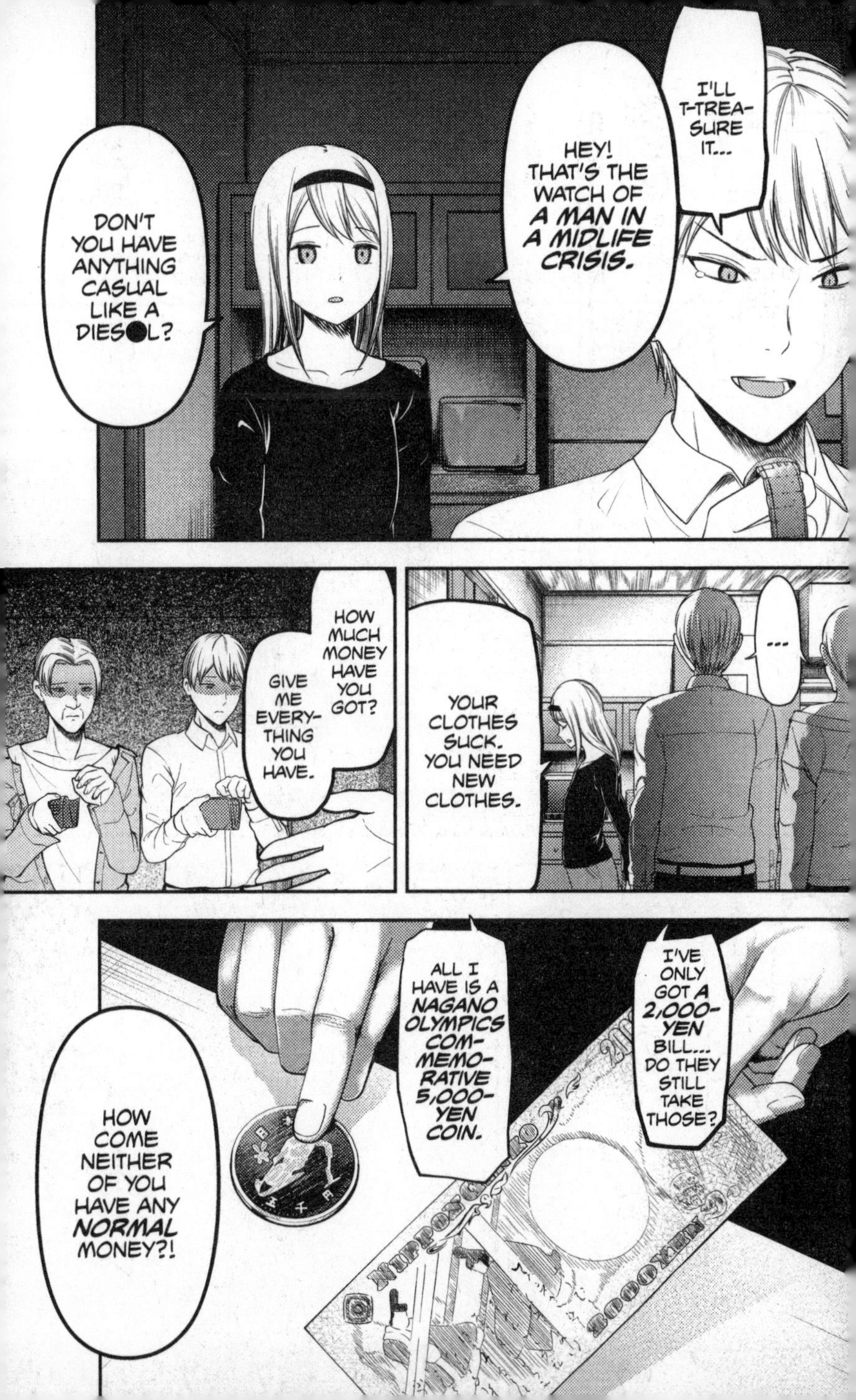
I'LL T-TREASURE IT...
HEY! THAT'S THE WATCH OF *A MAN IN A MIDLIFE CRISIS.*
DON'T YOU HAVE ANYTHING CASUAL LIKE A DIES●L?
...
YOUR CLOTHES SUCK. YOU NEED NEW CLOTHES.
HOW MUCH MONEY HAVE YOU GOT?
GIVE ME EVERYTHING YOU HAVE.
I'VE ONLY GOT *A 2,000-YEN* BILL... DO THEY STILL TAKE THOSE?
ALL I HAVE IS A *NAGANO OLYMPICS COMMEMORATIVE 5,000-YEN COIN.*
HOW COME NEITHER OF YOU HAVE ANY *NORMAL* MONEY?!

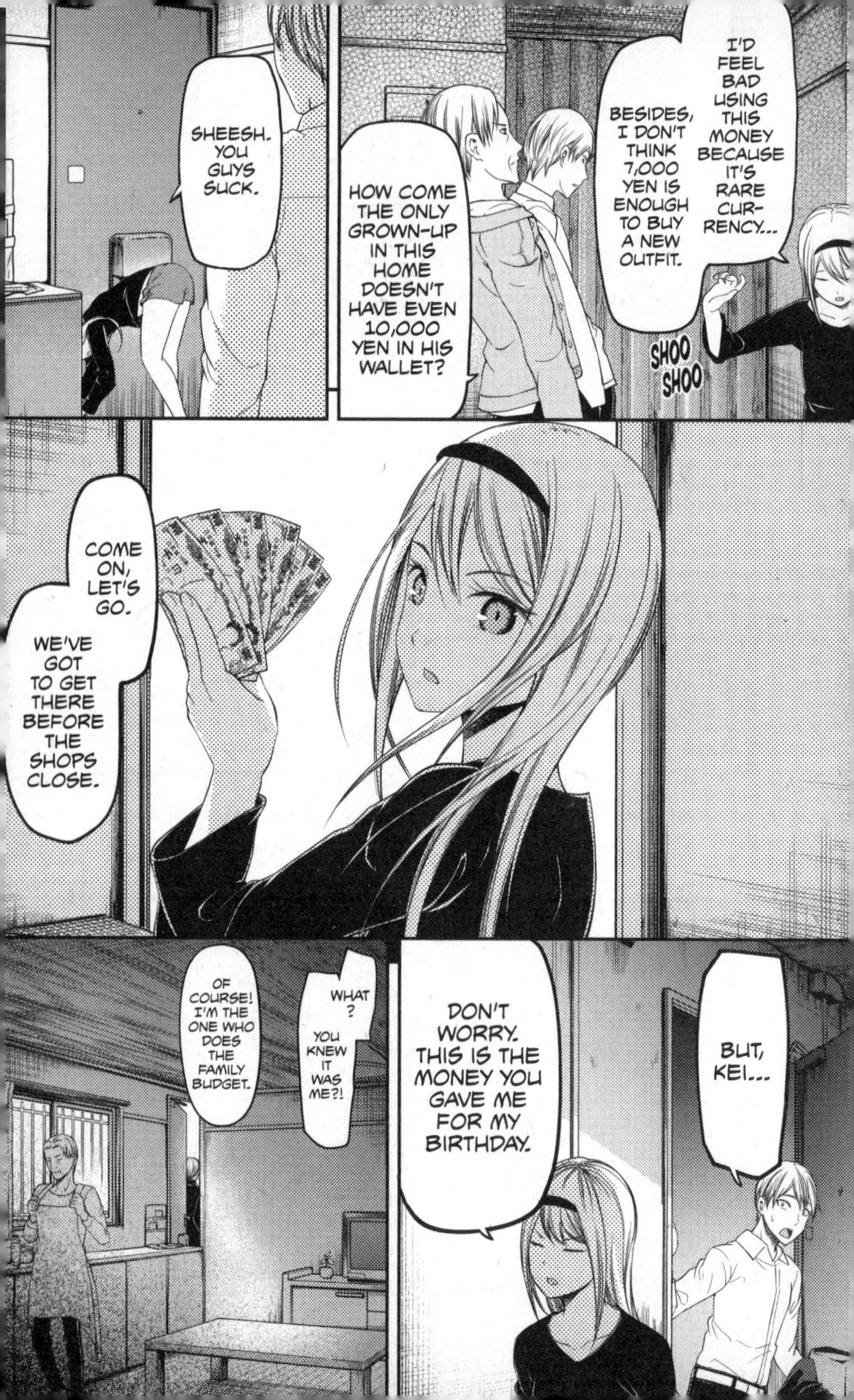
I'D FEEL BAD USING THIS MONEY BECAUSE IT'S RARE CURRENCY...
BESIDES, I DON'T THINK 7,000 YEN IS ENOUGH TO BUY A NEW OUTFIT.
SHOO SHOO
HOW COME THE ONLY GROWN-UP IN THIS HOME DOESN'T HAVE EVEN 10,000 YEN IN HIS WALLET?
SHEESH. YOU GUYS SUCK.
COME ON, LET'S GO.
WE'VE GOT TO GET THERE BEFORE THE SHOPS CLOSE.
BUT, KEI...
DON'T WORRY. THIS IS THE MONEY YOU GAVE ME FOR MY BIRTHDAY.
WHAT?
YOU KNEW IT WAS ME?!
OF COURSE! I'M THE ONE WHO DOES THE FAMILY BUDGET.

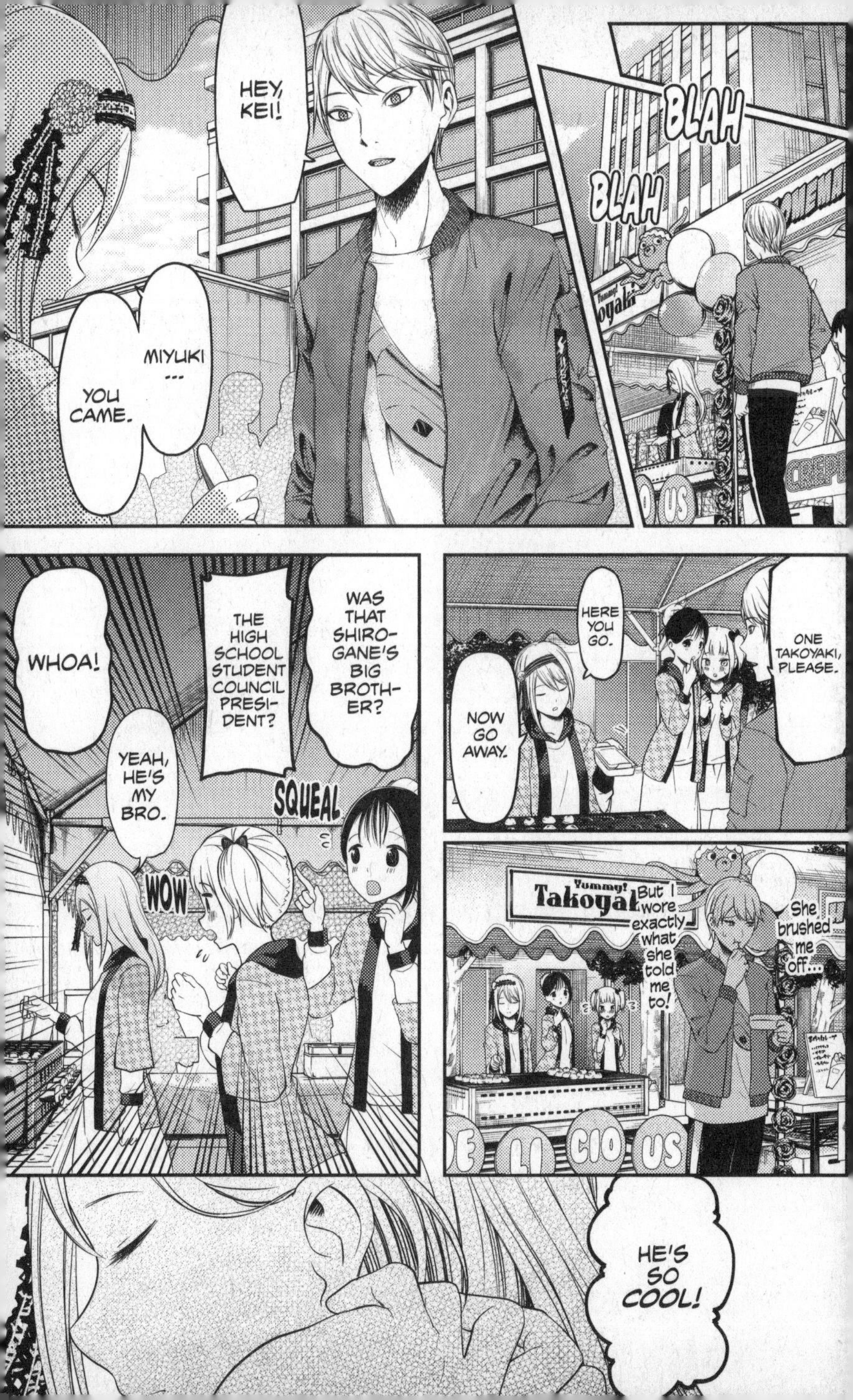
BLAH
BLAH
HEY, KEI!
MIYUKI... YOU CAME.
ONE TAKOYAKI, PLEASE.
HERE YOU GO.
NOW GO AWAY.
She brushed me off...
But I wore exactly what she told me to!
DE LI CIO US
WAS THAT SHIROGANE'S BIG BROTHER?
THE HIGH SCHOOL STUDENT COUNCIL PRESIDENT?
WHOA!
YEAH, HE'S MY BRO.
SQUEAL
WOW
HE'S SO COOL!

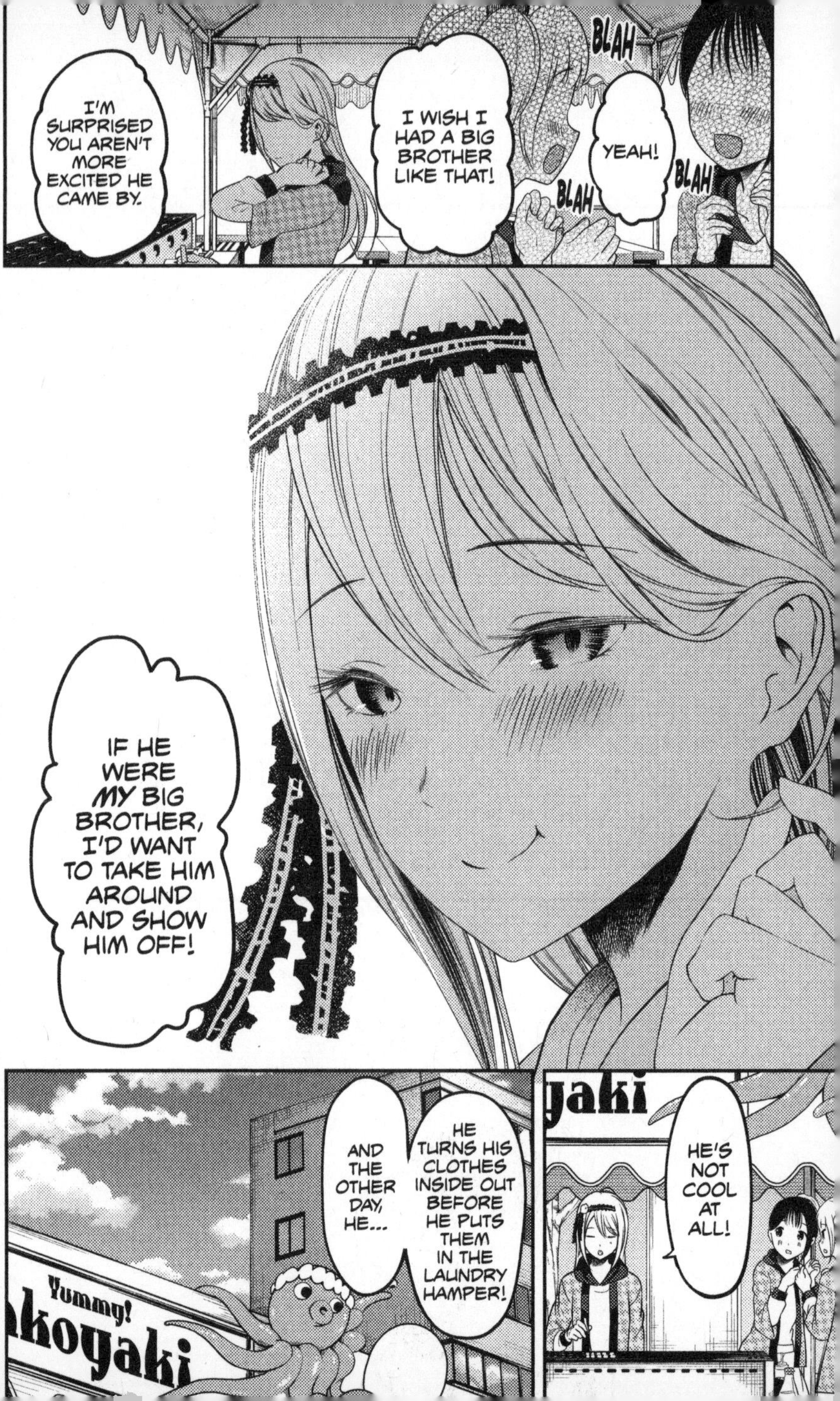
BLAH
YEAH!
BLAH
BLAH
I WISH I HAD A BIG BROTHER LIKE THAT!
I'M SURPRISED YOU AREN'T MORE EXCITED HE CAME BY.
IF HE WERE *MY* BIG BROTHER, I'D WANT TO TAKE HIM AROUND AND SHOW HIM OFF!
yaki
HE'S NOT COOL AT ALL!
HE TURNS HIS CLOTHES INSIDE OUT BEFORE HE PUTS THEM IN THE LAUNDRY HAMPER!
AND THE OTHER DAY, HE...
Yummy!
akoyaki

Student
council president
Shirogane is
sooo cool...

KAGUYA-SAMA
LOVE IS WAR

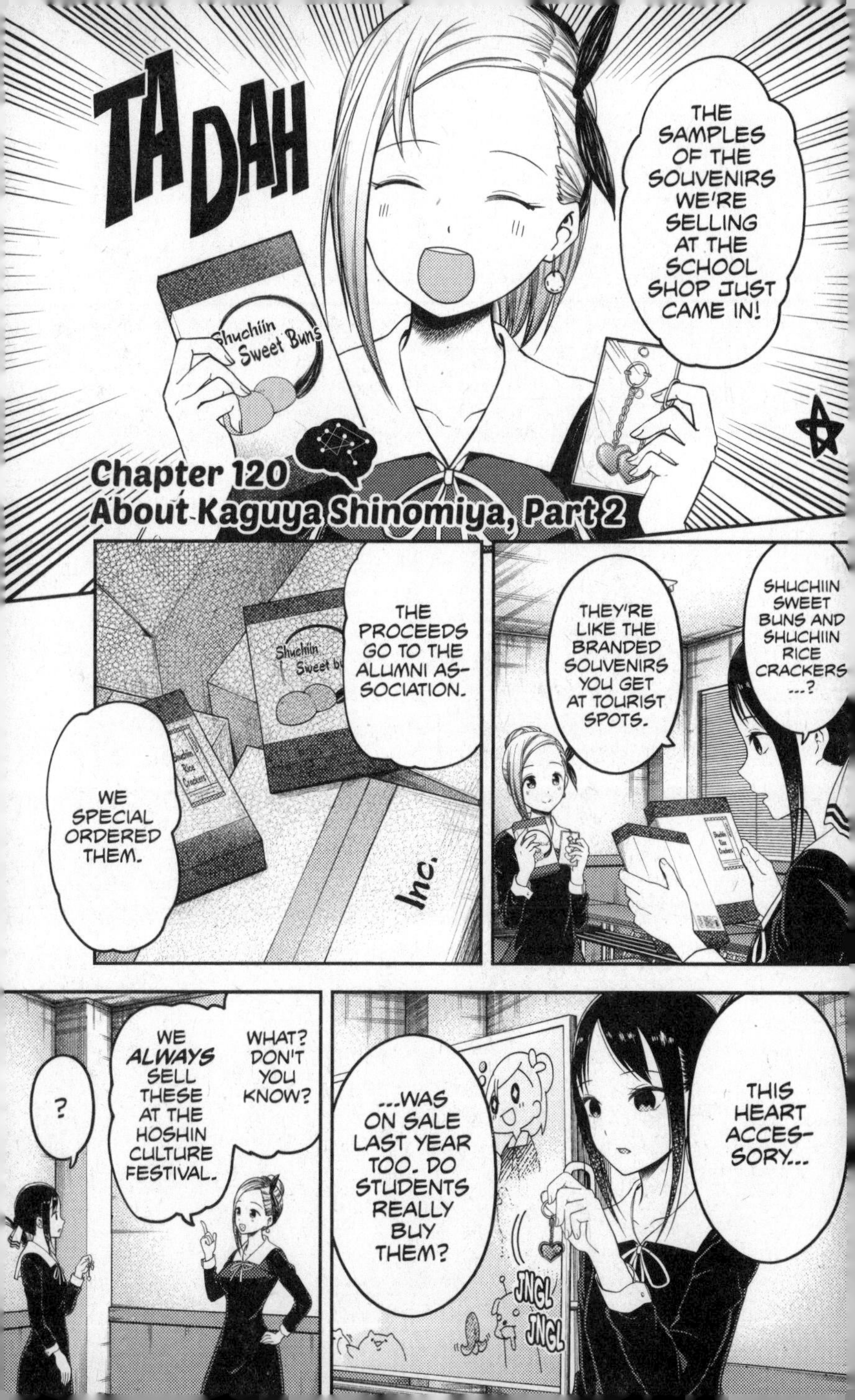
THE SAMPLES OF THE SOUVENIRS WE'RE SELLING AT THE SCHOOL SHOP JUST CAME IN!
TA DAH
Shuchiin Sweet Buns
Chapter 120
About Kaguya Shinomiya, Part 2
SHUCHIIN SWEET BUNS AND SHUCHIIN RICE CRACKERS ---?
THEY'RE LIKE THE BRANDED SOUVENIRS YOU GET AT TOURIST SPOTS.
THE PROCEEDS GO TO THE ALUMNI AS-SOCIATION.
WE SPECIAL ORDERED THEM.
Inc.
THIS HEART ACCES-SORY...
...WAS ON SALE LAST YEAR TOO. DO STUDENTS REALLY BUY THEM?
JNGL
JNGL
WHAT? DON'T YOU KNOW?
WE *ALWAYS* SELL THESE AT THE HOSHIN CULTURE FESTIVAL.
?

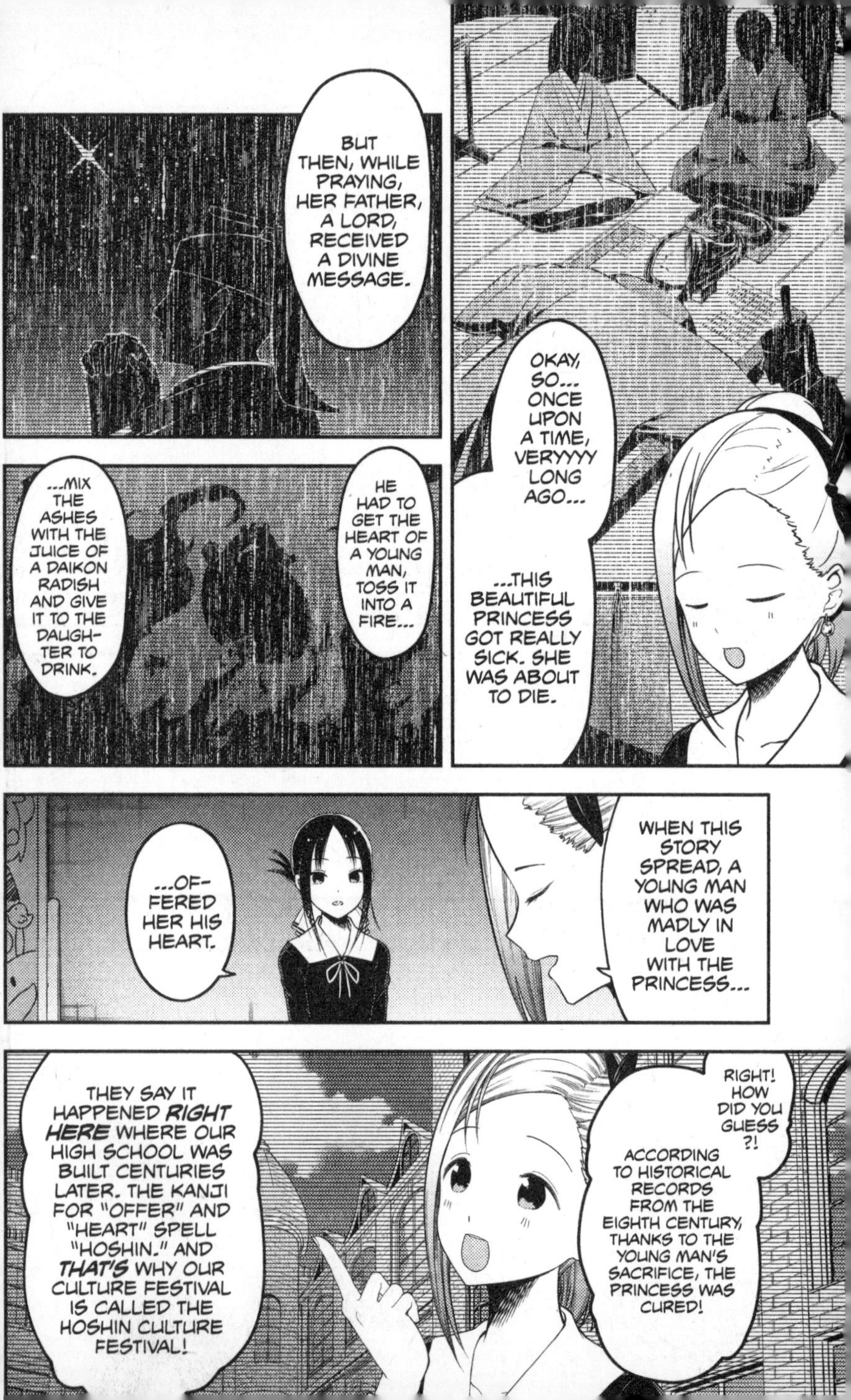
OKAY, SO... ONCE UPON A TIME, VERYYYY LONG AGO...
...THIS BEAUTIFUL PRINCESS GOT REALLY SICK. SHE WAS ABOUT TO DIE.
BUT THEN, WHILE PRAYING, HER FATHER, A LORD, RECEIVED A DIVINE MESSAGE.
HE HAD TO GET THE HEART OF A YOUNG MAN, TOSS IT INTO A FIRE...
...MIX THE ASHES WITH THE JUICE OF A DAIKON RADISH AND GIVE IT TO THE DAUGH-TER TO DRINK.
WHEN THIS STORY SPREAD, A YOUNG MAN WHO WAS MADLY IN LOVE WITH THE PRINCESS...
...OF-FERED HER HIS HEART.
RIGHT! HOW DID YOU GUESS?!
ACCORDING TO HISTORICAL RECORDS FROM THE EIGHTH CENTURY, THANKS TO THE YOUNG MAN'S SACRIFICE, THE PRINCESS WAS CURED!
THEY SAY IT HAPPENED ***RIGHT HERE*** WHERE OUR HIGH SCHOOL WAS BUILT CENTURIES LATER. THE KANJI FOR "OFFER" AND "HEART" SPELL "HOSHIN." AND ***THAT'S*** WHY OUR CULTURE FESTIVAL IS CALLED THE HOSHIN CULTURE FESTIVAL!

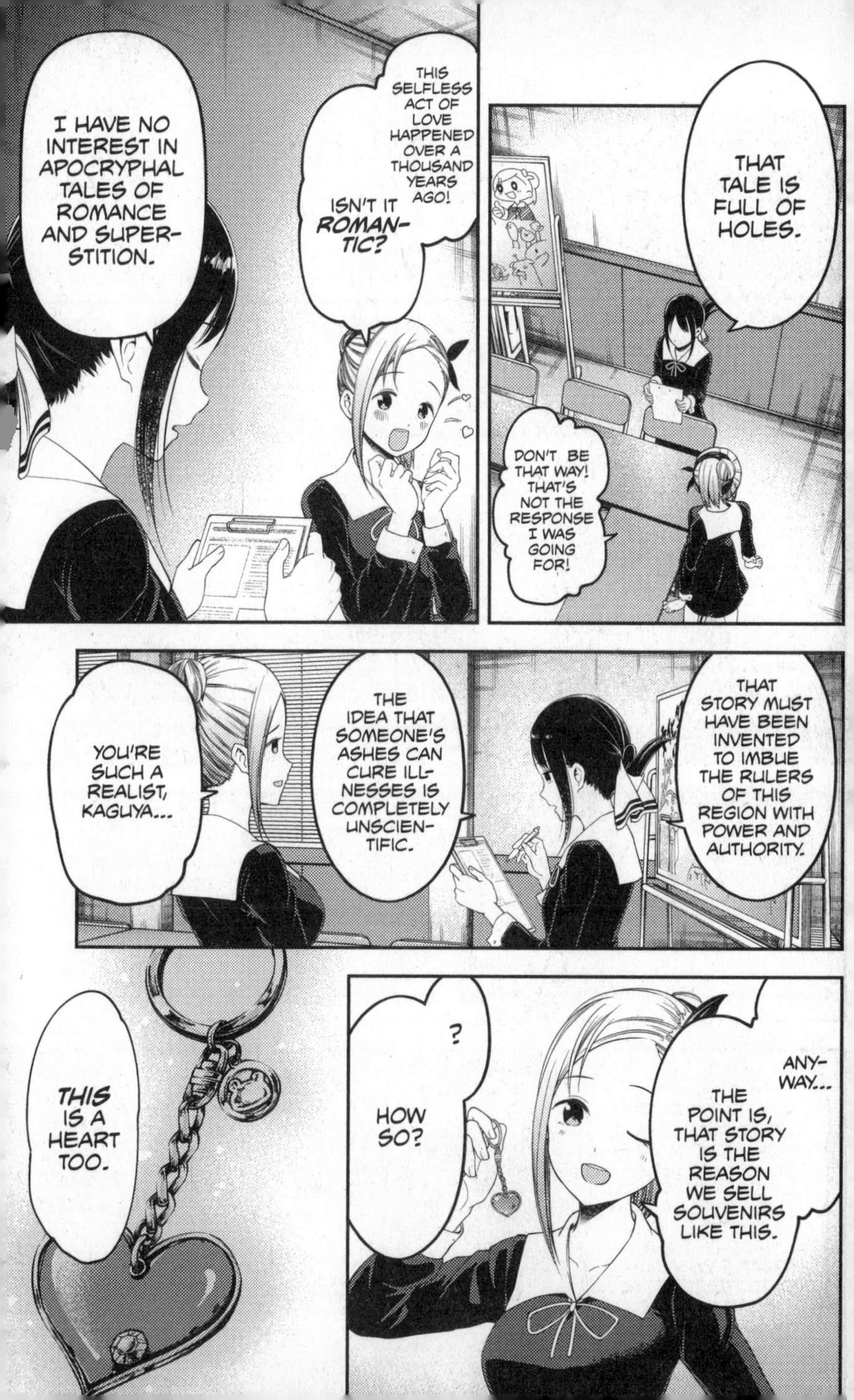

THAT TALE IS FULL OF HOLES.
DON'T BE THAT WAY! THAT'S NOT THE RESPONSE I WAS GOING FOR!
THIS SELFLESS ACT OF LOVE HAPPENED OVER A THOUSAND YEARS AGO!
ISN'T IT *ROMANTIC?*
I HAVE NO INTEREST IN APOCRYPHAL TALES OF ROMANCE AND SUPERSTITION.
THAT STORY MUST HAVE BEEN INVENTED TO IMBUE THE RULERS OF THIS REGION WITH POWER AND AUTHORITY.
THE IDEA THAT SOMEONE'S ASHES CAN CURE ILLNESSES IS COMPLETELY UNSCIENTIFIC.
YOU'RE SUCH A REALIST, KAGUYA...
ANYWAY...
THE POINT IS, THAT STORY IS THE REASON WE SELL SOUVENIRS LIKE THIS.
?
HOW SO?
THIS IS A HEART TOO.

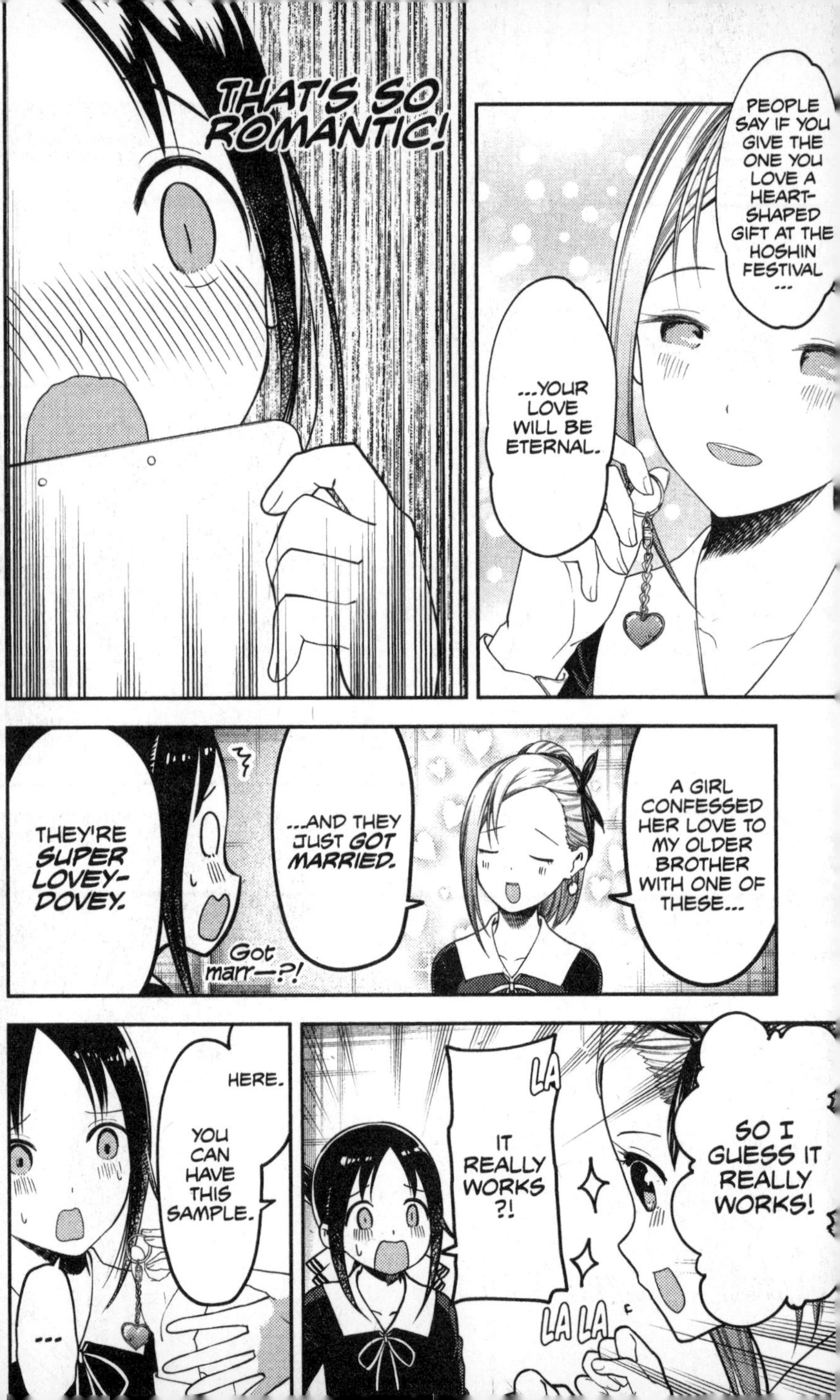
PEOPLE SAY IF YOU GIVE THE ONE YOU LOVE A HEART-SHAPED GIFT AT THE HOSHIN FESTIVAL...
...YOUR LOVE WILL BE ETERNAL.
THAT'S SO ROMANTIC!
A GIRL CONFESSED HER LOVE TO MY OLDER BROTHER WITH ONE OF THESE...
...AND THEY JUST GOT MARRIED.
Got marr—?!
THEY'RE SUPER LOVEY-DOVEY.
SO I GUESS IT REALLY WORKS!
LA
LA LA
IT REALLY WORKS?!
HERE.
YOU CAN HAVE THIS SAMPLE.
...

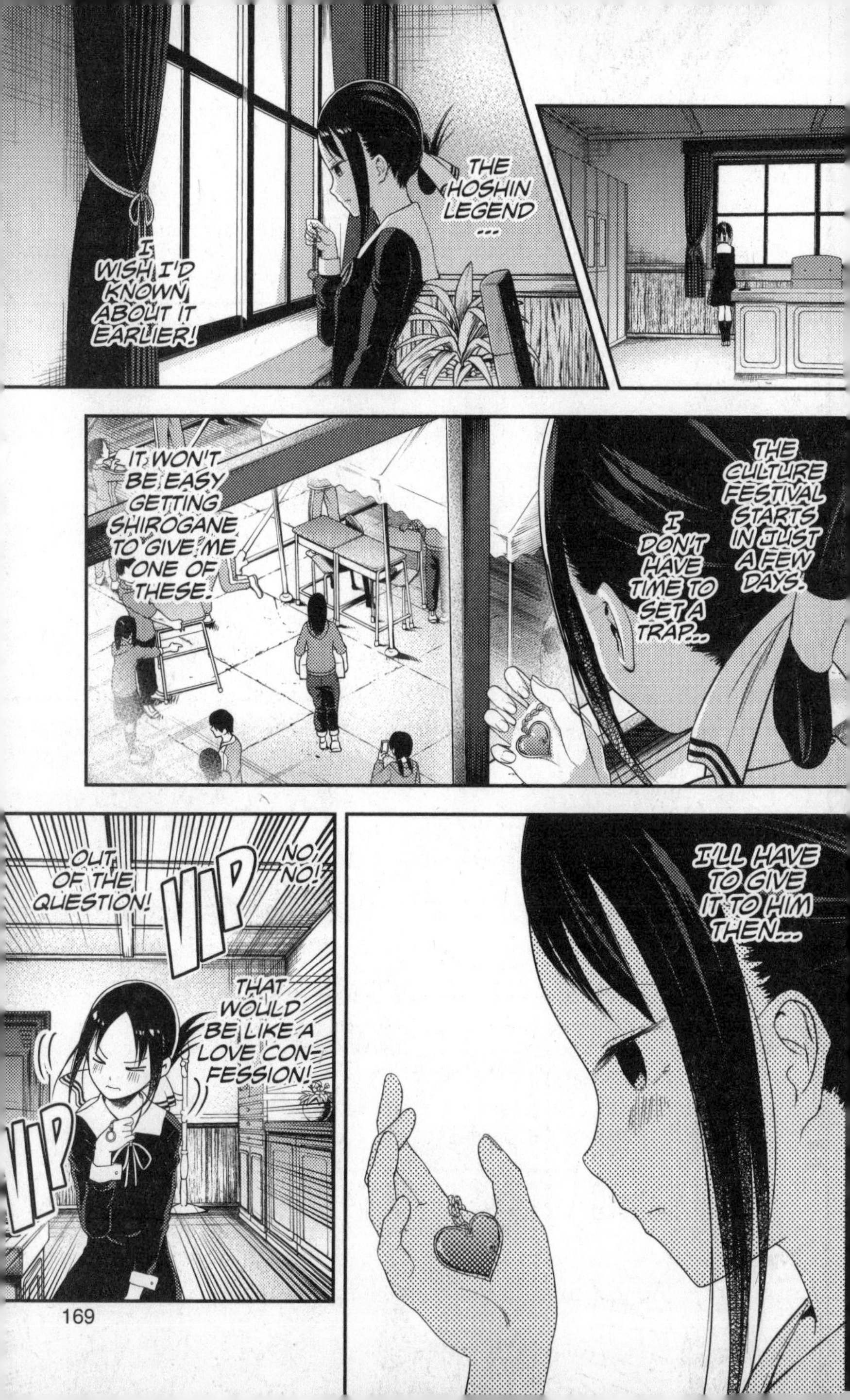
THE HOSHIN LEGEND...
I WISH I'D KNOWN ABOUT IT EARLIER!
THE CULTURE FESTIVAL STARTS IN JUST A FEW DAYS.
I DON'T HAVE TIME TO SET A TRAP...
IT WON'T BE EASY GETTING SHIROGANE TO GIVE ME ONE OF THESE.
I'LL HAVE TO GIVE IT TO HIM THEN...
NO! NO!
VIP
OUT OF THE QUESTION!
THAT WOULD BE LIKE A LOVE CON-FESSION!
VIP

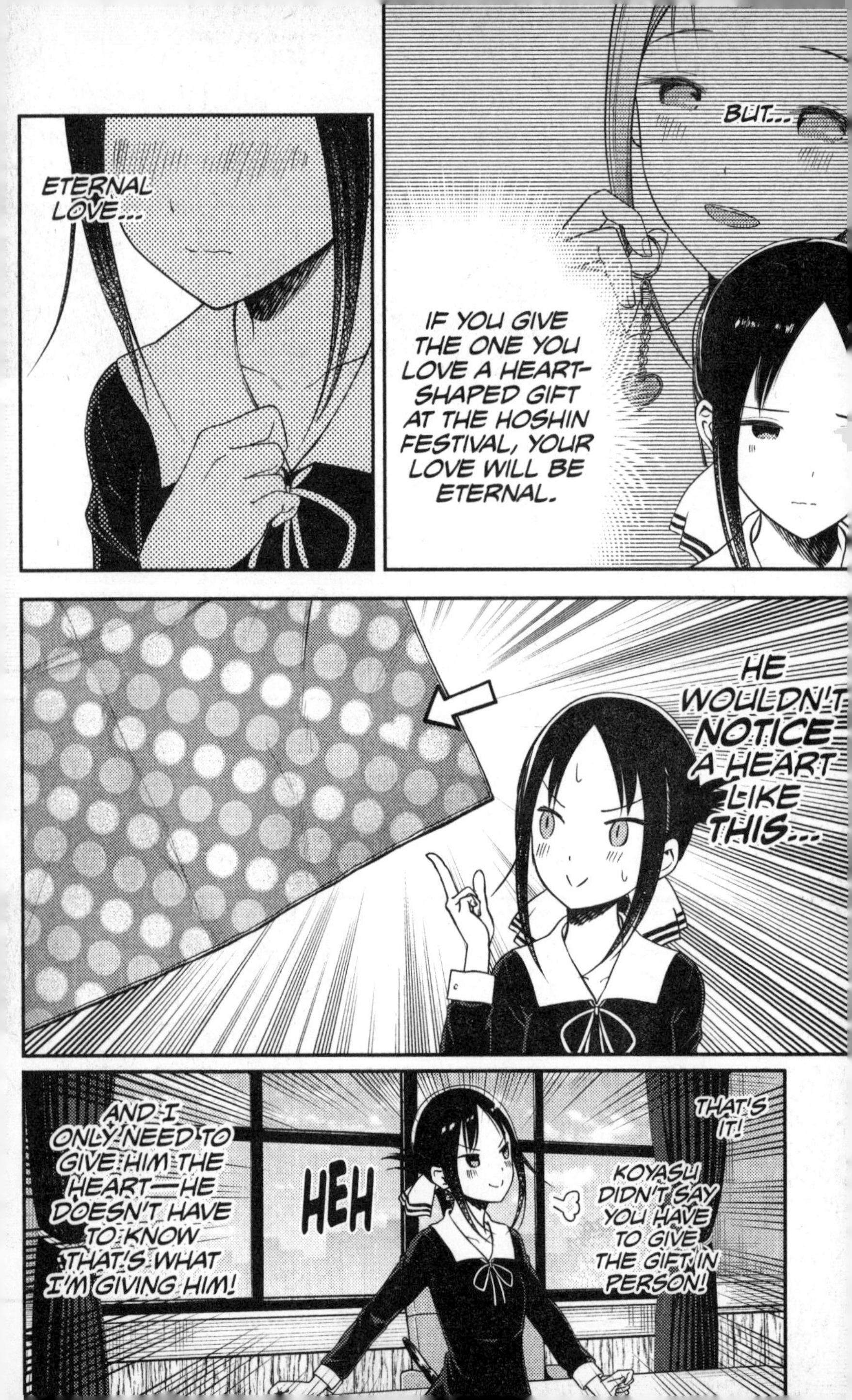
BUT...
IF YOU GIVE THE ONE YOU LOVE A HEART-SHAPED GIFT AT THE HOSHIN FESTIVAL, YOUR LOVE WILL BE ETERNAL.
ETERNAL LOVE...
HE WOULDN'T NOTICE A HEART LIKE THIS...
THAT'S IT!
KOYASU DIDN'T SAY YOU HAVE TO GIVE THE GIFT IN PERSON!
HEH
AND I ONLY NEED TO GIVE HIM THE HEART—HE DOESN'T HAVE TO KNOW THAT'S WHAT I'M GIVING HIM!

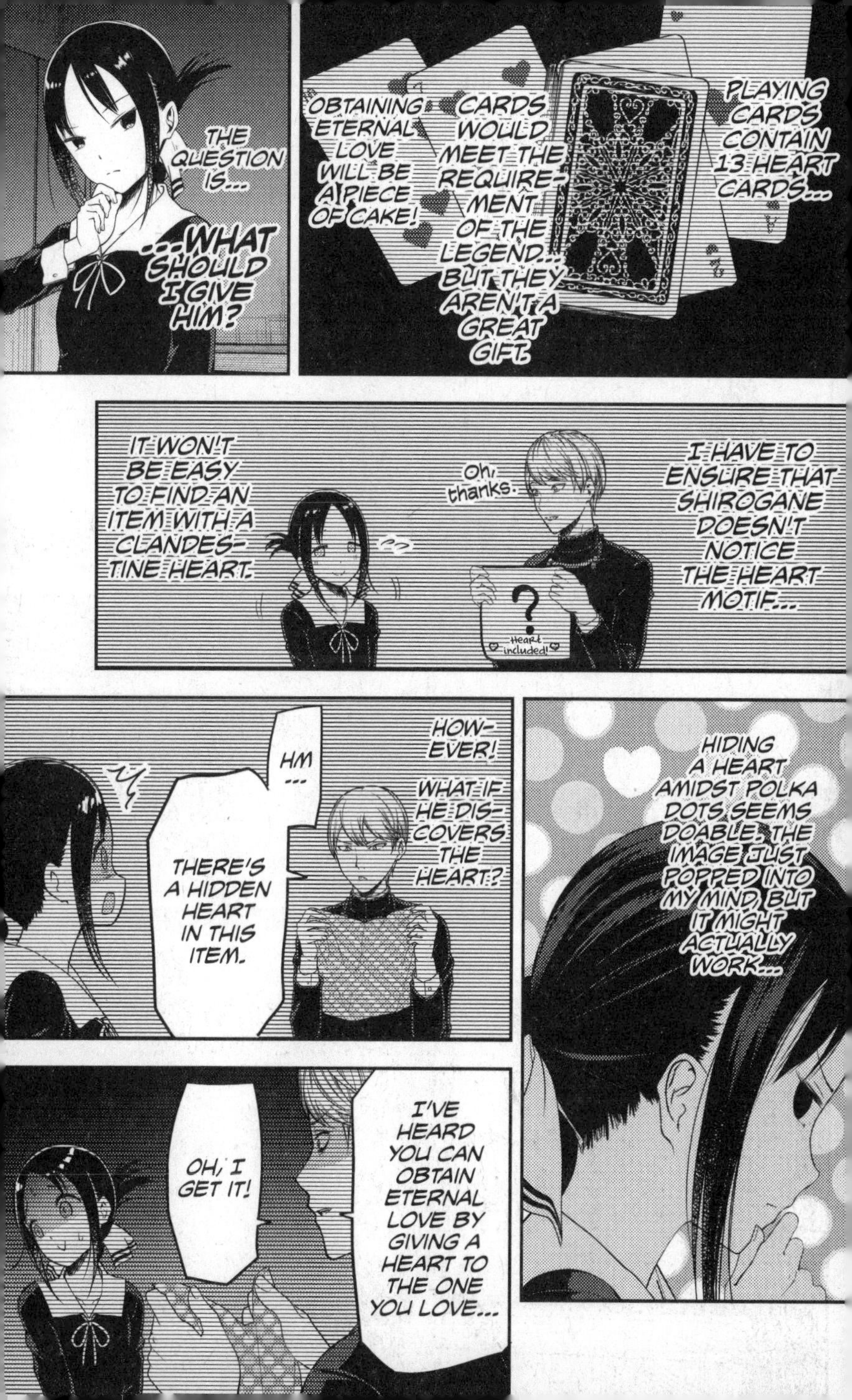
PLAYING CARDS CONTAIN 13 HEART CARDS...
CARDS WOULD MEET THE REQUIRE-MENT OF THE LEGEND... BUT THEY AREN'T A GREAT GIFT.
OBTAINING ETERNAL LOVE WILL BE A PIECE OF CAKE!
THE QUESTION IS...
...WHAT SHOULD I GIVE HIM?
I HAVE TO ENSURE THAT SHIROGANE DOESN'T NOTICE THE HEART MOTIF...
Oh, thanks.
?
Heart included!
IT WON'T BE EASY TO FIND AN ITEM WITH A CLANDES-TINE HEART.
HIDING A HEART AMIDST POLKA DOTS SEEMS DOABLE. THE IMAGE JUST POPPED INTO MY MIND, BUT IT MIGHT ACTUALLY WORK...
HOW-EVER!
WHAT IF HE DIS-COVERS THE HEART?
HM...
THERE'S A HIDDEN HEART IN THIS ITEM.
I'VE HEARD YOU CAN OBTAIN ETERNAL LOVE BY GIVING A HEART TO THE ONE YOU LOVE...
OH, I GET IT!

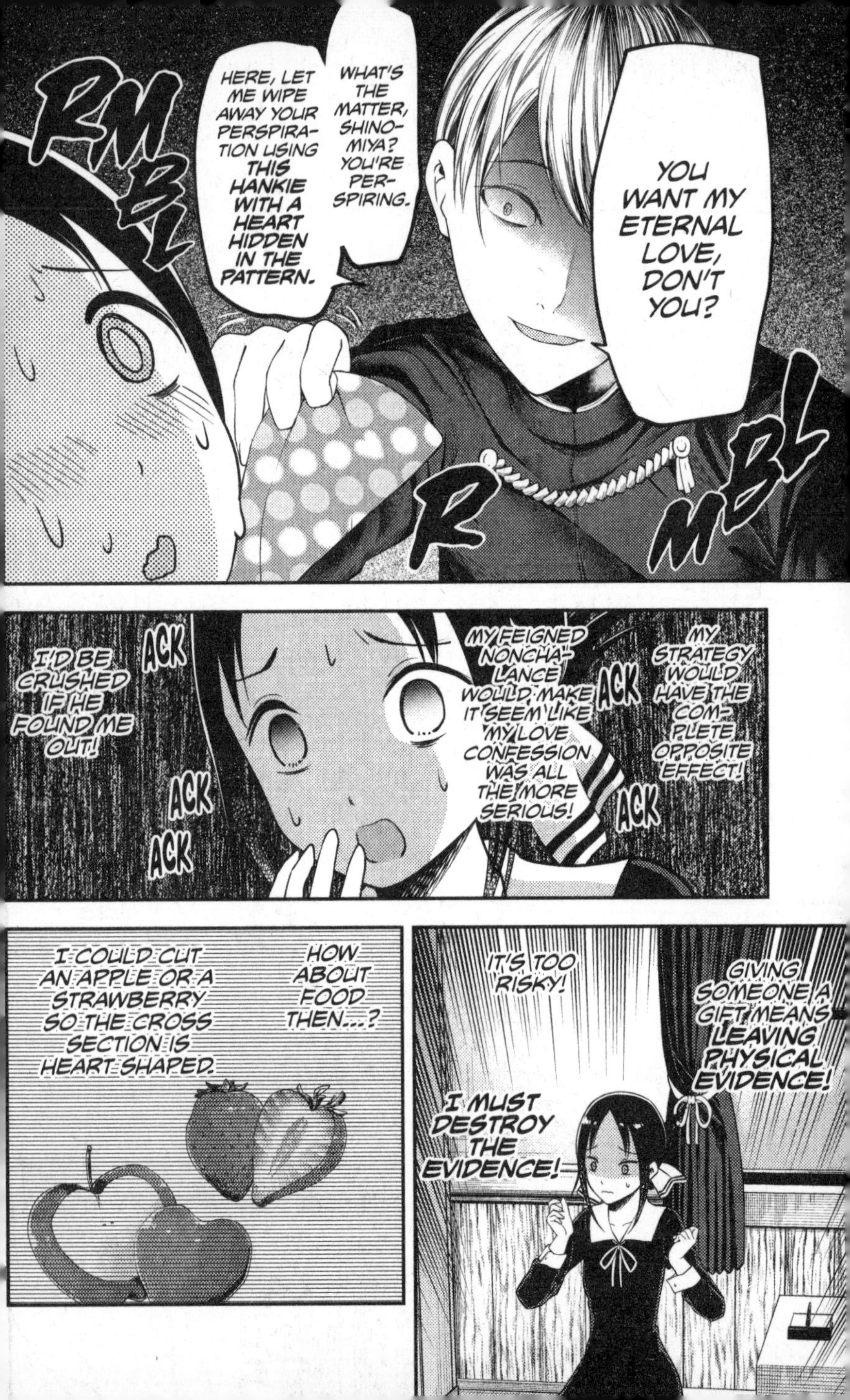
YOU WANT MY ETERNAL LOVE, DON'T YOU?
WHAT'S THE MATTER, SHINOMIYA? YOU'RE PERSPIRING.
HERE, LET ME WIPE AWAY YOUR PERSPIRATION USING THIS HANKIE WITH A HEART HIDDEN IN THE PATTERN.
RMBL
RMBL
MY STRATEGY WOULD HAVE THE COMPLETE OPPOSITE EFFECT!
ACK
ACK
MY FEIGNED NONCHALANCE WOULD MAKE IT SEEM LIKE MY LOVE CONFESSION WAS ALL THE MORE SERIOUS!
ACK
I'D BE CRUSHED IF HE FOUND ME OUT!
ACK
ACK
GIVING SOMEONE A GIFT MEANS LEAVING PHYSICAL EVIDENCE!
IT'S TOO RISKY!
I MUST DESTROY THE EVIDENCE!
HOW ABOUT FOOD THEN...?
I COULD CUT AN APPLE OR A STRAWBERRY SO THE CROSS SECTION IS HEART SHAPED.

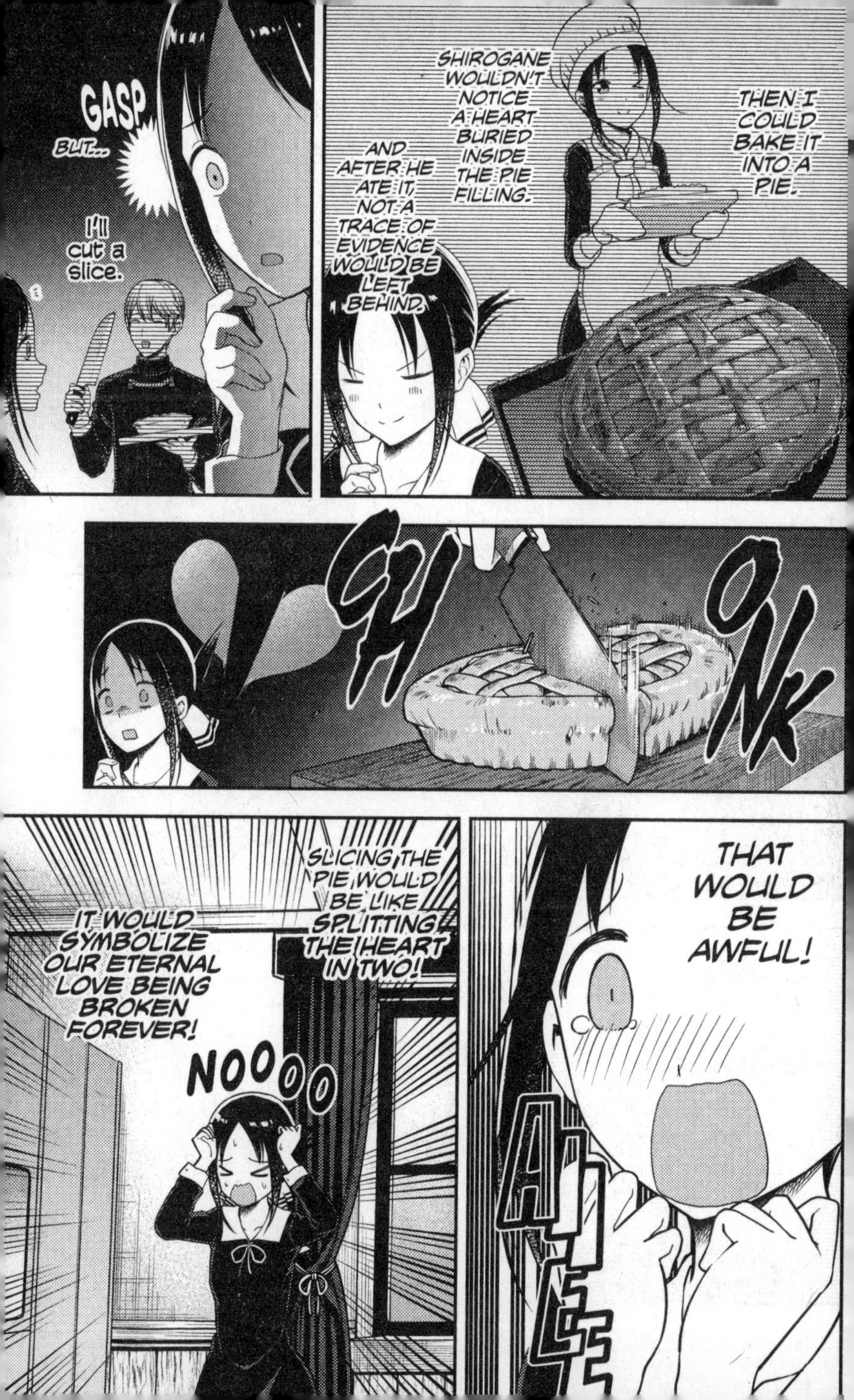
THEN I COULD BAKE IT INTO A PIE.
SHIROGANE WOULDN'T NOTICE A HEART BURIED INSIDE THE PIE FILLING.
AND AFTER HE ATE IT, NOT A TRACE OF EVIDENCE WOULD BE LEFT BEHIND.
GASP
BUT...
I'll cut a slice.
THAT WOULD BE AWFUL!
SLICING THE PIE WOULD BE LIKE SPLITTING THE HEART IN TWO!
IT WOULD SYMBOLIZE OUR ETERNAL LOVE BEING BROKEN FOREVER!
NOOOOO

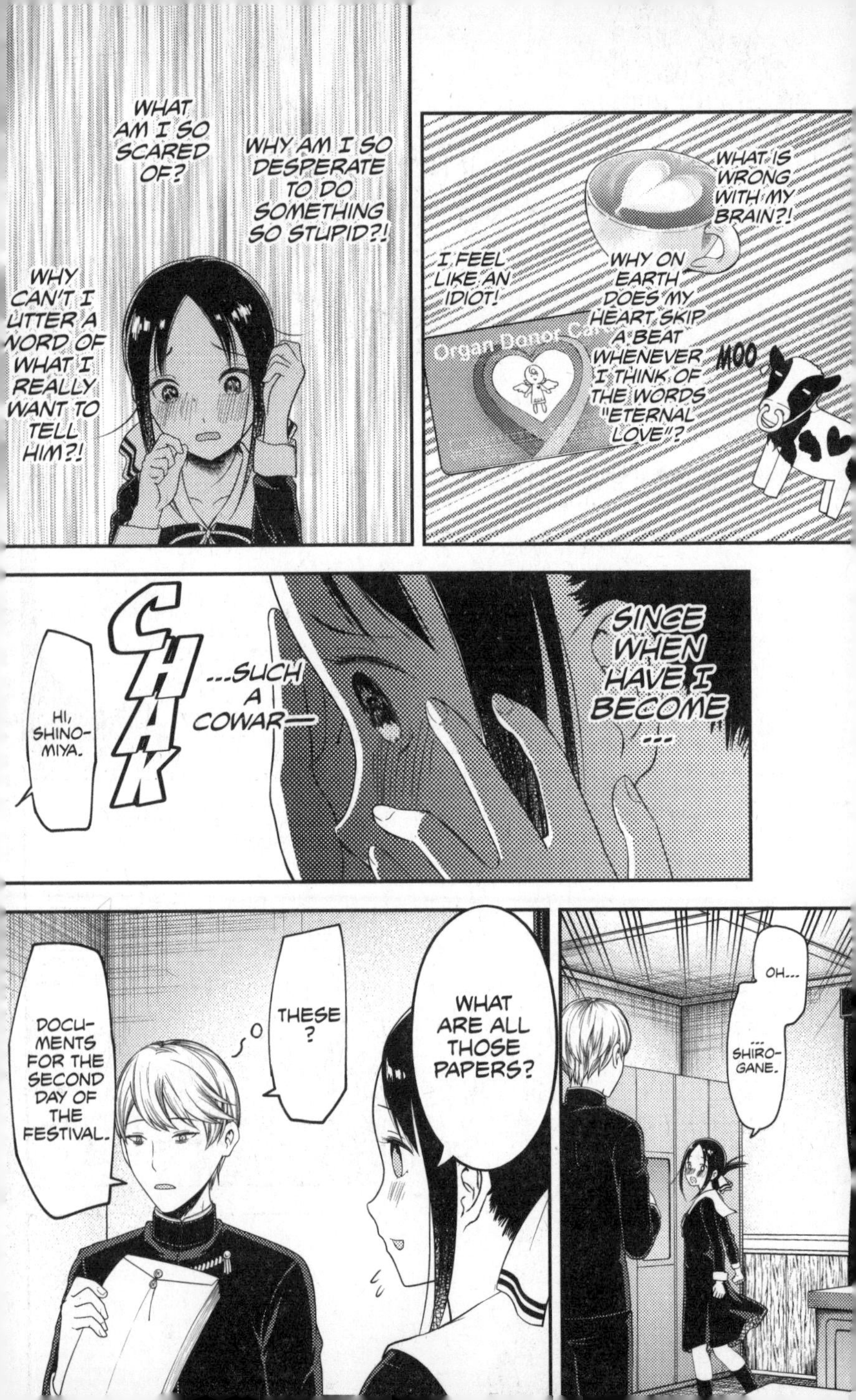
WHAT IS WRONG WITH MY BRAIN?!
WHY ON EARTH DOES MY HEART SKIP A BEAT WHENEVER I THINK OF THE WORDS "ETERNAL LOVE"?
MOO
I FEEL LIKE AN IDIOT!
Organ Donor
WHY AM I SO DESPERATE TO DO SOMETHING SO STUPID?!
WHAT AM I SO SCARED OF?
WHY CAN'T I UTTER A WORD OF WHAT I REALLY WANT TO TELL HIM?!
SINCE WHEN HAVE I BECOME ...
...SUCH A COWAR—
CHAK
HI, SHINOMIYA.
OH...
...SHIROGANE.
WHAT ARE ALL THOSE PAPERS?
THESE?
DOCUMENTS FOR THE SECOND DAY OF THE FESTIVAL.

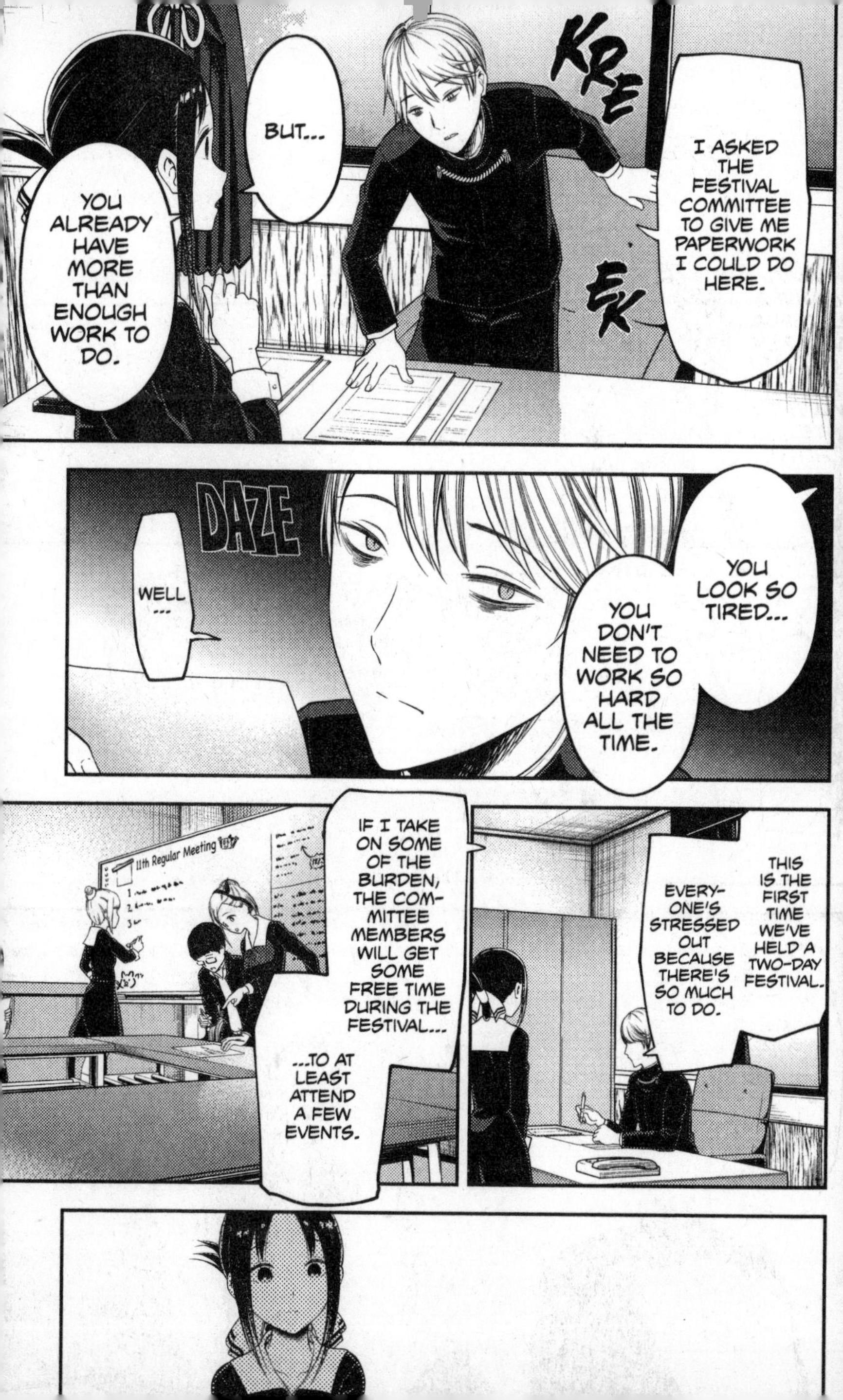
KREEK
I ASKED THE FESTIVAL COMMITTEE TO GIVE ME PAPERWORK I COULD DO HERE.
BUT...
YOU ALREADY HAVE MORE THAN ENOUGH WORK TO DO.
YOU LOOK SO TIRED...
YOU DON'T NEED TO WORK SO HARD ALL THE TIME.
DAZE
WELL...
THIS IS THE FIRST TIME WE'VE HELD A TWO-DAY FESTIVAL.
EVERYONE'S STRESSED OUT BECAUSE THERE'S SO MUCH TO DO.
11th Regular Meeting
IF I TAKE ON SOME OF THE BURDEN, THE COMMITTEE MEMBERS WILL GET SOME FREE TIME DURING THE FESTIVAL...
...TO AT LEAST ATTEND A FEW EVENTS.

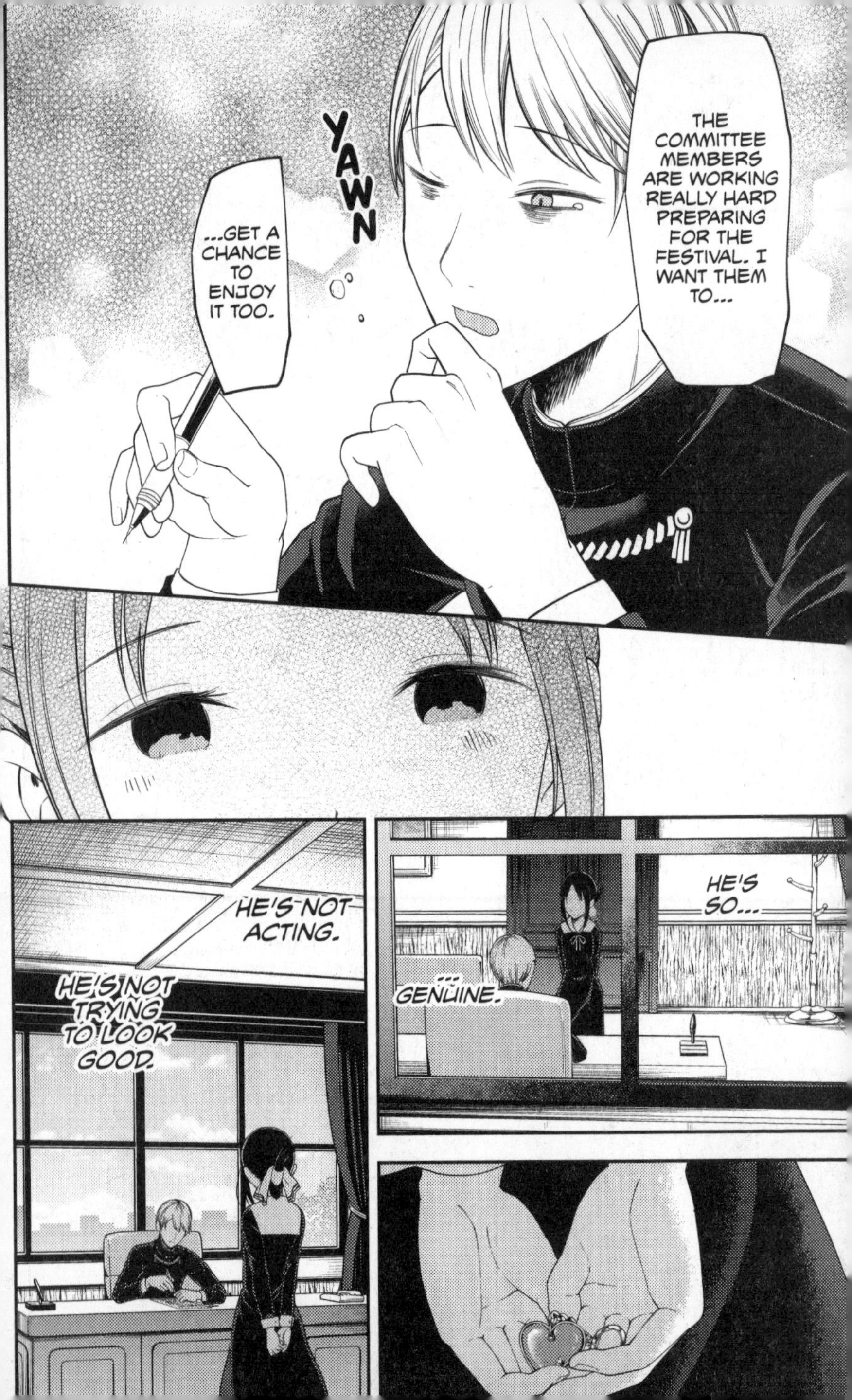
THE COMMITTEE MEMBERS ARE WORKING REALLY HARD PREPARING FOR THE FESTIVAL. I WANT THEM TO...
YAWN
...GET A CHANCE TO ENJOY IT TOO.
HE'S SO...
...GENUINE.
HE'S NOT ACTING.
HE'S NOT TRYING TO LOOK GOOD.

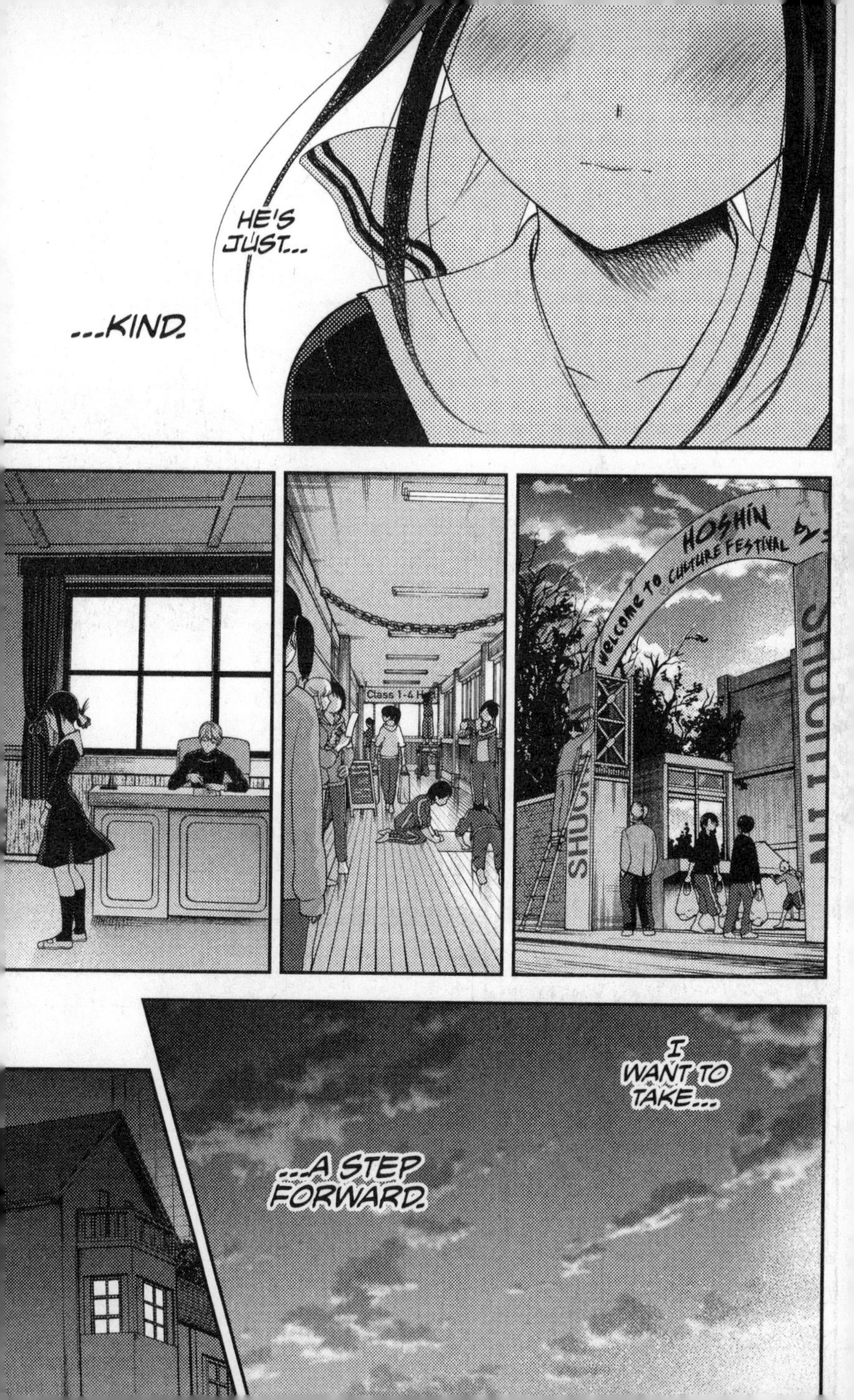
HE'S JUST...
...KIND.
HOSHIN
WELCOME TO CULTURE FESTIVAL
Class 1-4
I WANT TO TAKE...
...A STEP FORWARD.

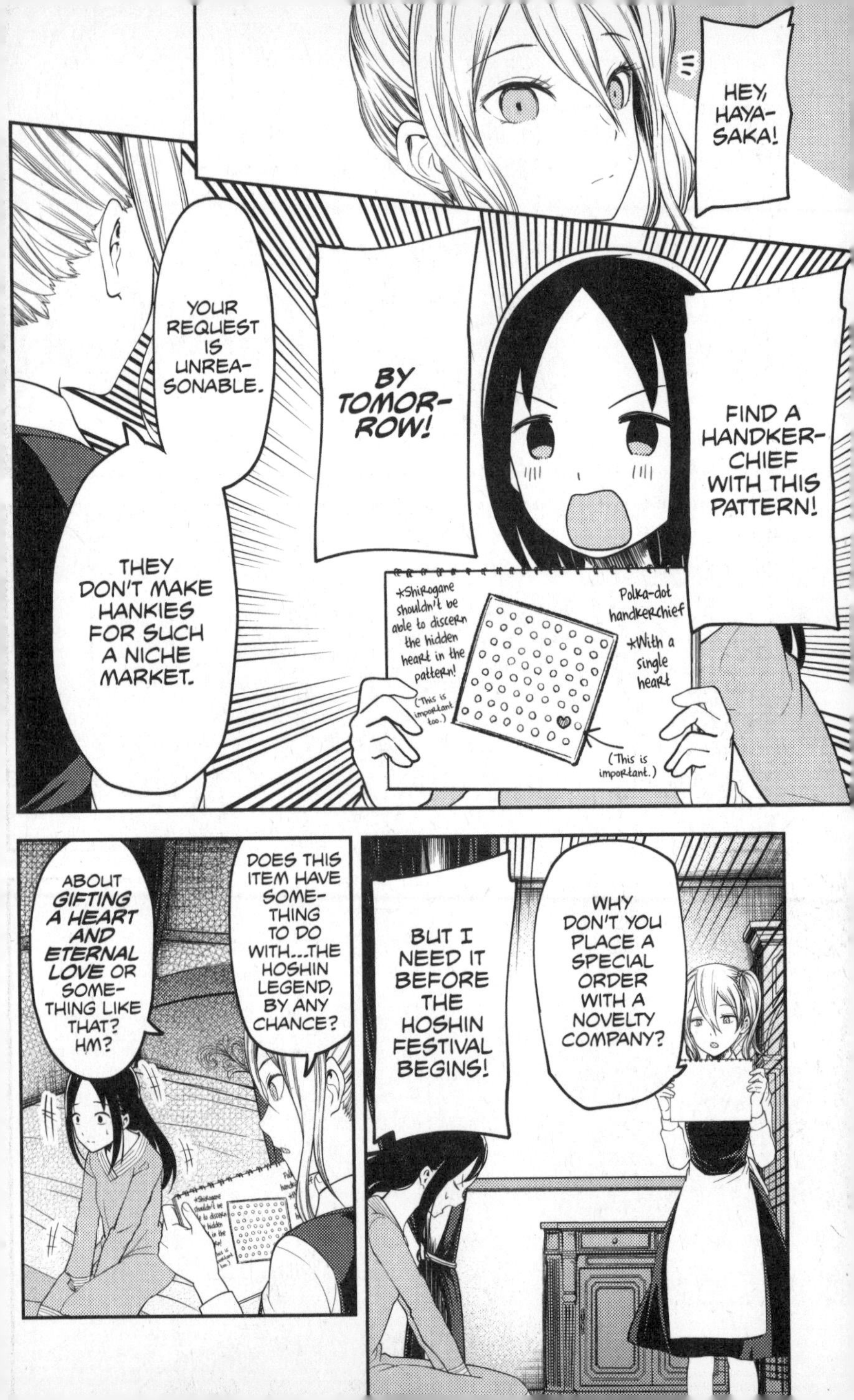
HEY, HAYA-SAKA!
FIND A HANDKER-CHIEF WITH THIS PATTERN!
BY TOMOR-ROW!
Polka-dot handkerchief
*With a single heart
*Shirogane shouldn't be able to discern the hidden heart in the pattern!
(This is important too.)
(This is important.)
YOUR REQUEST IS UNREA-SONABLE.
THEY DON'T MAKE HANKIES FOR SUCH A NICHE MARKET.
WHY DON'T YOU PLACE A SPECIAL ORDER WITH A NOVELTY COMPANY?
BUT I NEED IT BEFORE THE HOSHIN FESTIVAL BEGINS!
DOES THIS ITEM HAVE SOME-THING TO DO WITH...THE HOSHIN LEGEND, BY ANY CHANCE?
ABOUT GIFTING A HEART AND ETERNAL LOVE OR SOME-THING LIKE THAT? HM?

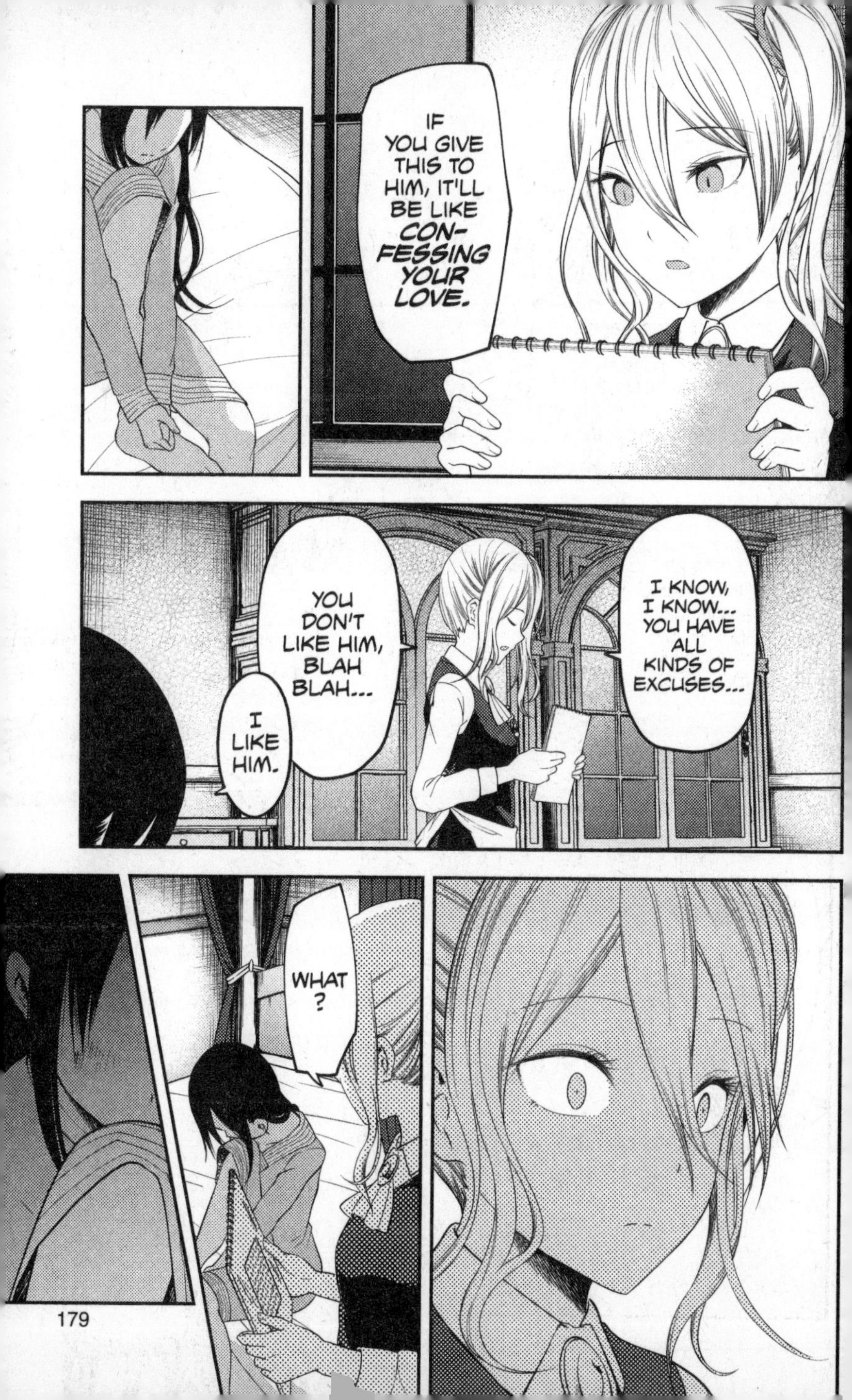
IF YOU GIVE THIS TO HIM, IT'LL BE LIKE CON-FESSING YOUR LOVE.
I KNOW, I KNOW... YOU HAVE ALL KINDS OF EXCUSES...
YOU DON'T LIKE HIM, BLAH BLAH...
I LIKE HIM.
WHAT?

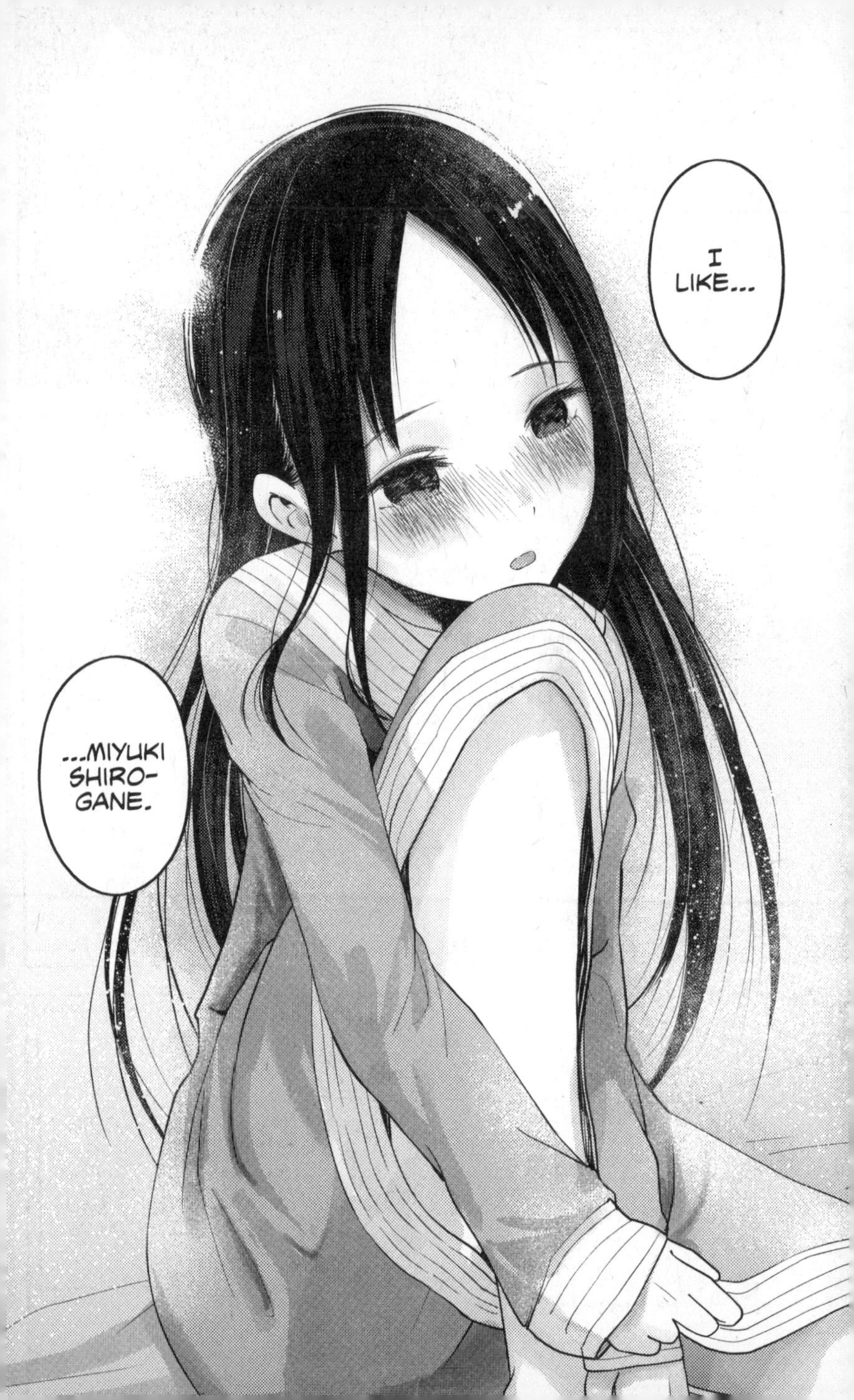
I LIKE...
...MIYUKI SHIRO-GANE.

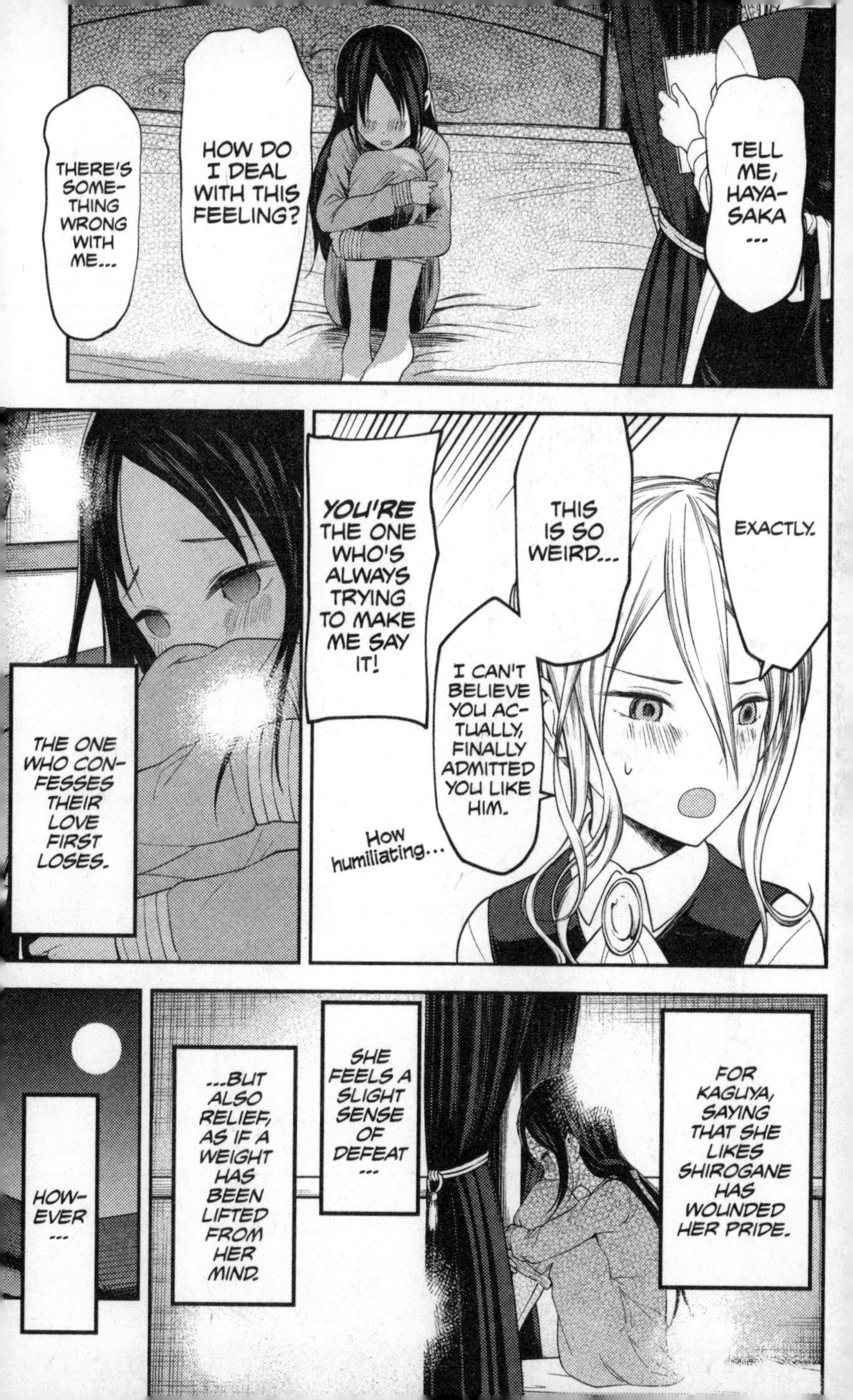
TELL ME, HAYASAKA...
HOW DO I DEAL WITH THIS FEELING?
THERE'S SOMETHING WRONG WITH ME...
EXACTLY.
THIS IS SO WEIRD...
YOU'RE THE ONE WHO'S ALWAYS TRYING TO MAKE ME SAY IT!
I CAN'T BELIEVE YOU ACTUALLY, FINALLY ADMITTED YOU LIKE HIM.
How humiliating...
THE ONE WHO CONFESSES THEIR LOVE FIRST LOSES.
FOR KAGUYA, SAYING THAT SHE LIKES SHIROGANE HAS WOUNDED HER PRIDE.
SHE FEELS A SLIGHT SENSE OF DEFEAT...
...BUT ALSO RELIEF, AS IF A WEIGHT HAS BEEN LIFTED FROM HER MIND.
HOWEVER...

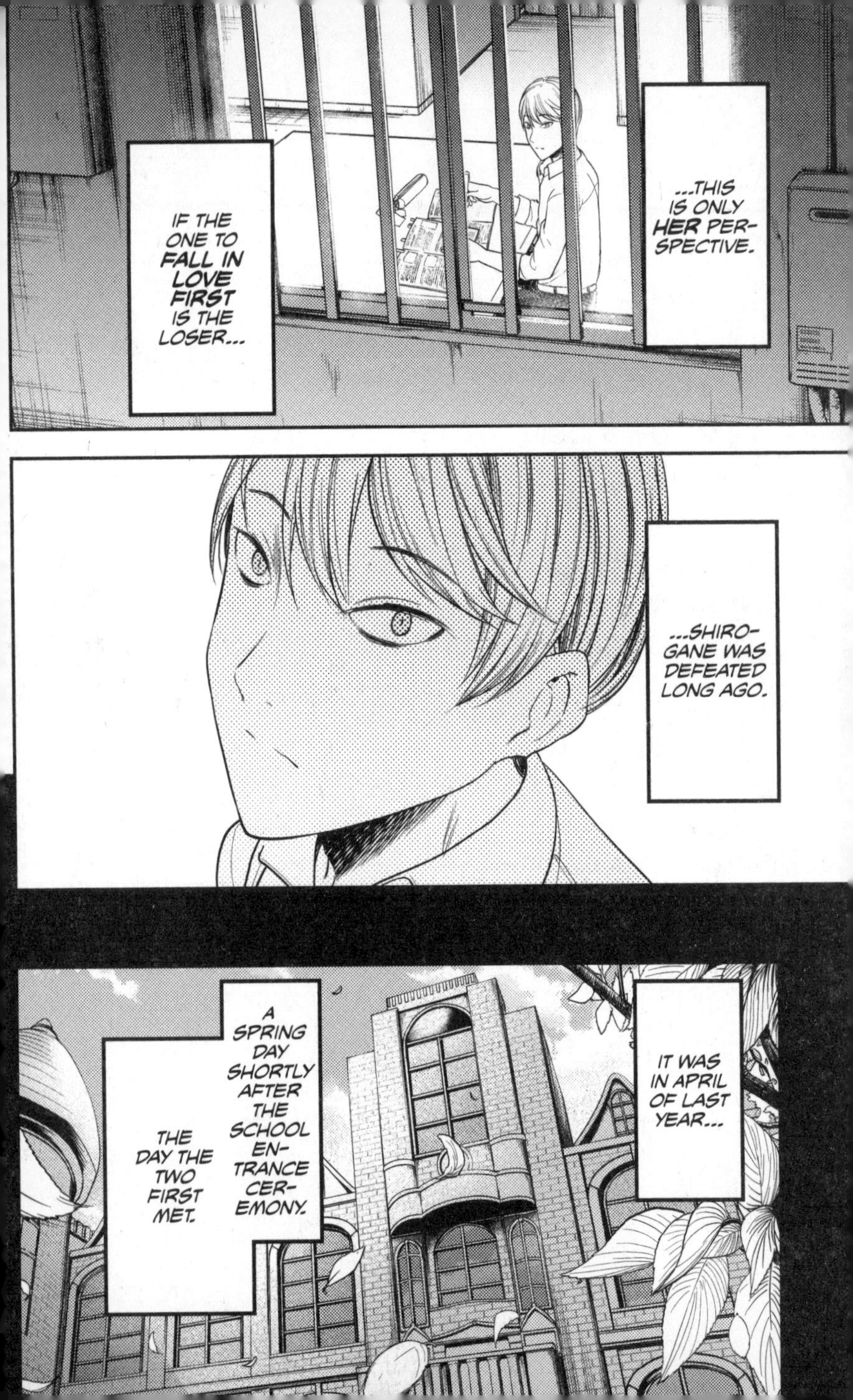
...THIS IS ONLY HER PERSPECTIVE.
IF THE ONE TO FALL IN LOVE FIRST IS THE LOSER...
...SHIROGANE WAS DEFEATED LONG AGO.
IT WAS IN APRIL OF LAST YEAR...
A SPRING DAY SHORTLY AFTER THE SCHOOL ENTRANCE CEREMONY.
THE DAY THE TWO FIRST MET.

I can't believe she finally broke down...
THIS WAS THE BIGGEST NEWS STORY OF THE YEAR FOR HAYASAKA.

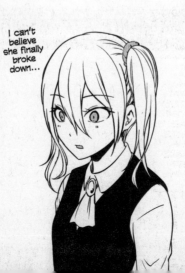

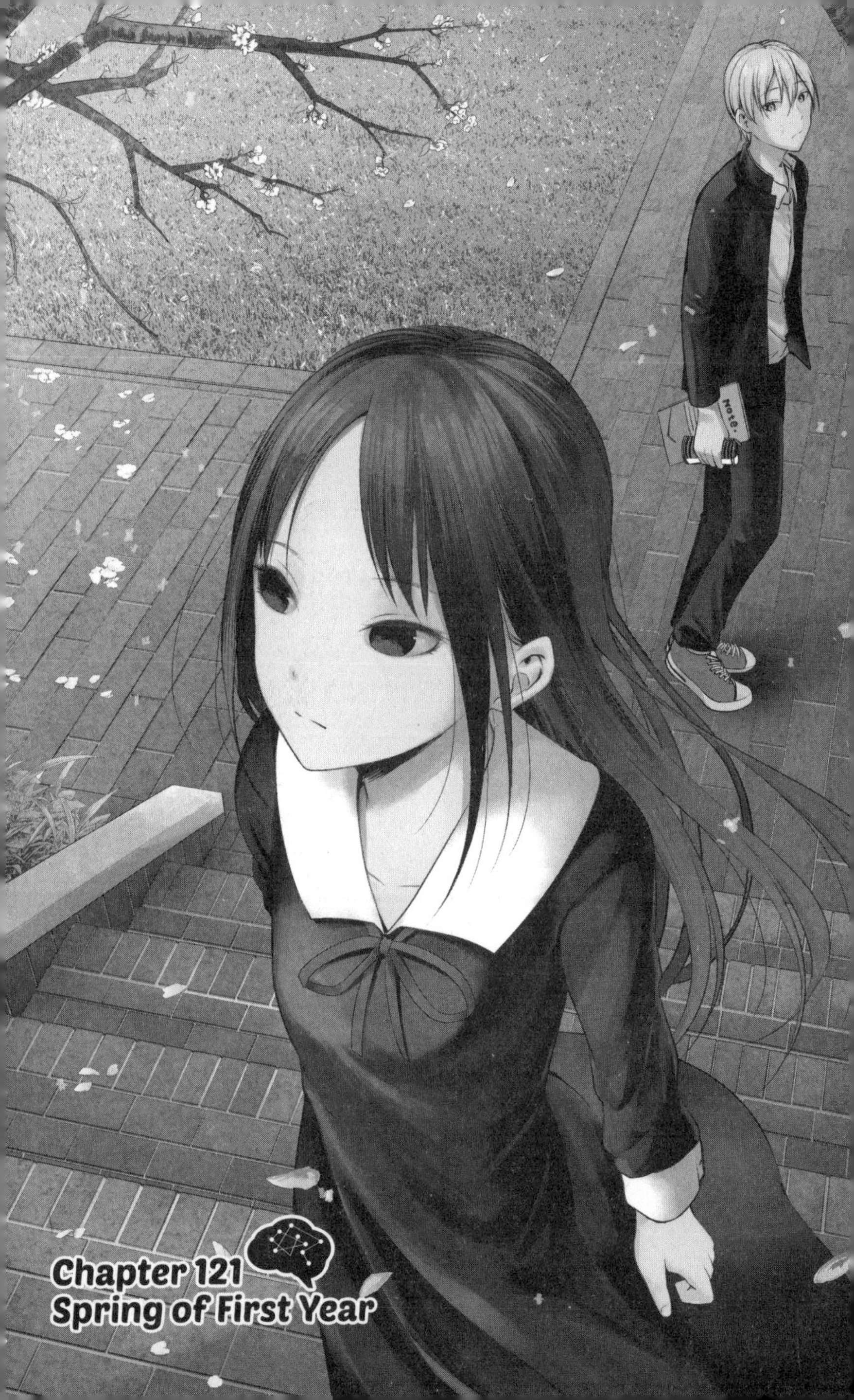
Note.
Chapter 121
Spring of First Year

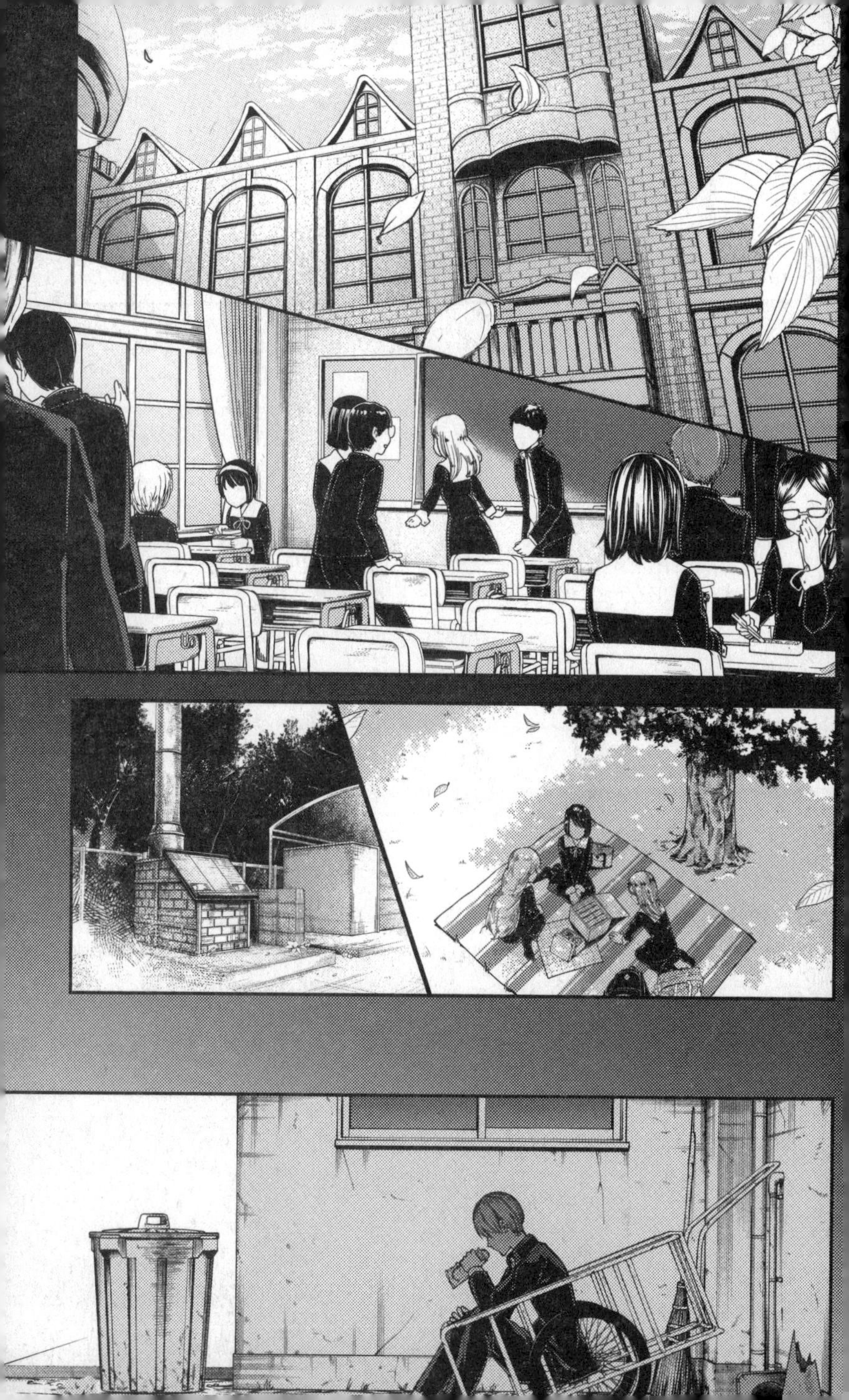

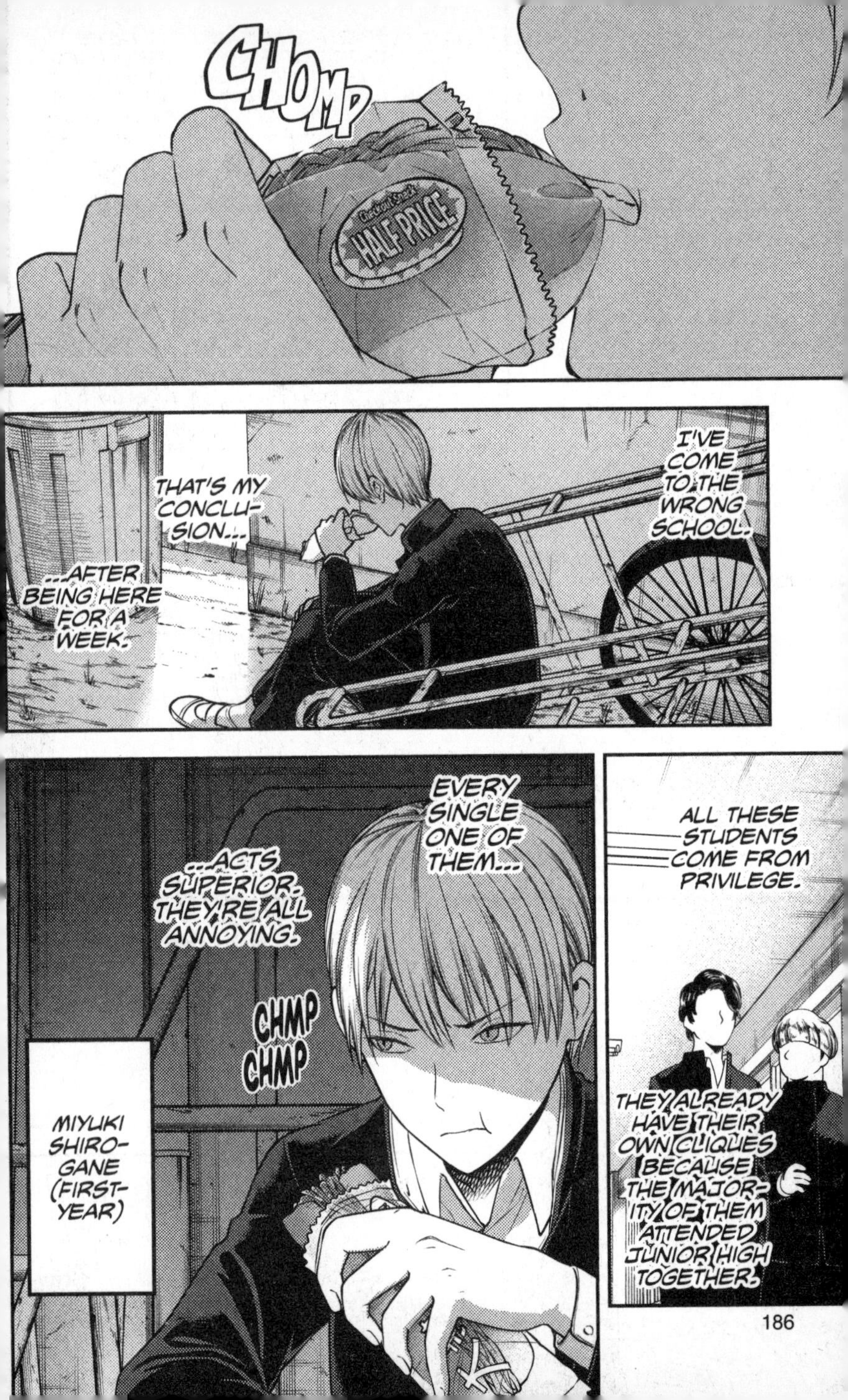
CHOMP
HALF PRICE
I'VE COME TO THE WRONG SCHOOL.
THAT'S MY CONCLUSION...
...AFTER BEING HERE FOR A WEEK.
ALL THESE STUDENTS COME FROM PRIVILEGE.
THEY ALREADY HAVE THEIR OWN CLIQUES BECAUSE THE MAJORITY OF THEM ATTENDED JUNIOR HIGH TOGETHER.
EVERY SINGLE ONE OF THEM...
...ACTS SUPERIOR. THEY'RE ALL ANNOYING.
CHMP CHMP
MIYUKI SHIROGANE (FIRST-YEAR)

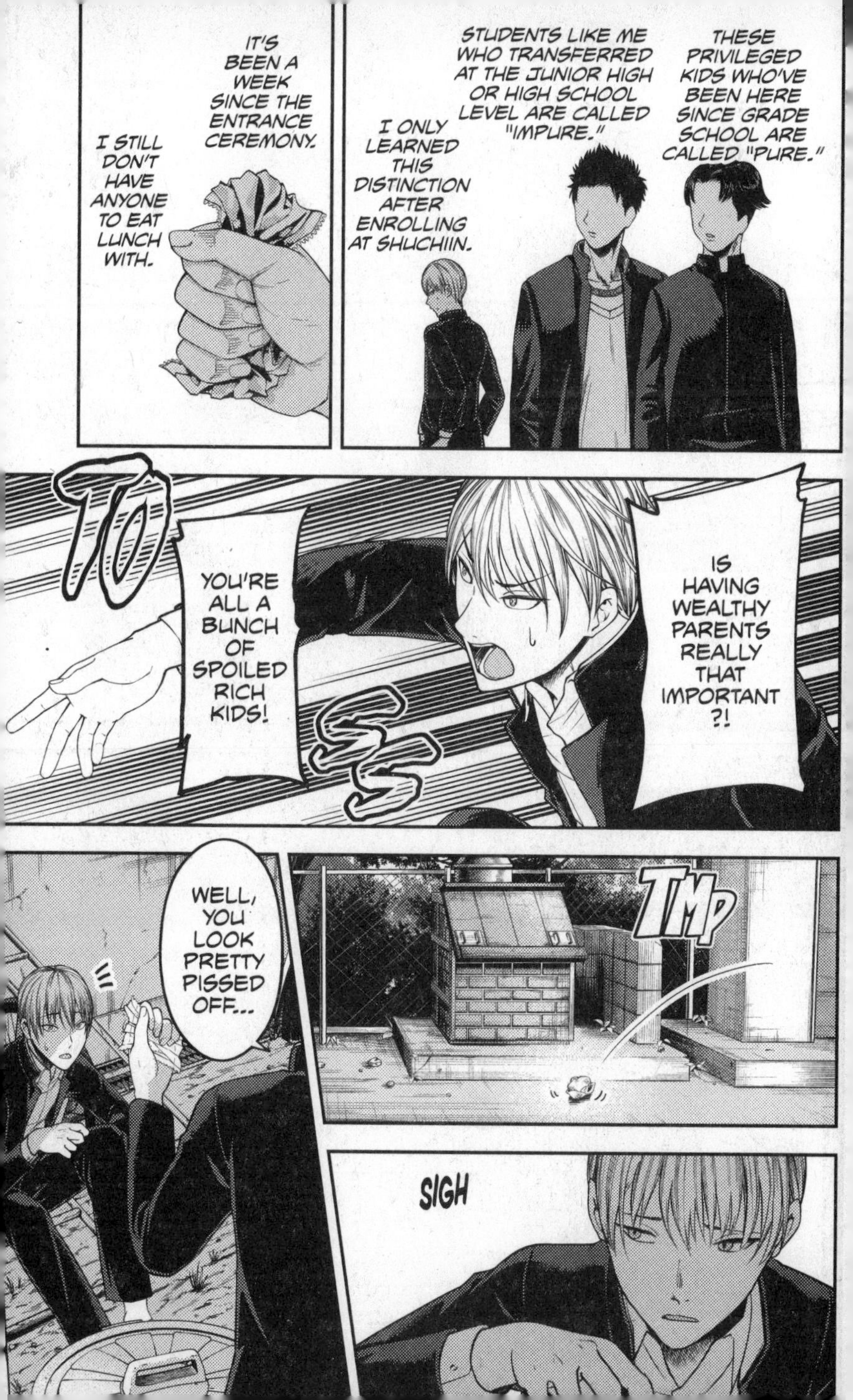
THESE PRIVILEGED KIDS WHO'VE BEEN HERE SINCE GRADE SCHOOL ARE CALLED "PURE."
STUDENTS LIKE ME WHO TRANSFERRED AT THE JUNIOR HIGH OR HIGH SCHOOL LEVEL ARE CALLED "IMPURE."
I ONLY LEARNED THIS DISTINCTION AFTER ENROLLING AT SHUCHIIN.
IT'S BEEN A WEEK SINCE THE ENTRANCE CEREMONY.
I STILL DON'T HAVE ANYONE TO EAT LUNCH WITH.
IS HAVING WEALTHY PARENTS REALLY THAT IMPORTANT?!
YOU'RE ALL A BUNCH OF SPOILED RICH KIDS!
TO
TMP
SIGH
WELL, YOU LOOK PRETTY PISSED OFF...

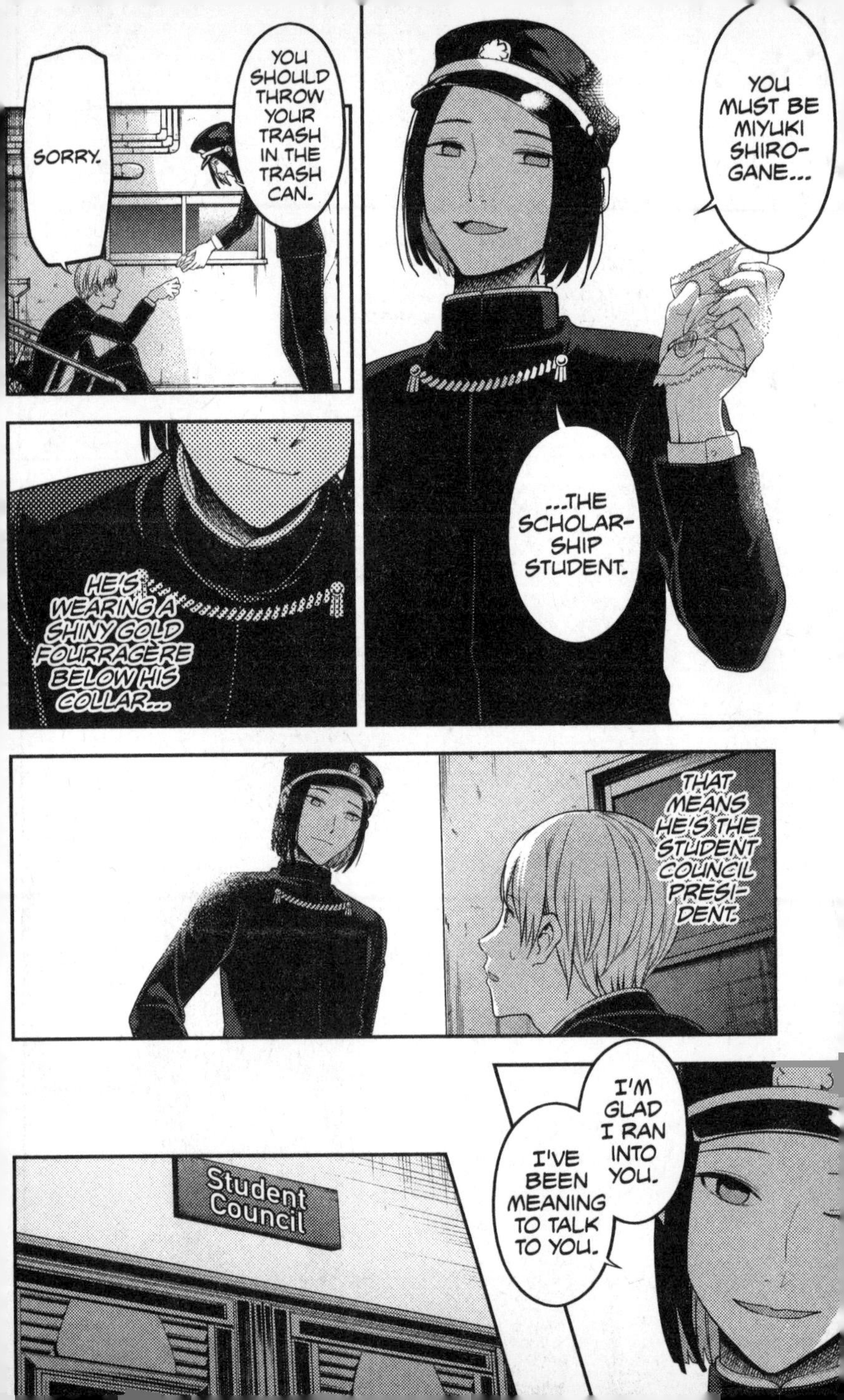
YOU MUST BE MIYUKI SHIROGANE...
...THE SCHOLARSHIP STUDENT.
YOU SHOULD THROW YOUR TRASH IN THE TRASH CAN.
SORRY.
HE'S WEARING A SHINY GOLD FOURRAGÈRE BELOW HIS COLLAR...
THAT MEANS HE'S THE STUDENT COUNCIL PRESIDENT.
I'M GLAD I RAN INTO YOU.
I'VE BEEN MEANING TO TALK TO YOU.
Student Council

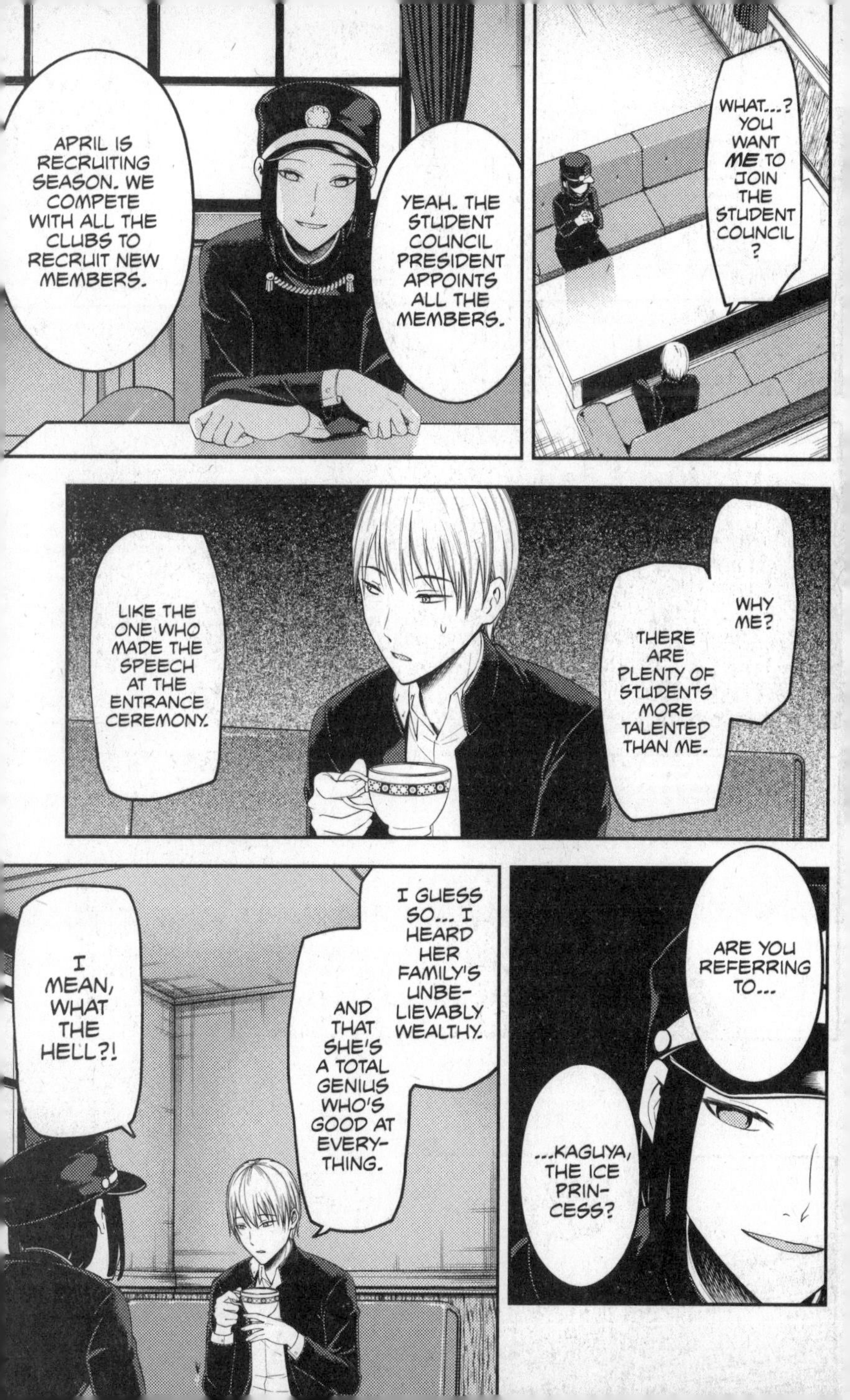
WHAT...? YOU WANT ME TO JOIN THE STUDENT COUNCIL?
YEAH. THE STUDENT COUNCIL PRESIDENT APPOINTS ALL THE MEMBERS.
APRIL IS RECRUITING SEASON. WE COMPETE WITH ALL THE CLUBS TO RECRUIT NEW MEMBERS.
WHY ME?
THERE ARE PLENTY OF STUDENTS MORE TALENTED THAN ME.
LIKE THE ONE WHO MADE THE SPEECH AT THE ENTRANCE CEREMONY.
ARE YOU REFERRING TO...
...KAGUYA, THE ICE PRINCESS?
I GUESS SO... I HEARD HER FAMILY'S UNBELIEVABLY WEALTHY.
AND THAT SHE'S A TOTAL GENIUS WHO'S GOOD AT EVERYTHING.
I MEAN, WHAT THE HELL?!

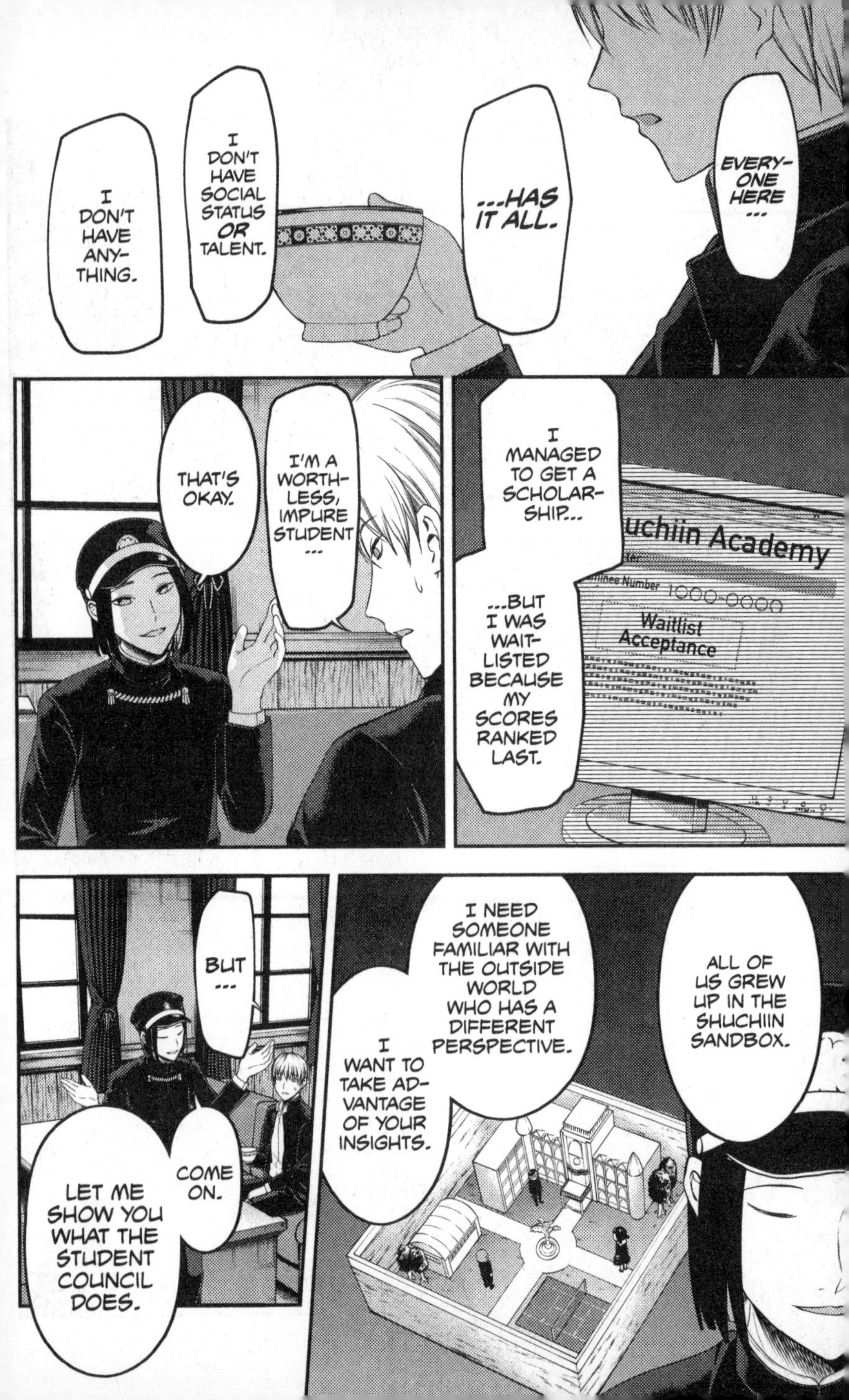
EVERYONE HERE...
...HAS IT ALL.
I DON'T HAVE SOCIAL STATUS OR TALENT.
I DON'T HAVE ANYTHING.
I MANAGED TO GET A SCHOLARSHIP...
uchiin Academy
1000-0000
Waitlist Acceptance
...BUT I WAS WAITLISTED BECAUSE MY SCORES RANKED LAST.
I'M A WORTHLESS, IMPURE STUDENT...
THAT'S OKAY.
ALL OF US GREW UP IN THE SHUCHIIN SANDBOX.
I NEED SOMEONE FAMILIAR WITH THE OUTSIDE WORLD WHO HAS A DIFFERENT PERSPECTIVE.
I WANT TO TAKE ADVANTAGE OF YOUR INSIGHTS.
BUT...
COME ON.
LET ME SHOW YOU WHAT THE STUDENT COUNCIL DOES.

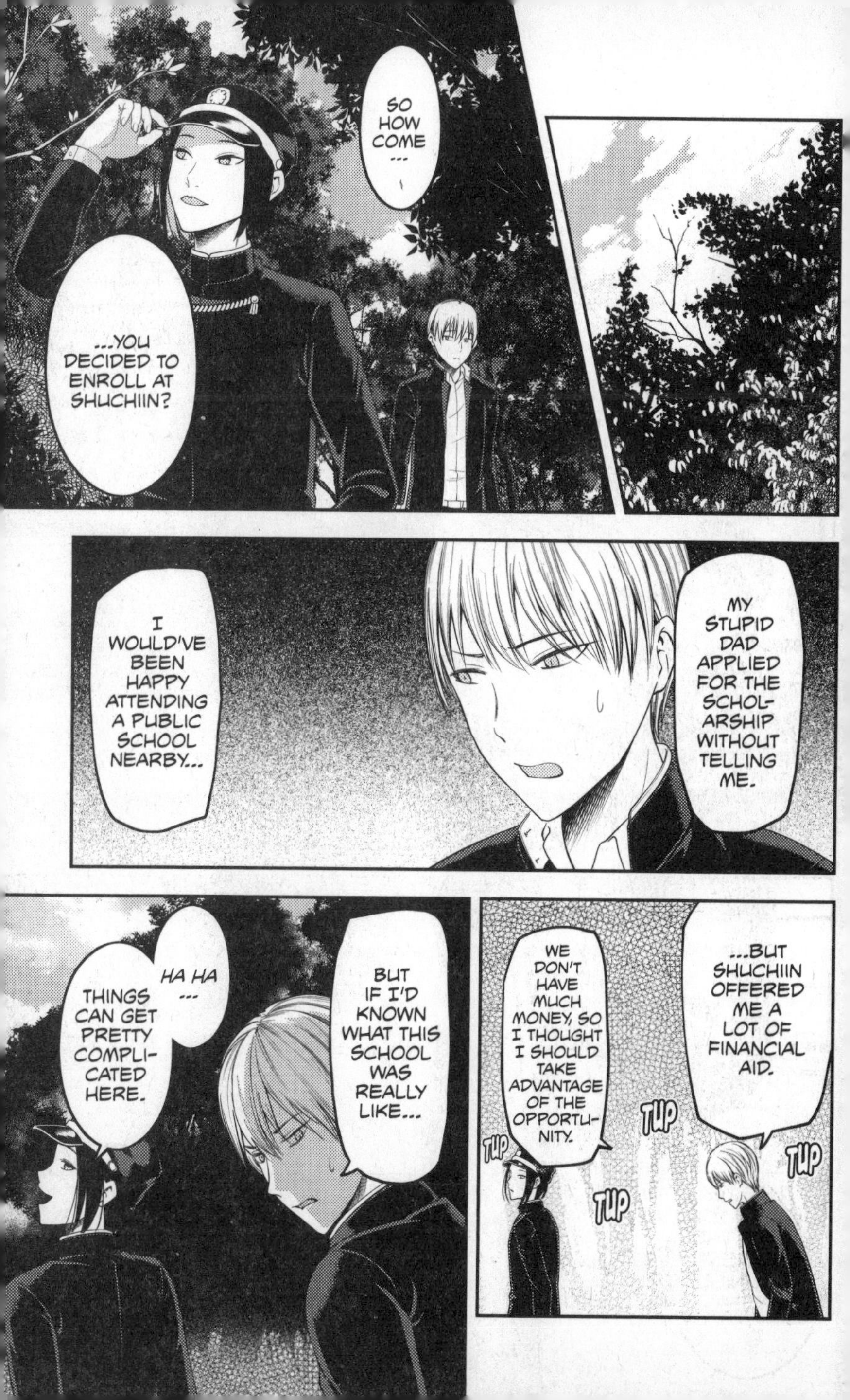
SO HOW COME ---
...YOU DECIDED TO ENROLL AT SHUCHIIN?
MY STUPID DAD APPLIED FOR THE SCHOLARSHIP WITHOUT TELLING ME.
I WOULD'VE BEEN HAPPY ATTENDING A PUBLIC SCHOOL NEARBY...
...BUT SHUCHIIN OFFERED ME A LOT OF FINANCIAL AID.
TUP
TUP
WE DON'T HAVE MUCH MONEY, SO I THOUGHT I SHOULD TAKE ADVANTAGE OF THE OPPORTUNITY.
TUP
TUP
BUT IF I'D KNOWN WHAT THIS SCHOOL WAS REALLY LIKE...
HA HA ---
THINGS CAN GET PRETTY COMPLICATED HERE.

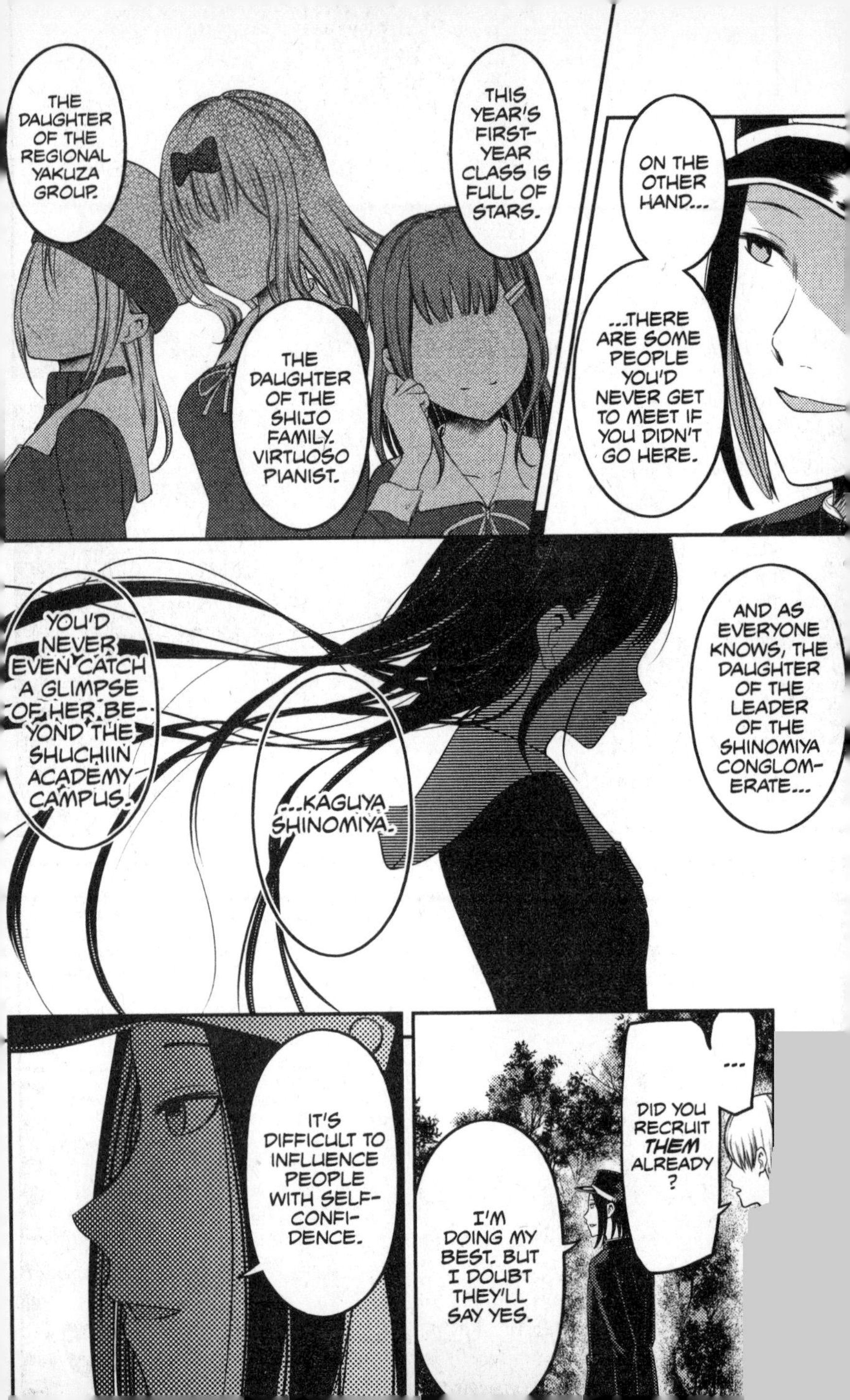
ON THE OTHER HAND...
...THERE ARE SOME PEOPLE YOU'D NEVER GET TO MEET IF YOU DIDN'T GO HERE.
THIS YEAR'S FIRST-YEAR CLASS IS FULL OF STARS.
THE DAUGHTER OF THE SHIJO FAMILY. VIRTUOSO PIANIST.
THE DAUGHTER OF THE REGIONAL YAKUZA GROUP.
AND AS EVERYONE KNOWS, THE DAUGHTER OF THE LEADER OF THE SHINOMIYA CONGLOMERATE...
...KAGUYA SHINOMIYA.
YOU'D NEVER EVEN CATCH A GLIMPSE OF HER BE-YOND THE SHUCHIIN ACADEMY CAMPUS.
...
DID YOU RECRUIT *THEM* ALREADY?
I'M DOING MY BEST. BUT I DOUBT THEY'LL SAY YES.
IT'S DIFFICULT TO INFLUENCE PEOPLE WITH SELF-CONFI-DENCE.

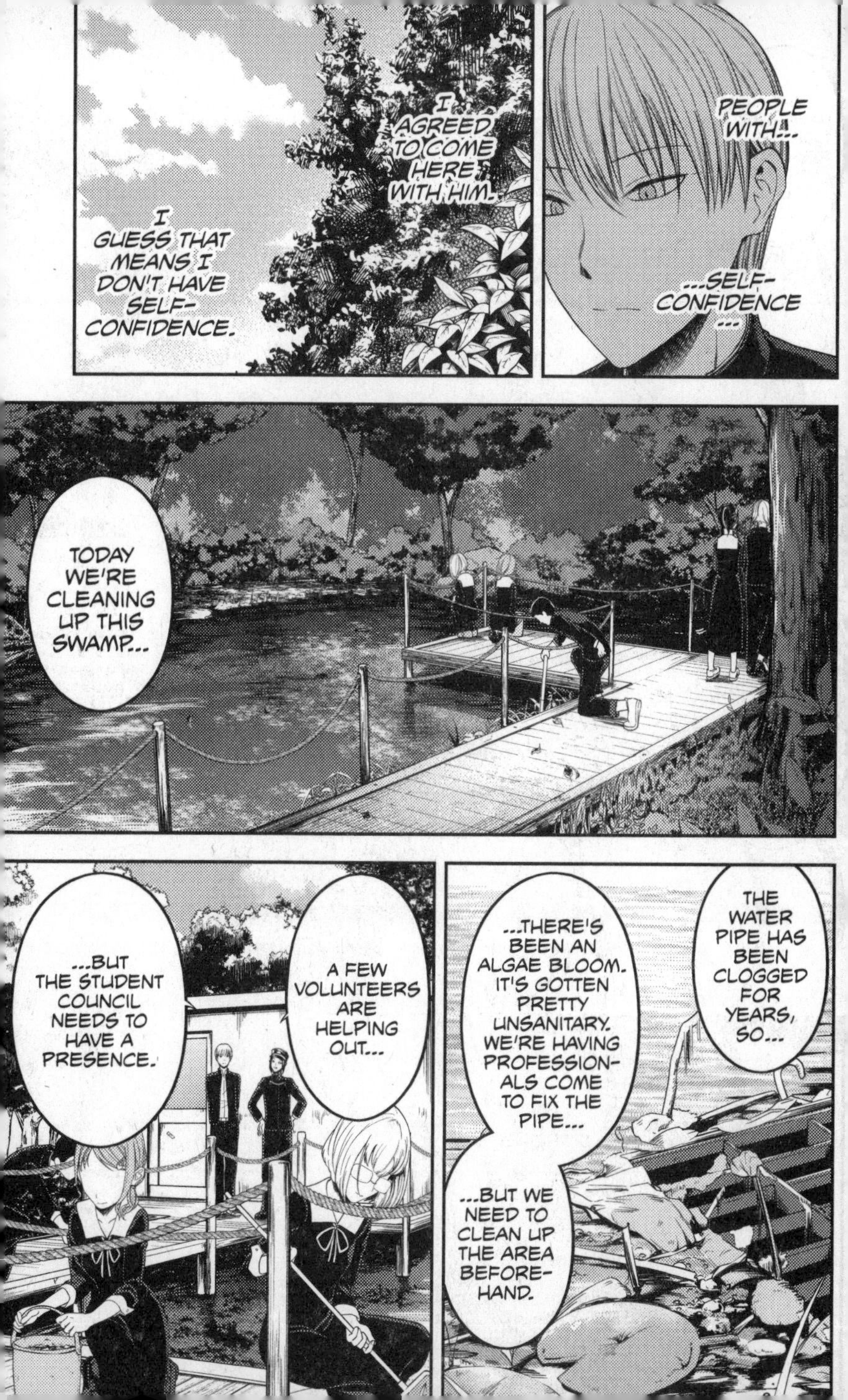
PEOPLE WITH...
...SELF-CONFIDENCE...
I AGREED TO COME HERE WITH HIM.
I GUESS THAT MEANS I DON'T HAVE SELF-CONFIDENCE.
TODAY WE'RE CLEANING UP THIS SWAMP...
THE WATER PIPE HAS BEEN CLOGGED FOR YEARS, SO...
...THERE'S BEEN AN ALGAE BLOOM. IT'S GOTTEN PRETTY UNSANITARY. WE'RE HAVING PROFESSION-ALS COME TO FIX THE PIPE...
...BUT WE NEED TO CLEAN UP THE AREA BEFORE-HAND.
A FEW VOLUNTEERS ARE HELPING OUT...
...BUT THE STUDENT COUNCIL NEEDS TO HAVE A PRESENCE.

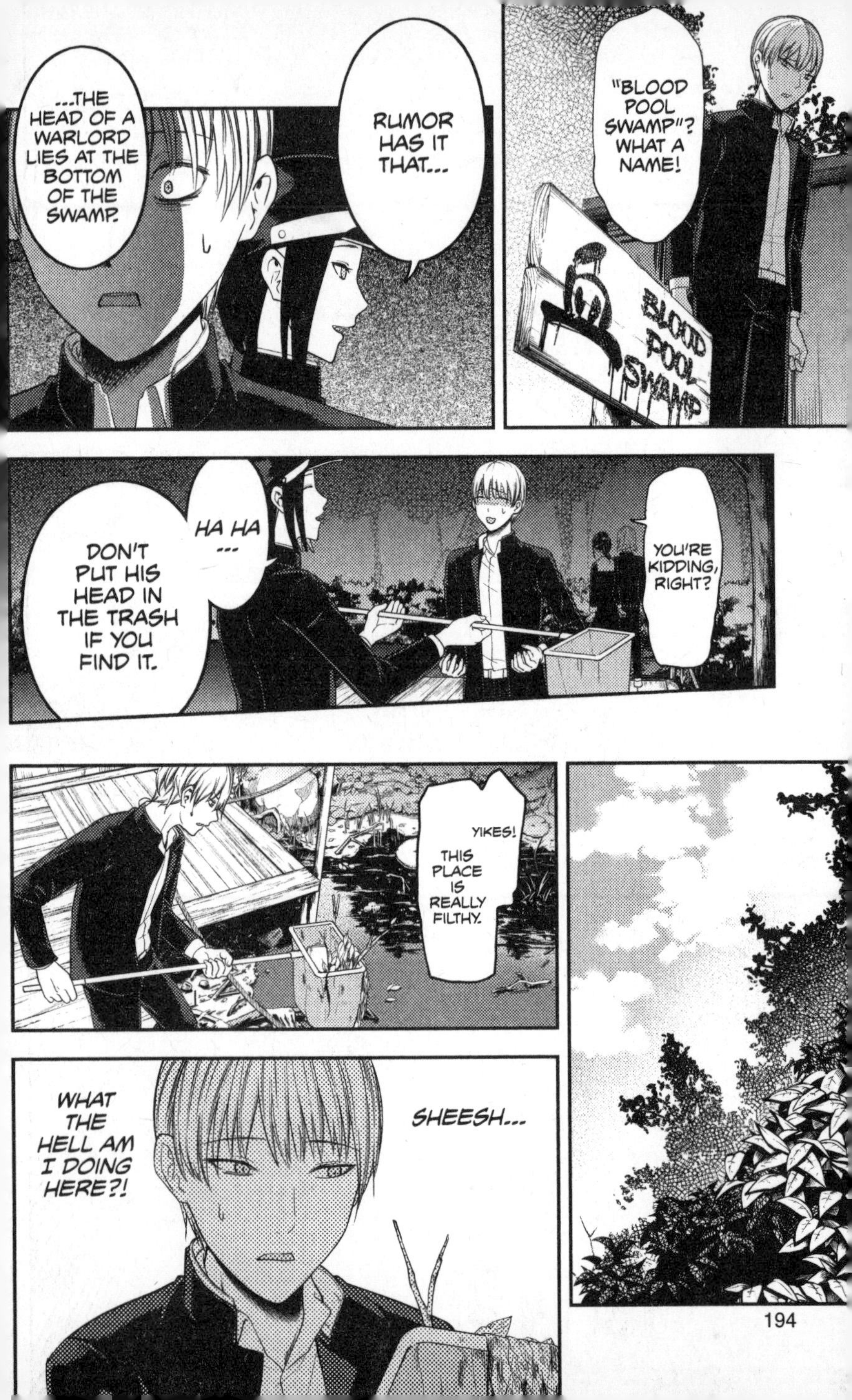
BLOOD POOL SWAMP
"BLOOD POOL SWAMP"? WHAT A NAME!
RUMOR HAS IT THAT...
...THE HEAD OF A WARLORD LIES AT THE BOTTOM OF THE SWAMP.
YOU'RE KIDDING, RIGHT?
HA HA...
DON'T PUT HIS HEAD IN THE TRASH IF YOU FIND IT.
YIKES!
THIS PLACE IS REALLY FILTHY.
SHEESH...
WHAT THE HELL AM I DOING HERE?!

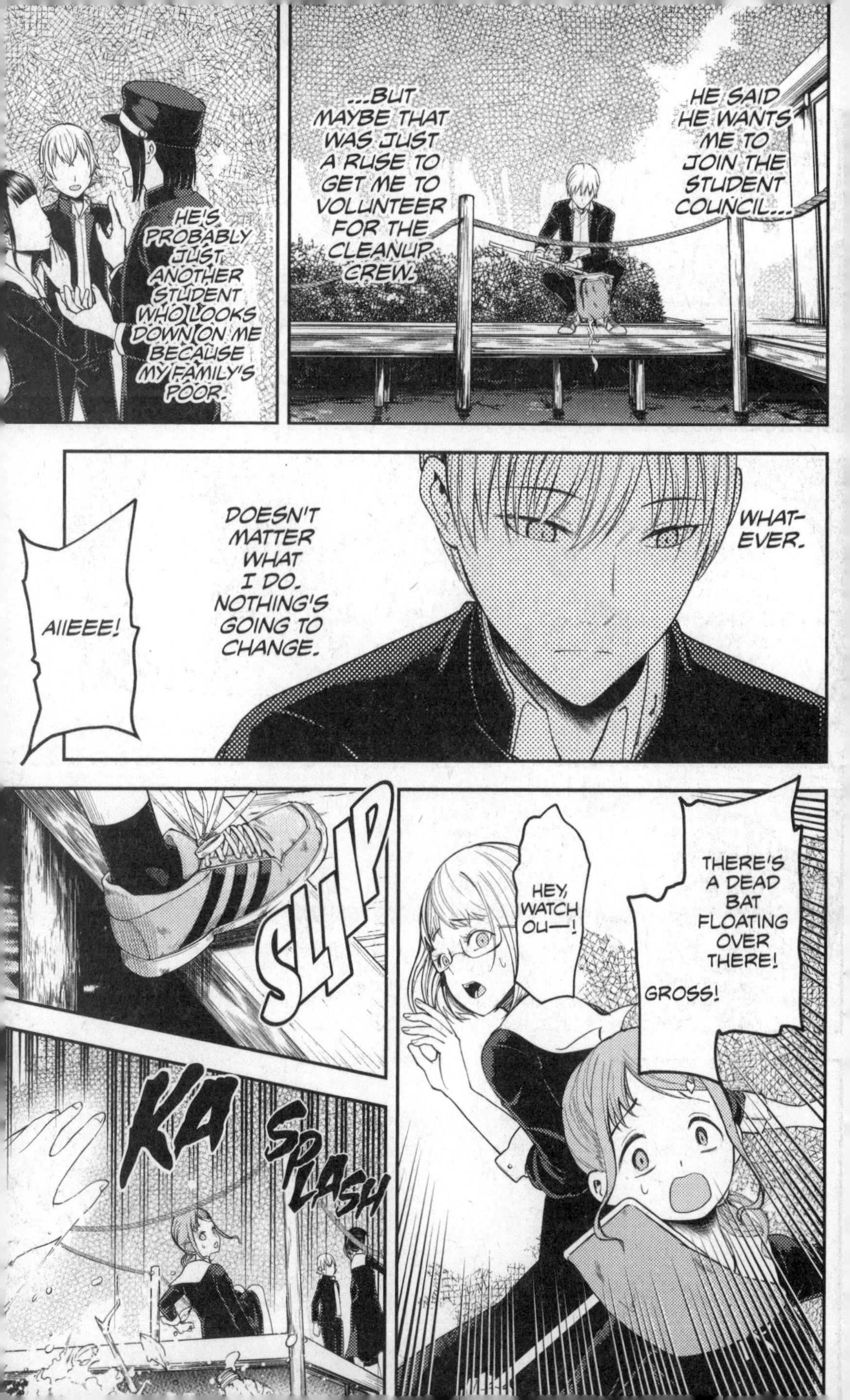
HE SAID HE WANTS ME TO JOIN THE STUDENT COUNCIL...
...BUT MAYBE THAT WAS JUST A RUSE TO GET ME TO VOLUNTEER FOR THE CLEANUP CREW.
HE'S PROBABLY JUST ANOTHER STUDENT WHO LOOKS DOWN ON ME BECAUSE MY FAMILY'S POOR.
WHAT-EVER.
DOESN'T MATTER WHAT I DO. NOTHING'S GOING TO CHANGE.
AIIEEE!
THERE'S A DEAD BAT FLOATING OVER THERE!
GROSS!
HEY, WATCH OU—!
SLIP
KA
SPLASH

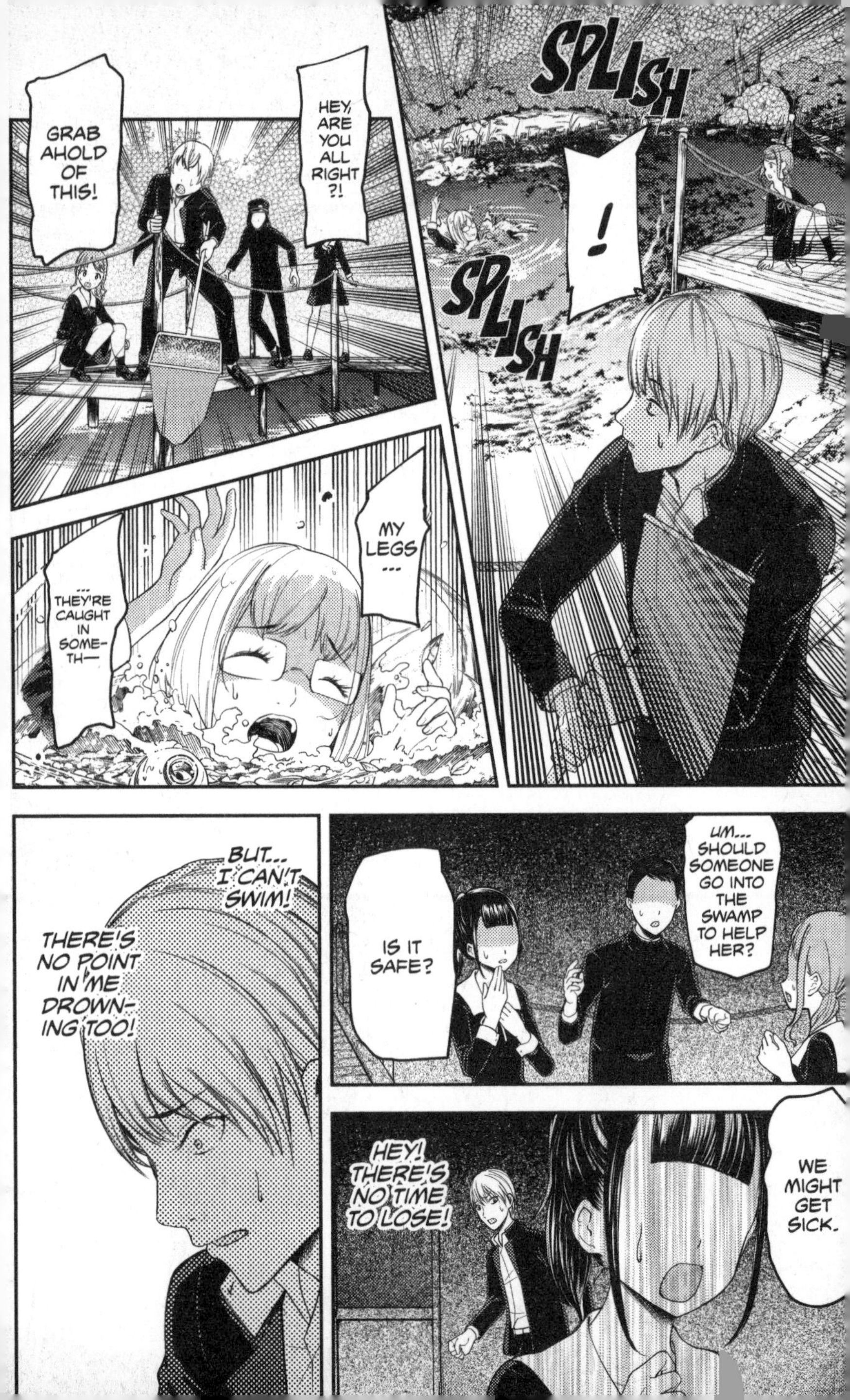
SPLISH
!
SPLISH
HEY, ARE YOU ALL RIGHT?!
GRAB AHOLD OF THIS!
MY LEGS...
...THEY'RE CAUGHT IN SOMETH—
UM... SHOULD SOMEONE GO INTO THE SWAMP TO HELP HER?
IS IT SAFE?
WE MIGHT GET SICK.
HEY! THERE'S NO TIME TO LOSE!
BUT... I CAN'T SWIM!
THERE'S NO POINT IN ME DROWNING TOO!

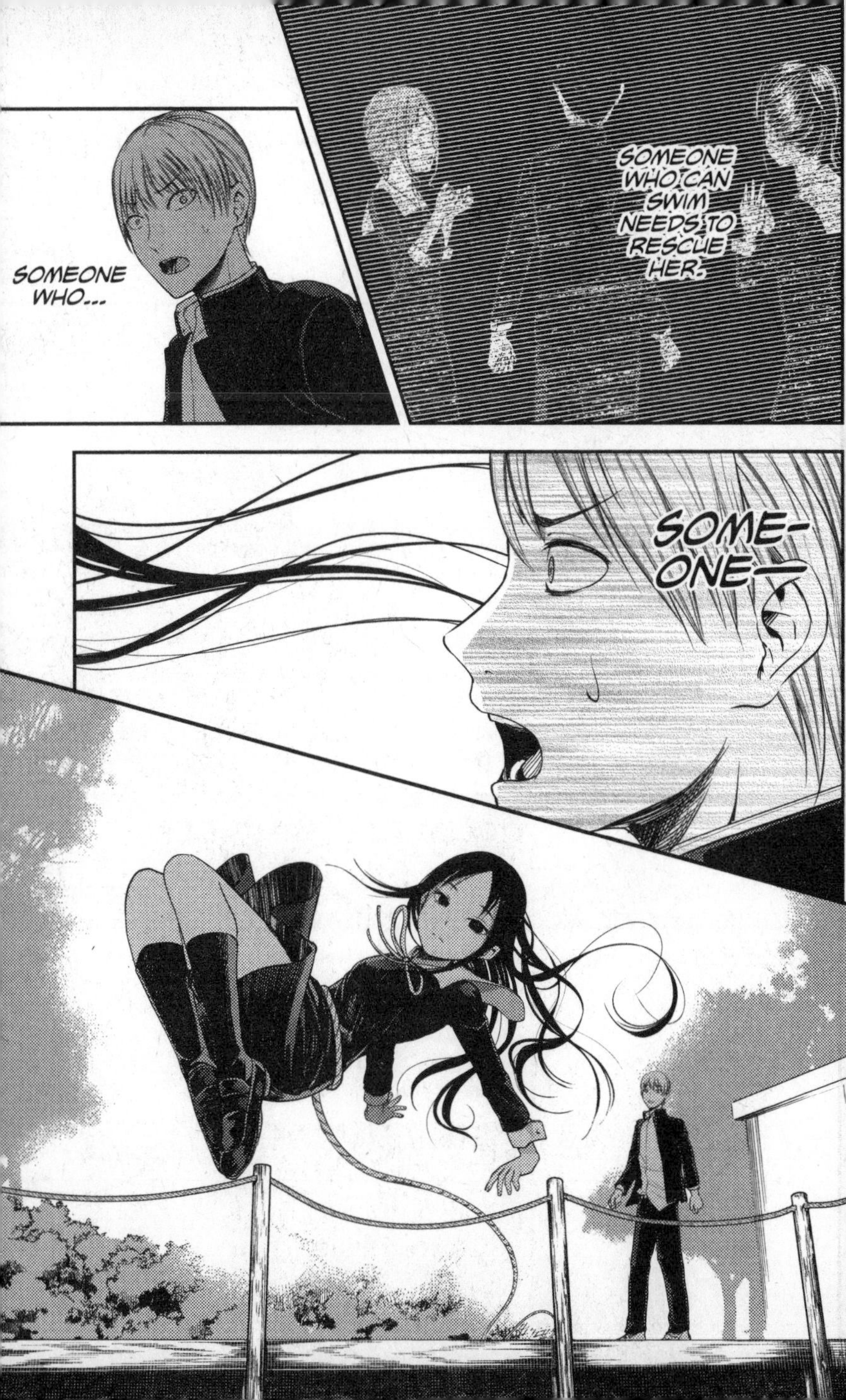
SOMEONE WHO CAN SWIM NEEDS TO RESCUE HER.
SOMEONE WHO...
SOME-ONE—

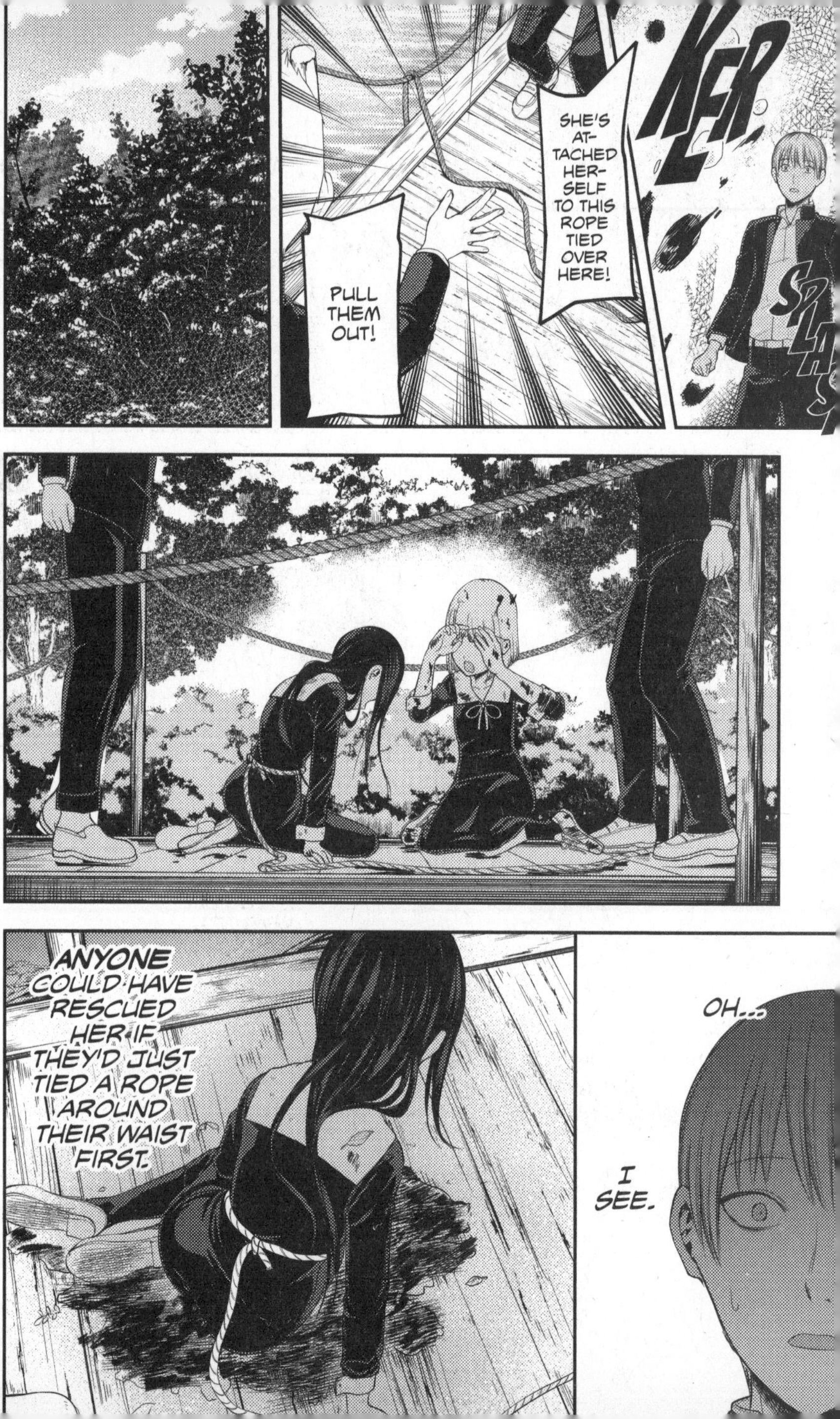
KER
SPLAS
SHE'S ATTACHED HERSELF TO THIS ROPE TIED OVER HERE!
PULL THEM OUT!
OH...
I SEE.
ANYONE COULD HAVE RESCUED HER IF THEY'D JUST TIED A ROPE AROUND THEIR WAIST FIRST.

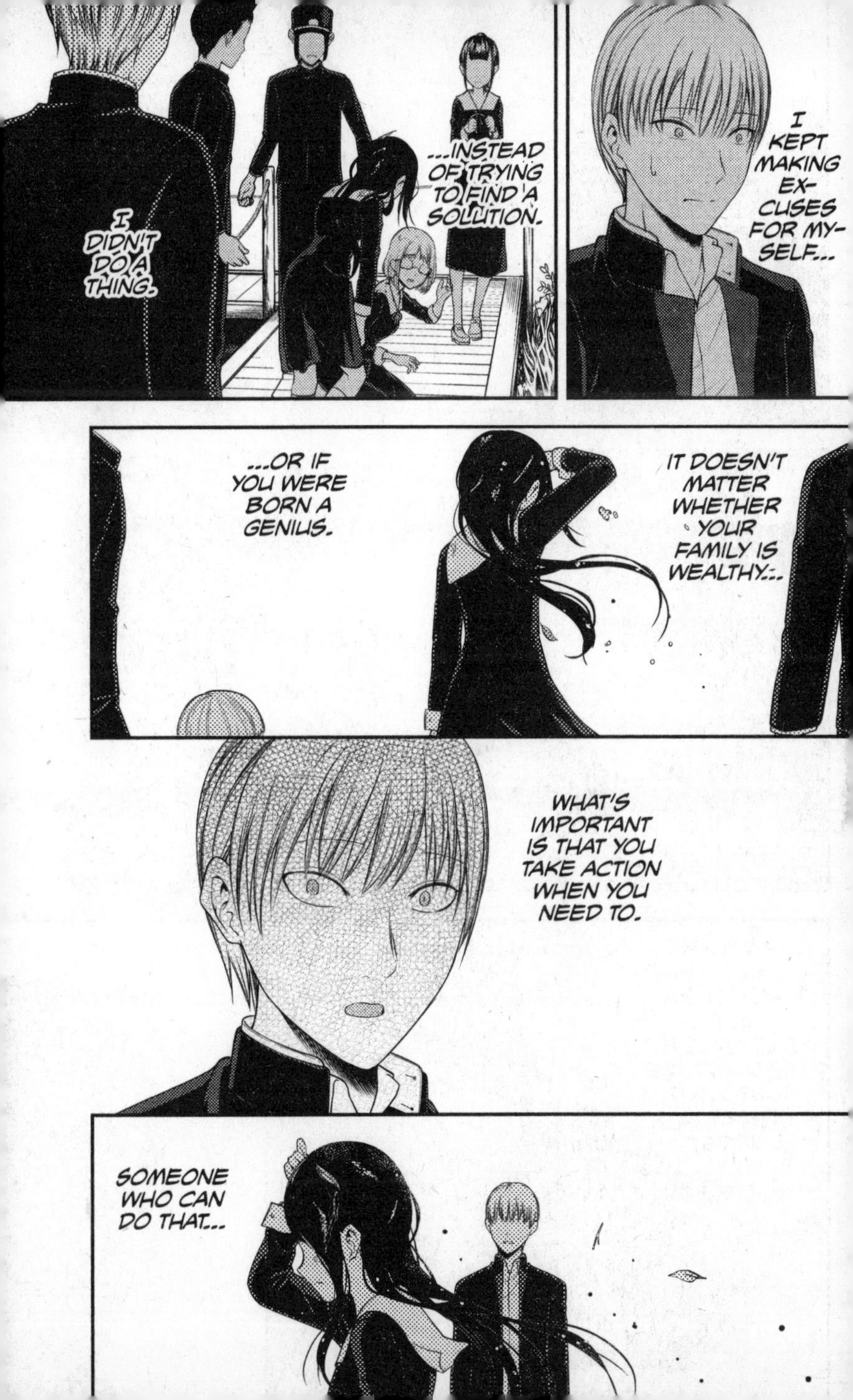
I KEPT MAKING EX-CUSES FOR MY-SELF...
...INSTEAD OF TRYING TO FIND A SOLUTION.
I DIDN'T DO A THING.
IT DOESN'T MATTER WHETHER YOUR FAMILY IS WEALTHY...
...OR IF YOU WERE BORN A GENIUS.
WHAT'S IMPORTANT IS THAT YOU TAKE ACTION WHEN YOU NEED TO.
SOMEONE WHO CAN DO THAT...

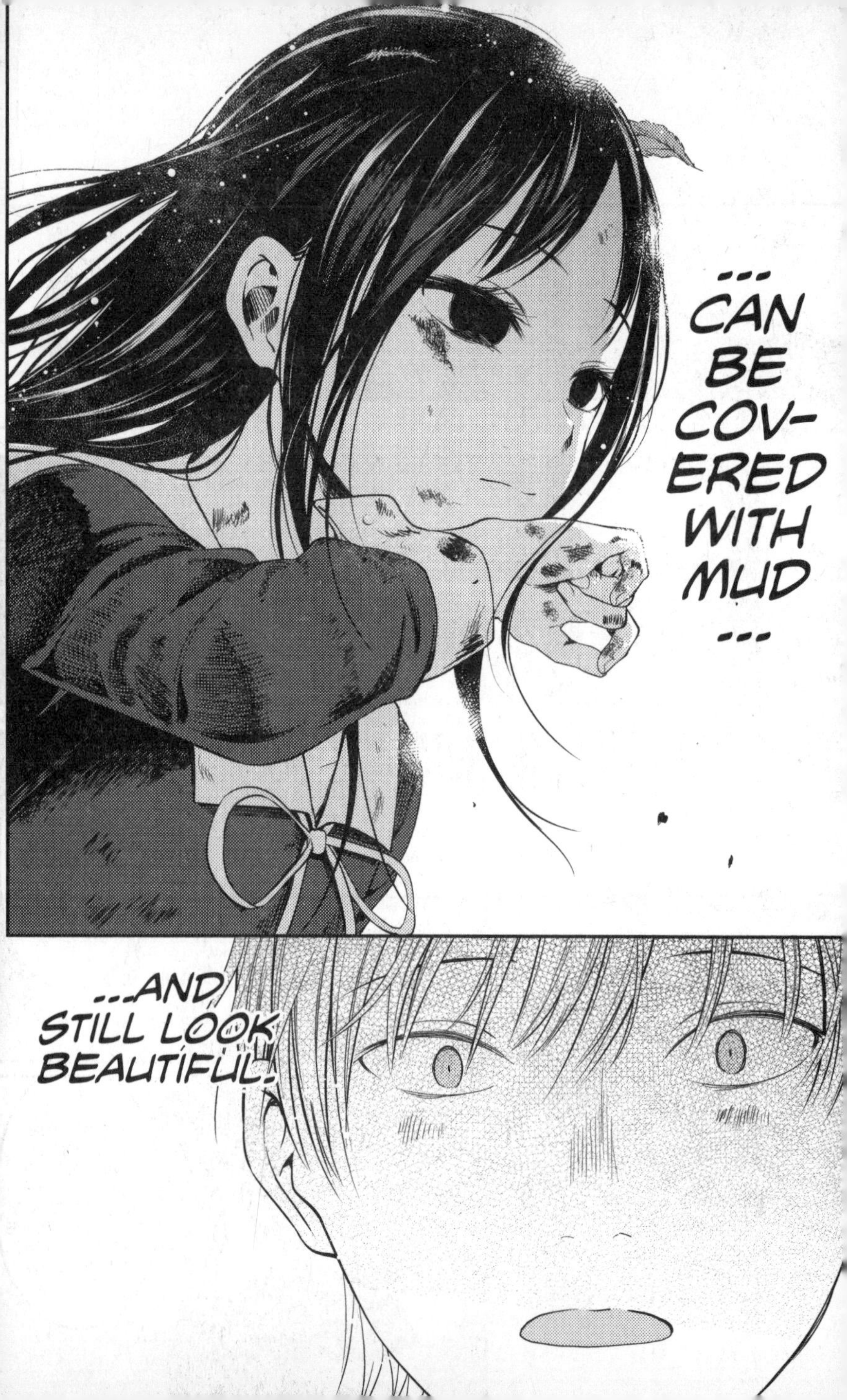
...CAN BE COVERED WITH MUD ...
...AND STILL LOOK BEAUTIFUL.

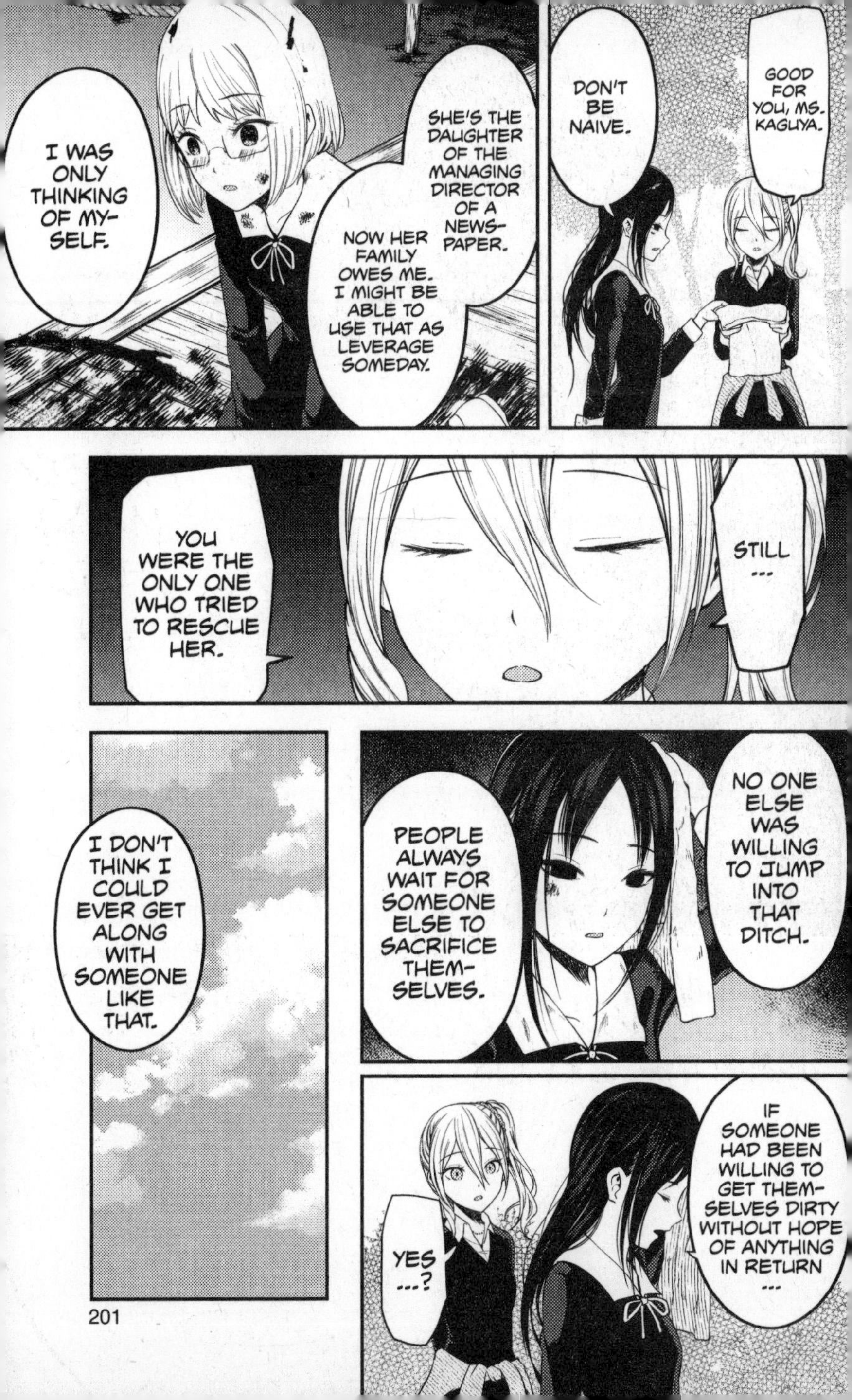
GOOD FOR YOU, MS. KAGUYA.
DON'T BE NAIVE.
SHE'S THE DAUGHTER OF THE MANAGING DIRECTOR OF A NEWS-PAPER.
NOW HER FAMILY OWES ME. I MIGHT BE ABLE TO USE THAT AS LEVERAGE SOMEDAY.
I WAS ONLY THINKING OF MY-SELF.
STILL...
YOU WERE THE ONLY ONE WHO TRIED TO RESCUE HER.
NO ONE ELSE WAS WILLING TO JUMP INTO THAT DITCH.
PEOPLE ALWAYS WAIT FOR SOMEONE ELSE TO SACRIFICE THEM-SELVES.
IF SOMEONE HAD BEEN WILLING TO GET THEM-SELVES DIRTY WITHOUT HOPE OF ANYTHING IN RETURN...
YES...?
I DON'T THINK I COULD EVER GET ALONG WITH SOMEONE LIKE THAT.

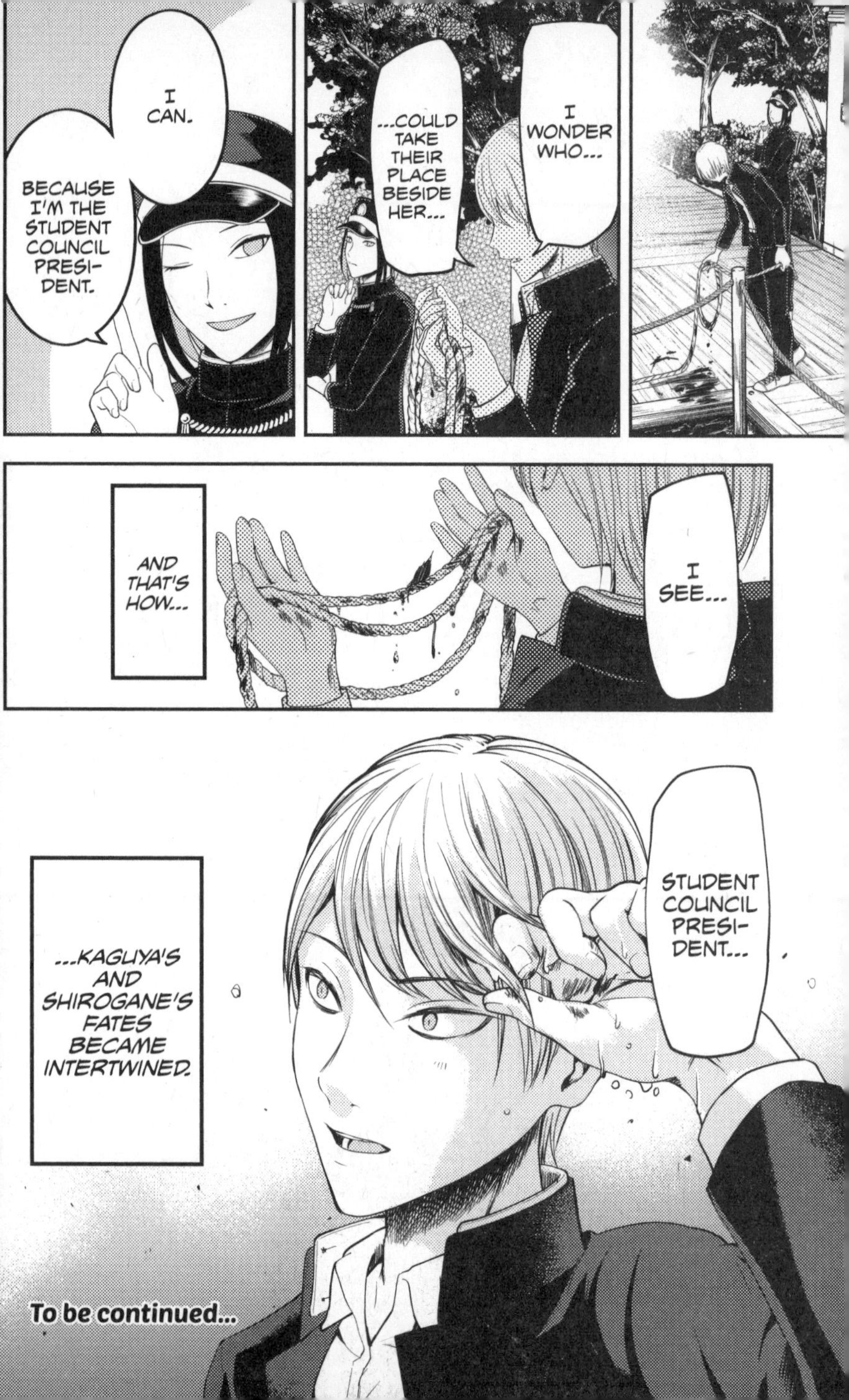
I WONDER WHO...
...COULD TAKE THEIR PLACE BESIDE HER...
I CAN.
BECAUSE I'M THE STUDENT COUNCIL PRESIDENT.
I SEE...
AND THAT'S HOW...
STUDENT COUNCIL PRESIDENT...
...KAGUYA'S AND SHIROGANE'S FATES BECAME INTERTWINED.
To be continued...

Continued
in the
summer
episode...

IF YOU KNOW HOW TO LIVE, THEN YOU KNOW HOW TO DIE.

AKA AKASAKA

Aka Akasaka got his start as an assistant to Jinsei Kataoka and Kazuma Kondou, the creators of *Deadman Wonderland*. His first serialized manga was an adaptation of the light novel series *Sayonara Piano Sonata*, published by Kadokawa in 2011. *Kaguya-sama: Love Is War* began serialization in *Miracle Jump* in 2015 but was later moved to *Weekly Young Jump* in 2016 due to its popularity.

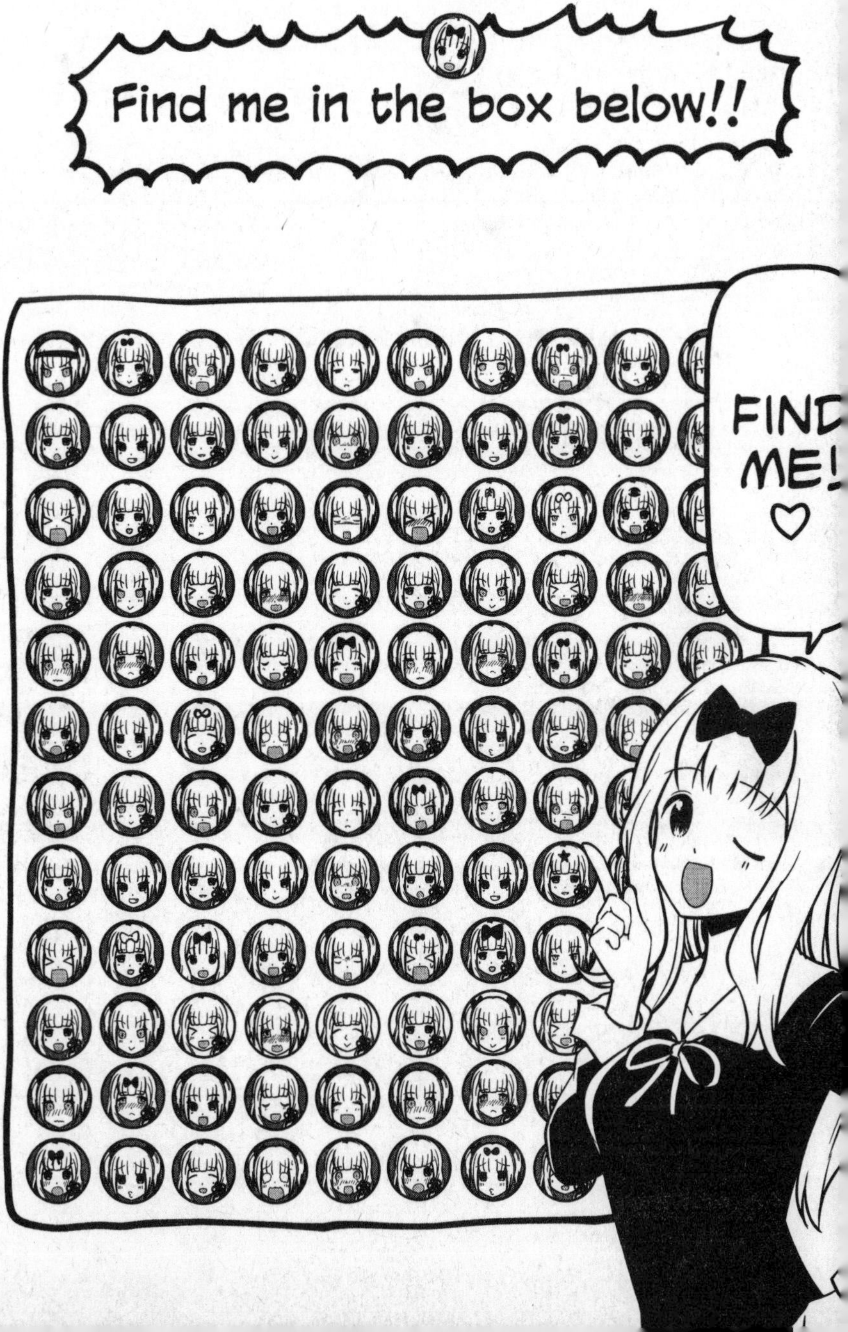
Find me in the box below!!
FIND ME! ♡

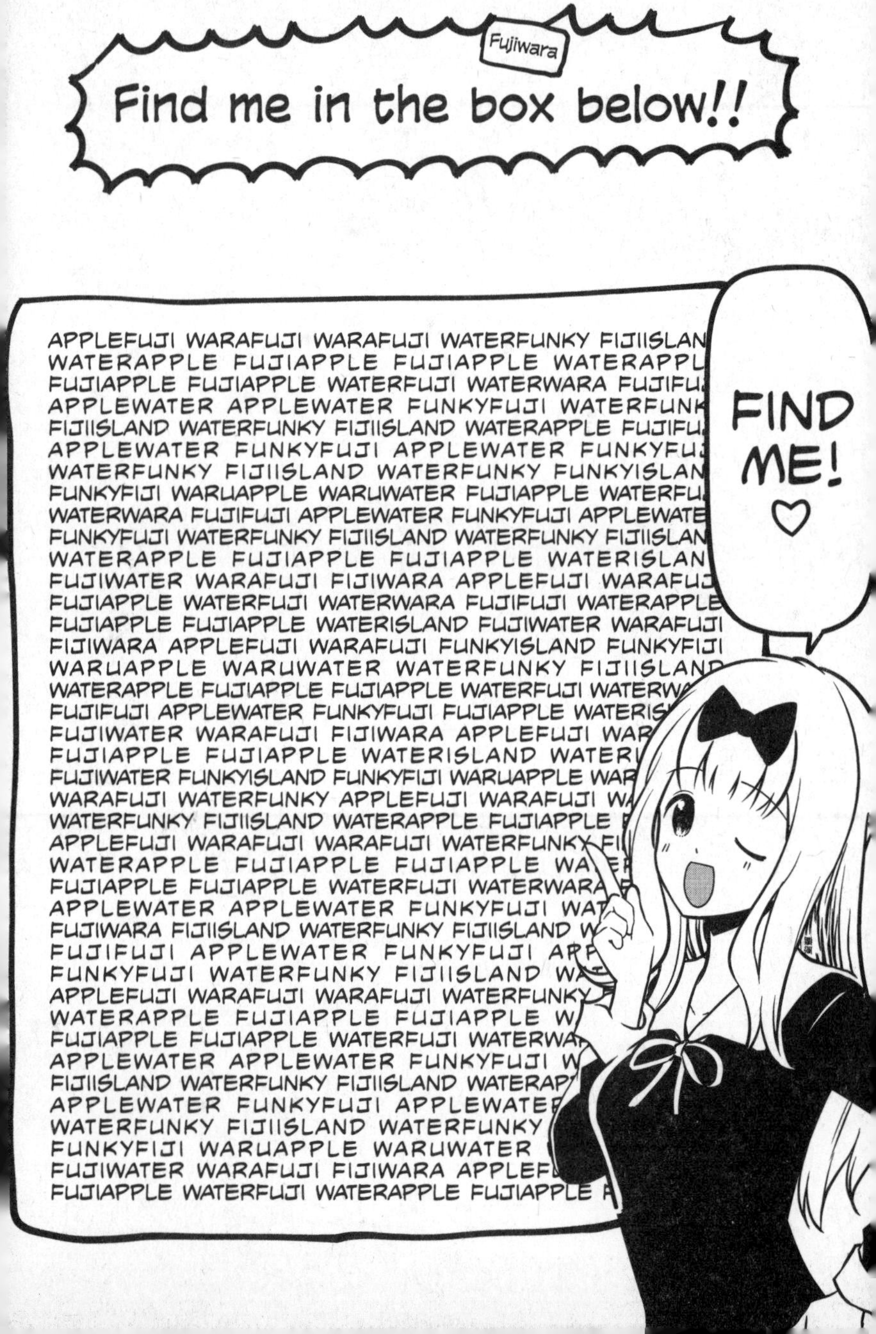
Fujiwara
Find me in the box below!!
FIND ME! ♡
APPLEFUJI WARAFUJI WARAFUJI WATERFUNKY FIJIISLAN
WATERAPPLE FUJIAPPLE FUJIAPPLE WATERAPPL
FUJIAPPLE FUJIAPPLE WATERFUJI WATERWARA FUJIFU
APPLEWATER APPLEWATER FUNKYFUJI WATERFUNK
FIJIISLAND WATERFUNKY FIJIISLAND WATERAPPLE FUJIFU
APPLEWATER FUNKYFUJI APPLEWATER FUNKYFU
WATERFUNKY FIJIISLAND WATERFUNKY FUNKYISLAN
FUNKYFIJI WARUAPPLE WARUWATER FUJIAPPLE WATERFU
WATERWARA FUJIFUJI APPLEWATER FUNKYFUJI APPLEWATE
FUNKYFUJI WATERFUNKY FIJIISLAND WATERFUNKY FIJIISLAN
WATERAPPLE FUJIAPPLE FUJIAPPLE WATERISLAN
FUJIWATER WARAFUJI FIJIWARA APPLEFUJI WARAFU
FUJIAPPLE WATERFUJI WATERWARA FUJIFUJI WATERAPPLE
FUJIAPPLE FUJIAPPLE WATERISLAND FUJIWATER WARAFUJI
FIJIWARA APPLEFUJI WARAFUJI FUNKYISLAND FUNKYFIJI
WARUAPPLE WARUWATER WATERFUNKY FIJIISLAND
WATERAPPLE FUJIAPPLE FUJIAPPLE WATERFUJI WATERW
FUJIFUJI APPLEWATER FUNKYFUJI FUJIAPPLE WATERIS
FUJIWATER WARAFUJI FIJIWARA APPLEFUJI WAR
FUJIAPPLE FUJIAPPLE WATERISLAND WATER
FUJIWATER FUNKYISLAND FUNKYFIJI WARUAPPLE WAR
WARAFUJI WATERFUNKY APPLEFUJI WARAFUJI W
WATERFUNKY FIJIISLAND WATERAPPLE FUJIAPPLE
APPLEFUJI WARAFUJI WARAFUJI WATERFUNKY
WATERAPPLE FUJIAPPLE FUJIAPPLE WA
FUJIAPPLE FUJIAPPLE WATERFUJI WATERWARA
APPLEWATER APPLEWATER FUNKYFUJI WAT
FUJIWARA FIJIISLAND WATERFUNKY FIJIISLAND W
FUJIFUJI APPLEWATER FUNKYFUJI AP
FUNKYFUJI WATERFUNKY FIJIISLAND WA
APPLEFUJI WARAFUJI WARAFUJI WATERFUNKY
WATERAPPLE FUJIAPPLE FUJIAPPLE W
FUJIAPPLE FUJIAPPLE WATERFUJI WATERWA
APPLEWATER APPLEWATER FUNKYFUJI W
FIJIISLAND WATERFUNKY FIJIISLAND WATERAP
APPLEWATER FUNKYFUJI APPLEWATE
WATERFUNKY FIJIISLAND WATERFUNKY
FUNKYFIJI WARUAPPLE WARUWATER
FUJIWATER WARAFUJI FIJIWARA APPLEF
FUJIAPPLE WATERFUJI WATERAPPLE FUJIAPPLE

KAGUYA-SAMA
LOVE IS WAR

SHONEN JUMP MANGA EDITION

12

STORY AND ART BY
AKA AKASAKA

Translation/Tomoko Kimura
English Adaptation/Annette Roman
Touch-Up Art & Lettering/Stephen Dutro
Cover & Interior Design/Alice Lewis
Editor/Annette Roman

KAGUYA-SAMA WA KOKURASETAI~TENSAITACHI NO REN'AI ZUNO SEN~
© 2015 by Aka Akasaka
All rights reserved.
First published in Japan in 2015 by SHUEISHA Inc.,Tokyo.
English translation rights arranged by SHUEISHA Inc.

Printed in Canada

Published by VIZ Media, LLC
P.O. Box 77010
San Francisco, CA 94107

10 9 8 7 6 5 4 3 2 1
First printing, January 2020

VIZ MEDIA
viz.com

SHONEN JUMP
shonenjump.com

COMING NEXT VOLUME

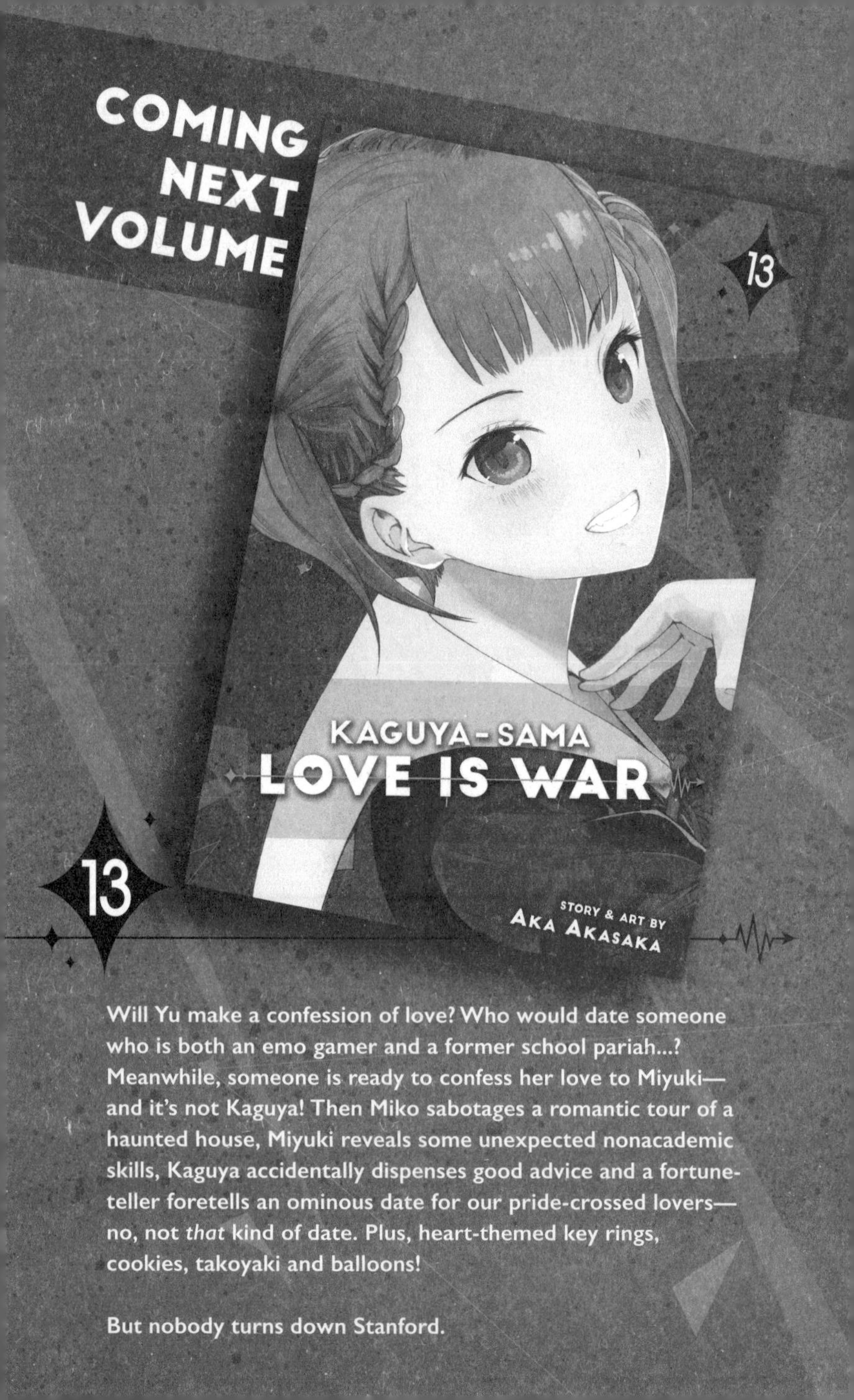
13
KAGUYA-SAMA
LOVE IS WAR
STORY & ART BY
AKA AKASAKA

13

Will Yu make a confession of love? Who would date someone who is both an emo gamer and a former school pariah...? Meanwhile, someone is ready to confess her love to Miyuki—and it's not Kaguya! Then Miko sabotages a romantic tour of a haunted house, Miyuki reveals some unexpected nonacademic skills, Kaguya accidentally dispenses good advice and a fortune-teller foretells an ominous date for our pride-crossed lovers—no, not *that* kind of date. Plus, heart-themed key rings, cookies, takoyaki and balloons!

But nobody turns down Stanford.